SLAVE POPULATION AND ECONOMY IN JAMAICA, 1807–1834

B. W. HIGMA

CAMBRIDGE UNIVERSITY PRESS
CAMBRIDGE
LONDON · NEW YORK · MELBOURNE

Published by the Syndics of the Cambridge University Press
The Pitt Building, Trumpington Street, Cambridge CB2 1RP
Bentley House, 200 Euston Road, London NW1 2DB
32 East 57th Street, New York, NY 10022, USA
296 Beaconsfield Parade, Middle Park, Melbourne 3206, Australia

First published 1976
First paperback edition 1979

Printed in the United States of America

Library of Congress Cataloging in Publication Data

Higman, B W 1943–
Slave population and economy in Jamaica, 1807 – 1834

Bibliography: p.
1. Slavery in Jamaica – History. I. Title.
HT1096.H53 301.44'93 75-28627
ISBN 0 521 21053 4 hard covers
ISBN 0 521 29569 6 paperback

CONTENTS

To my mother and father

PREFACE

Although recognizing the existence of the Slave Registration and Compensation Records, the bibliographer of the second volume of the *Cambridge History of the British Empire,* published in 1940, felt confident in commenting that 'these records are very detailed, but are disappointing in their content of historical material'. The analysis of the slave population of Jamaica presented in this book is based on but a fraction of the material contained in that series. This reassessment of the importance of the Slave Registration and Compensation Records stems from the fact that the political aspects of slavery and its abolition now attract less attention than the nature of slavery and its impact on individuals and populations, and from the application of new techniques to the analysis of demographic data. In this book an attempt is made to outline the structure of the slave population of Jamaica in the years between the abolition of the slave trade and emancipation, and its interrelationships with the plantation economy founded on the manipulation of slave labour. Because these economic–demographic interrelations were so closely bound, it is difficult to decide whether an analysis of them should begin with the economy or the population. Here the economy is discussed first, in order to describe the context within which the slaves moved and had their being. But it is an aim of the work to show that, in the period 1807–34, demographic change had a significant impact on the economy. The focus is strictly on the plantation economy as a system operated for the benefit of the masters, and on the slave population as a labour force manipulated towards that end. To this extent the perspective is, inevitably, that of the masters rather than that of the slaves. The economic life of the slaves and the social history of slavery are discussed only in so far as they touch on this central theme. But it should be obvious that the demographic patterns established here have important implications for the wider understanding of slave society.

The core of this book is a Ph.D. thesis in history presented to the University of the West Indies in 1970. That thesis was based entirely on Jamaican sources, but I have since had the opportunity of making use of the complementary materials available in the United Kingdom and to explore the archives of the other West Indian territories, as well as undertaking additional research in the Jamaican archives. This work has been supported generously by the Government of Jamaica, the University of the West Indies, the Leverhulme Trust, and the Research Institute for the Study of Man. For their critiques of the work, and parts of it, in various stages of preparation, I thank Roy Augier, Edward Brathwaite, Colin Clarke, Stanley Engerman, Barry Floyd, Robert Fogel, Elsa Goveia, Jack Greene, Douglas Hall, Audrey Johnson, Howard Johnson, Franklin Knight, and Richard Sheridan. Frank Innes loaned some microfilm at a vital stage; Ron Read and Errol Caby helped greatly with the computing, which was carried out at the Computer Centre of the University of the West Indies; Kathleen Falconer provided some research assistance; Sandra Pearce and Alan Hodgkiss drafted the figures, in the Department of Geography at the University of Liverpool. The editors of *Population Studies* and *The Journal of Interdisciplinary History* kindly granted permission to use material originally published in their journals. I must also thank Marlay Stephen of the University of Sydney for his encouragement in the early stages of my interest in West Indian history. For the help so willingly given by all these people I am sincerely grateful. The mistakes are all mine.

B. H.

CONVENTIONS, ABBREVIATIONS AND SYMBOLS

Conventions

Money values are expressed in £ Jamaica currency, unless otherwise specified. (£1.4 currency equals £1.0 sterling, throughout the period.)

Laws are Jamaica laws, unless otherwise specified.

People of 'colour' are people of mixed race. (For the Jamaica classification of gradations of colour see Chapter 7.)

Abbreviations

A.P	Accounts Produce (Jamaica Archives, Spanish Town)
J.H.A.V.	*Jamaica, House of Assembly, Votes*
P.P.	*British Parliamentary Papers*
R.R.S.	Returns of Registrations of Slaves (Jamaica Archives, Spanish Town)
T.71	Slave Registration and Compensation Records (Public Record Office, London)

Symbols

r coefficient of correlation
R coefficient of multiple correlation

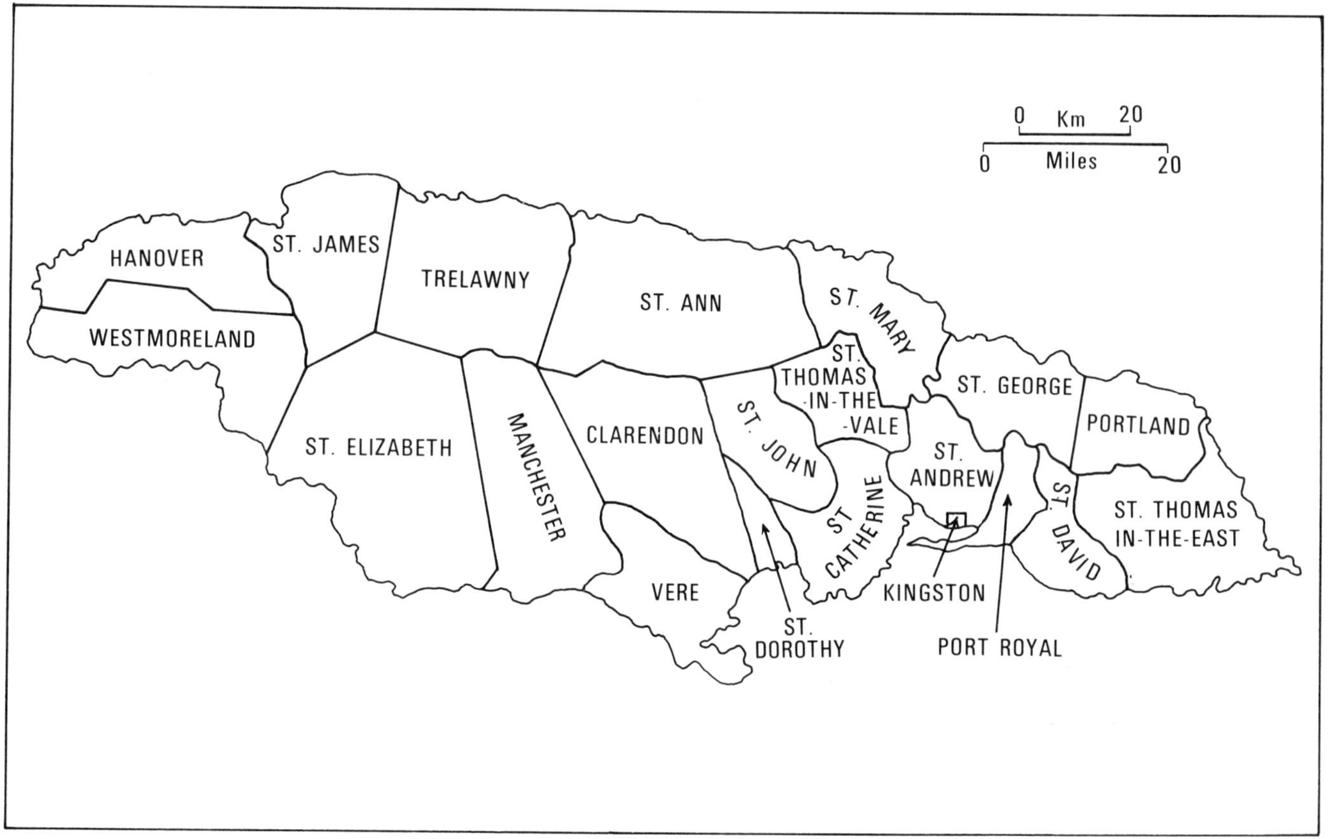

Figure 1. Jamaica Parishes, 1814–34.

CHAPTER 1

SLAVES, LIVESTOCK, MACHINES

When in the early nineteenth century the Jamaica planter sat down to count the cost and calculate his wealth or impending ruin he began by inventorying his changing capital stock. His mill and works were relatively durable. But the other kinds of power he manipulated, slaves and livestock, depreciated rapidly. They were vulnerable to debility, senility and mortality, the scourges of all living things, aggravated by the enervation of the torrid zone. So when he considered his ability to crush the cane, peel the ginger, chip the logwood or carry to port the produce of his land the planter was at pains to note the capacity of each of the units of power at his disposal. First, he divided his slaves into males and females, and then for each one, by name, he noted age, colour, country of birth, condition or state of health and, if he were particular, their disposition towards their masters. Second he listed his livestock and for each (for they had 'as fine or finer names than the negroes themselves'[1]) he noted sex, breed, age, colour, condition, state of fatness and whether creole.[2] The planter then ordered his slaves and livestock into groups according to their capacity and in relation to his needs. These lists of groups began with the strongest and most productive and descended to the weak and useless. For instance, on Irwin Estate in the parish of St. James the slaves were listed in the following order: first field gang, second gang, third gang, tradesmen, penkeepers, domestics, watchmen, grasscutters, invalids and young children; and the livestock: working stock, bulls, young working stock, mules, cows, calves and fattening cattle.[3]

Since the tasks to be performed on the planter's land, in his works and in his residence were varied, he did his best to use his forces of power for multiple purposes. Whereas his mill was an inflexible form of capital equipment, his slaves and livestock could be moulded to perform various tasks and to fit into new ones as they aged. Hall has argued that the planter's conception of slaves as very flexible, 'multi-purpose' capital equipment probably discouraged him from investing in agricultural implements such as ploughs and limited his readiness to teach slaves skills.[4] Yet the planter did at the same time see limitations to the flexibility of his working force and the source of these limitations was in part the very fact that he thought of the slave as 'a mere machine', and the black man as 'a connecting link in the great chain of being, between white men and brutes'.[5] These limitations applied to both slaves and livestock, hence they were not simply a result of that 'underlying contradiction' of slavery which is supposed to have disturbed Jamaica whites, namely that the slave was also a person, a social being.[6] True, the planter did not slaughter the deformed offspring of his slaves (as he did the calves of his cows), or select their mates, or castrate them; nor was he akin to those mythological figures who lay with the beasts of the field; nor could he hold conversation with an ass. But there was here a thin red line. The planter was capable of a duality of mind. Even Edward Long, whose anthropological theories were public ideology in the colonies,[7] recognized that Africans lived in societies and had built large towns; at the same time he believed that there was in the whole of creation a gradation from the inanimate to the animate, and that resemblances could be found between even a man and a fish.[8] The white was thus able to think of a slave at one time as an object of carnal desire or a potential criminal and at another as a mere unit of power to be weighed against a steer, mule, plough or wheelbarrow.

At least some of the aspects of the slaves' social status which limited their flexibility were also possessed by livestock. The colour of slaves, for example, is generally thought to have affected occupational allocations because the planter had a feeling of kinship with the slaves of colour,[9] but in fact the whites attached superstitions to colours. In the case of slaves, these superstitions related to ideas about the ability of people of different degrees of blackness or whiteness to perform manual labour under the vertical sun. There was also a custom of choosing working cattle on the basis of colour. Lewis reported that 'the only horned cattle said to be fit for Jamaica work, are those which have a great deal of black in them. The white are terribly tormented by the insects, and they are weak and sluggish in proportion to their quantity of white.'[10] In 1823 Roughley claimed that it was 'an old custom or superstition' in Jamaica to favour red, black or brindle working stock; good strong beasts of brilliant varied hues were put to the butcher's knife while weak, meagre ones of the favoured colours were put under the yoke.[11] In the same way, mulatto and quadroon women were brought into the shade of the great house to perform domestic tasks, while their black sisters – whether weak or strong – toiled in the fields.

When a slave grew old he was put to light tasks or was invalided. When a working steer or spayed heifer became old it was fattened and sold to the butcher. Here the mule tended to have more social status than the slave since it was often permitted to roam the estate lands foraging and breaking fences;[12] the aged slave was rarely released from labour altogether. A few slave-owners are said to have disposed of slaves who had become useless by throwing them down sink holes and gullies,[13] but generally aged slaves were unsaleable and by the early nineteenth century could only be manumized under bond, thus forming a potential source of inflexibility in the slave system. Slaves, in this respect, tended to be less flexible units of power than cattle (which also produced manure and meat).

In addition to the long-term sources of inflexibility in the slave population, there is reason to expect that the abolition of the slave trade in 1807 placed new stresses on the system. From the middle of the eighteenth century the planters had been generally agreed that it was cheaper to purchase slaves from the African slave traders than to 'breed' them.[14] Their preference was for slaves who were black, male and between 15 and 30 years of age. When the supply of African slaves was cut off the planter was faced with either a diminishing work force or the need to support a larger proportion of females and children if the estate was to maintain its numbers. These processes led to decreasing gross receipts in the first case and decreasing productivity per slave in the second. Both meant loss to the planter. The question arises, then, whether the economic decline of Jamaica was not related to the changing structure of the slave population.

An analysis of the relationship between the slave population of Jamaica and the plantation economy which it supported involves two distinct, yet intertwined, questions. How did the nature of the economy affect the growth and structure of the slave population? What was the impact of demographic change on the growth and structure of the economy? In the study of slavery in the Americas both of these questions have been, and remain, the focus of considerable debate.

Differences in the rate of growth or decline of the slave populations of the New World were recognized by the beginning of the nineteenth century at least. The most obvious contrast was that between the Caribbean and mainland North America. Wilberforce in 1804, and Humboldt in 1826, observed that whereas the sugar colonies of the Caribbean and northeastern Brazil suffered natural decreases the slave population of the United States experienced a rapid increase.[15] But these patterns reflected, and were confused by, varying levels of participation in the Atlantic slave trade.[16] Beyond these gross variations there were also contrasts between the Caribbean sugar colonies themselves, some even achieving natural increases before emancipation.[17] Further, Eblen has suggested that, in the case of the black population of nineteenth-century Cuba, what on the surface appears to be a natural decrease was in fact an increase if the native-born are isolated from the demographically abnormal foreign-born group.[18] Explanations of these contrasting patterns of population growth and decline were first looked for in the metropolitan institutional differences of the slave-masters, and the relative humaneness of the slave systems.[19] As the patterns of survival have become increasingly complex, however, the causes have similarly become less certain. The puzzle remains far from resolution. Thus one aim of the following discussion will be to ask whether the slaves of Jamaica multiplied and grew the more they were afflicted with hard bondage and all manner of service in the field, or whether their experience differed from that of the Egyptian captivity of the children of Israel.

The second question, that concerning the impact of demographic change on economic growth and structure, has an equally important place in the historiography of slavery. Writing in 1841, Merivale argued that the population dynamics of slavery could induce the termination of the system. Normally, he said, 'slave labour is dearer than free *wherever abundance of free labour can be procured*' and thus 'the limit of the profitable duration of slavery is attained whenever the population has become so dense that it is cheaper to employ the free labourer for hire'.[20] This idea was developed by Nieboer who distinguished between situations of 'open' and 'closed' resources, the land/labour ratio of the former providing the base for slave/plantation systems.[21] In the 1920s Ragatz broadened the attack on the economic efficiency of slavery, claiming that by the end of the eighteenth century the West Indian slave system 'was proving ruinous as a form of labor and must inevitably have come to an end through the operation of simple economic laws, even had there been no general clamor against it'.[22] The idea was taken up in the 1930s by Williams (strongly influenced by Ragatz) and Thompson, who saw population expansion as the essential factor in an evolutionary economic-demographic process leading inevitably to the unprofitability and breakdown of slave/plantation systems.[23] More recently, Goveia, extrapolating from her study of the Leeward Islands to the British West Indian colonies as a whole, has contended that

> the growing density of the slave population concentrated on their sugar estates and the increasing expense of their traditional methods of agriculture under the slave system were among the most important factors contributing to the lack of competitive efficiency which was already affecting the economic fortunes of most of these territories by the end of the eighteenth century. By that time, however, the West Indians could no longer afford to regard slavery simply as the economic expedient for supplying labour which it had been originally. The slave system had become more than an economic enterprise which could be abandoned when it ceased to be profitable. It had become the very basis of organized society throughout the British West Indies, and therefore it was believed to be an indispensable element in maintaining the existing social structure and in preserving law and order in the community.[24]

Finally, Patterson, referring specifically to Jamaica, holds that 'the abolition of slavery in 1834 was simply the official seal of ruin on a system that had already collapsed'.[25]

In this historiographical development three separate issues seem to have become confused. Firstly, did the British West Indian plantation economy suffer a decline in the period from the end of the eighteenth century to emancipation? Secondly, was the slave system a cause of this decline? Thirdly, by what processes could this economic decline lead to the ending of slavery and the slave trade? The answer to the first of these questions is not in dispute,[26] but it does not follow that the slave system was necessarily unprofitable or inefficient as a system of production. Further, the abolition of the slave trade and of slavery can be related to economic decline without looking for the sources of this decline within the slave system itself. Even if the inefficiency of the slave system was at the root of the decline of the West

Indian plantation economy, the view that evolutionary economic-demographic processes within the slave/plantation system could induce its disintegration without the necessity for external intervention is open to serious criticism of a strictly economic nature and without regard to the maintenance of a conception of society.[27] A full analysis of all of these issues is beyond the scope of this study. Here the emphasis will fall on the impact of the demographic character of the slave system on the economy of Jamaica. But the ramifications of this single issue for the general interpretation should be apparent.

PART I

ECONOMY

CHAPTER 2

DISTRIBUTION OF THE SLAVE LABOUR FORCE

It is generally conceded that of all the British West Indian colonies Jamaica's economy was the most diversified in the period of slavery. Having admitted this much, however, it is usual to underscore the dominance of sugar and the plantation. The 'minor staples' and other economic activities are seen as strictly marginal. Thus while Jamaica is accepted as an exception to the rule of monoculture the degree of deviance is thought to be insignificant.[1]

There is no doubting the dominance of sugar. What is required is a measure of the *extent* of that dominance. Here an attempt will be made to provide such a measure for the period immediately before emancipation.[2] Since the concern of this analysis is with the links between the structure of the economy and the slave population, emphasis will be placed on the distribution of the slaves between the different forms of economic activity. This is not the same as assessing the contribution of sugar to the wealth of Jamaica or the export sector, or tracing the dependence of other activities on the sugar plantation system. But it has often been assumed that because sugar was the principal export crop it also determined the distribution of the slave labour force. Hence a description of the pattern of activities and institutions on the sugar estate is sometimes thought to suffice as the basis for an analysis of Jamaican slave society.[3] It is necessary to test the adequacy of this assumption. For outside the sugar estates there was a varied set of occupations and activities, in a varied set of environmental situations (both physical and social), in which the slaves could be involved. If it is agreed that these various forms of economic activity may have had different effects on the growth and structure of the slave population, and vice versa, the importance of the exercise will be even more apparent.

Sources and methods of analysis

For Jamaica in the early nineteenth century there are available island returns of exports, lists of taxable livestock by parishes, and occasional estimates of the numbers of estates and pens in each parish, but little more. The area under cane, coffee or grass, for example, is unknown. Hence the materials for regional analysis based on parish data are strictly limited. But Jamaica possesses a rich source of data which makes it possible to study the output of individual properties and, thus, to determine the functional pattern of land and labour use at the holding level. From 1740 to 1927 all persons acting for owners who were absentees, minors, lunatics, heirs or otherwise not directly in control of their properties, or deceased, were required to return annual accounts of their produce to the Island Secretary.[4] For each property recorded, these Accounts Produce list everything sold within the island, produce shipped for sale, and the quantity of the year's output left undisposed at the date of the return. In addition to the produce of the land, receipts from the hire of slaves and from the sale of sundry items of movable personalty were also included. Often the value of production is not stated in monetary terms, but merely in quantities of weight or volume. For the period immediately before emancipation, the bald statements of gross receipts found in the Accounts Produce can be related to the demographic structure of the slave labour force located on the same properties by reference to the Returns of Registrations of Slaves. These returns provide a census of the slave population, by slave-holding, in 1817, while triennial returns continuing to 1832 listed all movements in the population. (The Returns of Registrations of Slaves will be discussed in detail in Chapter 5 below.)

In 1832, the year chosen for study, there are Accounts Produce for 960 properties[5] on which were located 167,858 slaves, or 53.6 per cent of the slave population.[6] Although this is an impressive proportion, it must be recognized that the Accounts Produce are heavily biased towards particular sectors of the economy. In the first place, the productions of urban slaves are excluded. Most of the properties recorded were large, the average size being 174.8 slaves as compared with 25.1 for the island as a whole. Since none of the holdings were managed by resident proprietors,[7] little can be learnt from the Accounts Produce about the relative productivity of resident and absentee proprietorship.[8] Some of the properties were frankly unprofitable, being in the hands of receivers and mortgagees. It may also be that there was a certain slackness in the production when deceased estates passed into the hands of administrators or trustees. Alternatively, some attorneys may have taken the opportunity to sell off as much of the realizable assets as possible, when they were paid by commission, since their appointment would not be assured under a new owner. Yet, in spite of these considerations, it remains true that the holdings on which the majority of the slaves were located, at least, were chronically subject to these problems.

Attorneys and overseers were often castigated as mendacious knaves who would conceal or falsify production or receipts whenever it suited them. It is true that some were lax in returning their Accounts Produce.[9] But if they stole a part of the produce and sold it on their own account it is impossible to trace this. It was probably more common for attorneys and overseers to work private deals, rather than actually concealing output.[10] In such cases the prices charged would be abnormal, so by applying standard values to all sales it is possible to remove these aberrations. Occasionally the Accounts Produce list the sale of horses and rum from the property to the overseer and none of these suggest that the overseers undercharged themselves. By 1832

Jamaica was basically a money economy (in an accounting sense), though barter was still carried on.[11] The general reliability of the Accounts Produce is not affected by barter since all transactions can be reduced to money terms.

The year 1832 has been chosen for analysis because it fits the terminal date of the Returns of Registrations of Slaves (analysed in most detail in the demographic section of this study). This reduces the problem of changes in ownership, thus maximizing the level of success achieved in fitting the Accounts Produce to the Returns of Registrations of Slaves.[12] In general, the Accounts Produce were sworn early in 1833 for the calendar year 1832, while the Returns of Registrations of Slaves were made at the end of June 1832.[13] The year 1832 was one of good weather. In 1831 there was a drought over the entire island, and in May an attorney in St. Thomas-in-the-East reported that it was 'suffering from the most severe drought which has visited the island since the year 96 – nearly the whole of the rivers and springs in this parish, being entirely dried up'.[14] But in June there were fine rains and by October the canes were said to be unusually forward.[15] In 1832 the crop, although interrupted by heavy rains in some areas, produced good yields.[16] But in the western parishes some estates were devastated in the rebellion of Christmas 1831 and their output was diminished significantly. At the island level, however, the rebellion seems to have had little impact; in fact the production of sugar and coffee was greater than in 1831.

In order to classify the 960 properties for which Accounts Produce are available, it is necessary first to reduce the data to a consistent measure of output. Three possible solutions to the problem need to be considered.[17] The first involves an assessment of the area devoted to each crop or of the volume of production. This cannot be applied directly to the Accounts Produce, since little is known of regional variations in yields and it is difficult to include livestock or the jobbing of slave labour in such a scheme. Secondly, the volume of production can be converted to standard annual man-days of labour input. This measure is very useful since it changes least over time, but it involves the assumption that inputs are uniform over space. The average man-days required to produce a hogshead of sugar could probably be determined,[18] but there is a paucity of relevant data relating to the minor staples, timber and livestock. Hence this measure is not applicable to the Accounts Produce. The third method of measurement is based on the monetary value of production. Although these values are not always stated directly in the returns, the relevant data are ready to hand within the Accounts Produce themselves. This is the approach adopted. All of the forms of produce have been assigned standard values (in Jamaica currency); because the data are thin, regional variations in price or quality have had to be ignored. The technical problems involved and the weights, measures and values employed are discussed in Appendix I. The justification for using this measure lies in the fact that the area and man-day measures could only be determined in many cases via the monetary. Its chief limitation is that since prices and yields vary, value may be a poor measure of the planter's intentions and expectations; but this also applies in part to the volume and man-day measures.[19]

The gross receipts of each of the 960 Accounts Produce properties have been grouped according to seventeen sources of income. Next, each property has been classified in terms of its combination of land and labour uses, following the method developed by Weaver.[20] Every source of income (or 'crop') contributing more than 1 per cent of gross receipts is considered. The mixture of crops is compared with a theoretical curve by means of calculating the standard deviations, so that the most efficient description of the combination of crops on each property can be selected. It is assumed that, ideally, a monocultural unit would obtain 100 per cent of its income from a single crop, a two-crop combination 50 per cent from each of two crops, and so on. The actual production of each property is compared with this ideal pattern to discover which kind of combination it most closely resembles. For example, a property receiving 54 per cent of its income from the sale of sugar, 24 per cent from pimento, 13 per cent from logwood, 5 per cent from livestock and 2 per cent from ginger, would be classified as a sugar–pimento–logwood three-crop combination. In practice, the combination selected will depend to a certain extent on the way in which the crops are classified before analysis, but a balance can be struck between attempting to extract the last drop of information relating to land and labour use and finding a manageable range of combinations.

Patterns of land and labour use

Sugar, rum and molasses accounted for 76 per cent of the total receipts of the 960 properties included in the Accounts Produce for 1832 (Appendix 1). Coffee (12 per cent) and livestock (6 per cent) were important, but after these only pimento (allspice) and jobbing labour exceeded 1 per cent. Of the other sources of income only pasturage, cartage and wharfage contributed more than £10,000, together making up 1.2 per cent of total receipts. But these percentages display the bias of the Accounts Produce rather than the true distribution of contributions to the Jamaica economy. It was the small plantations and settlements producing the minor staples, the pens and the jobbing gangs which were the least likely to appear in the Accounts Produce because their owners most commonly lived in the island and managed their own affairs. In 1832 the total exports of Jamaica were officially valued at £3,940,019 (or £2,814,299 sterling),[21] almost exactly the same amount as that estimated for the total receipts of the Accounts Produce properties (£3,916,794). But receipts from exports on the latter amounted to only about £3,000,000. Thus the Accounts Produce properties, with only 53.6 per cent of the slave population, produced 76 per cent of the total value of Jamaica exports in 1832. This demonstrates clearly the partiality of the

Table 1. *Size and export-orientation of the crop combinations, 1832* (Accounts Produce properties)

Crop combination	Number of properties	Number of slaves	Slaves per holding	Produce exported (%)	Produce sent to Kingston (%)
Sugar	527	117,670	223.28	78.40	4.76
Coffee	176	22,562	128.19	69.52	12.32
Coffee–labour	15	1,513	100.86	42.00	12.90
Coffee–livestock	11	1,885	171.36	50.84	0.30
Pimento	15	1,287	85.80	30.89	2.82
Livestock	56	5,529	98.73	1.03	0.00
Livestock–pimento	11	1,263	114.81	16.57	2.43
Labour (jobbing)	25	1,338	53.52	1.24	0.14
Livestock–labour	34	4,205	123.67	0.46	0.95
Wharfage	6	148	24.66	0.00	0.00
Sugar–pimento	4	682	170.50	63.63	7.43
Coffee–pimento	4	354	88.50	11.31	0.00
Livestock–dyewoods	4	412	103.00	8.34	0.00
Pimento–livestock–labour	4	532	133.00	17.61	7.78
Total	960	167,858	174.84	71.16	5.32

Source: Appendixes 1 and 2.

Accounts Produce. But it also shows that they represent a considerable proportion of the total economy.

Less than 50 per cent of the slave population of Jamaica was located on sugar estates in 1832. This estimate is arrived at by two different methods. The total value of sugar (muscovado) produced on the 960 Accounts Produce properties was £2,399,878 (Appendix 1). This was the produce of 540 estates, 527 of which have been classified as sugar monocultures and on which there were 117,670 slaves (Table 1). The thirteen properties on which sugar formed part of a mixed-crop combination were slightly larger than the monocultural estates, with a total of 3,410 slaves (Appendix 2). Thus the total value of sugar (produced on the 960 properties) was made by 121,080 slaves. Now, it is known that 78.40 per cent of the production of the sugar estates (including rum and molasses) was exported, and 4.76 per cent was sent to Kingston (Table 1); some of the latter was consigned to agents who later exported the sugar (but little of the rum), and it cannot be assumed that the remainder was all sold within the island since it includes that proportion of the crop 'undisposed' at the end of the year. Thus it is probable that more than 80 per cent of the production of the island's sugar estates was in fact exported. Using the same parameters as applied to the Accounts Produce properties, the total value of all sugar exported from Jamaica can be estimated from the published volumetric returns: £2,339,934.[22] If only

78.4 per cent of the island's sugar production was exported, total output was worth about £2,985,000. Thus the Accounts Produce properties made 78 per cent of the total sugar output, and if the productivity of slaves on sugar estates not included in the Accounts Produce was similar there must have been a total of about 154,500 slaves on sugar estates in 1832. This is an upper-limit estimate because the quantity of sugar exported was probably greater than 78 per cent (both because of the problems of undisposed and re-consigned sugar, and because of the inclusion of rum in the export figures in Table 1), and also because the unrecorded estates were probably smaller than average.

The second approach to the problem, with regard to sugar, is via the number of estates. The best estimate of the number of sugar estates operating around 1832 puts the total at 670.[23] Applying the average slave population on the monocultural Accounts Produce estates gives a total of 149,600 slaves. This is very close to the 154,500 estimated from the ratio of exports to production. It can be concluded that in 1832 no more than 155,000 slaves were settled on estates producing sugar, or almost 50 per cent of the total slave population of Jamaica.

The same method can be applied to coffee. About 70 per cent of the total output of the Accounts Produce properties cultivating coffee was exported (Table 1). The value of coffee exported from Jamaica in 1832 can be put at £643,312, so the value of total production cannot have exceeded £919,000. The plantations included in the Accounts Produce, then, contributed 51 per cent of total output, and the total number of slaves on monocultural coffee plantations cannot have been more than 45,000.

Plantations producing pimento as a monoculture exported only 31 per cent of their output. Since Jamaica exported pimento to the value of £55,585, the upper limit of total production can be put at £150,000. Thus there were probably no more than 3,000 slaves on monocultural pimento plantations in 1832.

Diversified plantations producing the minor staples, livestock pens and jobbing gangs exported only a small proportion of their total output, hence it is unsafe to attempt to estimate their real extent from the Accounts Produce sample using the methods applied to sugar, coffee and pimento. Nor are there any reliable estimates of the absolute numbers of these units. According to the census of 1844 there were 378 'breeding pens' in the island in that year.[24] Around 1832, 405 holdings were referred to as 'pens' in the Returns of Registrations of Slaves (1832), the Accounts Produce (1832), or the Claims for Compensation (1834).[25] But 47 of them were located on the periphery of Kingston, in lower St. Andrew, and most of these probably fell into the class of 822 units termed by the 1844 census 'pens with residence and woodland and pasture'. A rough estimate of 400 pens producing livestock and perhaps some minor export staples in 1832 is likely to be close to the truth, and applying the Accounts Produce norm of 100 slaves per pen (Table 1) results in a total of 40,000 slaves located on such units.

Around 1832, 494 properties were referred to as 'plantations'. About 350 of these have already been classified as coffee plantations and 30 as pimento plantations, thus there must have been at least 120 diversified plantations cropping the minor staples. In 1844 there were said to be 671 coffee plantations in Jamaica, and between 1832 and 1847 some 465 (with 49,383 slaves located on them in 1832) had been abandoned.[26] This suggests that the 45,000 slaves attributed to coffee plantations above is deficient, but it is probable that the later estimates were not confined to monocultural coffee plantations and included many properties which produced coffee as only one of a broader group of staples. It is conservative to suggest that there were 200 plantations in addition to the 380 already identified in 1832, and that (assuming the Accounts Produce average of 100 slaves for each of these diversified units) there must have been at least 20,000 slaves on such plantations.

The number of slaves worked in jobbing gangs and on wharves (independent of the urban ports) cannot be determined from the Accounts Produce. Jobbing and wharfage were often adjuncts to estate and plantation operations, but more frequently they were carried on by resident white smallholders.[27] Only six holdings in the Accounts Produce for 1832 are classified as wharves; but using the scattered references in the returns it is possible to identify at least 24 wharves, operating independently of the urban ports. Assuming 25 slaves at each of these (Table 1), gives a total of 600 slaves on the wharves. In 1834 the Assistant Commissioners appointed to value the slaves for the compensation of their masters at emancipation found 2,329 on 'wharves, shipping etc'.[28] But 819 of these slaves were in Kingston, and probably another 500 in the other urban ports. Thus a total of 1,000 slaves located on wharves outside of the towns is likely to be an upper-limit estimate. In 1834 the Assistant Commissioners of compensation classified 19,558 slaves as 'prædial unattached', which category corresponds roughly to that of the jobbing gangs. Thus 20,000 slaves worked in jobbing gangs forms an upper-limit estimate for 1832.

The results of the preceding calculations are gathered together in Table 2. The urban slave population has been estimated from the Returns of Registrations of Slaves for 1832, according to assumptions described in Chapter 5 below. Thus far 4,000 slaves have not been accounted for, and there seems to be no rule at hand to determine how they should be distributed. It is only certain that they were not in the towns or on wharves or sugar estates. It is improbable that they were worked in jobbing gangs or on monocultural pimento plantations. Most of them were probably settled on small holdings producing the minor staples, livestock or provisions. But redistribution along these lines would have little impact on the general pattern. It must be noted, however, that the category 'jobbing' does not fit easily into the classification adopted in Table 2. The sugar estates were the greatest employers of the jobbing gangs, but they also worked extensively on coffee and pimento

Table 2. *Estimated distribution of slaves, 1832*

	Number	Percentage
Sugar	155,000	49.5
Coffee	45,000	14.4
Livestock pens	40,000	12.8
Urban	25,000	8.0
Minor staples plantations	20,000	6.4
Jobbing gangs	20,000	6.4
Pimento	3,000	0.9
Wharves	1,000	0.3
Other	4,000	1.3
Total	313,000	100.0

Source: see text.

plantations in the picking season, and on the public roads. Even if the jobbers' slaves worked exclusively on sugar estates, this would increase the share of sugar to only 56 per cent of the total slave population. Slaves permanently settled on coffee and pimento plantations or on pens were also occasionally hired by the sugar estates, but it is fair to conclude that in 1832 at least 40 per cent of the slaves of Jamaica spent no part of their time labouring on sugar estates. In many cases, certainly, they laboured on units which supplied the sugar estates with goods and services, but this did not involve them personally in the labour regime or the social institutions peculiar to sugar.

The industrial distribution of the slave labour force is only one way of measuring the relative importance of the different sectors of the economy. Other approaches may place the emphasis elsewhere. Sheridan, for example, does so in his estimation of the wealth of Jamaica in the eighteenth century. The Jamaica poll tax roll of 1768, according to Sheridan, showed 40.6 per cent of the slave population located on coffee, cotton, ginger, pimento and other plantations and establishments, or in Kingston;[29] a proportion similar to that found for 1832. But by following through the ramifications of sugar Sheridan concludes that at least 84 per cent of the slaves were 'involved either directly or indirectly in the sugar industry', around 1773.[30] Even when arguing from the distribution of the slaves in 1768, noted above, Sheridan allows the non-sugar sector a contribution to his total wealth estimate of only 14 per cent. Although it was certainly not as land- or capital-intensive as the sugar sector,[31] this seems an understatement of its wealth–labour ratio. The Accounts Produce data for 1832 do not permit comparable wealth estimates, but some crude labour–output ratios can be constructed. Average gross receipts produced per slave varied between the different crop-combina-

Table 3. *Estimated value of slave-produced income, 1832*[a]

	Gross income (£'000 currency)	Percentage
Sugar estates	4,007	58.5
Coffee plantations	863	12.6
Livestock pens	713	10.4
Urban	500	7.3
Minor staples plantations	480	7.0
Jobbing gangs	172	2.5
Pimento plantations	77	1.1
Wharves	42	0.6
Total	6,854	100.0

[a] The 'others' category in Table 2 is here included with the minor staples plantations, for which an average £20 gross receipts per slave has been assumed (on the basis of the A.P. crop-combination norms). For the urban slaves a £20 average has been assumed from the annual hire rates for domestics and tradesmen (Appendix 1).
Source: see text.

tion types,[32] and if these ratios are applied to the distribution of slave labour estimated in Table 2 an assessment of the gross income generated by the slaves (for their masters) in each of the sectors can be made (Table 3). This does enhance the role of sugar, but only to a small extent. Since jobbing was strictly labour-intensive, its addition to the sugar sector results in a total contribution to gross income of only 61 per cent. Only if it is assumed that, in 1832, all of the slaves labouring on pens and wharves, in jobbing gangs, and in the towns were producing intermediate goods and services for the sugar industry, can the importance of the sector be pushed towards 80 per cent. Its role is similar if the export sector is isolated. While these aspects of the economy were of great concern to the masters, from the point of view of the experience of the slaves sugar was significantly less important.

CHAPTER 3

AGRICULTURE

Having established, in broad outline, the relative importance of the sectors of the economy of Jamaica around 1832, it is necessary now to consider the character of these various enterprises. In this chapter, the size, internal organization and spatial distribution of the agricultural units will be described. Forms of economic activity other than agriculture will be discussed in Chapter 4.

When classified into crop-combination types,[1] it appears that 816 of the 960 Accounts Produce properties for 1832 are best described as monocultures (Appendix 2). A further 109 were two-crop combinations, but only 35 involved combinations of more than two crops. Once again, these figures display the bias of the Accounts Produce data. Yet even in terms of the probable distribution of the total slave labour force (Table 2 above) it can be estimated that about 75 per cent of the rural slave population was located on monocultural units, producing sugar, coffee, pimento or livestock. Sugar was rarely combined with other crops. Of the 540 Accounts Produce properties making sugar, only 13 produced other crops to a significant extent. Coffee was more frequently combined with other crops: 40 of the 216 coffee-producing properties were diversified. Livestock, on the other hand, was the sole significant source of income on only 56 of the 144 properties involved in its production. It was a basic ingredient in all of the more diversified properties. The inclusion of livestock serves as an index of what were called 'pens' and shows that they were often diversified by the production of minor staples, lumber and jobbing labour. Pimento, also, was most often produced as part of a diversified combination of crops.

Sugar estates

The dominance of sugar resulted in a significant correlation between the distribution of estates and the density of the slave population.[2] Sugar estates were strung along the entire length of the north coast; they were also concentrated on the Recent alluvial plains of coastal St. Thomas-in-the-East and the Plantain Garden River, on the plains of Westmoreland, Vere, St. Catherine and Liguanea, and in the interior basins of the upper Black and Rio Minho Rivers, at Lluidas Vale and St. Thomas-in-the-Vale (Figure 2). No significant correlations have been found between the distribution of sugar estates and altitude, slope, relative relief or rainfall (Table A3.2).

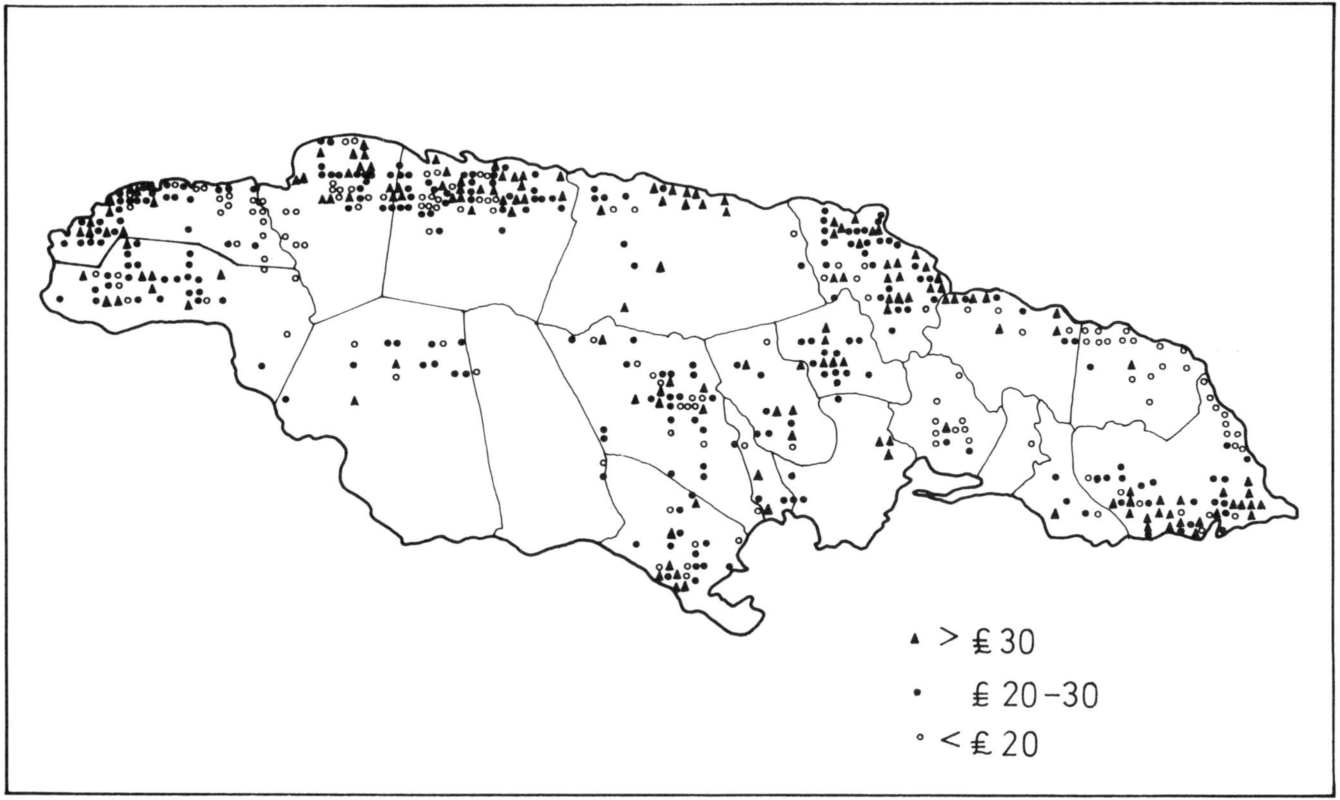

Figure 2. Sugar estates: Production per slave, Accounts Produce properties, 1832. Each symbol represents average gross receipts per slave on one estate.

But, although one planter asserted that 'sugar would grow anywhere almost',[3] the planters generally expressed fairly strong preferences for particular physical situations. Sugar cane does flourish in a wide variety of soils,[4] but the soil must always be well drained though retentive of moisture. In Jamaica, the favoured soils were the clays, clay loams and alluvial loams. The best was said to be a 'black mould upon clay'[5] or a deep and mellow 'brick mold' ('a compound of very fine particles of clay, sand, and black mold') which was easy to work, needed no manure, retained moisture well during drought and yet was well drained.[6] It was regarded second only to the 'ashy loam' of St. Kitts as a sugar-growing soil. Although Edward Long argued that apart from the problem of transportation inland situations were the best for estates, it was generally thought that these required more cultivation, manure and labour.[7] The value of the fertility of the few interior basins which were settled was, however, well recognized. The best land was believed to be nearly level, but it was also desirable to have an aspect to the sun, and sufficient slope to facilitate drainage.[8] Hilly land was liable to wash away and gully. On the north coast, Portland and St. George faced the greatest natural disadvantages of climate and transport.[9] Sugar needed not only adequate rainfall, but a marked dry spell in which the crop could be taken off. Cultivation was probably retreating from the marginal hillsides and the wettest and drought-prone parts of the island around 1832,[10] tempering the view that 'Providence has so diversified the landscape, that a variety of grounds present themselves to the view, of hill and dale, promising welfare to this benevolent, useful, and desirable plant . . .'[11]

The internal organization, and the annual and daily cycles of work on sugar estates have often been described and need not be repeated here.[12] Some regional variations in the patterns need to be outlined, however. A basic distinction was made between 'planting' estates and 'ratooning' or 'dry-weather' estates. On planting estates a proportion of new canes had to be planted each year, requiring much effort in the digging of cane holes. These estates were found most commonly on strong stiff soils,[13] which were suited to ploughing – yet the overseers preferred to employ jobbing gangs. In 1832 a planter of St. James stated that planting estates were common in his own parish, and in Westmoreland and Hanover.[14] Others believed that they were general in the interior, 'upper' Clarendon being cited specifically.[15] Ratooning or dry-weather estates, on the other hand, were believed to extend along the entire south side of the island and to occur often on the coastal edge of the north. Here the well-drained light soils meant that the canes did not rot in the ground and only a few plants had to be replaced each crop. After the cane had been cut the estate livestock was penned on the cane pieces to manure them.[16] These estates were believed to be very profitable ones, especially because the need to employ jobbing gangs was less than on the planting estates.

Regional variations also occurred in the seasonal pattern of production. On the south side of the island the crop was taken off between December and June, or August at the latest; sugar could not be shipped after 1st August without paying double insurance, and if stored until January it lost weight through drainage.[17] On the north side the crop generally extended from March to November. On the ratooning estates of the north coast a full plant was made between October and December, and a minor spring plant between March and May. In most parts of the south side an autumn plant was preferred (July to November), but 'in Vere and St. Dorothy's, the seasons being different, they give preference to a late fall or early spring [plant], because the seasons are not to be depended upon'.[18]

The nature of the output of the sugar estates varied little. Most of them occasionally sold their old, meagre livestock to pen-keepers for fattening or to butchers for killing. The only other important variations occurred in the relative proportions of sugar, rum and molasses produced. On the Accounts Produce estates, 80.3 per cent of the value of production came from sugar, 19.2 per cent from rum, and only 0.5 per cent from molasses. There was some variation between estates in these proportions, but the percentage of rum rarely fell below 15 and rarely rose above 25 per cent of the total value of production. Using the export figures, Eisner computed a ratio of 2.32 gallons of rum per hundredweight of sugar in 1832.[19] But the data derived from the Accounts Produce, which comprehend total production, give a ratio of 3.11, since almost 50 per cent of the rum produced in Jamaica was consumed in the island.[20]

Coffee plantations

Monocultural coffee production was concentrated into two distinct regions of Jamaica (Figure 3). In the west there was the area of rocky limestone hills centred on Manchester, and in the east the area of soils formed on shales and conglomerates, on fairly steep slopes, centred on the Port Royal Mountains and extending west through mountainous St. Mary and St. George. Between these two major regions was an area of thinly scattered plantations, stretching through St. Ann, St. John and St. Thomas-in-the-Vale,[21] where coffee was produced but was not significant enough to be described as a monoculture. The cultivation of coffee expanded rapidly, especially in the 1790s, following the drastic reduction of the British import duty in 1783.[22] The western coffee-producing region was still being settled at the beginning of the nineteenth century, and the parish of Manchester itself was not created until 1814.[23] At the same time, coffee plantations were already being abandoned in the eastern region as a result of erosion.[24]

Coffee required a deep virgin soil.[25] In Manchester, the most favoured soil was the 'loose friable greasy red earth' over white marl or limestone rock which occurred on the Carpenters and May Day Mountains, though there were also plantations north of Mile Gully.[26] 'The most favourable situation

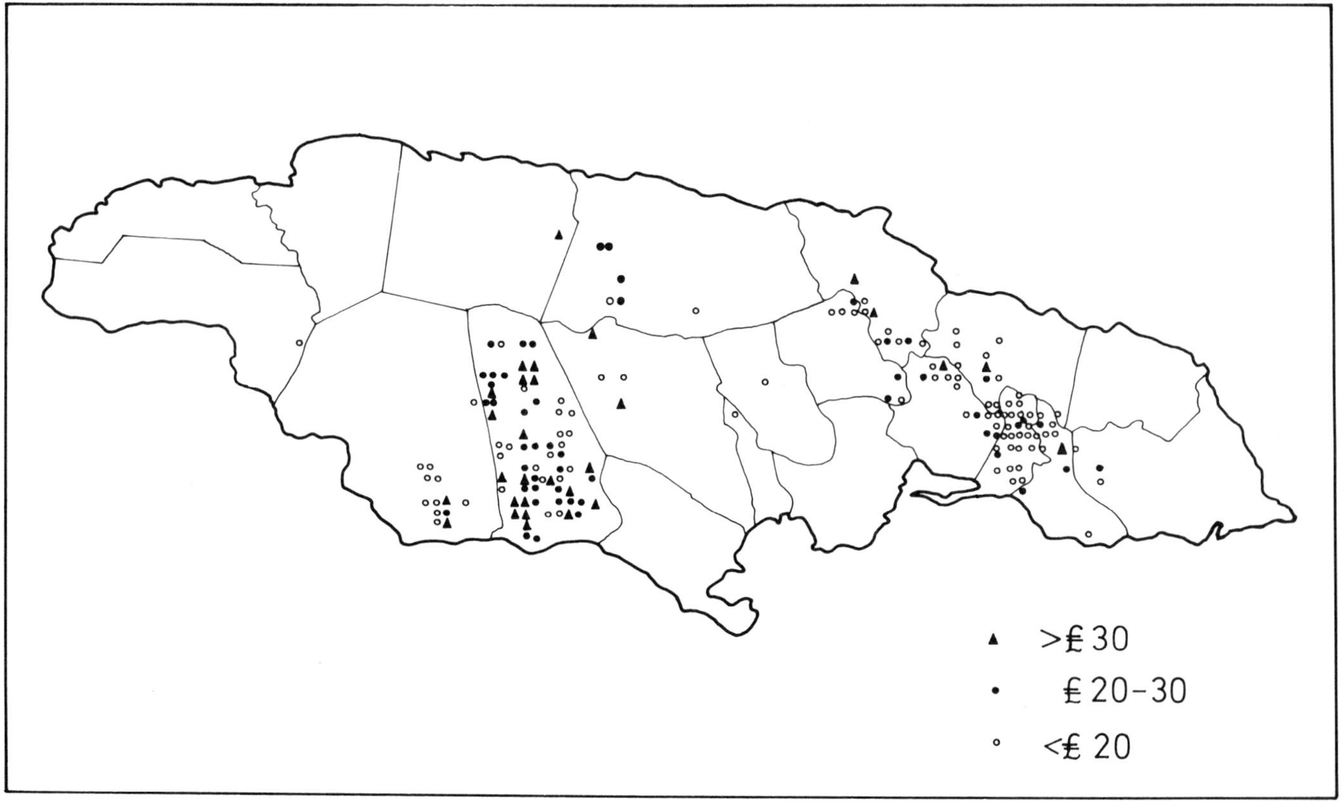

Figure 3. Coffee plantations: Production per slave, Accounts Produce properties, 1832. Each symbol represents average gross receipts per slave on one plantation.

for a coffee plantation', wrote Porter, 'is the side of a hill, exposed to the east, and where the earth is watered by occasional soft rains or refreshed by dews.'[27] In establishing a new plantation the general practice was to cut the lower branches from the trees and to burn these together with the brushwood on the site, the ashes manuring the soil. In the three- to four-year gestation period Indian corn and Angola peas were planted between the rows of coffee, and the slaves would also be employed establishing separate provision grounds.

Once the plantation was established, the tasks involved in its operation were restricted to weeding, pruning, picking the crop and roasting the berries on barbecues. Thus many planters organized their slaves on a task-work basis, especially in the picking season.[28] Kelly, a bookkeeper on Industry Plantation in St. George, reported that the only work not carried out on a task basis was the drying of the berries on the barbecues since this required constant attention.[29] The length and seasonal pattern of the crop time are uncertain. One attorney claimed that it lasted only six weeks,[30] but on Hermitage in Manchester it ran from December to March[31] and on Radnor in Port Royal it extended into October and November.[32]

In 1825 there were 206 slaves on Radnor Plantation, and three white men. Radnor covered 950 acres and an additional 37 acres were used as a pen.[33] (In 1832 the average coffee plantation had only 128 slaves, compared to 223 on sugar estates: Table 1 above.) At Radnor, most of the slaves were organized into three gangs, as on sugar estates, while others worked as carpenters, sawyers, masons, stockmen and domestics. When the slaves were served with cloth they were divided into seven 'classes': in the first three were 13 slaves who were given twenty-four to twenty-eight yards of oznaburgs and pennistones, in the fourth and fifth classes there were 164 slaves receiving twelve to fifteen yards, and in the sixth and seventh 40 receiving from six to ten yards.[34] At Christmas in the same year, 1825, the division was a little different: head people, great gang, second gang, third gang and children. The head people were given 12 lb. of fish, two bottles of rum and a quarter of sugar, whereas those in the third gang got only 4 lb. of fish, half a bottle of rum and half a pint of sugar.[35] Thus the pattern of occupation, status and preference was similar to that on sugar estates. But on coffee plantations smaller than Radnor this similarity must have been less.

At Radnor, the employment of the tradesmen, domestics and stockmen varied little from day to day and season to season. There was a greater amount of flexibility in the field gangs. Two extracts from the plantation journal illustrate the range of duties:[36]

Monday, 31 October 1825. The first gang weeding Abrahams piece. Second and third gangs picking coffee on Garden Flat. Carpenters and masons as before [in the horse and mule stable]. Pruners pruning McGillivray's piece. Two hands in the woods getting rafters, posts to repair and build huts in the field. 1 hand repairing the sheep penn. One boy cutting grass and one with two jacks [asses] carrying the same for the mules.

Monday, 14 November 1825. First gang, males, supplying [planting] young coffee on Garden Flat, females, cutting thatch. Second and third gangs picking coffee on Love's piece. Carpenters preparing stuff to make a house at the pen (St. Andrews). Masons at odd jobs, 2 hands building huts in the field . . .

The only regular employment not mentioned in these two entries is the carriage of the coffee to the wharf. Most of the bags were carried by mules, but some were transported by the slaves on their heads.[37]

The coffee plantation was less 'industrialized' than the sugar estate. This meant that the organization of labour was less strictly regimented – especially as a result of the widespread use of the task system – and that occupational allocations were more flexible. The corollary of this was that the occupations were relatively standardized, and that the slave living on a coffee plantation had less opportunities to learn trades and skills. Similarly, slaves on coffee plantations were less subject to a seasonal regime, and a prolonged crop period, than their fellows on sugar estates.[38]

Pimento plantations

Pimento (allspice) was the only other significant crop produced as a monoculture. But whereas most of the properties producing sugar or coffee were monocultural, most of those producing pimento were diversified. In fact 167 of the 960 Accounts Produce properties marketed pimento in 1832 but there were only fifteen monocultural plantations. The latter were concentrated into a narrow zone along the coast of St. Ann, only two plantations falling outside this area (one being in St. Mary and the other in St. John). In contrast to this specialist concentration, the production of pimento as part of a wider combination of crops was very widespread. As in the eighteenth century,[39] there were many pimento walks in eastern Trelawny and St. Ann, but there was also a sprinkling around the western coasts, a few extending across from St. Elizabeth to St. Ann and some more extending east along the mountain ridge. In St. Ann the pimento grew on red limestone soils, but elsewhere it grew on a variety of soils, notably black marl, in areas of heavy precipitation.

The labour demanded by pimento was thought to be minimal, and considerably less than that required by coffee.[40] The trees were indigenous, and said to be seeded by birds in ruinate land.[41] Porter noted that 'the mode usually practised in Jamaica is to select a piece of ground in the vicinity of another plantation, or in an hitherto uncultivated district where the plant is of spontaneous production'.[42] All that was required was to cut out the vegetation other than pimento. Sometimes, however, it seems that the planters took greater pains and planted the trees into walks or groves. Apart from the occasional bushing of the walks, the major effort came at the harvest (probably between July and September) when the branches were broken, the berries picked, spread on barbecues to dry, fanned and then bagged and carried to port for shipment. As with coffee, this work was often carried out on a task basis. One reference to the picking of pimento 'on the halves' has been found,[43] so some planters may have maintained only a minimal number of slaves throughout the year and employed jobbers' slaves to harvest the crop. But since the monocultural pimento plantations had an average of 86 slaves in 1832 (Table 1 above) it would seem unlikely that they needed to hire jobbing gangs. Nothing definite is known about the organization of the slaves into occupational groups on the pimento plantations; it can only be presumed that the pattern was roughly the same as that on coffee plantations, though on a smaller scale.

Pens

Livestock formed the sole source of income on a significant proportion of properties but, unlike sugar, coffee and pimento, it was raised for sale within the island and not for export. The pens were dependent on the demand for pasturage and stock from the estates and plantations. In consequence, they were widely distributed, though generally restricted to the gently sloping coastal plains and the relatively level uplands of eastern St. Ann. The distribution of the Accounts Produce properties for 1832 classified as pens, producing only livestock for sale, shows concentrations in eastern Hanover, eastern St. Ann, St. Elizabeth, Vere and St. Catherine. It has already been established, however, that the proportion of pens included in the Accounts Produce was small, so an independent check on this pattern is required. This can be found in the poll tax rolls. A tax of 10d was levied on every horse, gelding, mare, colt, filly, mule-colt and follower of breeding mares, every bull, cow, heifer, calf and follower of breeding cows, and every young steer for sale.[44] Thus not all livestock were taxed; exempt were working animals on estates and plantations (mules, spayed heifers and planter's steers).[45] The ratio of slaves to taxable stock, as a result, tends to over-emphasize those areas where livestock was kept on pens in contrast to those on estates and plantations; hence it serves well as a measure of the distribution of pens.[46] This ratio shows the chief pen parishes to be St. Elizabeth (1.12 livestock per slave) and St. Ann (0.95 : 1), followed by St. Catherine (0.73 : 1), Westmoreland (0.68 : 1) and St. Dorothy (0.64 : 1). Parishes in which pens were not significant, with ratios of less than 0.25 : 1, were Trelawny, St. John, St. Andrew, Port Royal and Portland. The island average was 0.44 : 1.

Pens competed with sugar estates for space in the lowlands, but generally they were pushed into the backlands and into the pockets of gently sloping land surrounded by hills.[47] According to Long, the pens of St. Elizabeth were chiefly concentrated in the dry and infertile savannahs between the mountains of the eastern part of the parish, where sugar estates were rare.[48]

The development of Guinea grass encouraged the extension of pen-keeping, but it was believed that the best livestock for estate work was that bred on 'common pasture' or savannah.[49] The best of these lands were spread along the southern plains.

The pens were said to rank with the sugar estates in 'respectability and responsibility', and to be of less trouble and expense to the proprietor.[50] They were also extolled because they contributed to Jamaica's economic self-sufficiency and augmented the creole, resident white population.[51] For the slaves, life on a pen meant less regimentation than on a sugar estate, a greater dispersion of isolated, individual occupations and a greater degree of contact with a resident master's family. On many pens the slaves were divided into gangs but their duties were most strictly ordered when they were employed in agricultural tasks. The great gang, made up of the ablest people, chipped logwood, mended fences and planted corn. The second gang, comprising the aged and adolescent, was put to cleaning the pastures of weeds, clearing corn pieces, shelling corn and so on. The small gang of juveniles carried bundles of grass to the stables and wild vine to the hogsty. In addition to the gangs, a considerable number of slaves were employed in the stables as groomsmen, horse breakers, saddlers and cleaners. Others had to dig pits so that the jackasses could mount the mares, to build yards, stables and fences, and to spay the heifers. Yet others were mounted stockmen.[52] Some of the pens not only bred working stock for sale to the planters but also fattened animals for sale to butchers or, in a few cases, for slaughter in their own butcheries. The labour exacted on pens was not light, but the occupations of the slaves did involve a degree of independent action and skill which was wanting for the majority on sugar estates, were less demanding physically and probably provided more opportunities for shirking. The degree of control which the master could exert over the slave labour force was also limited by the difficulty of implementing the task system on pens, in contrast to the opportunities on coffee and pimento plantations. But on the pens the proprietor was more often resident, and the slaves belonged to smaller communities than those on sugar estates or coffee plantations.

Patterns of diversification

Whereas the majority of the Accounts Produce properties for 1832 were based on income from a single significant source, a considerable number of the proprietors found it profitable to tap two or more sources. The nature of these combinations of income-sources, and the reasons for them, will be discussed in this section.[53]

The properties which have been classified as two-crop combinations were made up principally of mixtures of the four major monocultures – sugar, coffee, pimento and livestock (Appendix 2). They extended only to incorporate dyewoods, which were not produced monoculturally. But they also included jobbing labour and cartage, which did form the sole significant source of income on some units (and as such will be discussed in Chapter 4). The most important of the two-crop combinations was that linking livestock and jobbing. With an average of 124 slaves, these properties were larger than both pen and jobbing monocultures. Their spatial distribution fits most closely the pattern of pens, hence it is probable that the masters jobbed the strongest slaves most of the time, while making them perform the heaviest tasks on the pens when they were not engaged elsewhere and keeping the aged and young on the property all of the time.

Properties combining coffee and jobbing had an average of 101 slaves, falling between the monocultural coffee plantations (128 slaves) and the jobbing gangs (54 slaves). It is possible that the seasonal demands of coffee meant that the planter tried to find employment for some of his slaves on other properties when his own harvest was completed. Other reasons for this combination are suggested by the distribution of the coffee–jobbing properties. All of them were located on the margins of the specialized coffee regions of Manchester and Port Royal. It may be hypothesized that the environmental conditions of these marginal areas were found unsuited to profitable coffee production and hence the planters sought alternative sources of income. Support for this may be found in the fact that the value of production per slave was considerably less on the coffee–jobbing properties than on the monocultural plantations (£13.5 compared to £19.2). On the other hand, the spatial marginality of these properties may have been the cause of their diversification, since they were closer to the sugar areas where their labour was in demand.

Jobbing was a fairly crude method of diversifying the use of slave labour. It had the advantage of flexibility, but at the same time it was dependent on the demands of other planters who preferred to purchase slaves of their own[54] or to use jobbers' slaves only for the heaviest tasks. As a result of this uncertainty, many planters tried to maintain full control of the occupations of their slaves while diversifying the use of the land in their possession. The most important of these types were combinations of livestock with coffee and with pimento.

In contrast to the distribution of coffee–jobbing properties, some of the coffee–livestock units were located in the centre of the monocultural coffee region of Manchester. None of them were in Port Royal, but there the slopes were too steep for effective livestock-rearing. Those in Manchester exploited the juxtaposition of contrasting land types, the hill and hollow landscape noticed by Long and others. Grove Place Plantation, for example, was located in a depression at the foot of Mile Gully Mountain, where the soil was said to become less suited to coffee but excellent for Guinea grass.[55] In 1832, when it was in the hands of a receiver, Grove Place covered 3,493 acres, maintaining 575 head of livestock.[56] There were 308 slaves on the plantation.[57] The total value of production in 1832 was £7,776, of which £5,738 came from coffee and £1,692 from the sale of working cattle, mules, horses and fat cattle. Minor sources of income were pimento, jobbing, cartage and the hire of slaves.[58] The size of Grove Place probably meant that it was able to comprehend more than one land type within its boundaries, but it was often the case that a proprietor held two separate lots of land which he integrated by using the same group of slaves on both. A measure of internal complementarity existed, principally in the supply of livestock for the coffee-producing part of the property. This pattern was similar to that in which sugar estates maintained their own pens to supply working livestock. But the demand for livestock was much greater in sugar than coffee, so that these pens were generally operated as autonomous units with an independent slave labour force (in the ratio of one pen to two or three estates).

On all but one of the eleven coffee–livestock properties the most important source of income was coffee. This explains the localization of the units within the major coffee regions, and it also suggests that the pens were appended to provide livestock for the plantations rather than as a primary land use directed towards cash sales. The exception was Carton Pen in St. Ann which raised working livestock for sale to the estates and also served an important function as a centre for fattening stock.[59] Here coffee was produced either to make use of the pen's large slave population (165 in 1832)[60] or to exploit varied land types within its boundaries.

Of the eleven livestock–pimento properties, pimento was most important on six and livestock on five. The nature of the pimento crop suggests that it was included on pens when the trees happened to be present, and whether it was harvested or not depended on the price and the availability of slaves at the right time of the year. This is borne out by the fact that nine of the properties were called 'pens' and only two 'plantations'. On the other hand, all but two of them were located in the region of monocultural pimento production centred on St. Ann, even though pimento was very widespread. Thus pimento only became significant on pens which were located where it was most profitable to grow and harvest the crop. Similarly, the four sugar–pimento properties were all situated in eastern St. Ann, though in every case sugar was the primary source of income. Of the four coffee–pimento properties, however, only two were in St. Ann while the others were in St. Elizabeth and Port Royal. In general, it seems that pimento was included in crop combinations only when there were available stands on the properties, though in some cases it may have indicated planned land and labour use.

Four properties clustering around the southern end of the Westmoreland–St. Elizabeth border combined the production of livestock and dyewoods. In each case dyewoods formed the secondary source of income and the theory of availability applied to pimento probably applies here as well. Logwood and fustic, the principal dyewoods, were widely distributed and were exploited by many properties, though mainly on the southern side of the island to the west of Spanish Town, and with a definite concentration in St.

Elizabeth and Westmoreland. The logwood was first introduced from Honduras in 1715 but as it was self-sown it had overrun extensive tracts by the 1780s.[61] It was commonly planted for hedges and fences.[62] The trees were cut into billets and the bark and white sap was chipped off; the red heart was exported for use in dye-making, while the chips were sometimes used for medicinal purposes.[63]

Of the two-crop combinations perhaps the most interesting are those involving sugar. But care must be taken in interpreting their significance. Most sugar estates sold their old, meagre livestock when they could, but the contribution of this to their income was always small. And planters tried to reduce their costs by breeding their own working stock,[64] but this did not normally provide an income. In 1832 an abnormal pattern occurred on two sugar estates in Hanover which had been burned in the rebellion and were in the hands of receivers; here sales of livestock became significant only because the output of sugar was unusually small, and because the estates were forced to sell off their working livestock.[65] Pedro River Estate, the third sugar–livestock property, was not involved in the rebellion, being located in St. Ann near the junction with Clarendon and St. John. But it, too, was in trouble. Its sugar and rum had to be carted twenty miles to the coast, and by 1832 it had begun selling its working livestock to pen-keepers in the Moneague district. In 1832 there had been 234 slaves on the property but by 1834 only 28; and by 1847 the estate had been abandoned.[66] It can be concluded, then, that sugar and livestock did not form elements of a combined property economy, as sources of cash income, except when planters were in straitened circumstances.

The three properties which combined sugar and coffee were also in difficulties. But, unlike the sale of livestock, such diversification involved planned land and labour use. One of them, Leicesterfield Plantation in upper Clarendon, covered 4,053 acres and was thus able to comprehend both the hills and limited river flats of the region. Coffee provided 69 per cent and sugar 29 per cent of its gross income, but average production per slave was only £14, much less than on the normal sugar or coffee property.[67] On the other sugar–coffee properties, sugar was the principal crop. Both were situated in limited, gorge-like river valleys. At Dallas Castle on the Cane River in Port Royal the slaves produced an average of only £8 in 1832. By 1847 it, like Leicesterfield, had been abandoned.[68] But on the third sugar–coffee property, Windsor Castle in St. David, production per slave was not abnormal (£24), and there is nothing to suggest economic difficulty.[69] Here at least there seems to have been a conscious and successful combination of land and labour use.

Some forms of diversification stemmed from the special locational advantages possessed by particular properties. Thus the pens which also received a significant income from cartage were all located in lower Clarendon and St. Dorothy, well placed to act as carriers for goods passing from the ports to the interior estates. All of these pens were well diversified: they engaged in making lime and jobbing, and they grew corn and rented out their pastures.[70] Corn and provisions entered the cash economies of several properties in combination with livestock, jobbing, cartage, coffee, pimento and lumber. But it is well known that the greatest volume of Jamaica's ground provisions was produced by the slaves, outside the plantation economy. In 1832 it was noted that 'the great bulk of the provisions are raised by negroes belonging to plantations'.[71] But corn and provisions did enter the plantation economy in areas scattered around the major urban markets of the eastern parishes. They were generally part of an extended pattern of diversification.[72] The varieties of ground provisions sold by the planters were not generally specified, but they included yams, cocos and plantains. Similarly, many properties rented their grass pieces for pasturage, but a few cut the grass and sold it in bundles. Most of the latter were located along the road from Spanish Town to Kingston, well placed to supply the urban markets.[73] Like provisions and cartage, this type of diversification was a product of unique locational advantages which enabled grass to compete with sugar.

Diversification, then, was the product of several factors. In some cases it was simply the result of economic hardship; here the planter exploited whatever was at hand – timber, pimento, logwood, livestock or his resources of jobbing labour. Others planned the employment of their slaves to encompass both jobbing on estates and the production of livestock and minor staples. More importantly, a number of proprietors perceived the several potentialities of the diverse land types within their control and organized their use accordingly, combining sugar, coffee, pimento, livestock and a whole range of minor staples. A few were able to diversify because of the special advantages of their locations in relation to the total economy – grass, cartage and ground provisions being the major examples. Beyond these four types of diversification there was a large number of small proprietors who must have found it profitable to produce more than one crop as a protection against climatic and market uncertainty. It is difficult to estimate what proportion of the pens and plantations fell into this class since they are under-represented in the Accounts Produce, but an approach to the problem can be made through the generic labels (the common nouns) attached to property names.

Estates, plantations, pens and settlements

Around 1832 four generic labels were in common usage in Jamaica: 'estate', 'plantation', 'pen' and 'settlement'.[74] Using three systematic lists[75] it is possible to map the application of these terms to particular property names. Although some of the smaller slave-holdings were not given generic labels in any of the three sources, the coverage obtained is very much more comprehensive than that provided by the Accounts Produce (Figures 4–7).

The word 'estate' was synonymous with a sugar estate,[76] but it was acceptable usage to refer to an estate as a 'sugar plantation' and the words were often interchanged.[77] Yet the general principle of naming all properties producing sugar 'estates' was followed very closely, as is shown by a comparison of the distribution of the sugar monocultures found in the Accounts Produce (Figure 2) with the properties termed estates (Figure 4). Even when sugar was combined with other crops the property was called an estate. A few properties in Manchester and Port Royal where there was no sugar were named estates either in error or in an attempt to acquire status, but it remains true that mapping the word 'estate' gives as accurate a picture of the distribution of sugar cultivation as any other source.

'Plantation' was a more general term than 'estate', but when used by itself it was meant to comprehend properties cultivating coffee, pimento, ginger, cotton, arrowroot and other minor staples.[78] Because of this generality its pattern of distribution is not as easy to interpret. Comparison with the distribution of coffee monocultures (Figure 3) leaves many gaps, and even a map of all Accounts Produce properties producing coffee fails to account for a very dense belt of plantations in St. George and Portland, and a sparser collection centred on St. John (Figure 5). The map of pimento production fills most of the gaps in St. Ann and eastern Trelawny. But plantations were rare in the far western parishes and pimento-growing in that region must have occurred on units other than plantations. The only way to account for the unexplained plantations of St. George, Portland and St. John, is to argue that they were probably coffee producers on a small scale, the proprietors being resident, or that they had changed their pattern of land use without changing their names.[79]

Senior, in 1835, said that a 'pen' was the same as an English breeding-farm, and 'on it are bred horses, mules, steers, (i.e. oxen), and all kinds of stock, and from which the butcher is supplied with fat cattle for the market'.[80] Long in 1774 referred to 'breeding-pens', 'grass-pens' and 'farms',[81] and Moreton in 1790 to 'grass-penns' or 'farms'.[82] In 1832 properties called pens (Figure 6) were concentrated in St. Ann, St. Elizabeth and the southern plain running from Vere to St. Catherine. Pens required level land as much as the sugar estates. A large number of pens were also located on the Liguanea Plain of lower St. Andrew, but this concentration must be explained as a variant of the system of nomenclature; these were large residential holdings.[83] Properties producing minor export staples together with livestock were commonly called pens, and many of these were located in the western parishes.

The most tantalizing of all the generic labels attached to property names is 'settlement'. This term was highly localized in its application. Most of the settlements were in Hanover, especially to the south of Lucea in the district of Dias, and from this core they thinned out rapidly, there being only three east of Rio Bueno (Figure 7). According to Senior, a 'settlement' might be merely a residence, 'or it may produce, to a trifling extent, all the articles

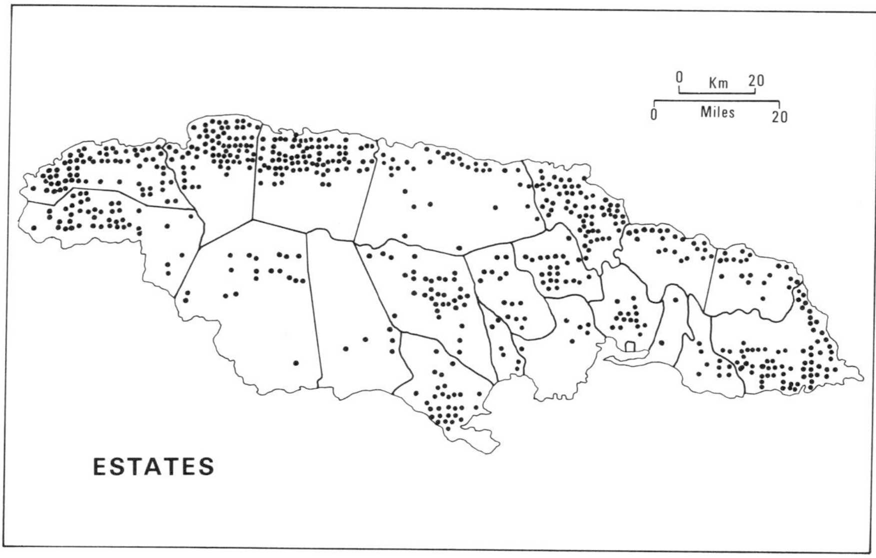

Figure 4. Holdings described as 'estates', 1832.

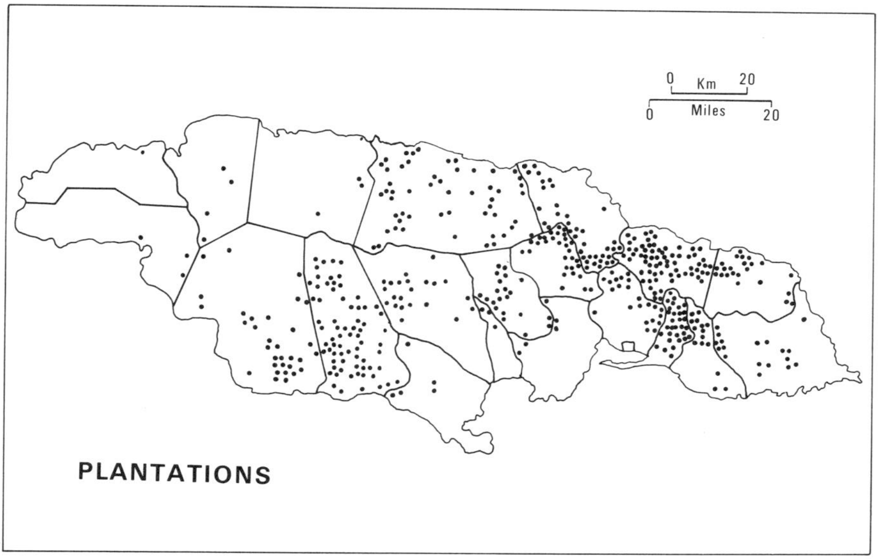

Figure 5. Holdings described as 'plantations', 1832.

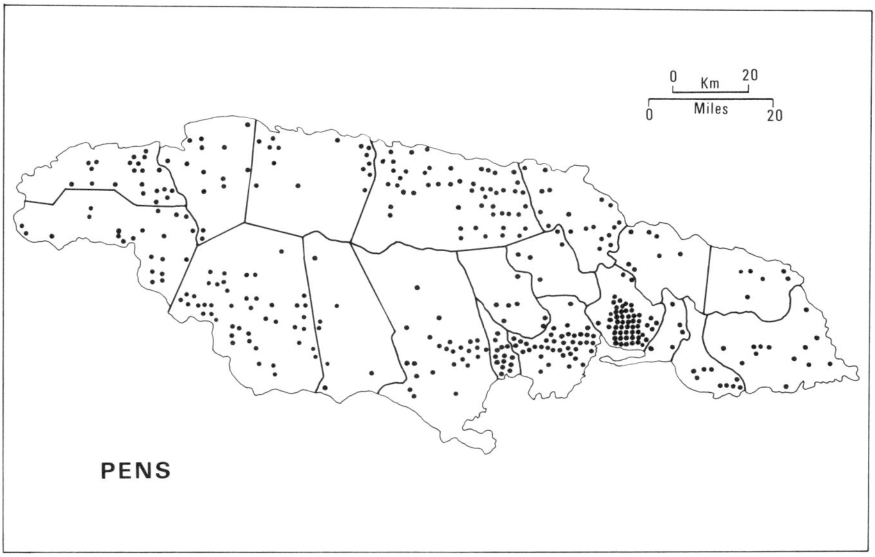

Figure 6. Holdings described as 'pens', 1832.

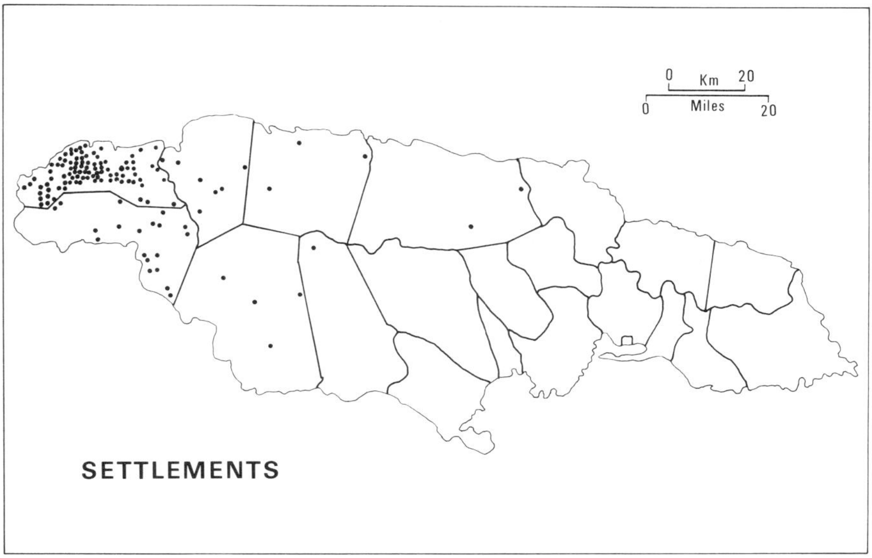

Figure 7. Holdings described as 'settlements', 1832.

cultivated on the plantation. On most of these possessions are found either logwood, fustic, lignum-vitae, or ebony.'[84] The concentration on dyewoods helps to explain their western localization. None of the settlements in Hanover found their way into the Accounts Produce (suggesting a very high rate of resident proprietorship), but the sizes of the slave-holdings provide a hint as to their nature. Almost half of them supported less than five slaves and only 18 out of 116 had more than twenty slaves, the largest having seventy-nine. In 1819 'Struy Settlement' in Westmoreland, with fourteen slaves, covered 100 acres planted out in Guinea grass and provisions.[85] In 1832 'a desirable mountain settlement' was offered for lease in St. John, together with a small gang of slaves; it covered 200 acres under coffee, pimento, provisions, fruit trees and hardwood.[86] Scattered references to settlements in the Accounts Produce confirm this emphasis on the minor staples, but also show that livestock and jobbing may have been important sources of income.[87] But no adequate explanation seems to be at hand for the peculiar distribution of the settlements.

This analysis of naming patterns does not solve all of the problems involved in attempting to fix the pattern of land and labour use around 1832, but does fill some of the gaps in the Accounts Produce data. It certainly demonstrates that the small, strongly diversified unit was both common and widely dispersed, even if it did not dominate the economy or the slave population.

Summary

In Jamaica around 1832 the various types of agricultural enterprise carried on by the slave-owners differed significantly in their degree of diversification and localization, and in their size and internal organization. At the property level, sugar was rarely combined with other crops; coffee was largely produced as a monoculture, though it also formed part of the output of many mixed-crop, minor staples plantations; pimento and livestock were most often part of a broader range of activities; all other crops were produced on diversified units. Thus there was a correlation between size and diversification, the largest units (in terms of their slave populations) being the most strictly monocultural and the smallest the most strongly diversified. For the latter, diversification was a response to uncertainties of climate and market, whereas the larger properties which showed significant diversification took advantage of contrasting land types within their boundaries or maximized the use of a slave labour force in excess of their basic needs.

Excepting the southwestern region, the coastal plains of Jamaica were settled by sugar estates intermixed with pens, and sugar spread in a belt through upper Clarendon, St. John and St. Thomas-in-the-Vale. Monocultural coffee plantations created regions of strong specialization, centred on Manchester and Port Royal. Pimento, as a monoculture, was confined to coastal

St. Ann. Pens specializing in livestock production spread out of the sugar regions into St. Elizabeth, Manchester and upland St. Ann. But about 25 per cent of the rural slaves were settled on small diversified holdings producing minor staples, livestock, provisions, and timber, and selling their labour to estates and plantations; these were widely scattered and overlapped the margins of the monocultural zones, especially in the western parishes.

The extent of resident proprietorship was closely related to the degree of diversification and the size of units. Thus the smaller the holding the greater the chances of contact between slave and master. But, in general, the smaller and more diversified the unit, the greater were the opportunities for the slaves to be involved in semi-independent, isolated tasks. On the other hand, the range of occupations and skills in which the slave might be engaged was greater on monocultural sugar estates than on small diversified units. This greater degree of occupational differentiation on the sugar estates went together with a relatively marked seasonal pattern of activities.

CHAPTER 4

OTHER ECONOMIC ACTIVITIES

Whereas the forms of agricultural enterprise in Jamaica displayed a certain, significant, degree of diversity, there is no doubt that the economy was essentially an agricultural one. In terms of the distribution of the slave labour force in 1832 (Table 2) it can be estimated that almost 90 per cent of the slaves worked on agricultural units. The only slaves outside this category were those living in towns or attached to wharves. But it is necessary to investigate the extent to which slaves living on agricultural holdings were engaged in strictly 'agricultural' occupations. In particular, the character and focus of activity of the jobbing gangs need to be compared with the patterns established for the agricultural units and for the towns. Thus the objective in this chapter is to establish the location and milieu of those slaves whose occupations were non-agricultural, the size of the units in which they were worked, and the internal organization of these units.

Extractive industries

Slaves worked as fishermen, salt-rakers, lime-burners and charcoal-burners. Those involved in the first two of these occupations were located on the coast, generally in or near the towns. The others were more widely dispersed. Slave fishermen were usually members of small units, belonging to urban whites. Their activities permitted a relatively high degree of independent action. Some fishermen were attached to larger units, however. Fish for consumption on sugar estates (both coastal and inland) was often caught by slaves from the estates, this being their only occupation.[1] One of the few Accounts Produce properties to sell fresh fish on a significant scale was Great Salt Pond Pen, in St. Catherine, which had 203 slaves attached to it in 1832.[2] In that year it sold fish worth £348, probably in the Kingston and Spanish Town markets; it also sold a quantity of salt.

Lime-burners, too, had a relatively independent existence. Some estates established permanent lime kilns, but in many cases the slaves went into the bush to build and burn piles of stone and hardwood to produce white lime. Many of the units employing slave lime-burners were small. In 1817, for example, an owner offered for sale his land and 25 slaves at Manatee Bay, in St. Catherine, together with the vessel and canoes used by the slaves to carry to the Kingston market the lime and timber produced.[3]

In general, the production of fish, lime, salt and charcoal formed part of a highly diversified economy, on small units belonging to resident proprietors. Often they were produced together with timber and dyewoods, which may also be regarded as extractive industries but have been discussed within the context of agriculture. The manner in which pimento was exploited might equally qualify it for classification as an extractive industry. Thus the distinction between the latter and agriculture is not clearly defined.

Manufacturing

The problem of separating the manufacturing sector from the agricultural is even greater than that of distinguishing the extractive industries. A considerable proportion of the slave labour force was involved in the manufacture of sugar and rum, but there is little utility in attempting to separate them from the agricultural sector.[4] The technology of sugar processing meant that it could not be carried out at any distance from the plantation, and many slaves spent part of the year in the field and part in the factory. On the other hand, some slaves worked throughout the year as coopers, blacksmiths, coppersmiths, wheelwrights, millwrights, 'engineers', shipwrights, sail-makers, caulkers, block-makers, joiners, turners, cabinet-makers, tailors and seamstresses,[5] producing items which did not necessarily have to be made within the island. They raised hogsheads, built and repaired carts and boats, hammered out items of mill equipment, sewed clothes and so on. Most of the output of those on estates and plantations was not produced for sale, but comprised essential inputs. Slaves working in the towns, however, did generally produce for the local market.

It is not always easy to identify the occupations of slaves belonging to white 'manufacturers,' so that the extent of their involvement, relative to that of free people employed by the masters, is uncertain. For instance, in 1826 the inventory of a St. Mary coppersmith recorded that he owned only one slave, a 'coppersmith negro'.[6] But the extent of his property in equipment and materials suggests that he also employed free tradesmen. On the other hand, in 1827 a Kingston dyer, with only a small quantity of dye-stuffs, acids and tools of trade, held one slave whose occupation is unknown.[7] In the same way, slaves worked for distillers (in Kingston), coopers, millwrights, merchant tailors, joiners and watchmakers.[8] Although some of these slaves may have been domestics or labourers, the general dependence of the masters on the skills of the slaves[9] suggests that many of them were involved in the industrial processes related to their master's profession or trade.

The slaves employed in manufacturing were usually men. One Kingston shipwright, for example, owned thirteen slaves, all of them men: three were sailmakers, four caulkers, two blacksmiths, two labourers, one a pitch boiler and another a carpenter.[10] Another held forty-six male slaves and six females, all but four of them aged between 20 and 60 years. Among these men were twelve shipwrights, ten caulkers, four joiners, three labourers, two blacksmiths, two block-makers, a turner, a pitch boiler, a blind bellows blower, a blind lath-wheel turner, a sailor, a store and water man, a cook, a mulatto waiting-man, a waiting-boy and two invalids. Of the women, two were house cleaners, one a seamstress, one a washerwoman and another acted as nurse for the 'negro yard'.[11]

A general estimate of the number of slaves employed in manufacturing can be made from the compensation commissioners' valuation returns of 1834. These classified 17,873 of the slaves as 'head tradesmen' and 'inferior tradesmen', or 5.7 per cent of the total slave population (Table 4). But some of these tradesmen were engaged in building and construction. On sugar estates, the masons and carpenters were about as numerous as the coopers and

Table 4. *The occupational distribution of the slave population, as classified by the assistant commissioners for compensation, 1834*

	Number of slaves	Percentage of slaves	Average compensation paid per slave (£)
Predial attached			
Head people	14,043	4.51	43.44
Tradesmen	11,244	3.61	43.81
Inferior tradesmen	2,635	0.85	28.96
Field labourers	107,053	34.41	37.26
Inferior field labourers	63,923	20.55	17.94
Total	198,898	63.94	31.74
Predial unattached			
Head people	1,329	0.43	43.46
Tradesmen	1,133	0.36	44.19
Inferior tradesmen	322	0.10	29.25
Field labourers	11,670	3.75	37.20
Inferior field labourers	5,104	1.64	18.50
Total	19,558	6.29	33.02
Non-predial			
Head tradesmen	1,759	0.57	43.34
Inferior tradesmen	780	0.25	28.80
Head people attached to wharves, shipping etc.	1,428	0.46	42.38
Inferior people attached to wharves, shipping etc.	901	0.29	31.76
Head domestic servants	12,883	4.14	40.82
Inferior domestic servants	19,083	6.13	27.36
Total	36,834	11.84	33.55
Children aged less than six years	39,013	12.54	7.69
Aged, diseased, non-effective	15,692	5.04	6.07
Runaways	1,075	0.35	17.70
Total	311,070	100.00	27.68

Sources: T.71/684 and 851; R. M. Martin, *History of the Colonies of the British Empire* (London, 1843), p. 8.

smiths. If the same proportion held in the towns, it follows that only 3 per cent of the slaves were involved in manufacturing. Nearly 80 per cent of these slaves were permanently settled on agricultural holdings, most of them large sugar estates. Only 8 per cent of them lived in the towns, the remainder belonging to jobbing gangs. The valuers, interestingly, classified tradesmen as predials whereas domestics were always regarded as non-predials whether they lived on agricultural units or in towns.

Using a wide definition, Starobin estimated that 5 per cent of the United States slave population was involved in 'industrial slavery' in the 1850s.[12] If slaves involved in building, transportation and extractive industries are excluded from his estimate, to fit the definition of the manufacturing group used above, the proportion for the United States appears to be very similar to that in Jamaica.[13] But in the United States the manufacturing industries employing slaves in the 1850s were more diverse and urbanized than those found in Jamaica in 1834.

Building and construction

The above analysis of the manufacturing group's relationship to the slaves classified as tradesmen in 1834 suggests that the carpenters, masons and bricklayers employed in building and construction numbered about 9,000, or 3 per cent of the total slave population. Once again, most of these slaves were settled on large agricultural units. The concentration was probably even greater than for the manufacturing group. Kingston's slave and white population was decreasing, so that little new building took place during the 1820s.[14] On the other hand, in the jobbing gangs the carpenters and masons probably outnumbered the coopers and smiths, in contrast to the pattern on estates and plantations. But whether attached to large rural holdings or to small urban units, these slaves possessed a degree of 'independence'.[15] Slaves employed in construction work on the public roads, bridges and buildings, however, were denied this relative freedom.

Transportation

On a sugar estate, slaves described as cartmen, wainmen or waggoners spent their time carrying canes to the mill, moving other produce or equipment about within the estate, and carting to and from the wharves its produce and supplies. Usually, they formed only a small proportion of the estate's labour force. But a few fairly large units (of about 50 slaves) took advantage of their location between port, town and interior estates to obtain the great majority of their income from cartage.[16]

As well as employing their slaves to transport goods overland, many sugar estates maintained their own wharves to which were attached a small number of slaves. Other slave-owners operated wharves independent of the estates, serving numerous interior properties, particularly from the south coast ports. On the Accounts Produce units classified as wharves there was an average of 25 slaves, with a high degree of masculinity (Table 1). Often the slaves employed on wharves were hired from other slave-owners.[17]

Slaves worked as sailors on vessels engaged in the 'drogging' trade, carrying goods between the ports of Jamaica. Many of these slaves belonged to the colonial merchants. For example, a Kingston merchant, whose personal property was valued at £112,744 when he died in 1825, owned fifty-one slaves: seven of them were 'sailor negroes' and another seven 'wharf negroes'; thirteen were coopers and twelve carpenters, while two worked in the stores and ten in the house.[18] This merchant owned a schooner, as did some shipwrights possessing 'sailor negroes'.[19] Other slave sailors operated strictly within the ports, particularly those who acted as pilots and canoe-men (transporting passengers) within Kingston harbour.[20]

Slave cartmen, wharf labourers and sailors all came into close contact with urban life, whether they actually belonged to townsmen or rural holdings. Whatever the size of the unit to which they were attached, their mobility meant that they enjoyed a degree of independence even greater than that possessed by slaves employed in manufacturing or construction.

Distribution

In addition to marketing the produce of their provision grounds in the public markets,[21] slaves were also employed by their masters as hucksters, or higglers, selling goods for the benefit of the master. They sold fresh fish and meat, and dry goods, both in the town markets and in the countryside.[22] Other slaves belonged to urban shopkeepers.[23]

Domestic and other services

Slaves worked about the houses of their masters and overseers as waiting-boys, grooms, stable-boys, gardeners, barbers, washerwomen, cooks and house-women. In 1834 the assistant commissioners for compensation classified 12,883 slaves as 'head domestic servants' and 19,083 as 'inferior domestic servants', together comprising over 10 per cent of the slave population (Table 4). In Kingston, 67.5 per cent of the slaves were domestics; the town accounted for 40 per cent of the 'inferior' class but only 6 per cent of the 'head' servants (Table A3.16). The evidence for St. Catherine, the other highly urbanized parish, suggests a similar predominance of the inferior class of domestics in the towns. It follows that, in contrast to the general and town patterns, there must have been 10,000 head and 5,000 inferior domestics settled on agricultural holdings. This pattern is surprising, and perhaps it simply results from the size of the units – there would be less opportunities for slaves to become head domestics in the small urban units.[24] Thus the domestic group on estates was structured differently from the urban group not simply because of the contrast between town and rural life. But whether in town or country the domestic, in spite of his supposed superior status relative to the field slave, came into closest contact with the masters and lacked openings for independent activity.[25]

Some slaves, those belonging to tavernkeepers, for example, performed domestic duties outside the homes of their masters.[26] Others performed services as firemen, woodsmen and guides.[27] On the estates there was an important group of slaves with responsibility for the health of the slaves, beyond the occasional visits of white physicians. They were slave doctors, doctresses, midwives, nurses, yaws house nurses, and hospital attendants.

Jobbing

The masters sold the services of their slaves in three different ways. Firstly, and most commonly, slaves were jobbed as field labourers or road workers on a daily or piece-work basis, at rates ranging in 1832 from 1s 3d to 3s per day depending on the task performed (cleaning canes and cane hole digging being at the two ends of the scale). Secondly, slave tradesmen were jobbed at daily rates of 3s 9d to 5s, working as masons, carpenters, coopers, copper smiths and blacksmiths. Thirdly, some tradesmen were hired at yearly rates (generally £30), as were domestics and some other slaves.[28]

It is probable that the majority of the 20,000 slaves belonging to jobbing gangs (Table 2) spent most of their time performing agricultural labour or working on the public roads. In 1825 De la Beche argued that the number of gangs had been reduced by the abolition of the slave trade and that jobbing was then 'principally performed by persons who own more negroes than they can find employment for on their own properties'.[29] It is clear from the patterns of diversification established in Chapter 3 that by 1832 there were pens which sent jobbers to estates, plantations and pens; plantations which sent them to estates, plantations and pens; and so on. But there were still opportunities for the small white settler to take the classical route to colonial wealth, beginning with a few jobbing slaves. The process can be traced in the inventories of personal property. Many white carpenters and masons died owning no slaves, but others acquired one or two, and some had as many as thirty.[30] These whites possessed little other property. Some of them simply hired their slaves to the estates on which they themselves worked for a salary,[31] while others jobbed them elsewhere.[32] Sometimes these slaves were, like their owners, carpenters and masons, but most were not distinguished as tradesmen, being field or house slaves.[33] Yet the small white settlers rarely referred to themselves as jobbers,[34] preferring to be known by the trades which they continued to practise.

Jobbing was particularly common on the interior 'planting' estates, where there was a great demand for cane holing. Thus in upper Clarendon, reported a planter in 1832, 'it is a profitable species of traffic; and many men who have acquired property prefer buying jobbing gangs, and those gangs abound, and at certain seasons any number can be got at a day's notice'.[35] On the other hand, planters in Manchester complained that it was hard to find jobbing gangs to pick their crops of coffee.[36] Some gangs travelled long distances, however, the women (though they were few) carrying their children. Before commencing work they often had to build their own huts.[37] They were fed by their owner, and worked under their own 'driver'.[38]

Because of their specific skills, tradesmen were generally hired over greater distances than field labourers. Those hired for an entire year were often domestics or tradesmen, but in many cases they were small groups attached to deceased estates or pens and wharves on lease. These slaves frequently had to travel as far as Kingston.

Usually, the slave-jobber contracted directly with another free person for the sale of his slaves' labour. But sometimes he found it convenient to simply ask a fixed weekly or monthly payment from his slave and permit the slave to employ himself to others for a wage. Some estate tradesmen were encouraged to do this, especially before 1807, but in the towns the system applied to a whole range of occupations.[39] To a certain extent the system allowed the slave to choose his occupation as well as his employer, and this also suited the slave-owner. Thus, for example, most of the 'common prostitutes' in the towns were slaves. In 1832 a Wesleyan missionary reported that, although he could give no instances of a master allowing a slave out for his benefit, 'in many instances the master or mistress never inquires what course of life the slave follows, if she but pay him the weekly amount stipulated; for she is at perfect liberty to work as she pleases, or live as she pleases'.[40] Some slaves were simply given a paper to look for a new owner, paying a fixed sum until they could find a purchaser.[41]

Conclusion

The distribution of the slave labour force between specific occupations is not readily quantified. In any case, the boundaries between the categories were often vague, reducing the utility of any attempt at precision. But it is necessary to revise the pattern established on the basis of the types of holdings on which the slaves were settled (Table 2). Whereas only 8 per cent of the slave population was not located on agricultural units, immediately before emancipation, another 10 per cent was employed in non-agricultural tasks (Table 4). In terms of the active slave labour force (excluding children, aged and runaway slaves) the non-agricultural category accounted for slightly more than 20 per cent. Slaves had come to be employed in a wide range of occupations, which their owners did not find incongruous with the institution of slavery. Yet even in 1834 more than 70 per cent of the active slave labour force of Jamaica comprised field labourers.

PART II

POPULATION

CHAPTER 5

POPULATION DISTRIBUTION AND STRUCTURE

Sources and methods of analysis

The humanitarians believed that slavery was 'created and sustained' by the slave trade,[1] rather than the reverse. Once the supply of slaves from Africa had been cut off, said Wilberforce, 'they hoped that the amelioration of the state of the slaves in the West Indies would follow as a matter of course'.[2] Thus, when it became clear that the abolition had not provided this expected change, the humanitarians argued that the planters continued to think that the Act might be evaded and a supply of replacements obtained. To convince the masters that they were deluded the Saints adopted two lines of attack, both of them directed at the slave trade. In the first place, they maintained their attack on the international slave trade, and in this they were supported by the West Indian planters.[3] The second approach, which the planters saw as 'a violent infringement of their rights',[4] was to call for the registration of all slaves in the colonies, in order to identify and prevent any illicit importations. But, according to James Stephen, this aim was secondary to registration's 'direct and infallible tendency to improve the condition of the negroes'.[5]

In 1810 the humanitarians began to press for the introduction to Parliament of a Bill to establish the registration of slaves in Trinidad. The government forestalled this move by permitting James Stephen to draft an Order in Council, which was applied to the Crown Colony of Trinidad in 1812.[6] The Saints then delayed their campaign for a general Registration Act until 1815. But the colonial legislatures were strongly opposed to registration, arguing that it violated their right to control internal taxation. These constitutional claims weighed heavily on the government, and on Wilberforce,[7] and the Registry Bill was dropped. In turn, the West India interest was cajoled into entreating the colonial legislatures to pass Acts of their own instituting the registration of slaves.[8]

Thus towards the end of 1816 an Act was passed by the Jamaica House of Assembly which stated that

> Whereas the legislature of this island is anxious to shew, by every means in its power, the most sincere disposition to guard against any possible infringement of the laws for abolishing the slave-trade, for the evasion of which the return to peace may be thought to afford facilities; And whereas a more particular return of the slaves in this island, than has hitherto been required by the laws heretofore passed for that purpose, and an enrolment thereof, may be advantageous . . .

It was enacted

> That all and every person and persons, who shall be present in this island on the twenty-eighth day of June next, after the passing of this act, and shall then be in the possession of any slave or slaves within the same, whether as owner, mortgagee, trustee, guardian, executor, administrator, sequestrator, committee, receiver, assignee, lessee, attorney, agent, or otherwise howsoever, do and shall, on or before the twenty-eighth day of September then next, render in to the clerk of the vestry of the parish, where such slave or slaves, so possessed as aforesaid, shall be considered to be most permanently settled, worked, or employed, a true and perfect list or return in writing . . .

of all these slaves.[9] But although the Act was designed principally to check the smuggling of slaves (every person making a return being liable to forfeit £100 for each slave omitted), the second, vaguer aim has indeed proven advantageous to the historian at least. The Returns of Registrations of Slaves provide a wealth of demographic data which are both more reliable and richer in detail than those to be found in any other source.

Six triennial registrations were recorded in Jamaica, the first in 1817 and the last in 1832. In 1817 the return listed each slave by name, sex, colour, age, and country of birth, and noted their mothers' names (when the mother was alive and living on the same holding). Thereafter the returns listed the increase and decrease among the slaves in the preceding three years, whether by birth, purchase, removal, death, sale, gift, manumission, transportation, desertion or committal to the workhouse. In a column for 'remarks' the names of mothers were generally given, the names of persons from whom slaves were purchased or inherited and, occasionally, the causes of death.

The administration of the Jamaica Registration Act was relatively simple. Unlike some of the other colonies, Jamaica did not appoint a registrar or allocate any special rooms or clerks to the task.[10] At the end of 1816 the Assembly ordered the printing of the major clauses of the Act in the newspapers, together with forms of the schedules to be used.[11] The returns were made out by the slave-owners themselves and taken to the offices of the parish vestries, where they were collected by the clerk (between 28 June and 28 September). The owners paid the clerk a fee of 2s 6d per legal sheet.[12] Fees were also charged for extracts made from the returns. The clerk of the vestry then sent the returns to the Island Secretary in Spanish Town, who in turn transferred the separate returns to bound volumes, parish by parish, in alphabetical order, owner by owner. The originals were transmitted to the central Registry Office in London,[13] while a duplicate set was kept in the island.[14]

Although the slave-owner or his representative was required to swear that he had made 'a true, perfect, and complete list and return, to the best of my knowledge and belief', the reliability of the returns must be considered critically. In the first place, there is little evidence of the actual concealment of slaves. The cost to the master of registration was small, and registration was not used as a basis for the poll-tax in Jamaica. In Barbados, by contrast, the same man held the offices of registrar and treasurer; so when he called for returns of taxable slaves in 1817 he could remind the masters that 'as Registrar I shall have it in my power to detect all those persons who did not heretofore give in their slaves'.[15] Such threats were absent in Jamaica. Yet some cases of non-registration can be found, the most important being the slaves belonging to the Maroons. But regular returns of these slaves were made to the Assembly, and, although registration was a condition for compensation, the normal compensation rates were paid on them in 1834.[16] In any case the number of slaves held by the Maroons was small: 112 in 1832.[17] Some slaves were not registered for the first time until 1820, while a few appeared only in 1832. These cases tended to be exceptional. In 1832, for example, William Burton, a slave on Golden Grove Estate, St. Thomas-in-the-East, registered seven slaves bequeathed to him by his grandmother, Clarinda Benton, 'a very old Negro woman slave on Golden Grove Estate and who died in 1828' and had never returned them under the Act.[18] On the other hand, the planters vehemently denied such under-registration and claimed that the Act had put such fear into the slave-owners' hearts that many double returns were recorded, two individuals having an interest in the same slave both making returns.[19] Some examples of such dual registration can be found in the returns but they are recognized readily and can be excluded with ease; often they would seem to be the result of mere clerical duplication.

There is no evidence to suggest that there was any significant illicit importation of slaves into Jamaica after 1817.[20] Thus the Returns of Registrations of Slaves are not deficient from this point of view. It will be argued below,[21] in a comparison with the returns made as the basis for compensation in 1834, that the degree of under-registration is very unlikely to have been more than 1 per cent of the total slave population.

Criticism of the returns has been levelled chiefly at the data relating to fertility and mortality. Roberts, in particular, has argued that the returns take no account of children born within a triennium but dying before its end, thus ignoring infant mortality and understating total fertility and mortality.[22] But this criticism seems to be based on Roberts' study of the printed reports for British Guiana rather than on the Jamaica Registration Act or the original Jamaica returns,[23] for the reality is more complex than he suggests. The Jamaica Act was somewhat ambiguous, calling simply for a record of 'the total number of births and of deaths since the last return'.[24] Thus although it is undoubtedly true that much mortality and fertility of the type described by Roberts went unrecorded, it was not omitted universally.

A sample of the 1829–32 returns for St. James (Table 5) shows that about 13 per cent of the births registered in the parish involved children who were born and died within the triennium. The number of children born within the triennium and remaining alive at the date of registration tapers off with

Table 5. *Recorded infant mortality in St. James, 1829–32: A sample*

Age	Children born within the triennium: Alive on 28 June 1832	Children born within the triennium: Died before 28 June 1832
Months		
0–2	26	7
3–5	31	4
6–8	35	8
9–11	20	10
12–14	27	7
15–17	17	3
18–20	23	1
21–23	12	—
24–26	17	2
27–30	32	6
31–33	16	1
34–36	12	—
Years		
½	3	—
1	26	—
1½	8	—
2	29	—
2½	6	—
Total	389	49

Source: R.R.S., Liber 129, fos. 1–60.

increasing age, as would be expected, but it is clear that there must have been a good deal of under-registration among children less than two months of age. The data also suggest that mortality reached a peak at about twelve months, which is unlikely. Thus the omissions must occur especially within the first few months of life. In another study of three holdings over the entire registration period, 1817–32, it was found that 14 per cent of the 251 births registered related to children born and dying within a triennium.[25] The Account Book for one of these holdings, Old Montpelier, throws some light on the problem since it contains 'increase' lists for 1825 and 1827. In 1827 all the children born were described as being 'nine days old at date' and all appear in the registration return for 1829. In 1825 two children who died of tetanus on the sixth and seventh days after birth were listed in the Account Book but not registered.[26] On this estate the mothers of children surviving nine days received 13s 4d from the attorney. Thus it would seem that on these three holdings the under-recording of fertility was confined to mortality in the first nine days of life. In 1816 Sells, in his *Practical Remarks for the Management of Pregnant Women,* had recommended that plantation books should contain complete records of births, 'and not, as is too common a practice, to omit taking any notice of such as die within the ninth day'.[27] Contemporary estimates placed the mortality within this period at between 25 and 50 per cent of all live births.[28] There are also some apparently complete registration returns (including stillbirths) for Jamaica which suggest that the proportion might have fallen below 20 per cent.[29]

The application of these ratios to the returns in order to correct for the under-registration of births and deaths is complicated by the inconsistencies in practice. Thus some masters reported stillbirths, others excluded only those children dying within the first nine days of life, while others based their returns on plantation books which might have been made up quarterly, annually or triennially.[30] But it seems that both births and deaths should be inflated by roughly one-third.

Another kind of under-registration, not mentioned by Roberts, must be noted. When an owner sold or transferred all of his slaves he might make no return at the end of the triennium, while the purchaser would record only that he had bought so many slaves giving no list of the births and deaths between the previous return and the date of purchase. According to the Act, owners were required only to record increases and decreases 'as near as circumstances will admit'.[31]

In addition to these problems of under- and over-registration, the accuracy of the data concerning age, colour and place of birth needs to be considered. In general, the returns simply distinguish Africans and creoles. This presented the masters with few difficulties since the physical differences between the two groups were marked – most strikingly in the filed teeth and 'country' marks of the Africans.[32] The data concerning colour and age almost certainly contain more errors. Some returns generalized the colour of the slaves, simply calling them all negro or listing all those of mixed race as mulattoes. But since the gradation from black to white was a significant feature of slave society most of the masters in fact recorded the finer distinctions with care. Age presents the greatest difficulty. The Act required the master to state 'the age, or reputed age' of the slaves 'according to the best of the knowledge or belief of the party, who shall make attestation on oath to the truth of such list or return'.[33] Some of the returns noted that the ages listed were only 'reputed' or 'supposed' ages. Obviously this problem decreased as the proportion of creoles in the slave population grew, since the masters generally kept records of their dates of birth. For the Africans, in particular, the rounding of ages was common in the returns. But this applies to much census-taking and if the figures are not used too finely the problem can be accommodated. Barclay, an apologist for the slave system, suggested that the planters understated the ages of the Africans in order to maximize their saleable value;[34] but it was his purpose to prove the great antiquity to which slaves lived. If the registration returns are compared with lists kept in plantation books, inconsistencies in age and colour are rare, but the latter were often the source of the former so this accordance is not surprising. It was a general rule, however, that although some of the data appearing in the returns may have been supplied by the slaves themselves or the 'head people' on the holdings, it was always interpreted by the masters, the vast majority of whom were white.

The Returns of Registrations of Slaves with which this study is particularly concerned are those for 1817, 1820 and 1832. The 1817 returns contain the only direct and comprehensive age data, and these have been related to the first triennial return of 1820 in order to calculate age-specific mortality and fertility rates. Those for 1832 are used to establish a detailed picture of the slave population on the eve of emancipation. In particular, since they can be related to the compensation claims of 1834, they permit a fine analysis of the spatial distribution of the slaves.

The returns for 1832 covered the period 28 June 1829 to 28 June 1832.[35] Some of the data are sketchier than in earlier returns, perhaps because of the rebellion of Christmas 1831 – though only one owner stated that he could not make accurate returns because his books had been burnt.[36] But the vital data are all included and are comparable with those for previous returns.

When the subject of slavery was prominent in parliamentary debate, the British government willingly financed the Slave Registry Office in London, which produced calculations relating to sex, births, deaths and manumissions from the returns of 1817 to 1829.[37] But, perhaps because no summary returns were sent from Jamaica, only the total number of slaves was published from the returns of 1832.[38] The Jamaica House of Assembly, which had calculated some tables at the parish level from the earlier registrations, showed no more interest than Parliament in the one for 1832.[39] All attention was then directed to that great act of expiation, the compensation of the dispossessed masters, for which a new return was required even though each claim had to be accompanied by a certificate signed by the registrar of slaves stating that the number claimed was equal to that shown in the 1832 registration return, allowing for natural increase.[40] For 1832, then, the vital rates have to be calculated from the original returns.

Before attempting to analyse these returns it is necessary to discuss the question of spatial scale, which poses a fundamental problem in historical generalization. For Jamaica, the most obvious level at which to begin is the parish. But many problems relating to spatial and social patterns result from working with the parish. Jamaica's parishes (Figure 1) contained a great deal of diversity, all but three of them running from the coast to the spine of the island. The only urban centre separated from its rural hinterland was Kingston. This general problem was noticed in 1832 by John Baillie, a planter living in the western end of the island, when he argued that it was impossible to make laws relating to slave diet by parishes, 'for the estates in most of the parishes vary exceedingly between the sea side and the mountains, the soil and climate vary very much, and the seasons also'.[41] More generally, it may be noted that administrative regions are not usually determined by homogeneity but by a compromise between area, population and compactness. The result is that they approximate the most unsuitable units which could be devised to illuminate patterns of distribution and variations between land types.

It is a general rule that relationships and patterns can be identified best when the basic units of data and space are as small as possible. Units can always be aggregated but never divided. The Returns of Registrations of Slaves are very satisfactory, in this context, since they list individual slaves grouped by holdings. Hence the data are very malleable. But, in order to establish spatial patterns, it is also necessary to know where each holding was located and here the returns give little immediate help. Only in a small minority of cases are names of properties given. The names of slave-owners and their various representatives are, however, listed very fully in the claims for compensation made in 1834 and the associated returns of the valuers appointed by the Assistant Commissioners for Compensation, in which the property, town or place name of each unit is also given.[42] Thus it is possible to link a place-name to the great majority of the Returns of Registrations of Slaves. The interval of two years creates some difficulties but most of these can be solved by reference to the poll-tax givings-in.[43] Next, the place names can be located by using Robertson's excellent inch to the mile map of 1804, the inch to twenty chains cadastral survey of the later nineteenth century, the 1832 map of estates destroyed in the rebellion, and the modern 1 : 50,000 topographic map of Jamaica.[44]

With these data it would almost be possible to map every slave-holding in 1832, but the operation would be both tedious and unhelpful. It is more useful to impose a system of regions and aggregate the data within each of the regions. It should be noted that an attempt to do this was made by Cumper in 1956, using the poll-tax givings-in for 1831.[45] He estimated the total populations in three parishes subdivided into soil regions. The pitfalls involved in this approach are that the poll-tax returns were deficient, emphasizing the dominance of the large holding, and that to allocate the population to soil regions is to impose a degree of environmental determinism on the analysis. Rather than espouse any form of *a priori* interpretation it is better to impose a systematic pattern of grid lines on this point pattern of slave-holdings, so that a whole range of demographic, economic and ecological characteristics can be tested for co-variation. The advantage of this method is that the historian can approach the patterns uncommitted to any particular hypothesis and unhindered by the restrictions of bureaucratic needs. The grid units are neutral. They are uniform in size and shape (if square), yet readily aggregated without losing these qualities.

There is considerable debate about the optimum size of these square grid units, or quadrats, but the practical needs of each case are uppermost.[46] Curtis and McIntosh have proposed that (for botanical studies) the best quadrat size is twice the reciprocal of the density function, or $2(A/n)$, where

A is the total area and *n* the frequency of the most common plant species.[47] If this is applied to the slave population of Jamaica in 1832 the optimum quadrat size is found to be 0.03 square miles (when based on slaves) or 0.68 square miles (slave-holdings), and the number of quadrats required to cover the island would be 156,000 and 6,500 respectively. This is clearly impracticable in terms of the limits of confidence in allocating holdings to quadrats.

Jamaica is readily divided into about 1,000 square quadrats with sides of three kilometers and an area of 3.546 square miles by using the military grid on the 1 : 50,000 topographic map. These units are large enough to enable the accurate placing of the data. Some properties overlap more than one quadrat but it is necessary to regard them as points, taking the mill-site as the focus of population. Difficulties also occur where there was more than one place with the same name or where two contiguous, joint-owned holdings were registered together but fell into two quadrats. In the first case a qualitative decision as to importance has to be made, while in the second the population has to be concentrated into the dominant quadrat. Another problem is that jobbing gangs often moved from estate to estate, but were returned only for their owner's location or the place where they were 'considered to be most permanently settled, worked, or employed'.[48] But this involves a problem of interpretation rather than of allocation.

Only 1.58 per cent of the slaves registered in Jamaica in 1832 could not be located within this quadrat grid, but 8.39 per cent of the holdings were unlocated. If these slaves were distributed evenly among the parishes they could be ignored in the comparison of densities, but since this is not the case it is necessary to allocate them to quadrats using a standard procedure. It is assumed that they are not unlocated because of any peculiar locational characteristic but rather are submerged in the pattern of those already located. Since the units are generally small (having an average of 4.73 slaves per holding compared to 25.14 for Jamaica as a whole) they are best located with regard to the structure of holdings already located rather than the total population of each quadrat. For example, a quadrat containing twelve holdings each with less than twenty slaves is considered more likely to be the true location of a small holding, the name and owner of which may be hard to trace, than a quadrat containing only two large estates. Thus the number of slaves allocated to each quadrat was determined by multiplying the number of located holdings in the quadrat by the percentage of unlocated holdings in the parish and by the mean size of the unlocated holdings for the parish in which the quadrat fell. This expedient involves only minor changes in the densities of the rural quadrats but augments the urban populations to some extent. The adjusted totals have been used only to calculate the densities; the unadjusted totals are used to find the other demographic rates since these do not involve a fixed denominator but are self-contained relationships best left unadjusted so long as the assumption that the unlocated holdings were not demographically abnormal is justified.

Some small areas of the coast are cut off by the grid system and for convenience all of these oddments which were unpopulated were ignored unless they were larger than 20 percent of one quadrat (0.72 square miles).

In order to separate the urban and rural slave populations it has been necessary to adopt an *ad hoc* definition of a town. A liberal definition has been used in order to include settlements which had town names – Brown's Town and Chapelton, for instance. The rule used is that a town have at least ten slave-holdings and 40 slaves located at the same place name. This excludes, for example, Old Harbour Market, Martha Brae, Duncans and the Moneague. The resulting list fits fairly well with contemporary opinion[49] and with what is known of function.

The 1,239 quadrats of 3.546 square miles have also been grouped by fours to make 328 quadrats, each with an area of 14.184 square miles. The data are much more manageable at this scale and the problem of allocation is

Table 6. *Slave population density, 1832*

<table>
<tr><th>Parish</th><th>Total slaves</th><th>Area in square miles</th><th>Slaves per square mile</th><th>Slaves per cultivated square mile</th></tr>
<tr><td>Westmoreland</td><td>20,309</td><td>320.4</td><td>63.4</td><td>227.6</td></tr>
<tr><td>Hanover</td><td>20,907</td><td>177.1</td><td>118.0</td><td>178.3</td></tr>
<tr><td>St. James</td><td>22,249</td><td>240.6</td><td>92.5</td><td>225.1</td></tr>
<tr><td>Trelawny</td><td>25,196</td><td>352.6</td><td>71.5</td><td>200.9</td></tr>
<tr><td>St. Elizabeth</td><td>19,777</td><td>474.4</td><td>41.7</td><td rowspan="2">410.6</td></tr>
<tr><td>Manchester</td><td>18,453</td><td>339.8</td><td>55.3</td></tr>
<tr><td>St. Ann</td><td>24,708</td><td>481.0</td><td>51.4</td><td>250.3</td></tr>
<tr><td>Clarendon</td><td>16,849</td><td>289.0</td><td>58.3</td><td>181.8</td></tr>
<tr><td>Vere</td><td>8,191</td><td>178.9</td><td>45.8</td><td>106.9</td></tr>
<tr><td>St. Dorothy</td><td>5,252</td><td>47.6</td><td>110.3</td><td>271.6</td></tr>
<tr><td>St. Thomas-in-the-Vale</td><td>10,684</td><td>181.2</td><td>58.9</td><td>251.4</td></tr>
<tr><td>St. John</td><td>5,886</td><td>117.4</td><td>50.1</td><td>252.9</td></tr>
<tr><td>St. Catherine</td><td>8,187</td><td>137.1</td><td>59.7</td><td>167.2</td></tr>
<tr><td>St. Mary</td><td>23,237</td><td>205.2</td><td>113.2</td><td>256.1</td></tr>
<tr><td>St. Andrew</td><td>13,977</td><td>137.7</td><td>101.5</td><td>225.9</td></tr>
<tr><td>Port Royal</td><td>6,406</td><td>47.7</td><td>134.4</td><td>358.3</td></tr>
<tr><td>St. David</td><td>7,649</td><td>92.1</td><td>83.1</td><td>386.3</td></tr>
<tr><td>St. George</td><td>11,875</td><td>179.3</td><td>66.2</td><td>326.3</td></tr>
<tr><td>Portland</td><td>7,247</td><td>158.3</td><td>45.8</td><td>337.4</td></tr>
<tr><td>St. Thomas-in-the-East</td><td>23,306</td><td>247.8</td><td>94.1</td><td>267.8</td></tr>
<tr><td>Kingston</td><td>12,531</td><td>6.0</td><td>2088.5</td><td>3489.0</td></tr>
<tr><td>Total</td><td>312,876</td><td>4,411.2</td><td>70.9</td><td>247.4</td></tr>
</table>

Sources: Number of slaves calculated from R.R.S.; area of defunct parishes estimated from the 1 : 50,000 topographic map; cultivated area based on Robertson's map of 1804.

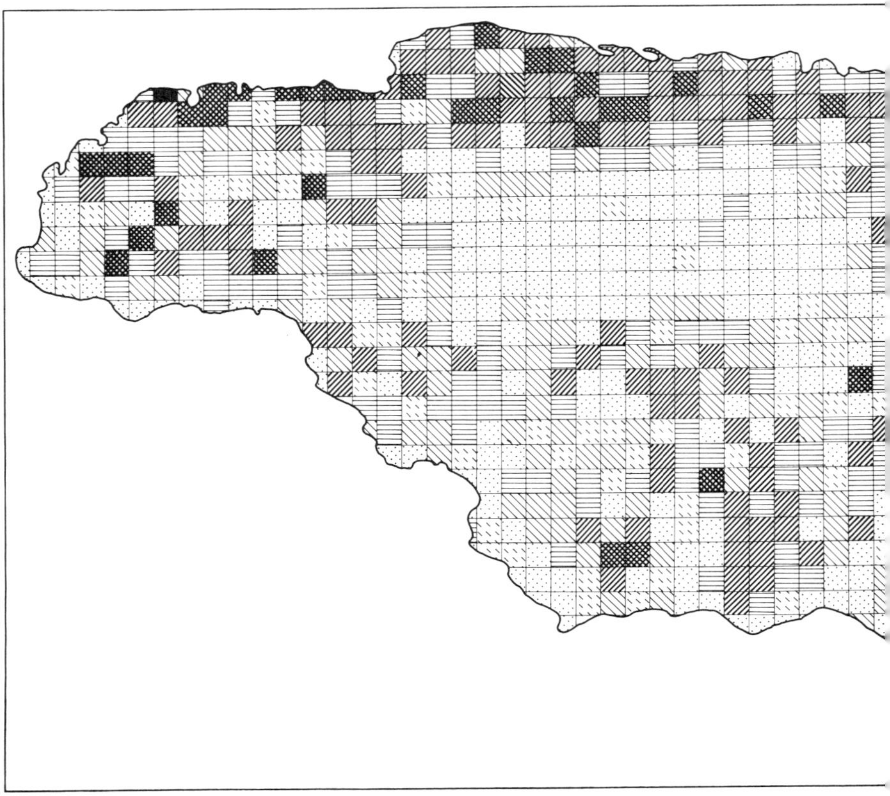

Figure 8. Slaves per square mile, by quadrats of 3.546 square miles, 1832. (Slaves

less. It has been used as the principal level of quadrat analysis.

Thus the analysis of the slave population will be carried out at three major levels of spatial generalization: parishes, quadrats of 14.184 square miles, and towns. At each of these levels the demographic data extracted from the Returns of Registrations of Slaves are related to economic, ecological and distance characteristics. The complete matrixes of correlation coefficients resulting from this analysis, together with definitions of the variables involved, are presented in Appendix 3 (Tables A3.1 to A3.3).[50]

Spatial distribution

The interpretation of the spatial distribution of the slave population within Jamaica brings out very clearly the problem of scale. In 1832 the Returns of Registrations of Slaves for the island listed a total of 312,876 slaves.[51] At the parish level, it appears that the slave population was concentrated into a dense band running across the island from Port Royal to St. Mary, with

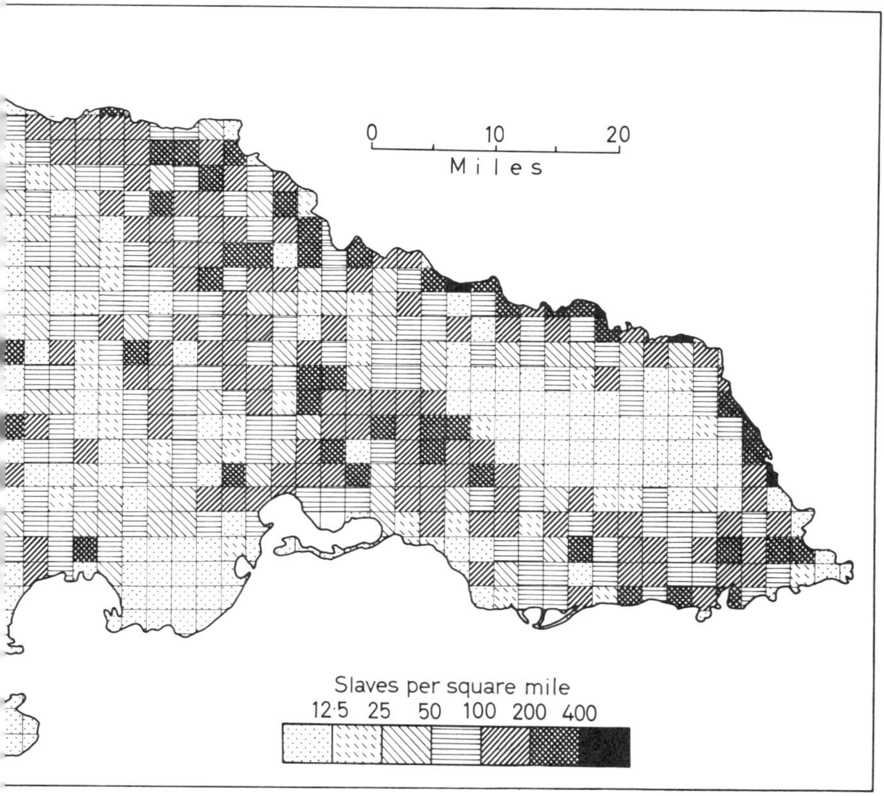

living in towns are not included in this map.)

other concentrations in the western parishes of Hanover and St. James, in St. Dorothy, and in St. David and St. Thomas-in-the-East (Table 6). The middle of the island appears relatively empty. But it is clear that the density of the population was closely related to the absolute size of the parishes, density increasing along with decreasing size. Thus the apparent thin spread of slaves in the larger parishes may be merely a function of their size.

That this contention is true is demonstrated by a comparison of the parish pattern with that based on quadrats (Figure 8). The slaves were not distributed evenly within the parishes. Thus, while the concentration of slaves in the band running across the island is confirmed at the quadrat level, the high density of St. Dorothy at the parish level disappears and merges into the dense areas of upper Clarendon along the Rio Minho, and this extends in a strip into the very dense areas of southern Vere. The southern parts of St. Thomas-in-the-East were just as dense as the band across the island. It is also apparent that there was a high-density strip running along the entire north coast, thinning out only in St. Ann and Portland. Some empty areas emerge: the Cockpit Country and adjacent parts of northern Manchester and southwestern St. Ann, the Blue Mountains, the Hellshire Hills, and Portland Ridge in Vere. But these areas apart – most of them still thinly settled, with the notable exception of northern Manchester – Jamaica was extensively peopled in 1832. Curtin's assertion that Jamaica 'still had a potential frontier in the American sense' appears doubtful.[52]

The area under cultivation in 1832 is not known, but a set of parish figures was compiled by Robertson in 1804 as part of his careful survey of the island.[53] His estimates have been used to determine the density of agricultural slaves in 1832 (Table 6). There was little significant change in the spread of agriculture, at the parish level, between 1804 and 1832, with the exception of the growth of coffee cultivation in Manchester. Thus these figures may be regarded as a fair approximation of the pattern in 1832. In general, the density of agricultural slaves declined from east to west, a product of the history of the spread of settlement within Jamaica.

At the parish level, there was an almost perfect correlation between the absolute density of the slave population and the number of slaves per cultivated acre ($r = .99$). But it must be recognized that all of the parish level correlations based on area are weighted by the inclusion of Kingston, and by the presence of varying proportions of urban slaves within the other parish populations. Since it is difficult to measure ecological factors at the parish level, not much would be gained by excluding Kingston. Thus it is best to examine the pattern at the quadrat level. At this scale the cultivated area is not known, but statistically significant correlations are found between density and the number of sugar estates in a quadrat ($r = .50$), the slave/white ratio ($r = .49$), the mean size of slave-holdings ($r = .47$), and the percentage of holdings with more than 100 slaves ($r = .51$). Thus the densest areas were those occupied by large properties rather than those settled by smaller units. The highest correlation found is that between slave population density and the density of the network of roads ($r = .54$), but although accessibility was a factor in the spread of settlement it is best to think of roads following people rather than the reverse. The role of accessibility is better measured by distance to the coast and to the nearest port, and here the relationships are much less clear, though significant. The effect on the density of the slave population of distance from a port was little greater than distance to the coast ($r = -.29$ and $-.27$, respectively), a reflection of the export orientation and internal self-sufficiency of the plantation economy.

No significant correlations were found between slave population density and ecological variables included in the analysis. Only absolute altitude may have had a limiting effect. The method used to measure the average slope of the land within the quadrats has inadequacies[54] and the total annual rainfall of an area may be a crude index of its effectiveness. Yet, despite these limitations, it seems that settlement was not strictly hindered by absolute altitude, and hence not by coolness, roughness, steepness, drought or deluge

This conclusion is a reflection of the diversity of economic uses to which the land had been put.

An attempt has been made to test the combined effect of the various economic, ecological and distance variables on the density of the slave population, using multiple regression analysis, at the quadrat level. Three of these variables taken together explain 28 per cent of the variance ($R = .53$), giving the following estimating equation:

$$Y_1 = 55.14 - 2.60X_{31} + 11.23X_{39} + 0.01X_{46}$$

where Y_1 is slaves per square mile, X_{31} is distance to the coast, X_{39} is number of sugar estates, and X_{46} is relative relief. This equation can now be used to predict the density of the slave population in each quadrat and the value obtained compared with the observed density in 1832, in order to see where the equation deviates from reality. This should help to discover the important variables which have been omitted from the analysis. The map of the residuals from regression shows that along much of the north coast of Jamaica density has been underestimated by the equation while on the south coast it has been overestimated. This may be explained by the intensity of the sugar industry on the north coast, based on the favoured 'brick mould' soil.[55] The overestimation of the Blue Mountains may be accounted for by the absolute altitude of the area, and that of the Cockpit Country as a result of its local roughness and paucity of arable land. Other local factors limiting the spread of settlement were the Great Morass at Negril, the Black River morasses, the desiccated limestones of Portland Ridge and the Hellshire Hills, and the droughtiness of upper Vere. The areas having more slaves than predicted by the equation are less readily explained in ecological terms, though small pockets of alluvial soil in inland valleys and poljes such as Lluidas Vale in St. John gained their great local densities in this way, surmounting the problem of accessibility. But it is apparent that what the equation leaves out of account are the environmental requirements of coffee which contrasted strongly with those of sugar. Since sugar itself had been pushed to the limits in terms of occupying marginal environments by 1832, it follows that the slaves were exposed to a wide variety of ecological conditions at that time.

In 1832 about 8 per cent of the slaves were not located on rural properties but lived in towns (Table 7). Almost exactly 50 per cent of these slaves were in Kingston. Of the other towns the largest were in the western end of the island and were fairly widely spaced (Figure 9). Those along the north coast east of Falmouth were smaller and closer together. Only a few of the smallest towns were located away from the coast, with the exception of the capital, Spanish Town. The port function was uppermost, as is shown by the use of the generic term 'bay' in eight of the town names. Service functions tended to be dispersed into the plantations themselves or to be centred in the smallest hamlets. In some cases the two functions were separated, as for example in the division between Old Harbour Bay and

Table 7. *Urban slave population, 1829–32*[a]

Town	Total slaves	Average slaves per holding	Males per 100 females	Births per 1,000	Deaths per 1,000			Natural increase per 1,000
					Males	Females	Total	
Lucea	760	5.16	81.60	16.6	41.4	13.3	25.9	−9.3
Green Island	146	4.34	103.23	23.8	15.6	10.8	13.2	+10.6
Savanna la Mar	1,344	5.53	83.69	23.0	12.1	14.4	13.4	+9.6
Montego Bay	2,237	5.45	85.24	25.9	27.0	21.0	23.7	+2.2
Stewart Town	60	5.50	89.66	12.1	25.6	11.5	18.2	−6.1
Rio Bueno	204	5.84	79.81	44.6	16.1	25.6	21.4	+23.2
Falmouth	1,388	5.28	90.68	21.3	21.6	25.1	23.4	−2.1
Lacovia	112	6.67	92.31	13.3	0.0	6.4	3.3	+10.0
Black River	312	7.62	107.35	24.8	18.3	27.0	22.5	+2.3
Brown's Town	43	3.90	95.00	34.2	35.1	0.0	17.1	+17.1
Ocho Rios Bay	53	4.36	84.62	27.8	0.0	12.8	6.9	+20.9
St. Ann's Bay	283	4.48	80.56	21.8	11.5	6.9	9.0	+12.8
Chapelton	99	6.36	270.83	11.2	82.1	55.6	74.9	−63.7
Old Harbour Bay	215	6.22	103.06	10.1	42.9	17.0	30.2	−20.1
Spanish Town	2,104	5.43	77.51	19.9	21.4	18.4	19.7	+0.2
Kingston	12,531	4.90	78.25	19.4	26.9	16.6	21.1	−1.7
Port Maria	361	4.18	73.12	10.4	39.2	17.9	26.9	−16.5
Annotto Bay	188	5.39	122.50	16.9	20.4	16.7	18.7	−1.8
Buff Bay	122	5.80	93.33	14.4	29.8	16.7	23.0	−8.6
Charles Town	60	2.52	82.76	25.2	13.9	11.5	12.6	+12.6
Port Royal	719	5.13	93.90	23.0	34.1	14.5	24.0	−1.0
Port Antonio	603	5.73	101.05	23.7	26.6	24.6	25.6	−1.9
Morant Bay	731	6.40	117.45	21.5	32.7	11.4	22.9	−1.4
Port Morant	46	3.23	100.00	15.9	79.4	31.8	55.6	−39.7
Bath	175	7.64	104.88	27.8	19.4	40.7	29.8	−2.0
Manchioneal Bay	88	4.88	84.44	36.1	17.5	14.8	16.1	+20.1
Total	24,984	5.31	83.29	21.7	27.3	18.6	23.0	−1.3

[a] Figures in the first three columns are for the year 1832, in the last five columns for the period 1829–32.
Source: R.R.S

Old Harbour Market. The sizes of the towns do not seem to have been related to the size or nearness of their neighbours, but to the size and transportation networks of their hinterlands, which are difficult to measure.

Little is known of the internal distribution of slaves within the towns, but some data are available for Kingston. Although the Kingston Parish and Poll-Tax Rolls for August 1832 list only 5,265 slaves, less than half the actual total, they do provide a breakdown by streets.[56] In the division west of King Street there were 1,640 slaves and to the east 3,625. The names of the masters are available but it is possible only to distribute the slaves along the streets evenly; thus Figure 10 is only a rough approximation to the real pattern. It may be that the slaves not listed for poll-tax belonged to masters situated in what appear to have been the most thinly peopled parts of the town. But

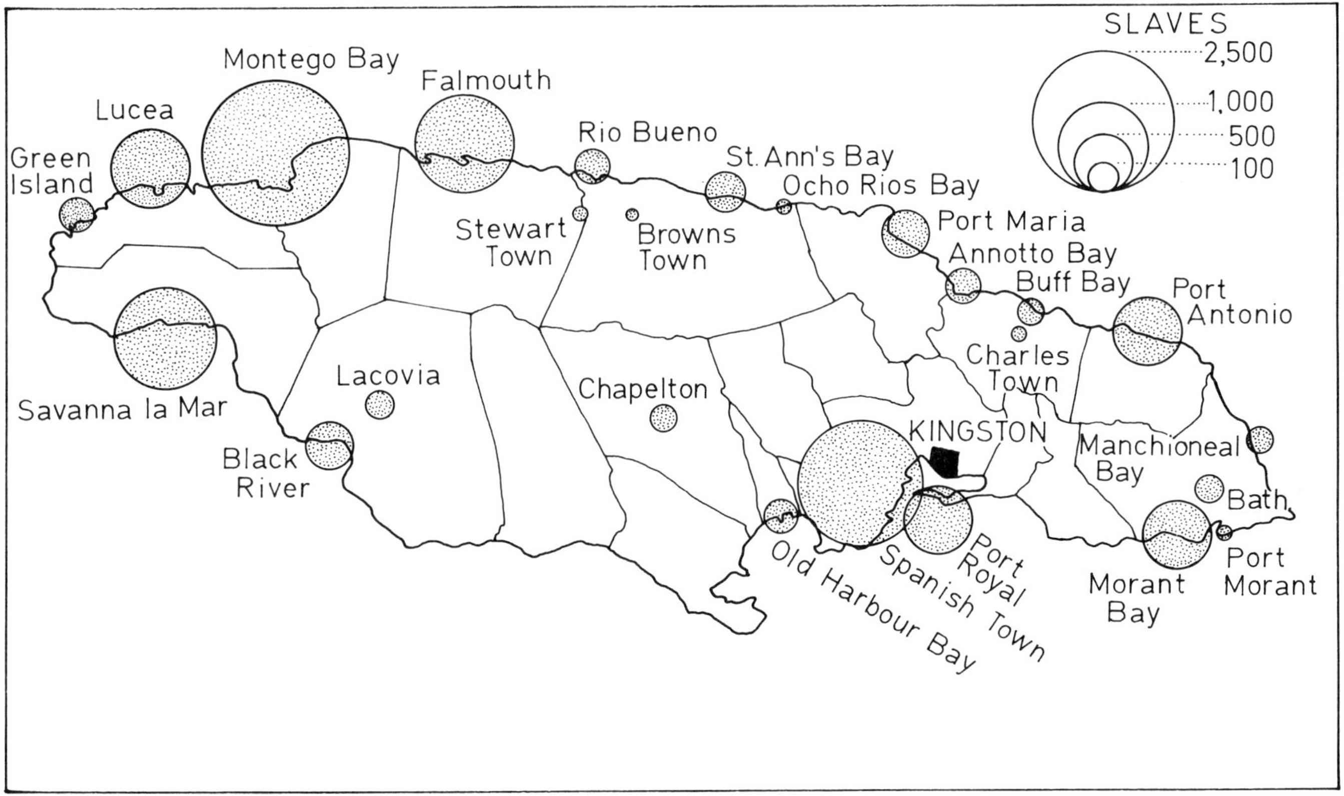

Figure 9. Town slaves (excluding Kingston), 1832.

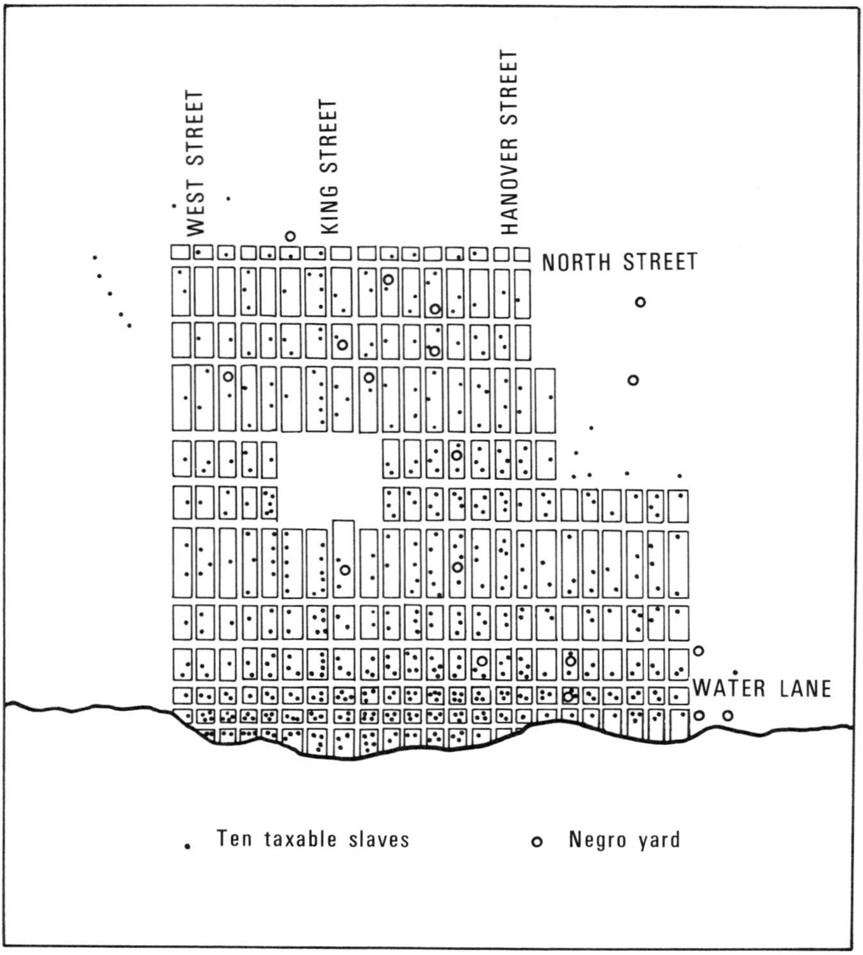

Figure 10. Distribution of slaves in Kingston, 1832.

it is certain that the greatest concentration of slaves was in the area south of Water Lane, around the wharves and merchant houses. The western side of King Street and the area between Church and Hanover Streets were also relatively densely populated by slaves. Exactly how the housing of the slaves was organized in this commercial section of the town is not certain. Some slaves lived with their masters. In 1831, for example, a house at the corner of Lawes Street and Mark Lane was offered for sale, 'containing a hall and two bed-rooms, with convenient out-offices: viz. one negro room, kitchen, horse stable, &c. with a fine shop attached thereto'. Some slaves lived on pens, mostly in the eastern part of Kingston parish away from the built-up area; but many more of the merchant masters had established pen residences in the parish of St. Andrews. Thus there may have been a growing residential separation of master and slave. The practice of permitting slaves to hire themselves out must have had a similar effect, allowing the slave to find his own landlord as well as his own employer. But from the early eighteenth century Spanish Town, Port Royal and Kingston had been said to be skirted by 'negro huts'. An Act of 1744 required that where four or more huts were built together they should be enclosed by a seven-foot fence, with only one gate.[57] The tax rolls for 1832 refer to eighteen 'negro yards', most of them located on the fringes of the Kingston urban area. These seem to have provided lodgings for slaves separate from their masters' premises. For instance, a small house on Duke Street was put up for sale in 1831, together with 'a negro yard, in Upper James' Street, with twelve negro rooms, kitchen, &c, &c.'[58] Few slaves were listed for the yards noted in the tax rolls, so it is probable that they accommodated slaves given 'board-wages' by their masters, together with free blacks. Thus it is possible that many slaves lived in yards not owned or controlled by their masters.

Population growth and movement

Thus far the analysis has been concerned with the spatial distribution of slaves in town and country around 1832. It is necessary now to consider changes in the total size of the slave population and in its distribution in the period between the abolition of the slave trade and emancipation. This discussion will be centred on the parish data, since the source materials which enable analysis at the quadrat and town levels are lacking for years other than 1832. Hence the range of explanatory variables accessible is less.

The abolition of the British slave trade in 1807 produced a period of secular decline in the population of Jamaica. Before 1807 the slave population had grown steadily, increasing from about 45,000 in 1700 to 328,000 by 1800, and reaching a peak of 354,000 in 1808.[59] The general trend in the size of the slave population, between 1800 and 1838, is shown in Figure 11. For 1800–16 the populations are based on the poll-tax givings-in, inflated by 10 per cent to conform with the registered populations for 1817–32.[60] The poll-tax totals moved erratically in 1810 and 1811, so that the apparent peak of 1811 should be ignored. The slave population grew only slowly between 1800 and 1805, but expanded more rapidly in the last three years of the slave trade. From 1808 to about 1826 the rate of decline was fairly gradual, the total slave population falling by roughly 20,000. After 1826 the rate of decline increased significantly, so that in the next six years, 1826–32, the population fell by another 20,000. If, however, the total number of slaves listed by the compensation commissioners in August 1834 is assumed to be accurate, it appears that the rate of decline during the period 1832–4 returned to the level of 1817–20 (and probably 1808–20). This reversal might be explained by the deficiency of the Returns of Registrations of Slaves, except that the slave-apprentice population seems to have continued the trend, actually showing an increase

Figure 11. Total slave population, 1800–38 (semi-log scale).

by 1838. In any case, applying the rate of decline for 1829–32 to the population listed for compensation in 1834 means that the 1832 population should have been 315,000, suggesting that the registration returns could have omitted no more than 2,000 slaves in that year, or less than 1 per cent. Further, it must be remembered that each claim for compensation was to be certified by the registrar of slaves, stating that the number of slaves claimed was equal to the number registered in 1832, making allowance for natural increase.[61] Thus the potential degree of divergence between the two populations was limited. It follows that the general trends in the pattern of population growth and decline need to be explained in demographic terms rather than in terms of errors in the source materials.

It may seem paradoxical that the period of greatest decline in the slave population, 1829–32, should be followed by an increase between 1834 and 1838. This apparent reversal can be better understood if, rather than looking at the absolute values, the rate of change in the rate of growth or decline is considered.[62] It appears that the rate of decline was in fact increasing less rapidly by 1832 than it had been about 1817, the rate of change probably reaching a maximum around 1826 (Figure 12). Thus the rapid decrease in the rate of decline between 1832 and 1834, and the growth after 1834, can be seen to follow reasonably smoothly from the pattern of change during the period 1817–32. But an explanation of this pattern of change can be approached only through a study of the age structure of the slave population, which must be postponed.[63]

In the period between the abolition of the slave trade and emancipation the slave population of Jamaica was essentially a closed population. Between 1800 and 1808 86,821 African slaves were brought to Jamaica and only 7,885 were re-exported.[64] After the closing of the African slave trade, slaves continued to be moved from colony to colony and from place to place within colonies, but as a result of this trade Jamaica had made a net gain of only

Figure 12. Percentage change in slave population per annum, 1817–38.

164 slaves by 1830.[65] Within this period Jamaica was a net importer of slaves only between 1815 and 1825.

For Jamaica the internal trade in slaves was much more important than the inter-colonial slave trade after 1808. Although the chances of the planter being able to maintain the age and sex structure he favoured were reduced, he could still be selective in his purchases of slaves and attempt to keep up his numbers. As a result a few parishes showed patterns of growth and decline which diverged from the pattern for the island as a whole. But, unlike the United States,[66] Jamaica lacked areas of natural increase capable of supplying slaves to newly settled regions or even stabilizing the regions of greatest decline. There is no evidence of the systematic 'breeding' of slaves for a market. Humanitarian pressure was applied to have the slaves attached to the soil[67] but, although this failed, speculation in the internal slave trade seems to have been very restricted. By 1831 it was unlawful to travel from place to place within Jamaica offering slaves for sale.[68] Selective purchase was also restricted by the law of 1735 which provided that all slaves sold under writs of *venditioni exponas* be in families, this provision being extended to all sales by 1791.[69]

The most significant changes at the parish level were the growth of Manchester and the decline of Kingston. The development of Manchester followed the removal in 1783 of the prohibitory duties levied on coffee imported into Britain. The parish itself was created only in 1814.[70] A similar growth, resulting from coffee cultivation, had occurred in Port Royal before 1808, but the eastern regions suffered from erosion and many of the slaves were moved to the coastal sugar estates.[71] Part of the increase in the population of Manchester resulted from natural increase rather than movement from other parishes (Table 8). Thus the decline of Kingston is more spectacular since, in spite of a natural increase in the slave population over most of the period from 1817 to 1832, the population fell from 17,954 to 12,552.

Table 8. *Movement of slaves between parishes, 1829–32*

From: / *Into:*	Westmoreland	Hanover	St. James	Trelawny	St. Elizabeth	Manchester	St. Ann	Clarendon	Vere	St. Dorothy	St. Thomas-in-the-Vale	St. John	St. Catherine	St. Mary	St. Andrew	Port Royal	St. David	St. George	Portland	St. Thomas-in-the-East	Kingston	*Total*	*Net Gain*
Westmoreland	X	25	27	1	30	3	0	0	1	0	0	0	1	0	0	0	0	0	5	0	0	93	—15
Hanover	14	X	108	6	5	1	0	0	0	0	0	0	0	0	0	0	0	0	0	0	11	145	—81
St. James	9	27	X	33	9	0	8	0	0	0	1	0	1	0	1	0	0	0	0	0	0	89	153
Trelawny	0	5	62	X	1	0	32	0	0	0	0	0	0	5	0	0	0	0	0	0	3	108	98
St. Elizabeth	40	0	26	1	X	48	0	9	0	0	0	0	0	0	0	0	0	0	0	0	2	126	51
Manchester	0	0	0	0	100	X	0	57	18	6	0	0	0	5	14	2	0	0	0	0	13	215	—147
St. Ann	0	0	5	134	5	0	X	0	0	0	25	5	56	10	3	0	7	5	0	0	4	259	—149
Clarendon	0	0	0	0	3	10	3	X	15	95	33	120	83	0	0	0	0	0	0	6	2	370	—184
Vere	0	0	0	0	0	0	0	12	X	1	0	11	1	0	0	0	0	0	0	0	2	27	109
St. Dorothy	0	0	0	0	0	0	0	9	1	X	0	3	8	0	0	0	0	0	0	0	4	25	200
St. Thomas-in-the-Vale	0	0	1	1	0	0	21	0	0	1	X	79	26	147	40	1	0	6	0	1	30	354	—209
St. John	0	0	1	0	0	0	1	27	1	26	1	X	47	63	1	1	2	0	0	3	7	181	141
St. Catherine	8	2	2	12	3	1	4	15	7	15	38	58	X	3	34	2	1	2	0	0	54	261	139
St. Mary	0	0	0	0	0	0	8	0	0	0	6	0	1	X	28	0	1	10	0	0	19	73	343
St. Andrew	4	2	1	2	5	2	0	39	78	1	19	41	34	102	X	28	4	50	2	127	240	781	—229
Port Royal	0	0	0	0	0	0	3	0	0	0	0	0	1	36	38	X	73	20	0	97	57	325	—243
St. David	0	0	0	0	0	0	1	0	0	0	1	0	0	0	97	1	X	1	10	121	22	254	—2
St. George	0	0	0	0	0	0	7	0	0	0	1	0	5	16	81	7	20	X	36	6	37	216	—68
Portland	0	0	0	0	0	0	0	0	0	0	0	0	28	0	4	0	0	21	X	21	0	74	—9
St. Thomas-in-the-East	0	0	0	0	0	0	0	1	0	71	3	0	10	0	3	1	118	1	10	X	33	251	172
Kingston	3	3	9	16	17	3	22	17	15	9	17	5	98	29	208	39	26	32	2	41	X	611	—71
Total	78	64	242	206	177	68	110	186	136	225	145	322	400	416	552	82	252	148	65	423	540	4,838	

Source: R.R.S.

After Kingston, the greatest loss of population occurred in the semi-urban parish of St. Catherine, which also showed a natural increase over the period 1817–32.

Apart from these changes at the parish level, there were attempts to push settlement into the interior of the island. Around 1832 the whites believed that the bulk of Jamaica was in estates, plantations and pens, but that there was still 'a great proportion of the island not yet cleared, and much bad soil'.[72] Although settlement had encroached on the wooded interior persistently throughout the eighteenth century,[73] it was the relative emptiness of the centre which continued to prey on the whites' minds. And this murky *terra incognita* was magnified by the belief that the total area of the island was 6,400 square miles rather than the actual 4,411.[74] Special efforts were made to maintain and protect settlers pressing into the interior. When settlements were established along the upper reaches of the Great River separating St. James and Hanover a special unit of militia, the Western Interior Regiment, was formed in 1807.[75] In 1812 the Southern Interior Regiment was set up in the area that was to become the parish of Manchester.[76] The windward company of the Western Interior Regiment saw service at Argyle in Hanover when the slaves there rebelled in 1824,[77] and in 1831 it was at the centre of the rebellion. So the whites threw their hands up in horror when Earl Mulgrave, Jamaica's new governor, announced at the close of 1832 that he planned to abolish the regiment because the communications of the district had so improved that the militiamen could attend the regular parish musters. They told Mulgrave that many of their properties had been laid waste by the rebels and that the accumulating population of the region had been checked. If the regiment was abolished, 'one of the most fertile districts of the island' would 'relapse into its primitive wild and neglected condition'.[78]

Schemes to render the entire island populous, secure and self-sufficient were popular, but generally unoriginal. Edward Long, who saw the interior as a healthy region suited to the Anglo-Saxon constitution, proposed the establishment of a central town together with small provision farms and coffee plantations. These farms could later be consolidated and incorporated into the plantation economy, and the small men move further into the woods.[79] In this way Jamaica could emulate the fertility of Barbados and Antigua, supply its own livestock and provisions rather than depending on North America, and live free of the depredations of montane rebels.

Only a month before the outbreak of the rebellion of 1831 the Assembly passed an Act 'to colonize the interior lands of this island, and form a permanent militia'.[80] It was based on the fear that security would be endangered if a large number of runaways were to assemble in the interior to descend on nearby plantations.[81] Justices and vestrymen were appointed as commissioners to acquire land and establish towns in suitable locations in each parish, for the settlement of paupers and other free people (excluding Maroons). All able males between the ages of 16 and 25 years were to be formed into a police. One-third of these were always to be on police duty in the towns, and of the remainder one-half (together with the women and children) were to cultivate the land for their own benefit and the other half for the general benefit of the establishment. The men were to be indented for a minimum of three years and given weekly rations. They were to live sober, moral, industrious lives and unions with their womenfolk were to be blessed by the church.

In none of these schemes for the settlement of the interior did the slaves play a central role. Rather the plans were designed to apply pressure to the slave population, to constrict it, to make the interior unattractive to the slave. The extension of the slave-based planting economy depended on private entrepreneurial decisions. And although the planter was warned that slaves might run away if moved to new locations, the slaves' preferences were of no importance in determining the distribution of population.

An attempt to explain the general pattern of population redistribution in the period 1817–32 can now be made. At the parish level, the rate of change in the size of the slave populations between 1817 and 1832 was correlated significantly with the birth rate of 1829–32 ($r = .56$) and sex ratio ($r = .60$), but not with mortality or natural increase (Table A3.1). Thus at the parish level, at least, the rate of total population change was not a simple function of natural increase but must also have depended on migration. There were also important negative correlations between growth and manumissions, colour, urbanization and non-predial occupations. Increases were associated with holdings in the range of 21 to 100 slaves ($r = .64$), an obvious connection with the expansion of coffee plantations in Manchester. Taken together, eleven of the variables included in this study[82] can account for 77 per cent of the variation in population change, but six of them can explain as much as 75 per cent ($R = .86$) and the multiple regression of these yields the following estimating equation:

$$Y_{24} = 150.46 - 0.77X_7 + 0.76X_{13} + 0.57X_{21} - 0.19X_{28} + 0.14X_{29} + 12.56X_{41}$$

where Y_{24} is slave population in 1832 as a percentage of that in 1817, X_7 males per 100 females (in 1832), X_{13} natural increase, X_{21} percentage deaths African, X_{28} manumissions, X_{29} runaways, and X_{41} livestock per slave. The residuals from this equation have not been calculated for all of the parishes, but it is proved to be a very good guide to the reasons for Kingston's decline though a failure in the case of Manchester. Thus it is clear that Kingston's losses were not strictly a result of sales of slaves to other parishes.

The actual movement of slaves, then, was only one of the factors involved in the variable growth rates of the parish populations between 1817 and 1832. In fact there was no significant correlation between population change in this period and net purchases of slaves during the period 1829–32, at the parish level ($r = -.03$). Yet there is no doubt that a considerable number of slaves were moved from place to place within the island. The Returns of Registrations of Slaves listed these movements only when they involved changes in ownership or changes in parish of residence. But changes in ownership did not always mean changes in location, so care is required in the interpretation of the data. When an owner sold all of his slaves he was not obliged to make a return at the end of the triennium, and it follows that when all of the purchases and sales recorded are totalled the purchases outweigh the sales. Thus the returns of purchases are much more exhaustive than those for sales. When slaves were moved from parish to parish, the parish from which they came was noted consistently, whereas other locational references were given only occasionally. Thus it is possible to trace the pattern of movement between parishes resulting from purchases and other types of gains.

In the three years 1829–32 some 4,838 slaves, or 1.5 per cent of the population, were moved from one parish to another (Table 8). Most moves took place between contiguous parishes, so apparent movement may be affected by parish size. The clustering along the diagonal in Table 8 demonstrates the short distances involved in most cases. Only the urban and peri-urban parishes of Kingston, St. Andrew and St. Catherine were involved in long-distance movement. Kingston alone sent out slaves to every other parish; and it also received slaves from all but the most remote rural parishes. Kingston and St. Andrew sent out the greatest numbers of slaves, though a significant proportion of this movement took place between these two parishes and this was probably only a shift of domestic slaves or a transfer from commercial to residential occupations. It was said in 1832 that 'the trades were overstocked' in Kingston.[83] After the urban parishes, the greatest receivers were St. Thomas-in-the-East, St. Mary and St. John. All of these had very high rates of natural decrease and it is clear that the movement of slaves was an attempt to replace the losses,[84] but the net gains were not sufficient to account for more than one-third of the natural decrease.

Twelve parishes were net 'exporters' of slaves in the period 1829–32 while nine were net 'importers'. But these parishes were intermixed spatially, so that it is difficult to define the main directions of movement. The greatest proportional gains were made by St. Mary, St. John, St. Catherine and St. Dorothy. A much more detailed pattern is obtained if the net gains and losses of the rural quadrats are mapped, but here the data relating to gains are overestimates and only the figures for losses can be relied on. The quadrats with net losses were widely scattered but there were concentrations in upper St. Andrew, the Port Royal Mountains, the inland areas of Manchester, St. Elizabeth and St. James, and, surprisingly, the uplands behind Morant Bay in St. Thomas-in-the-East. This suggests that the basic movement was from the interior towards the coast, resulting in an increasing concentration of population on the sugar estates.

The urban dominance of the pattern of movement suggests that many of the slaves involved may have been non-predials.[85] It is difficult to test this proposition, but some hints can be gleaned from the colour of the slaves, and the sex and African/creole ratios. In Portland, for example, only 10 per cent of the slaves sold were Africans but 35 per cent of the slaves purchased were Africans. At the same time, only two coloured slaves were sold (a mulatto and a quadroon) while thirty-four coloured slaves were purchased (seventeen samboes, sixteen mulattoes and one quadroon). In St. John, on the other hand, the proportions of coloured slaves sold and purchased were similar, and only a slightly greater proportion of Africans were purchased than were sold. But in St. John a considerably larger proportion of females were purchased than were sold. Thus there may well have been a flow of domestics and (coloured) tradesmen from the towns to the rural parishes (or the outports).[86] This was balanced by a movement of Africans, though in the eastern parishes the Africans, too, could have come from the towns. But, although the precise character of the movements may be uncertain and in spite of the planters' contention that the successful removal of slaves to new locations was a difficult thing,[87] it is clear that the flows created by the differential decline of the slave population after 1808 meant that by 1834 the slaves had a good idea of the nature of life in town and country and in the various rural parishes.[88]

Slave-holding size

The flow of slaves from the towns to the rural parishes, together with the flow from the interior coffee plantations to the coastal sugar regions following the abolition of the slave trade, suggests a concentration in the ownership of slaves. As a consequence, slaves would increasingly find themselves members of relatively large holdings. Thus Barclay, in 1826, claimed that after 1807 the small owners began to die out; the slaves moved from the free coloured and small tradesmen 'to the jobbing gangs of the middle class of white people', and from these to the large plantations.[89] De la Beche made a similar point when he argued that jobbing gangs were becoming less numerous because the abolition of the slave trade had 'in a great measure prevented overseers and others who had acquired some little money from investing it in this kind of property, as they cannot now recruit their numbers as formerly by purchase from the slave-ships'.[90] But, although it is true that between 1807 and 1834 many estates were amalgamated and there was a clear decline in the small urban holdings, the rate of natural increase tended to be relatively high on the smallest holdings and low on the largest. Thus the observations of Barclay and De la Beche, while applicable to the number of slave-holdings and hence of masters, do not necessarily mean that the slaves more often lived on large plantations.

Systematic data relating to slave-holding size begin only with the Returns of Registrations of Slaves, in 1817. There are, however, certain problems associated with the interpretation of these data. The number of returns did not equal the number of masters. Some of the masters possessed several holdings, while other units were jointly owned. Of the 252 holdings in Portland in 1832, for example, 5 were owned by two persons, 7 were joint owned (by a total of twenty-five persons), the estates of thirty-one absentees were managed by attorneys and agents, 6 were leased, 6 were in the hands of receivers, 4 were mortgaged, 25 were managed by executors and trustees, and 27 were controlled by guardians. A further complication was that the slaves living together in a single functional unit could be owned by several persons, each making a separate return.[91] This problem cannot be solved by simply aggregating all units with the same name, since it is evident that satellites of a major settlement often took its place name. On the other hand, the owner of two contiguous estates not operated as a single unit occasionally made one return for both. Thus the frequency distribution of size groups tends to be flattened somewhat.

In 1832 the average holding comprised 25 slaves. At the parish level, the average ranged from 53 in Vere to 5 in Kingston (Table A3.15). But it is clear that the usefulness of the average as an index of the distribution of large and small holdings depends on the proportion of the slave population living in towns. All of the towns conformed closely to the Kingston average of 5 slaves per holding (Table 7). Thus the parish of St. Catherine, dominated by Spanish Town, had the low average of 13 slaves per holding.

Although more than 50 per cent of the slave-holdings in 1832 consisted of units of 5 or less slaves, only about 4.3 per cent of the slaves lived in such units (Table A3.15). Only 25 per cent lived on units of less than 50 slaves, while another 25 per cent lived on units of more than 250 slaves. Almost 50 per cent of Jamaica's slaves were held in units of more than 150. This pattern may be compared with that in the United States in 1860 where 75 per cent of the slaves lived in units of less than 50 and 97 per cent of the masters held less than 50 slaves[92] (the latter figure being 88 per cent in Jamaica). In the United States (in 1860) there were only 312 plantations of more than 200 slaves, whereas Jamaica had 393 (in 1832). Much more than in America, the typical Jamaican slave lived on a large estate or plantation.

For 1817, slave-holding size has been analysed for a sample of six parishes only (Table 9). These parishes were representative of the range of economic and demographic diversity within Jamaica. It seems clear that between 1817 and 1832 there was a real decline in the proportion of slaves held in units of 50 or less, confirming the impressions of Barclay and De la Beche noted above. It is less certain, however, that there was a concentration into the largest plantations. Only in St. Elizabeth, Manchester and St. John was there an increase in the percentage in holdings of more than 200 slaves. The greatest gains appear to have occurred in the 101–200 slave group, though St. John showed a loss in it. Thus rather than a movement from the smallest

Table 9. *Slave-holding size in six parishes, 1817 and 1832*

	Percentage of slaves in size-group						
Slaves per holding	St. James	St. Elizabeth	Manchester	St. John	Portland	Kingston	Jamaica (total)
1817:							
1–50	26.4	37.5	27.3	26.4	29.8	96.1	
51–100	7.5	13.3	24.1	15.8	10.9	3.9	
101–200	23.8	17.0	24.4	19.6	24.8	—	
201–300	22.0	14.4	7.5	15.1	19.4	—	
301–400	10.6	17.8	13.9	5.1	4.0	—	
401–500	5.5	—	2.8	—	11.1	—	
501–600	4.2	—	—	8.3	—	—	
601–700	—	—	—	9.7	—	—	
Total	100.0	100.0	100.0	100.0	100.0	100.0	
1832:							
1–50	26.5	32.5	20.1	25.6	22.7	95.9	24.3
51–100	13.1	11.6	22.0	19.5	9.3	1.9	14.0
101–200	27.4	22.2	29.4	16.4	36.2	2.2	25.6
201–300	19.0	15.2	15.5	12.6	16.2	—	21.4
301–400	12.0	13.9	5.6	17.7	9.7	—	9.2
401–500	2.0	4.6	7.4	8.2	5.9	—	3.5
501–600	—	—	—	—	—	—	1.1
601–700	—	—	—	—	—	—	0.6
701–800	—	—	—	—	—	—	0.3
Total	100.0	100.0	100.0	100.0	100.0	100.0	100.0

Source: R.R.S. (1817 calculated directly; 1832 estimated: see Table A3.15).

to the largest holdings, it is probable that there was a concentration into the middle-sized units. This pattern fits well with the movement of slaves away from the towns and into the coastal sugar estates, established above, and with the demographic variations between the size groups which will be discussed in the next chapter.

Slave-holdings varied in size according to their economic function; the fertility and mortality experience of the slaves had only a minor effect since owners redistributed their numbers according to the rate of increase. The masters attempted to approximate the optimum size which they believed appropriate to the particular activity in which their slaves were engaged. It has been noted already that where the slave population was dense the units in which the slaves were settled tended to be relatively large. Thus there were strong correlations between the number of sugar estates in each quadrat and mean slave-holding size ($r = .47$) and the percentage of holdings with more than 100 slaves ($r = .46$). The largest estates tended to be located in the more level areas, near to the coast and ports, or in areas with good transportation networks. These relationships can be seen in a slightly different way by looking at the quadrats in which large holdings were dominant, the quadrats in which more than 25 per cent of the units comprised more than 100 slaves in 1832. In addition to the concentrations along the eastern littoral, there were other regions of dominance in the Queen of Spain's Valley, Vere, the upper reaches of the Rio Minho, and the Great, Negro and Morant Rivers. As a consequence it appears that large estates dominated both densely peopled areas along the coasts and river valleys, and isolated regions in the interior which were quite thinly populated. The latter formed those outposts which impressed contemporary writers by their loneliness and isolation.

Large and small slave-holdings were intermixed spatially, but only in a few of the quadrats where holdings of more than 100 slaves formed 25 per cent of the total did units of less than 21 slaves reach 60 per cent. The greatest region of small holdings was that in southern St. Elizabeth; the parish had long been known to contain a great number of free people of colour and small proprietors.[93] Other regions in which small holdings were dominant were found in the more rugged parts of the interior, unsuited to sugar or pen-keeping, and in the hinterlands of ports; the latter probably provisioned the townspeople and passing ships. Areas in which units of 21–100 slaves dominated were most numerous in the interior regions of considerable altitude and relative relief; these were the medium-sized coffee plantations.

It is probable that between 1807 and 1834 the average slave-holding was becoming larger. This resulted chiefly from the significant decline in the smallest, urban units, for it was counterbalanced by a decline in the largest holdings. But if this meant that the planters more often controlled units which they thought to approach an optimum size, it does not follow that they were satisfied with the change, for the abolition of the slave trade produced changes in the age–sex structure as well as in the size distribution of slave-holdings. For the slaves, this process of concentration into larger, optimum-sized units meant an increasing concentration into sugar estates and a decline in the opportunities for relatively independent economic activity which had often been associated with belonging to small, especially urban, holdings.

Sex ratio

In recruiting their slave labour force, the masters showed a clear preference for males when they made purchases from the slavers' ships. But after 1807 this imbalance gradually worked itself out. By 1817 there were only 74 more male than female slaves in Jamaica,[94] though contrasts between the African and creole sections of the population remained. Among the Africans there were 117.8 males for every 100 females, whereas there were only 91.4 creole males per 100 females.[95] After 1817 the males continued to decline relatively because the Africans among them formed an aging group and because

Table 10. *Slave sex ratios, 1817, 1829 and 1832*

Parish	Males per 100 females		
	1817	*1829*	*1832*
Westmoreland	95.1	94.1	92.7
Hanover	99.5	92.9	90.5
St. James	95.9	94.6	92.1
Trelawny	98.4	93.4	93.0
St. Elizabeth	101.5	97.9	95.7
Manchester	111.9	104.3	101.1
St. Ann	102.9	101.5	99.5
Clarendon	98.2	96.5	94.8
Vere	96.3	90.2	90.2
St. Dorothy	103.4	96.9	96.5
St. Thomas-in-the-Vale	102.2	94.4	92.9
St. John	95.4	96.1	93.1
St. Catherine	84.6	96.2	93.4
St. Mary	102.2	97.7	93.9
St. Andrew	106.0	101.1	100.2
Port Royal	112.2	100.0	99.9
St. David	111.4	104.4	102.4
St. George	112.4	101.8	99.5
Portland	101.3	94.2	93.6
St. Thomas-in-the-East	103.4	98.5	95.5
Kingston	81.4	79.7	78.5
Total	100.0	96.4	94.5

Source: J.H.A.V., 1817, p. 39; T.71/683, Bundle 9 (1829); R.R.S. (1832).

males – especially African males – suffered a heavy differential age-specific mortality in the groups above about 35 years.[96] The fall in the sex ratio between 1817 and 1832, from 100.0 to 94.5 was quite smooth. Extrapolating, it appears that about 1807 the sex ratio must have been 104. This suggests that in the last years of the slave trade to Jamaica the proportion of males imported is unlikely to have exceeded 60 per cent of the total.

The downward trend of the sex ratio at the island level was reflected faithfully in almost all of the parishes between 1817 and 1832 (Table 10). The major anomaly was the significant rise in the sex ratio in St. Catherine between 1817 and 1829, for which there is no obvious explanation. The levelling out of the ratio in Vere may be explained by the emergence of a positive natural increase in the slave population of this mature sugar parish. In terms of differences between the parishes, the most obvious feature was the femininity of Kingston and, in 1817, St. Catherine. The high ratio of females in Kingston was not peculiar to that town but was typical of urban slave society as a whole, though only Spanish Town and Port Maria were less masculine than Kingston in 1832 (Table 7, above). Of the 26 towns in 1832, 9 did in fact have an excess of males. At Charles Town there were almost three males for every female, though the Maroons (who owned at least 38 of the 99 slaves in the town) had a slight preponderance of females, in common with the creole slave population.[97] Apart from the major centres, the towns with the greatest femininity were mostly the larger ones in the western end of the island. These variations were a result of the domestic function of urban slavery – the larger the town the greater the proportion of masters anxious to demonstrate their social standing through the size of their domestic retinue.

In addition to the rural–urban contrast in the level of the sex ratio, Table 10 suggests that the ratio was significantly higher in the eastern parishes than western parishes. But it is not clear why the latter should be so, and when the pattern is mapped at the quadrat level this apparent east – west contrast largely disappears. In 1832 areas of male dominance clustered around the headwaters of the Great and YS Rivers, southern St. Elizabeth, Manchester, mountain Clarendon, the eastern and western boundaries of St. Ann, southwestern St. Catherine, and – as the parish figures show – most of St. David, Port Royal, St. Andrew and St. George. Areas of female dominance, with sex ratios of less than 90, were scattered through the interior and along the coast, the most significant concentrations being in Hanover/Westmoreland, southern Manchester and Portland. The regions in which the sex ratio fell between 90 and 100 bear a strong resemblance to those in which large properties were dominant, though with particular concentrations in St. Thomas-in-the-Vale and St. Mary. On the sugar estates included in the Accounts Produce (comprehending 117,670 slaves) the sex ratio was 92.

It is tempting to explain the variations in the sex ratio in terms of the historical expansion of settlement. It might be expected that where the land had to be cleared males would predominate, that newly established settlements would contain a high percentage of Africans and hence males. This may be true of some areas, such as northern Manchester and Port Royal, where expansion followed the coffee boom of the 1790s,[98] but it can hardly be argued as a general proposition. The spatial pattern of the sex ratio was in fact a product of differential purchasing, fertility and mortality. In the towns, natural increases were associated with femininity ($r = -.70$), but this relationship breaks down at the parish and quadrat levels. In the parishes, masculinity was related to the dominance of holdings in the 21–100 slaves group (suggesting a link with coffee), but in the quadrats it was positively correlated with only the smallest slave-holdings. The only other strong correlations were between femininity and urbanism, and masculinity and sugar estates, at the parish level. But the map evidence suggests a link between masculinity and coffee planting – the sex ratio on the coffee plantations included in the Accounts Produce being 101 – and this might be best explained in terms of the greater mortality of males on sugar estates, rather than the selectivity of coffee and sugar planters.

In general, it seems that the sex ratio fell as slave-holding size increased. Taking the holdings included in the Accounts Produce, there was a constant pattern, the sex ratio falling from 110 in the 1–50 size-group to 92 in units of more than 500 slaves (Table 25, below). A similar, though inevitably more complicated, trend appeared in 1817 in the six parishes analysed in detail (Table A3.14). The clearest case was the recently settled parish of Manchester, where the trend applied both to Africans and creoles. On the other hand, in Kingston in 1817 the sex ratio stood at 78 in the 1–50 group and 313 in the 51–100 group; and among the Africans the ratios were 80 and 561, emphasizing the domestic function of the smaller units in the towns.

The general trend of a fall in the sex ratio with increasing holding-size is somewhat surprising. It is true that the purchaser of a few slaves could be more selective than the large planter, but the proportion of African slaves possessed did not generally fall consistently as holding-size increased. More importantly, by 1817 differential mortality had worked to reduce the male proportion in the larger units, among both Africans and creoles. This factor must also be invoked to explain the continued fall in the sex ratio between 1807 and 1832 – and, probably, 1844 – even after the creoles became dominant, and in spite of an equality of the sexes at birth.[99]

Connected with these variations in the sex ratio over time and between size groups were variations in terms of age. But the latter showed some strong contrasts between parishes (Table A3.12). In Kingston males outnumbered females in no age-group; the sex ratio fell consistently with age, and with great rapidity after about 30 years (Figure 13). This pattern, although partly a result of differential mortality, must have reflected sex-specific migration; the movement of slaves away from Kingston to the rural parishes centred on males, whereas women remained tied to the domestic function. In contrast to the pattern in Kingston, the sex ratio in most parishes rose to about 50 years of age before falling off sharply. This contrast was not a product of the African/creole ratio, for Kingston's slave population in 1817 included a larger proportion of Africans than any other parish, with the exception of Manchester. Although the sex ratio for Africans was always higher than for creoles, in Kingston males outnumbered females among the Africans only in the age-group 25–34 years. Thus it would seem that, although there was a great demand for Africans in Kingston, this demand centred heavily on females. In the rural parishes the demand was for males, so that even in 1817 they generally outnumbered females consistently between the ages of 20 and 60 years. In 1817 in the newly settled coffee parishes of Manchester and Port Royal the sex ratio exceeded 150 in the 40–44 age-group. In the mature sugar parish of Vere, on the other hand, it came close to maintaining an equality between 0 and 55 years. These variations had important consequences for fertility, mortality and family structure.

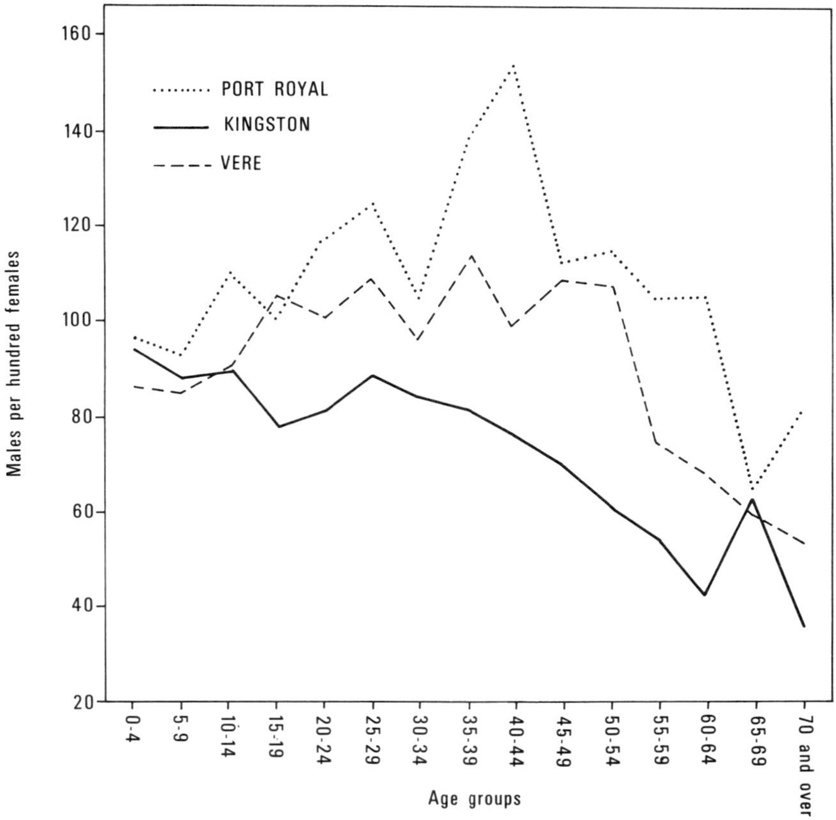

Figure 13. Age-specific sex ratios, Port Royal, Kingston and Vere slave populations, 1817.

Africans and creoles

There was a steady increase in the annual average number of slaves brought from Africa to Jamaica during the eighteenth century, the rate rising from about 2,000 in 1700 to 8,000 by 1790. Between 1792 and 1807 the rate rose to 10,700,[100] though there is little evidence of a rush to augment the slave population in the final years of the slave trade, with the exception of 1807 (Table 11). In 1789 the Assembly estimated that 25 per cent of the slaves in Jamaica were Africans,[101] but this is likely to have been an understatement for as late as 1817 – ten years after abolition – Africans made up 37 per cent of the slave population.[102] In 1817 there were 126,903 African slaves in Jamaica, but by 1844 only 33,519 of the total population had been born in Africa.[103] If it is assumed that there were no free Africans in 1817 and that the rate of decrease was constant between 1817 and 1844, it can be estimated that in 1832 there must have been about 73,500 African slaves, or 23.5

Table 11. *Slaves imported to Jamaica, 1800–8*[a]

	Slaves imported	Slaves exported	Net importation
1800	20,436	5	20,431
1801	11,309	270	11,039
1802	8,131	2,554	5,577
1803	7,846	2,036	5,810
1804	5,979	1,811	4,168
1805	5,006	398	4,608
1806	8,487	166	8,321
1807	16,263	336	15,927
1808	3,364	309	3,055
Total	86,821	7,885	78,936

[a] Years ending 30 September.
Source: Further Proceedings of the Honourable House of Assembly of Jamaica, . . . (London, 1816), p. 101. See also *P.P.*, 1806, XIII (265), *Accounts presented to the House of Commons, relating to the African Slave Trade*, pp. 775–804.

per cent of the total. But it is likely that the rate of decrease rose as the Africans aged between 1817 and 1844, so that the actual proportion in 1832 was perhaps nearer 25 per cent. Extrapolating, it follows that around 1807 Africans comprised roughly 45 per cent of the slave population of Jamaica.

If the Assembly's estimate of 1789 was anywhere near the mark, it appears that the slave population must have become as heavily Africanized in 1790–1807 as in any other period, with the exception of the late seventeenth century. This has important implications for an understanding of the process of 'creolization',[104] as does the fact that in the period 1792–1807 approximately 83 per cent of the slaves came from the Bight of Biafra (Ibos) and Central Africa (Congos), compared to 46 per cent over the entire history of the slave trade to Jamaica.[105] Equally important for creolization was the rapid decline in the African section after 1807. But even in those parishes in which Africans comprised less than 30 per cent of the slave population by 1817, they continued to form a majority in the age-groups above 30 years (Figure 14). At the other extreme, in Port Royal, where 50 per cent of the slaves were African in 1817, they dominated all age-groups above 20 years, and after 30 years of age accounted for 80 per cent of the total population. In general, Africans accounted for at least two-thirds of the total in all age-groups above 35 years. But by 1832 the Africans could in no parish have formed a majority in the age-groups under 35 years and, of course, the growth of the creole section meant that the older age-groups became increasingly insignificant, in numbers at least.

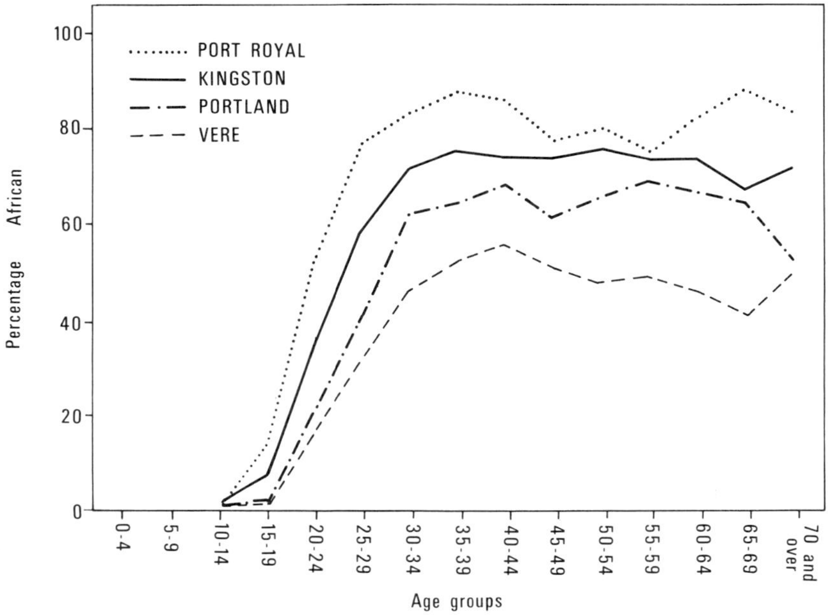

Figure 14. Percentage of slaves African, by age-groups, Port Royal, Kingston, Portland and Vere, 1817.

There were significant differences in the spatial distribution of Africans and creoles. In 1817 Africans approached a majority in the newly settled coffee parishes of Port Royal and Manchester, whereas in the sugar and pen parishes they accounted for about one-third of the slave populations, reaching a minimum in the mature sugar parish of Vere (Table 12). These contrasts were closely related to the level of the sex ratio, as noted in the previous section. In order to obtain a more detailed picture of the spatial distribution of Africans and creoles, however, it is necessary to use the Returns of Registrations of Slaves for 1829–32, in which the only systematic data available are those relating to deaths (Table 13). The figures for the eight parishes included in Table 12 do suggest a consistent relationship between the percentage of Africans in the total slave population and the percentage of deaths African, for 1817–20. Data for individual holdings, 1829–32, show a much greater degree of variability in this relationship, so that estimates based on deaths at the quadrat level are necessarily less certain. But the only significant correlation found between African and total deaths is that at the quadrat level, and it is positive ($r = .30$), supporting the view that the percentage of deaths African was a measure of the actual size of the African group. It is necessary to establish this relationship since it might be argued that a high percentage of African deaths could be associated with a large, young creole population, whereas a low percentage of African deaths may mean only that there was also a high percentage of

Table 12. *Percentage of African slaves, 1817, and percentage of deaths African, 1817–20*

Parish	Percentage of slave population African, 1817	Percentage deaths African, 1817–20
St. James	35.0	49.8
Manchester	49.2	59.9
Clarendon	31.8	38.5
Vere	28.6	39.6
St. John	33.0	36.2
Port Royal	50.0	58.1
Portland	35.1	45.8
Kingston	42.1	50.2
Jamaica	37.0	?

Source: R.R.S., the Jamaica total being calculated from the published statistics in *P.P.,* 1832 (721), p. 521.

Table 13. *Percentage deaths African, 1829–32*

Parish	Percentage deaths African, 1829–32			Estimated percentage African, 1829
	Males	Females	Total	
Westmoreland	34.5	32.1	33.5	(26)
Hanover	29.1	31.4	30.1	(23)
St. James	38.0	34.6	36.5	29
Trelawny	42.7	35.8	39.6	(32)
St. Elizabeth	33.8	32.4	33.2	26
Manchester	53.4	49.9	52.0	43
St. Ann	36.3	33.1	34.8	(27)
Clarendon	38.6	27.0	33.1	26
Vere	32.4	28.5	30.5	23
St. Dorothy	41.6	32.4	39.4	(32)
St. Thomas-in-the-Vale	37.9	26.8	33.0	(26)
St. John	35.9	28.6	32.5	26
St. Catherine	34.9	29.8	32.5	(26)
St. Mary	40.3	33.2	37.1	(29)
St. Andrew	43.2	33.5	39.0	(32)
Port Royal	46.6	48.0	47.3	39
St. David	51.4	40.5	46.5	(38)
St. George	50.6	43.4	47.4	(39)
Portland	32.0	33.0	32.5	25
St. Thomas-in-the-East	37.5	32.3	35.2	(28)
Kingston	43.7	37.8	41.0	32
Total	39.2	33.9	36.7	(29)

Source: R.R.S.

creole deaths, that is, that both the African and creole sections of the population were old.

Estimating from the linear relationship between deaths and total percentage African derived from the sample of parishes in Table 12, the percentage African for the island in 1829 is found to be 29 per cent. This comes close to the 27 per cent found by straight-line interpolation based on the 1817 and 1844 data, discussed above. The former percentage may be slightly high because the sample of parishes in Table 12 is weighted to the extremes. But the line may be used to estimate the percentage African in 1829 from the deaths 1829–32, with confidence for the parishes included in Table 12 and with less certainty for the others (shown in parentheses in Table 13). The important point is that the percentage deaths African proves to be a reliable index of the percentage African in the total populations.

At the parish level, large proportions of Africans – 38 per cent and above in 1829 – were found not only in Manchester and Port Royal, but also in St. George and St. David, suggesting that there was a heavily Africanized belt stretching across the eastern end of the island (as was predicted from the level of the sex ratio), a region much affected by the coffee boom of the 1790s. At the other extreme, Hanover and Vere stand out as the most heavily creolized of the parishes. At the quadrat level, working directly from the percentage of deaths African, the pattern becomes more complex. But two major concentrations of Africans emerge. The most important was that covering Manchester and spilling over into the adjacent parts of St. Elizabeth, Trelawny, St. Ann and Clarendon. The other was in the Port Royal Mountains, confirming the connection with coffee predicted from the parish pattern. Africans were at a minimum in the far western parishes – not only Hanover – and in the region centring on northern St. John. At the quadrat level, high percentages of African deaths were correlated, though weakly, with small to medium-sized slave-holdings, and with pens and plantations (Table A3.2). The major sugar-producing areas had relatively few Africans. This can also be identified in the properties included in the Accounts Produce sample. The percentage of deaths African on sugar estates (32 per cent) was much lower than that on coffee (46) and its associations with livestock (48) and pimento (43) (Table 24, below). Livestock and its combinations with pimento and dyewoods had percentages as low as that applying to sugar. But the highest percentage of deaths African (59) was found in the jobbing gangs. There were also high percentages – in excess of 40 per cent – in many of the towns, particularly in the eastern end of the island; but in contrast to the agricultural holdings these high percentages of Africans went together with low sex ratios.

A corollary of this concentration of Africans into particular locations and economic activities was their concentration into the smaller slave-holdings. The percentage of deaths African 1829–32 on the properties included in the Accounts Produce sample was at a peak in the 1–50 size-group (47 per cent), fell smoothly and rapidly to 29 per cent in the 201–250 group, then levelled out, reaching a minimum in the 401–500 group (Table 25, below). A similar pattern occurred in most of the parishes analysed for 1817, except that in Manchester the percentage African remained fairly constant as slave-holding size increased and in Kingston the percentage climbed to its maximum (71 per cent) in the largest urban holdings (Table A3.14). In all of the rural parishes the proportion of the African population living in units of less than 100 slaves exceeded the proportion of the total population in such units, whereas the Africans were generally under-represented in larger units. In most parishes more than 50 per cent of the Africans lived in units of less than 100 slaves; for creoles this seems to have been true only of Manchester in 1817, and there only barely. Creoles, therefore, dominated the larger holdings.

The concentration of Africans and males into the smaller slave-holdings was not a direct result of preferences of coffee planters and jobbers as contrasted to sugar planters. Apart from the demand for female domestics in the towns, all of the masters favoured adult male slaves, and hence Africans. Creoles fetched higher prices than Africans because they were 'seasoned' and less recalcitrant; yet the cost of 'breeding' slaves was thought to outweigh that of importing them.[106] For planters, and missionaries, a high percentage of Africans meant a high degree of uncivilized, recalcitrant behaviour – according to the Baptist Phillippo, the abolition of the slave trade 'lessened in an equal proportion that amount of ignorance, superstition, and profligacy, which was the necessary result of every fresh importation from Africa'.[107] But whereas the sugar estate populations had been in existence for long periods and the creoles on them were established, if not self-supporting, the jobbing gangs were more ephemeral units for which purchases were often made from slave ships; many of the coffee plantations, too, had been formed only in the late eighteenth century.[108] Thus it was the timing of the spread of settlement which determined the spatial distribution of Africans and creoles rather than any peculiar characteristics of the forms of economic activity in which they were involved.

Age structure

Age is one of the most important demographic characteristics, but unfortunately the data available in the Returns of Registrations of Slaves are relatively limited. As noted already,[109] their interpretation also involves more difficulties. Only in 1817 did the returns note the age of every slave, so that changes in the pattern can be traced accurately only by following individual slaves through the triennial returns, an extremely tedious task. Had the population been a quasi-stable one it would be possible, using model life tables, to attempt to find the age distribution from the birth rate, death rate, mortality schedule and rate of growth, but it is obvious that Jamaica did not conform to the assumptions of a quasi-stable population: minimal age-specific migration and relatively constant levels of fertility and mortality.[110]

In 1834 the valuers appointed by the assistant commissioners for compensation made returns of the number of children under six years of age in each parish, as at 1st August, and of the number of 'aged, diseased, or otherwise non-effective' slaves (Table A3.16). The 'aged' in the latter category included all slaves of 70 years or older,[111] but it seems that these accounted for varying proportions of the category in different parishes; hence its usefulness as an index of age structure is limited. These two extreme categories do, however, provide a rough picture of the age distribution at the time of emancipation. Children under six years of age made up 12.5 per cent of the total slave population. They exceeded 14 per cent only in St. Ann, Manchester and St. Elizabeth, the leading pen and coffee parishes. Elsewhere the percentage did not vary from the island average significantly. But the parish with the lowest percentage of children under six years, St. Mary (with 11.2 per cent), also had the largest number of aged (9.5 per cent). Variations from the island mean of 5.0 per cent aged were much greater than those of children under six years. Yet only Westmoreland (8.9 per cent) approached the high level of aged found in St. Mary, and it had a normal percentage of children. On the other hand, none of the parishes with large percentages of children had low percentages of aged, with the exception of St. Ann. By far the lowest percentage of aged occurred in Kingston (1.0) – probably a result of the age-specific migration out of the town in the early years of the century. Neither the percentage under six years or aged was correlated significantly with the vital rates – or, indeed, with any of the variables included in the analysis – so these measures were not mere surrogates of fertility, mortality, sex or the African/creole ratio. But it is clear that their value as an index of age structure is slight.

The age structure of nine sample parishes has been calculated from the Returns of Registrations of Slaves for 1817, distinguishing Africans and creoles, and slave-holding size-groups (Table A3.11). These parishes were representative of the main varieties of economic activity, stages of settlement and environmental conditions. The age distributions of these parishes present some strong contrasts, along with important similarities. A common feature of the total populations was an erosion of the age pyramid between about 15 and 25 years. Port Royal and Vere, at the extremes in terms of most of the demographic characteristics discussed so far, provide clear illustrations of this pattern (Figure 15). The erosion in the 15–24 age-group was much more obvious in Port Royal, with its large African section, than in the long-settled and heavily creolized parish of Vere. But in neither parish did the masters control the type of slave labour force which they idealized – one in which the population was concentrated into the major working age-groups, 15–44 years. Ten years earlier, at the abolition of the slave trade, they had controlled such a labour force. Twenty-five years after the abolition, with

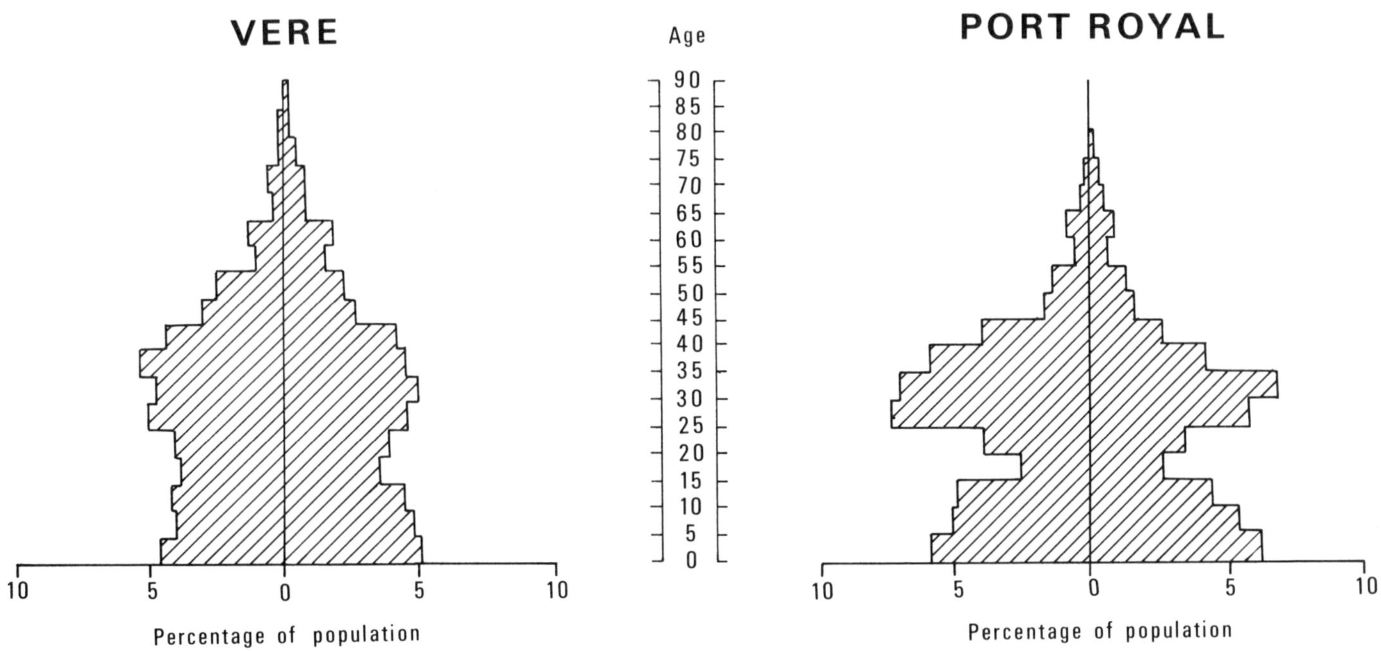

Figure 15. Age pyramids of Vere and Port Royal slave populations, 1817.

emancipation approaching, the erosion would inevitably be even more pronounced than it was in 1817.

A clearer understanding of variations in the age structure around 1817 can be obtained by separating the African and creole populations (Figure 16). The age structures of the two sections were always closely linked, so that the differences between the parishes remain strong. Thus where the African group was concentrated into the younger age-groups, the creole age profile was also relatively young. This, together with differences in the African/creole ratio, explains the contrast between the Port Royal and Vere age pyramids, noted above. In Vere the modal age-groups for Africans were 35–44 years, but in Port Royal 25–34 years. The contrast between creoles was even greater – in Vere only 38 per cent were under 15 years, but in Port Royal 65 per cent. In Port Royal the creole age profile was young, in Vere it was mature.

The remaining sample parishes ranged between these extremes. The only exception to this generalization is that the African age profile for St. James was somewhat flatter than that for Vere (Figure 17); this may have occurred because an abnormally small proportion of the Africans in St. James lived in the smaller slave-holdings, whereas in Vere most were probably in such units, in which the masters could be more selective in their purchases from the slave ships. Otherwise the age profiles of the parishes found their place between the extremes in close conformity to their type of economic activity and stage of settlement. In the other newly settled coffee parish, Manchester, the age structure of the slave population was very similar to that in Port Royal, though slightly more heavily weighted to the older age-groups. In Kingston the Africans were as heavily concentrated into the 25–39 age-groups as in these parishes, but the creoles were not dominated by the younger groups in the same way. The age pyramid shows the effect of an age-sex-specific migration out of Kingston, as suggested earlier. It is also notable that in Kingston the 0–4 group contained less slaves than the 5–14 age-groups, and this – while surprising – may also be linked with the effect on fertility of the movement of slaves. After the coffee parishes and Kingston, the most youthful creole age profiles were those of Portland, St. John and Clarendon, all long-established sugar parishes (with Portland experiencing a period of definite decline). The African population in Clarendon was slightly older than in the other two parishes, and as a result the creole section was relatively mature, lacking a heavy concentration in the 0–14 age-group. St. Elizabeth, a parish dependent on livestock and sugar, also had a fairly youthful creole age profile, though with a surprisingly small percentage in the 0–4 group. Finally, St. James, a late-developing sugar parish, had a creole population more mature than might be expected, rivalling Vere.

Age structure also varied between slave-holding size-groups within each of the parishes, but these variations were not altogether consistent. Once again, trends in the African section of the population were reflected in the

PORT ROYAL

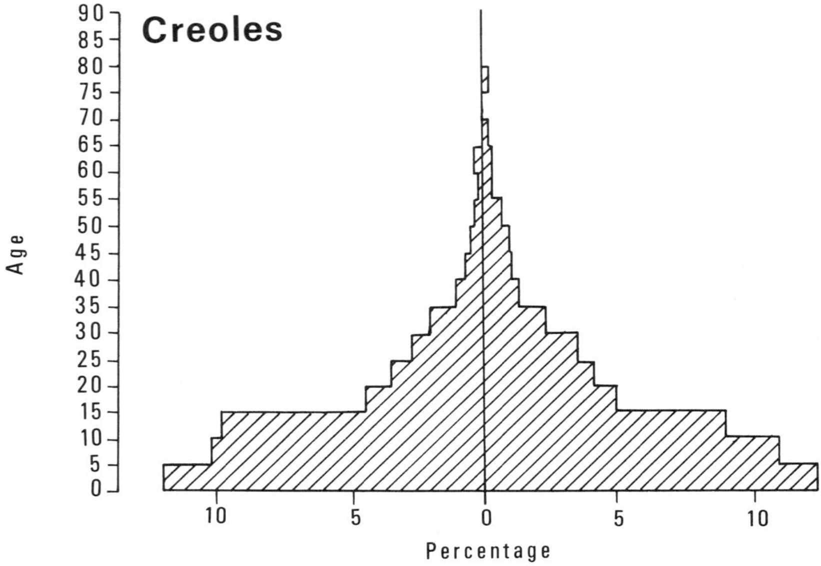

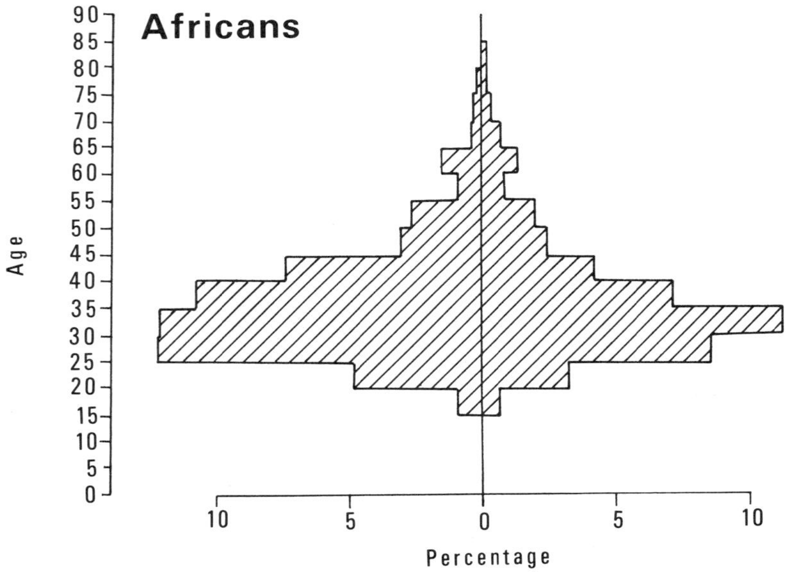

Figure 16. African and creole age pyramids of the slave populations of nine parishes, 1817.

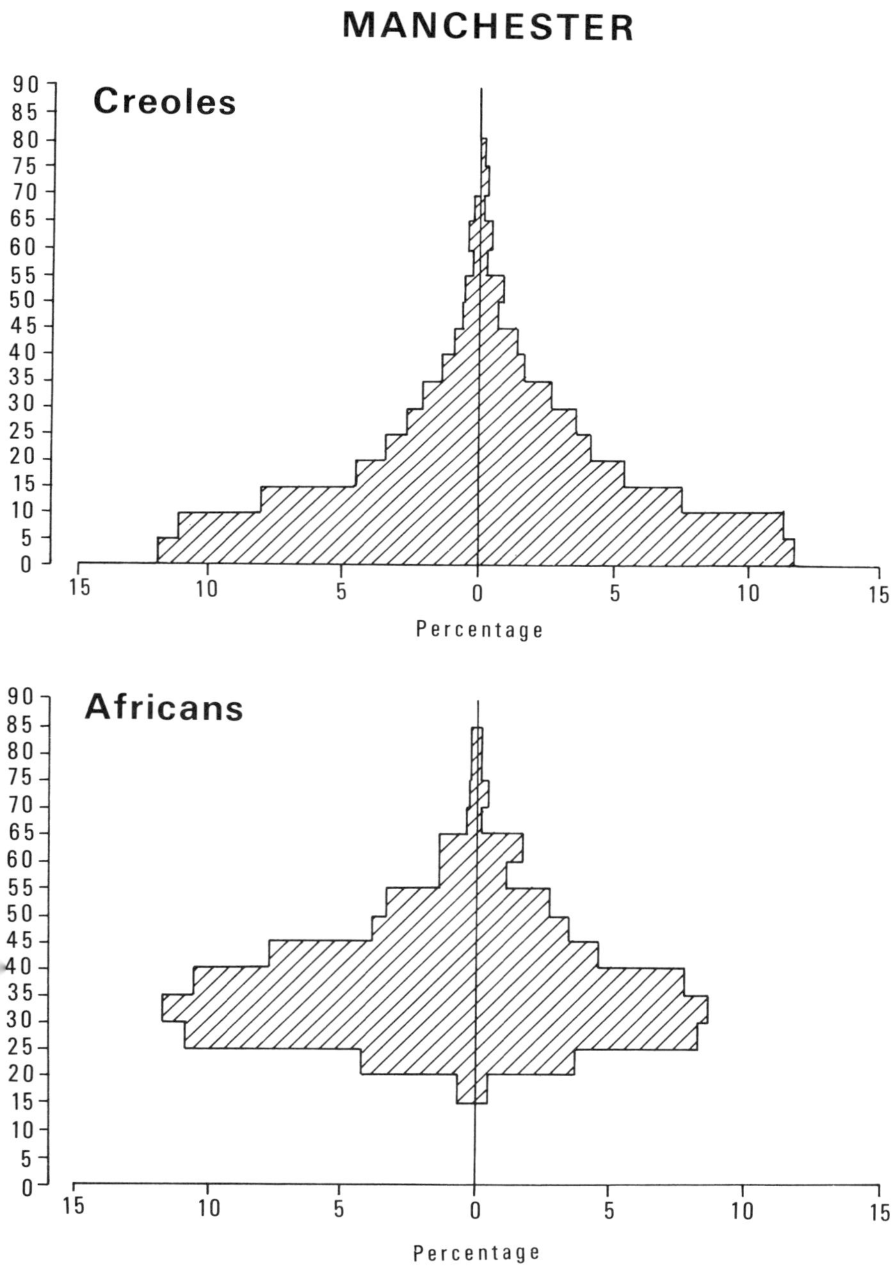

Figure 16. African and creole age pyramids of the slave populations of nine parishes, 1817. (Continued)

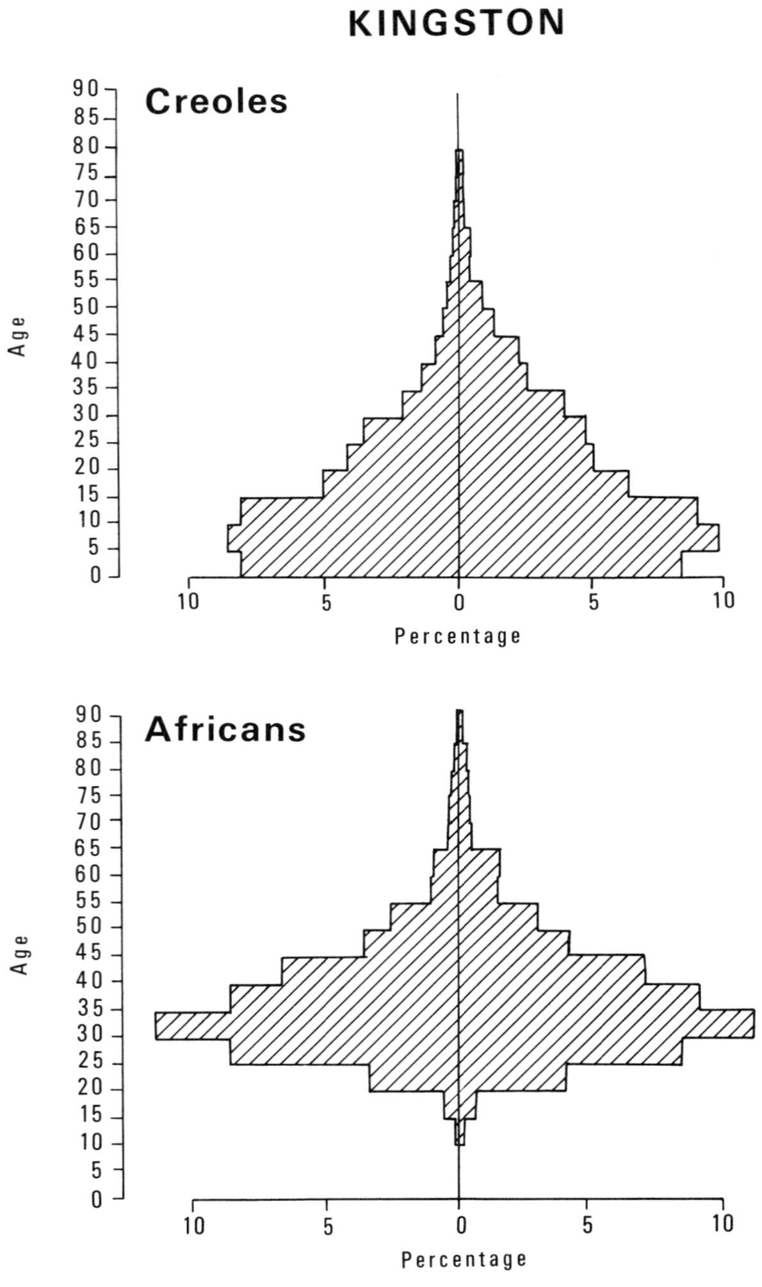

Figure 16. African and creole age pyramids of the slave populations of nine parishes, 1817. (Continued)

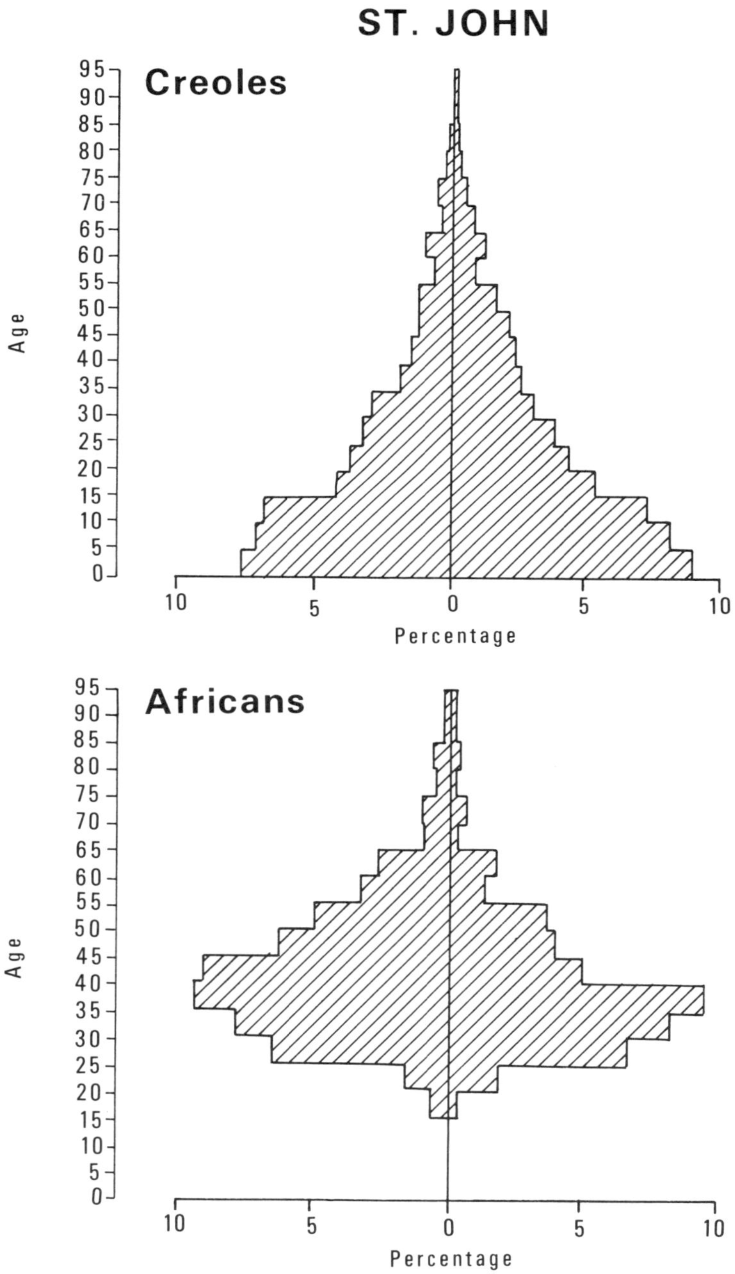

Figure 16. African and creole age pyramids of the slave populations of nine parishes, 1817. (Continued)

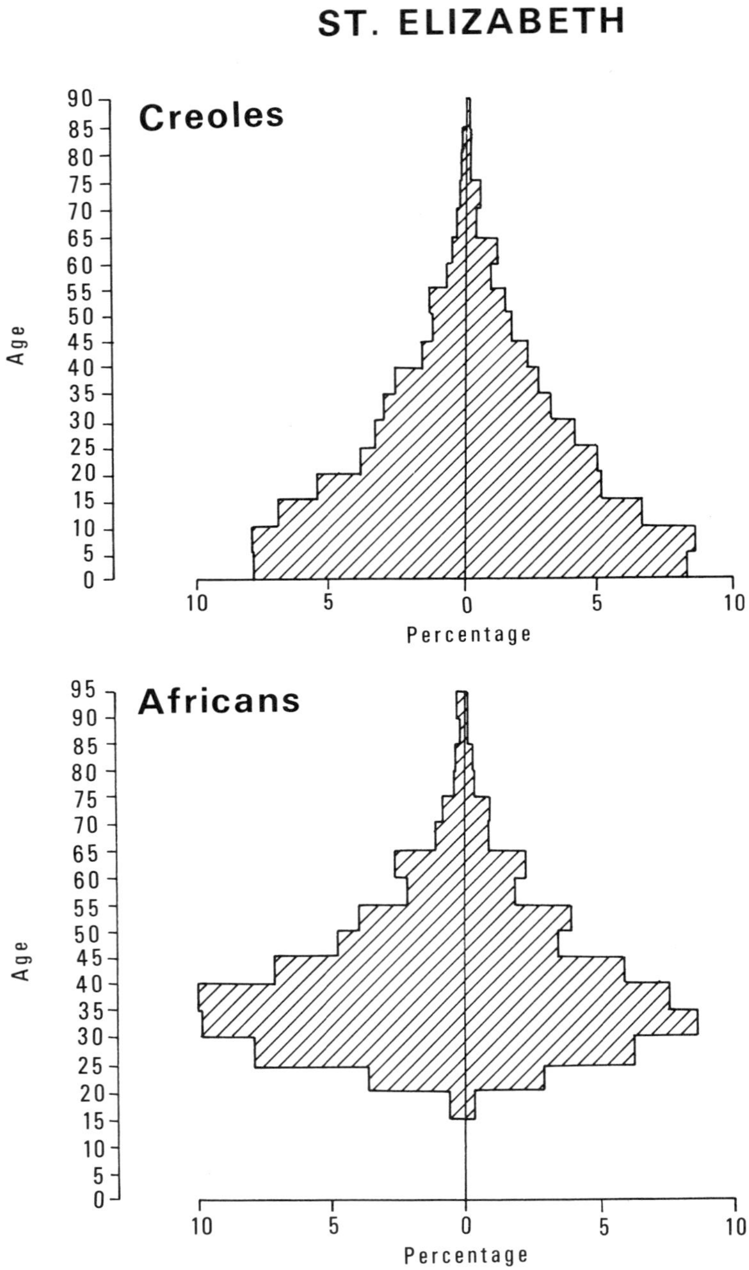

Figure 16. African and creole age pyramids of the slave populations of nine parishes, 1817. (Continued)

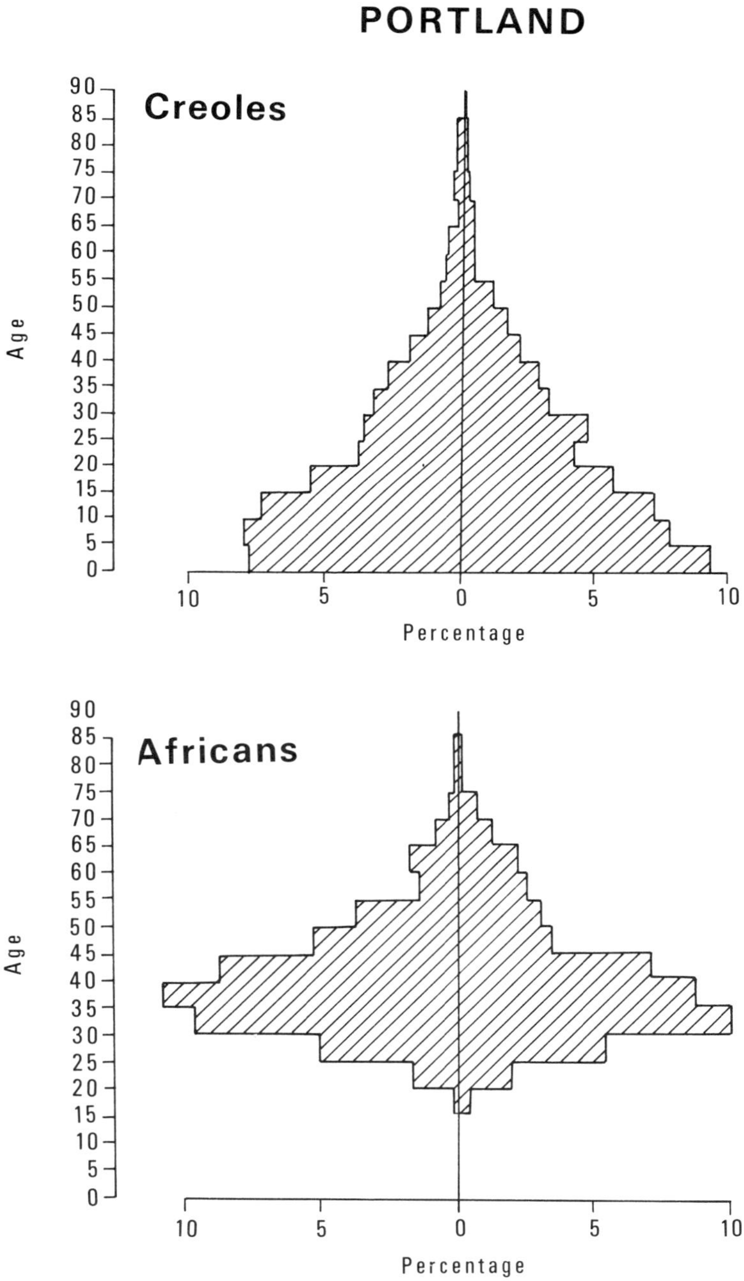

Figure 16. African and creole age pyramids of the slave populations of nine parishes, 1817. (Continued)

CLARENDON

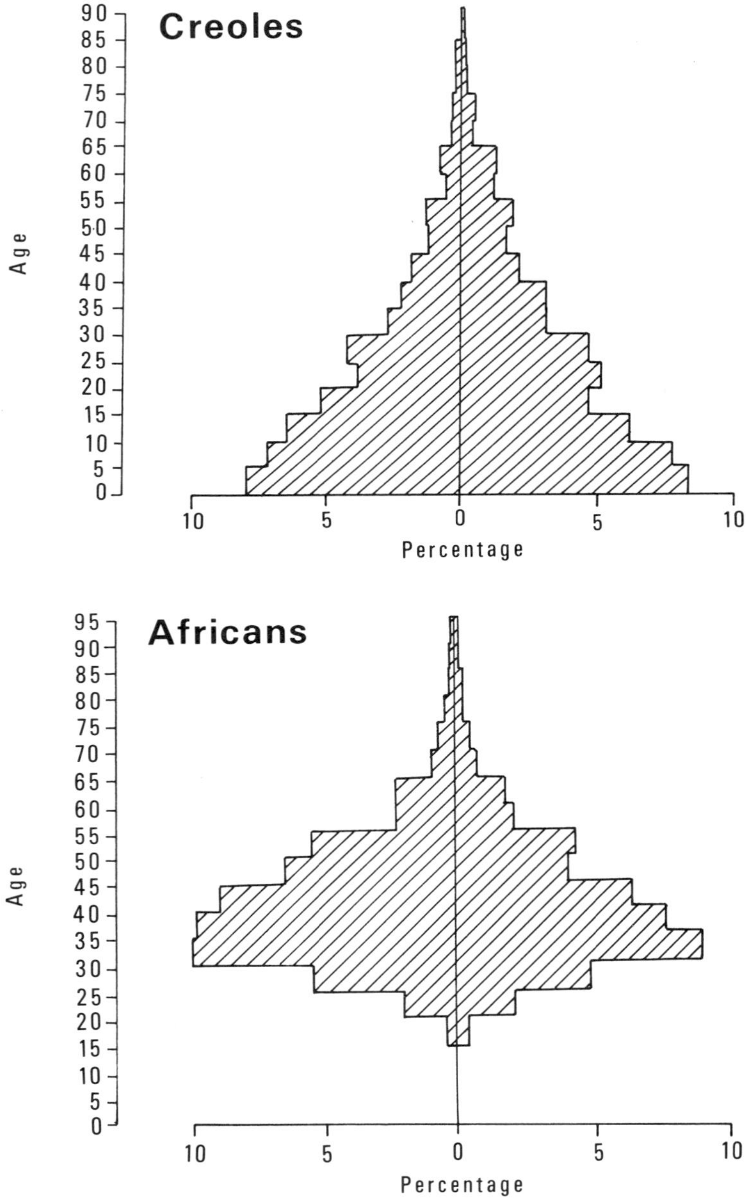

Figure 16. African and creole age pyramids of the slave populations of nine parishes, 1817. (Continued)

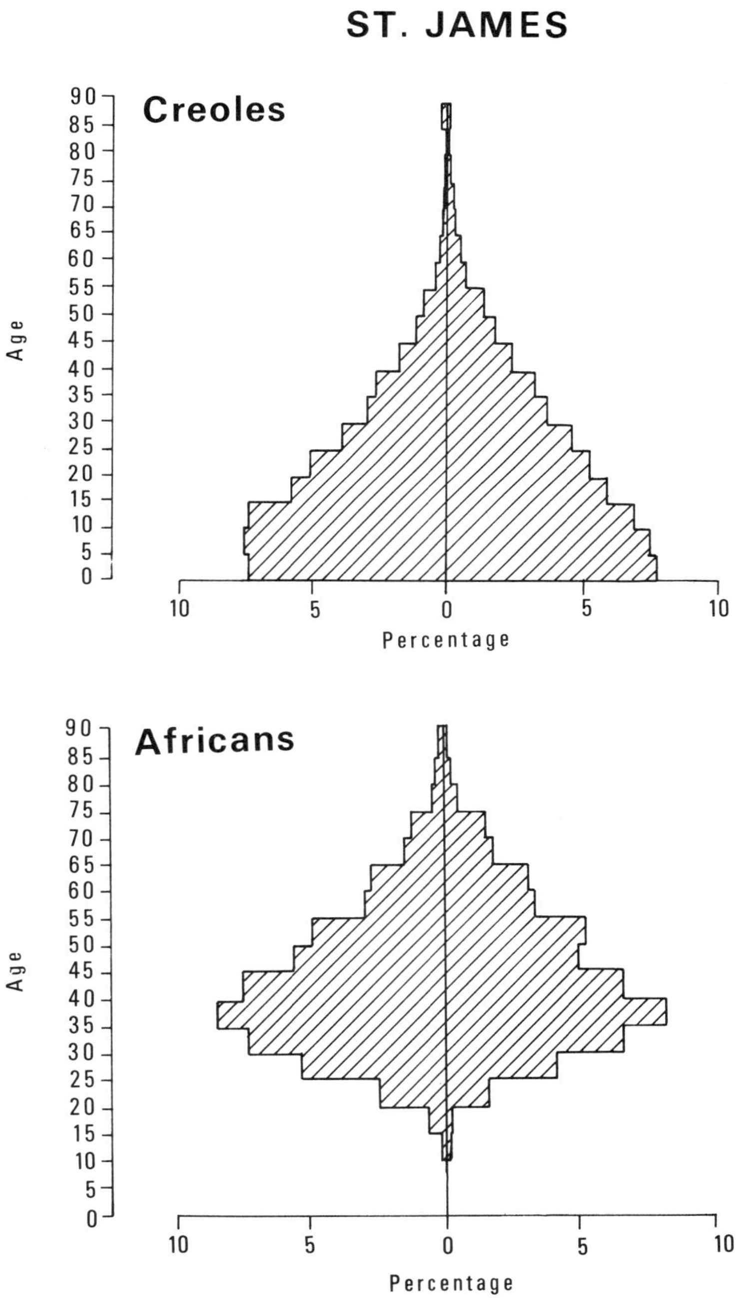

Figure 16. African and creole age pyramids of the slave populations of nine parishes, 1817. (Continued)

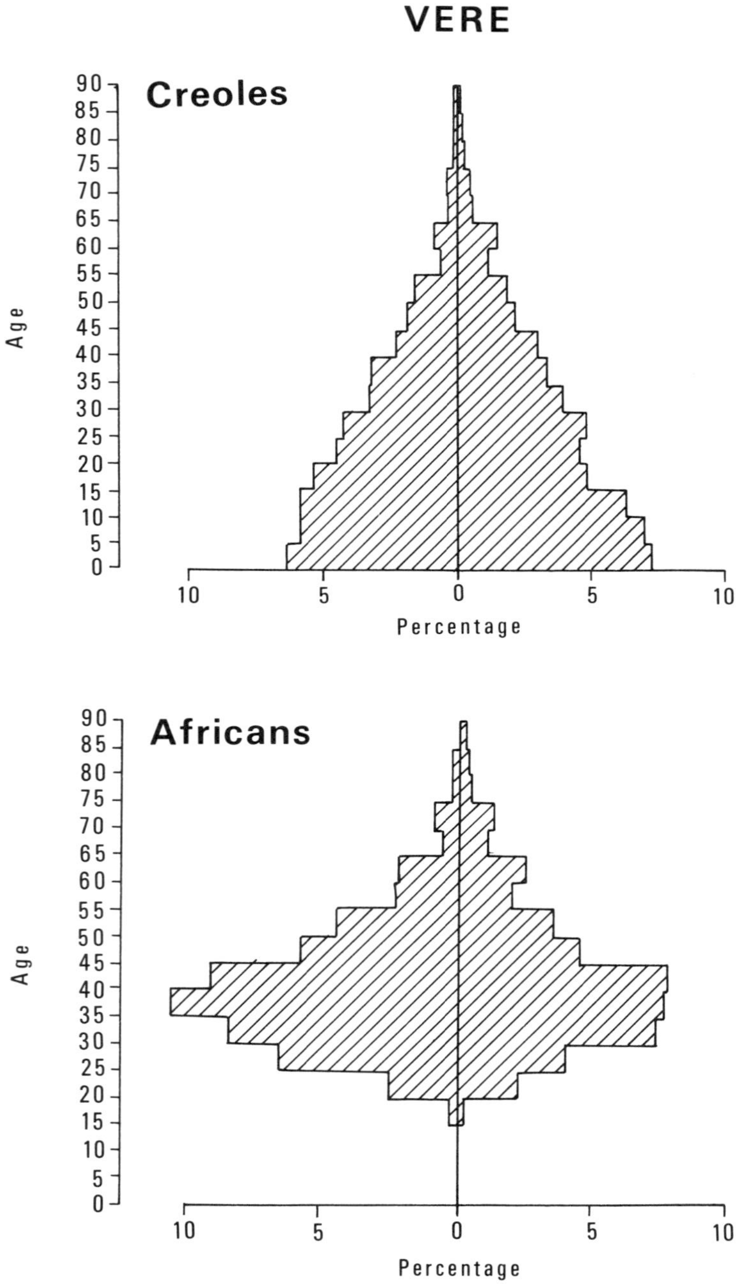

Figure 16. African and creole age pyramids of the slave populations of nine parishes, 1817. (Continued)

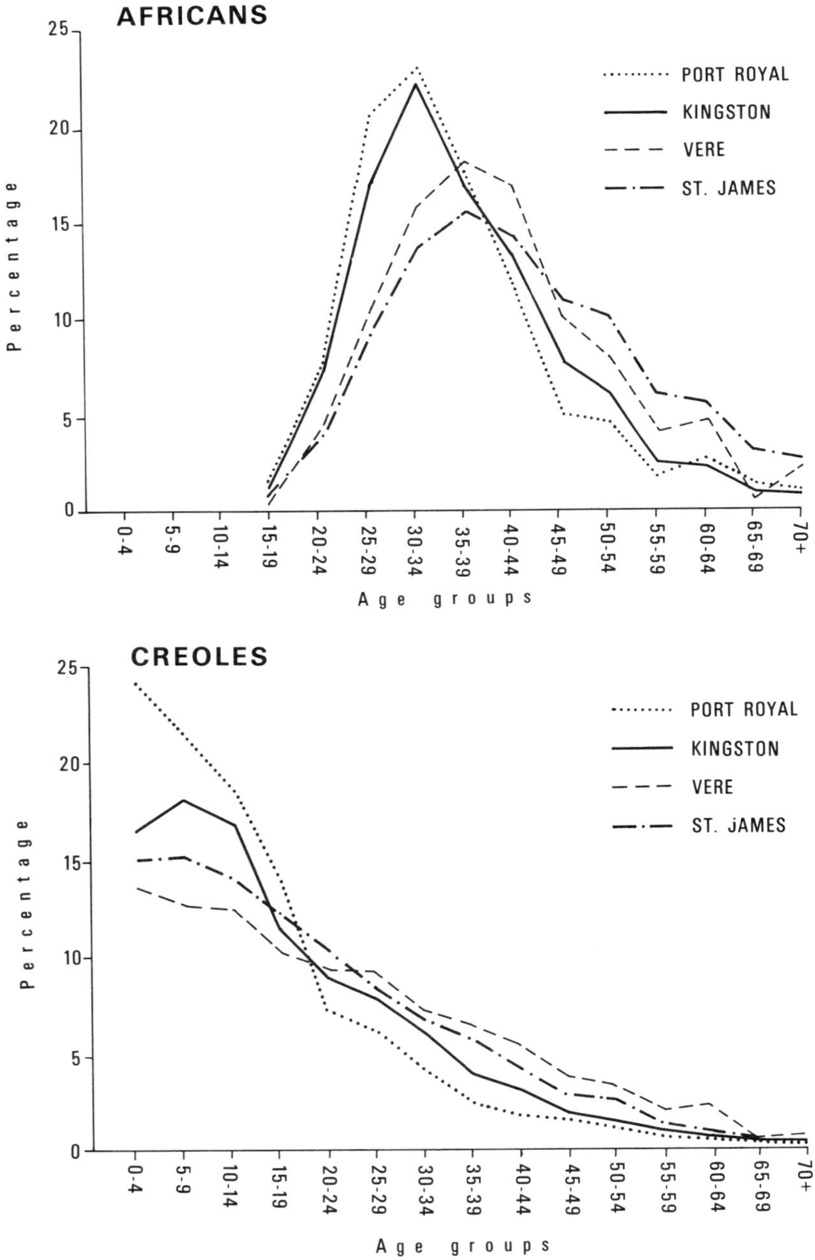

Figure 17. African and creole age profiles of the slave populations of Port Royal, Kingston, Vere and St. James, 1817.

creole group, and the pattern is best considered in terms of the former since the variations were greatest in that section. In accordance with the trends noticed for the sex ratio and the African/creole ratio around 1817, the African population (and hence the creole population) increased in maturity as slave-holding size increased, until about the optimal unit of 201–300 slaves. Thereafter there was a tendency – though a much less consistent one – for the African population to become more youthful as slave-holding size approached its maximum. The clearest case of this trend was the parish of Manchester. There the modal age-group for Africans rose from 25–29 years in the 1–50 slaves size-group, to a peak of 35–39 in the 101–300 groups, and then fell to 30–34 in the 301–400 group and 25–29 in the 401–500 group. In general, the shape of this curve of modal age-groups was roughly the inverse of the percentage African curve. Thus the smaller the percentage of Africans in a slave-holding size-group the older they tended to be. It is probable, therefore, that where creoles were replacing Africans there was less need to purchase Africans from the slave ships, hence both the African and creole populations came to be relatively mature. (It should be remembered that towards the end of the eighteenth century the Jamaica Assembly had passed a law to tax the importation of slaves over 25 years of age.[112]) In Kingston, conversely, the African population of the 51–100 size-group was older than that in the 1–50 group, even though the percentage African was at a maximum in the former. But in Kingston the smaller holdings tended to be much less stable, often speculative, units dependent on the slave trade, whereas the larger holdings were relatively long-established units dominated by males involved in manual labour and skilled trades for the merchant class.

The erosion of the middle age-groups of the slave population observed in 1817 was a continuing process. It can be seen at work in the twelve large estates listed in Table 14. On only one of these estates, Lysson's, did the percentage of slaves in the 18–42 years group increase between 1817 and 1829. Taking the twelve estates as a whole, it appears that there was a slight increase in the proportion under 18 years, an increase of 7 per cent in the oldest group, and a decrease of 9 per cent in the 18–42 group – the core of the slave labour force. Only on three of the estates was there a decrease in the proportion of slaves older than 42 years, so the erosion of the middle age-groups was a result of the aging of the African section and of age-specific mortality among the creoles, rather than the growth of a young creole population.

This process of erosion probably reached a peak on most Jamaican slave-holdings around 1834. By that date the Africans had almost passed out of the middle age-groups and were thus unlikely to further augment the older group. Relatively large proportions of creoles must have been passing into adulthood around 1832 (Figures 16 and 17). These trends can be illustrated by three properties owned by Lord Seaford in Hanover and St. James: Old

Table 14. *Age structure on twelve estates, 1817 and 1829*

Estate	1817 percentage Under 18 years	1817 percentage 18–42 years	1817 percentage Over 42 years	1829 percentage Under 18 years	1829 percentage 18–42 years	1829 percentage Over 42 years
Trelawny						
Orange Valley	41.9	34.0	24.1	46.2	31.8	22.0
Linton Park	35.4	46.2	18.4	34.8	34.8	30.4
Fontabelle and Southfield	31.5	44.8	23.7	25.7	38.1	36.2
St. Mary						
Hopewell	28.2	45.8	26.0	35.5	32.9	31.6
Llanrumny	25.6	52.9	21.5	32.7	32.7	34.6
Clarendon						
Fountain	30.4	50.8	18.8	27.4	35.6	37.0
Whitney	31.6	45.5	22.9	42.3	32.8	24.9
St. Elizabeth						
Bogue	38.0	39.9	22.1	39.9	39.6	20.5
Hampstead	33.8	50.0	16.2	34.3	23.6	42.1
St. Thomas-in-the-East						
Lysson's	31.6	41.6	26.8	28.5	48.4	23.1
Hector's River	32.3	43.0	24.7	37.4	32.4	30.2
Portland						
Golden Vale	37.1	44.8	18.1	34.4	40.1	25.5
Total	33.3	44.4	22.3	35.4	35.5	29.1

Source: Calculated from *P.P.*, 1832 (172), Lords, Vol. 1, Appendix A, pp. 566–77.

Montpelier, a long-established sugar estate; New Montpelier, established in the 1770s and having a large African section; and Shettlewood, a livestock pen – the three properties having a total population of 958 in 1817.[113] The age profile of the Africans on the three properties fell away consistently between 1819 and 1831 (Figure 18). This trend was reflected in the decline of the younger age-groups at New Montpelier which continued to 1831; at Old Montpelier and Shettlewood, with relatively small proportions of Africans, this trend was reversed by 1831, the younger age-groups beginning to grow again. The slowing down in the rate of population decline between 1817 and 1832, and the emergence of an increase by 1838 (Figure 12), can be understood in terms of these changes in the age structure. It is important to note that the modal creole age-group on Seaford's estates, 20–24 in 1831, can be related to births occurring between 1807 and 1811. The fecundity of the slave population, in terms of its age structure, was probably at a maximum about 1807, resulting from the considerable injections of Africans in the preceding decade, most of them in the child-bearing age-groups. After 1807 there was a significant decline in this potential, and renewed growth had to

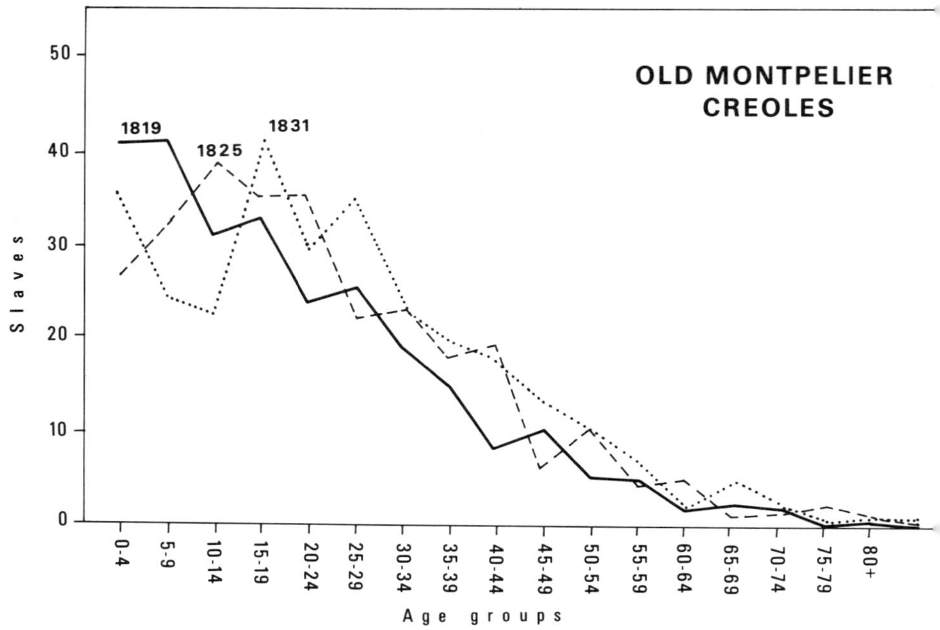

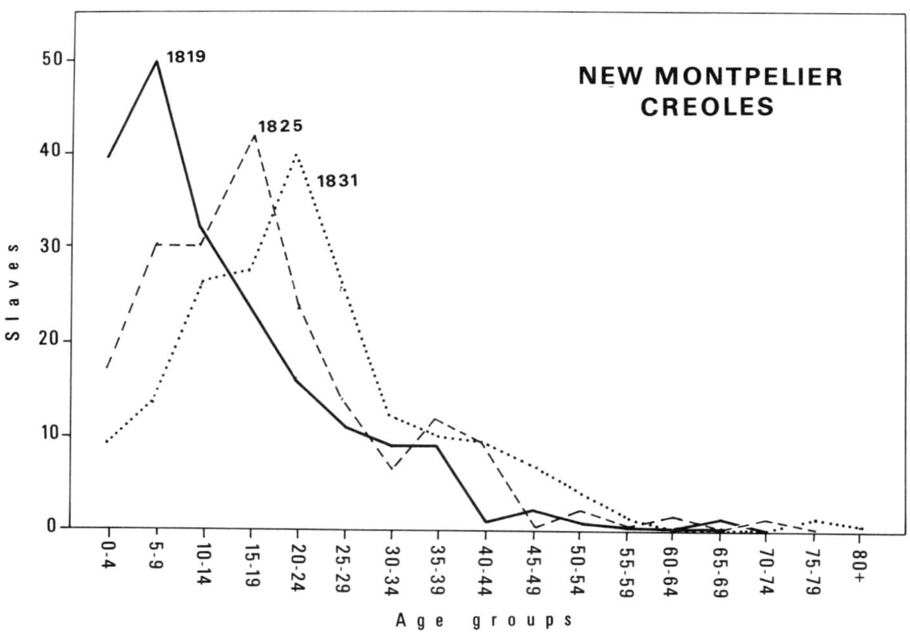

Figure 18. Age profiles of African and creole slaves at Old Montpelier, New Montpelier and Shettlewood, 1819–31. (The African profile combines all three properties.)

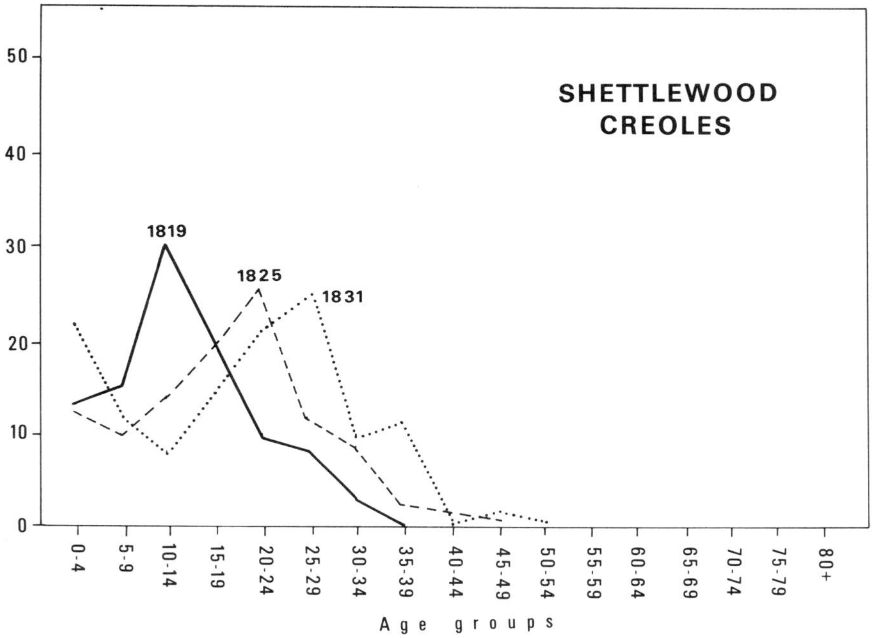

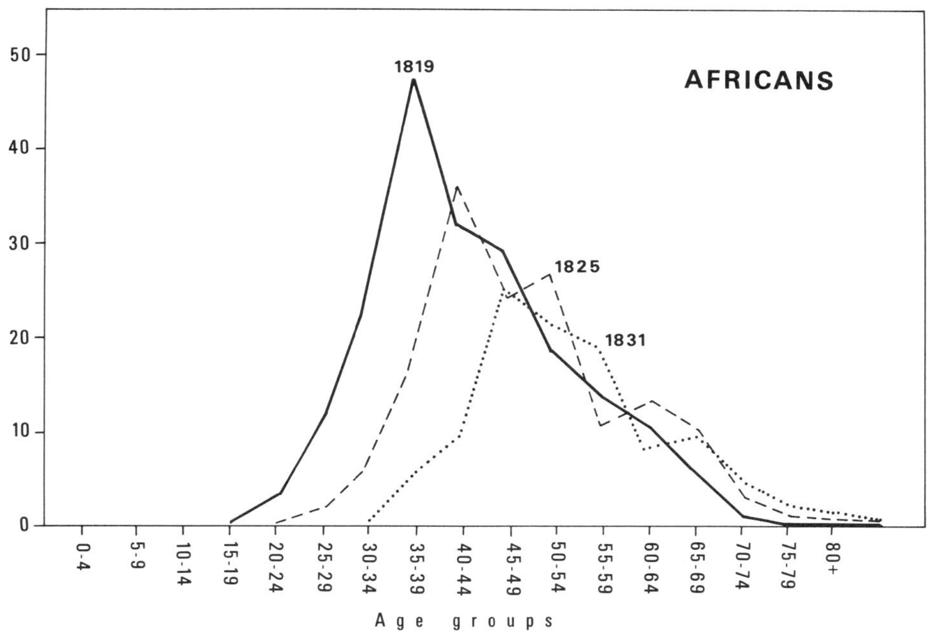

Figure 18. Age profiles of African and creole slaves at Old Montpelier, New Montpelier and Shettlewood, 1819–31. (The African profile combines all three properties.) (Continued)

wait until the wave of creoles born 1807–11 entered the most fertile age-groups after about 1825. Although the improvement in fertility (or mortality) may have resulted from changes in the attitudes of the masters,[114] the growth of the creole population after 1830 could also be explained simply in terms of the internal cycle of the age structure. If slavery had not been abolished in 1834, this internal cycle might have resulted in self-sustaining population growth or (following the analogy of the aftermath of the 1807–11 wave) a series of degenerating phases of decline and growth. Which of these alternatives is the most plausible depends on the levels of fertility and mortality prevailing, the capacity of the creole population to survive in spite of slavery.

CHAPTER 6

PATTERNS OF SURVIVAL

Those Englishmen who sought the abolition of slavery on moral grounds believed that the failure of the slaves to maintain their numbers put the seal of confirmation on all their other charges against the system. In 1832 Thomas Fowell Buxton, parliamentary leader of the Saints, told a select committee of the House of Lords that he regarded the decrease of the slave population as the best test of the physical suffering involved in slavery because 'it was a purely rational argument, it was addressed only to the understanding, it was an arithmetical proposition'.[1] Buxton was clearly a Malthusian, thus he saw it as a certain maxim of political economy that population ordinarily increases: 'the law of nature is clearly for an increase, and that increase can only be prevented by intense misery'. Not only was the slave population failing to press on the arithmetically determined means of subsistence, it was declining absolutely; thus the abolitionists felt no need to refer to vice or moral restraint. For them, it was a question of positive rather than preventive checks.

'After abusing us in detail', complained the Jamaica Assemblymen in 1815, 'we are attacked in mass, and told, that although we have refuted the items, the general charge of cruelty and oppression must be just, because the slaves have not increased, but diminished, in number, and a different and natural order of things is not likely to take place.'[2] The masters, while accepting that it was 'natural' for populations to increase and that 'the increase is the only test of the care with which they [slaves] are treated',[3] preferred to attribute the decrease to 'various preventive checks'.[4] The fertility of the ancients had been the subject of much debate in the eighteenth century, but it was agreed generally that slave populations, such as the Israelites, were prolific and that the poor who ate simple food were fertile whereas the luxurious rich were relatively barren.[5] Hence the apologists contended that slavery had been established in Africa in order to draw off the superabundance of population of that continent in which propagation was more exuberant than in temperate Europe.[6] Thus Malthus' theory of population was pressed into service to prove that the abolition of the slave trade would not terminate African misery. As a result Malthus called on Wilberforce to explain that he was by no means a supporter of the slave trade. But George Hibbert, representing the Society of West India Merchants and Planters, was able to reply that despite Malthus' disclaimer 'the principle he has advanced, and the reasoning he has introduced on this subject, remain unaltered'.[7]

The Jamaica planter thus faced a dilemma in his demographic theory. He believed that 'every region on this earth has its own climate, men, morals and religion', and that the 'wisdom and design' observable in all works of nature meant that 'all animal and vegetable life now existing on the globe is most beautifully adjusted . . . to the conditions under which it is placed'.[8] He also held the pre-Malthusian idea that those who perform manual labour are in general the healthiest part of mankind.[9] Why then did those who were so prolific in Africa fail to maintain their numbers in the equally exuberant tropical lands of the New World?

This question was answered readily by the humanitarians: the slaves decreased because of the unnatural positive checks imposed by the masters – insufficient food, excessive demands on labour, and physical brutality. The masters agreed that these factors would produce population decline, but claimed that cases of abuse were rare. They attempted to shift the blame from themselves to the slaves by arguing that the cause was not the Malthusian positive (mortality-increasing) check of 'misery', but the preventive (fertility-depressing) checks of 'vice' or even a perverted kind of 'moral restraint'.[10] Thus, they said, the 'African ideas' of the slaves led them to prefer promiscuity and polygamy rather than stable monogamy whereas, it was generally believed, 'to multiply and rear the human species, there must be marriage, or something to that effect'.[11] According to De la Beche: 'Another cause of decrease is the practice too many of the young women have, of procuring abortions in the early stages of pregnancy, from their dread that child-bearing will interfere with the pursuit of their favourite amusements, and their dislike of the restraint that it necessarily imposes on them.'[12] But to attribute the failure of natural increase to a debauched African character was to ignore the contrast between Africa and Jamaica. As Burnley noticed, the masters had 'attributed the decrease of the slave population to the national vices of the Negroes, in spite of the annual swarms proceeding from the African hive, testifying to the contrary'.[13] One of the few to face up to this dilemma was Edward Long; yet he remained puzzled. He argued that childbirth was less easy in Jamaica than in Africa, that slaves suffered from being moved to new locations, that the sexes had become unbalanced and that venereal disease was more common. But he also asserted that in Jamaica the slave was in a relative state of perfect freedom, having his life and sustenance guaranteed, in contrast to his abject condition in Africa.[14]

Because they were attempting to explain an absolute decline in population the masters were in difficulty with the Malthusian theory of population, but they were also forced to turn the pre-Malthusian social theory of fertility on its head, to claim that the slave population was a special case. One writer did this by denying that population increase was necessarily related to personal welfare.[15] When Rome ruled the world and wallowed in riches, he said, Italy was depopulated; the Irish, on the other hand, lacked sufficient food, shelter and raiment, but were extremely prolific.[16] He concluded that 'a decrease may arise from a variety of adventitious circumstances having no relation even to the personal welfare of the individuals of a community'.[17] This contention does possess a certain amount of theoretical validity. Natural decreases may occur, for example, in areas with abnormal age distributions resulting from migration, as was the case in Jamaica, especially after 1807. But obviously the masters were wrong to argue that, because these peculiar circumstances affected the population, Jamaica was not a land full of suffering.

To test these two major theses, one attributing the decline of the slave population to peculiar demographic conditions and the other to ill-treatment, the role of six factors will be examined: the sex ratio, the age structure, the labour required on particular types of properties, the amount of labour exacted, the size of slave-holdings, and the physical environment. All of these factors were used, singly and in various combinations, by contemporaries to explain the rate and regional variations of the natural decrease of the slave population of Jamaica. But before examining their validity it is necessary to describe briefly the spatial and temporal patterns of natural increase, mortality and fertility.

Natural increase

It has already been noted that the Returns of Registrations of Slaves understate fertility and mortality, particularly infant mortality. The rate of understatement varied between properties, but it is unlikely to have varied at the regional (parish, town or quadrat) levels. The 'birth rates' and 'death rates' discussed in this chapter should strictly be defined as rates based on the number of births and deaths registered. Thus the birth rates should be inflated by perhaps one-third and the deaths rates by a somewhat smaller ratio.[18] But since the precise ratio is uncertain, it has seemed best to present the rates in an unadjusted form. The rate of natural increase (the difference between the birth and death rates) can be calculated accurately independent of this problem.

It must also be noticed that there is a tendency to overstatement in the birth rates because they are based on the slave population only, excluding paternity by the white, free coloured and free black population. But the free population, whatever its role in procreation, was generally small; it was significant only in the towns and in the parishes of Kingston and St. Catherine where the birth rate is already known to have been low. An adjustment has been made to the death rates in the western parishes affected by the rebellion of Christmas 1831; all deaths attributed to the rebellion (179 in St. James, 132 in Hanover, 26 in St. Elizabeth, 23 in Westmoreland and 12 in Trelawny) have been excluded.[19] Although the rebels tended to fall into the age-groups with above-average mortality, very few of them would have died between Christmas 1831 and June 1832 if the rebellion had not occurred.

Between 1817 and 1832 deaths in the slave population were always in excess of births. During the period the rate of natural increase (or, rather, decrease)

Table 15. *Rate of natural increase, 1817–32*

	Natural increase per 1,000 per annum				
Parish	1817–20	1820–3	1823–6	1826–9	1829–32
Westmoreland	−7.4	−8.1	−5.1	−5.1	−5.2
Hanover	−5.9	−5.3	−6.2	−8.3	−8.4
St. James	−3.1	−7.7	−7.5	−5.4	−8.6
Trelawny	−1.0	−5.4	−5.2	−6.8	−6.6
St. Elizabeth	+5.8	+4.5	+5.0	+9.0	+7.4
Manchester	+5.1	+4.2	+6.0	+7.4	+6.4
St. Ann	+1.8	−0.6	+1.6	+2.6	+3.9
Clarendon	+1.2	−6.9	−2.4	−0.3	−7.1
Vere	−2.3	−1.9	+2.3	−0.7	+1.1
St. Dorothy	−2.8	−4.4	−3.3	+3.2	−6.6
St. Thomas-in-the-Vale	+2.1	−0.5	−4.2	−3.3	−9.6
St. John	+3.1	−5.5	−1.5	−5.3	−9.1
St. Catherine	+2.4	−0.4	+1.5	+6.2	−2.4
St. Mary	−6.1	−5.0	−6.9	−10.2	−12.8
St. Andrew	+3.6	+3.6	+4.0	−2.1	−4.6
Port Royal	+10.9	+4.8	+5.4	+4.8	+2.1
St. David	+2.9	−3.8	−4.9	−6.1	−4.1
St. George	−1.1	−3.7	−2.7	−15.6	−7.9
Portland	−2.5	+1.4	−2.9	−7.2	−4.7
St. Thomas-in-the-East	−5.7	−8.6	−4.9	−12.0	−10.5
Kingston	+3.0	+2.0	+0.2	+1.3	−1.8
Total	−0.7	−3.1	−2.1	−3.4	−4.8

Sources: T.71/683, Bundle 9 (1817–29); R.R.S. (1829–32).

fell fairly consistently, from —0.7 to —4.8 per thousand (Table 15). But not all of the parishes conformed to this general trend. In the period 1817–20 eleven of the twenty-one parishes actually showed positive natural increases, but only three of these improved their position in the years to 1832: St. Elizabeth, Manchester and St. Ann, the pen and coffee parishes. Port Royal also had a positive natural increase throughout the period but, rather than improving, the rate declined quite rapidly. Only one parish, the mature sugar parish of Vere, managed to emerge from a position of negative natural increase to one of consistent positive gains by the end of the period (Figure 19). By the 1829–32 triennium only five parishes showed positive natural increases. But the urban parishes – Kingston, St. Catherine and St. Andrew – maintained positive natural increases almost to the end of the period, falling away only in 1829–32. With the exception of Westmoreland, all of the parishes which had negative natural increases throughout the period showed a deterioration over the years. Thus only five parishes diverged from the general downward trend, and three of these had in fact entered the period with positive natural increases. It is difficult to extrapolate these trends into the period before 1817, but since

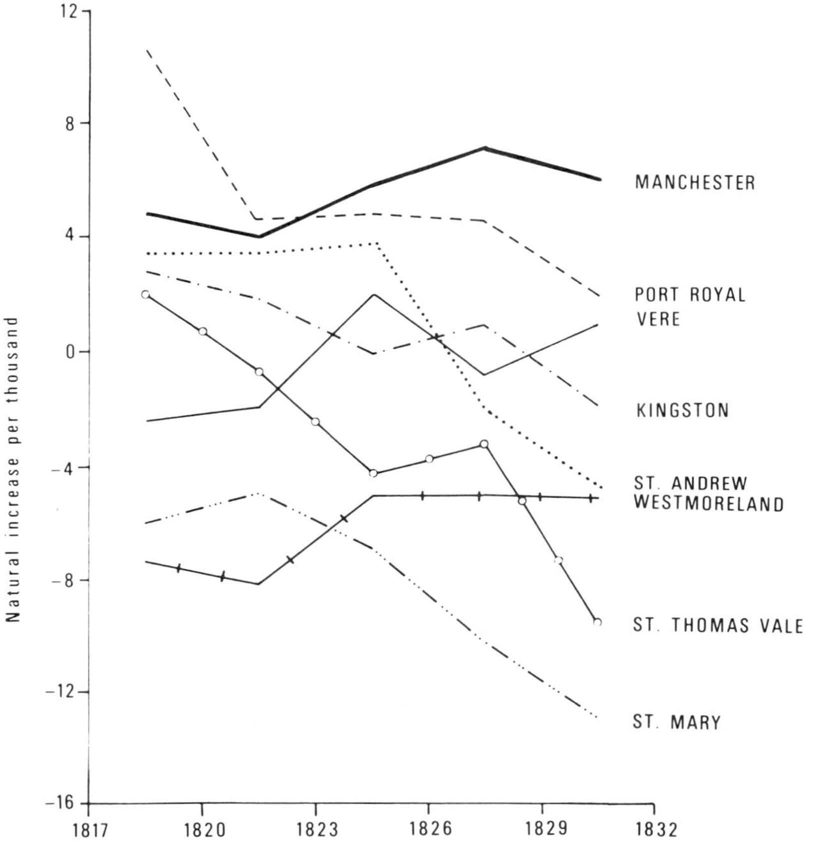

Figure 19. Rates of natural increase in the slave populations of eight parishes, 1817–32.

there was a close relationship between changes in the rate of natural increase from 1817 to 1832 and in the rate of decline in the total slave population (Figure 11), it appears that the rate of natural increase between 1807 and 1817 must have been very similar to that in the 1817–20 triennium. In the period following the abolition of the slave trade, then, the great deterioration in the rate of natural increase did not begin until about 1820.

The spatial distribution of variations in the rate of natural increase observed at the parish level during the period 1817–32 conformed closely to the pattern at the quadrat level for 1829–32 (Figure 20). Most of the parishes showing natural decreases contained small pockets of increase, the most notable being along the eastern edge of Westmoreland and in the mountainous interiors of Portland and St. George. Conversely, the parishes with increases all had pockets of decrease. But although the quadrat level map is complex, it brings out very clearly the great zone of unmitigated decrease stretching from

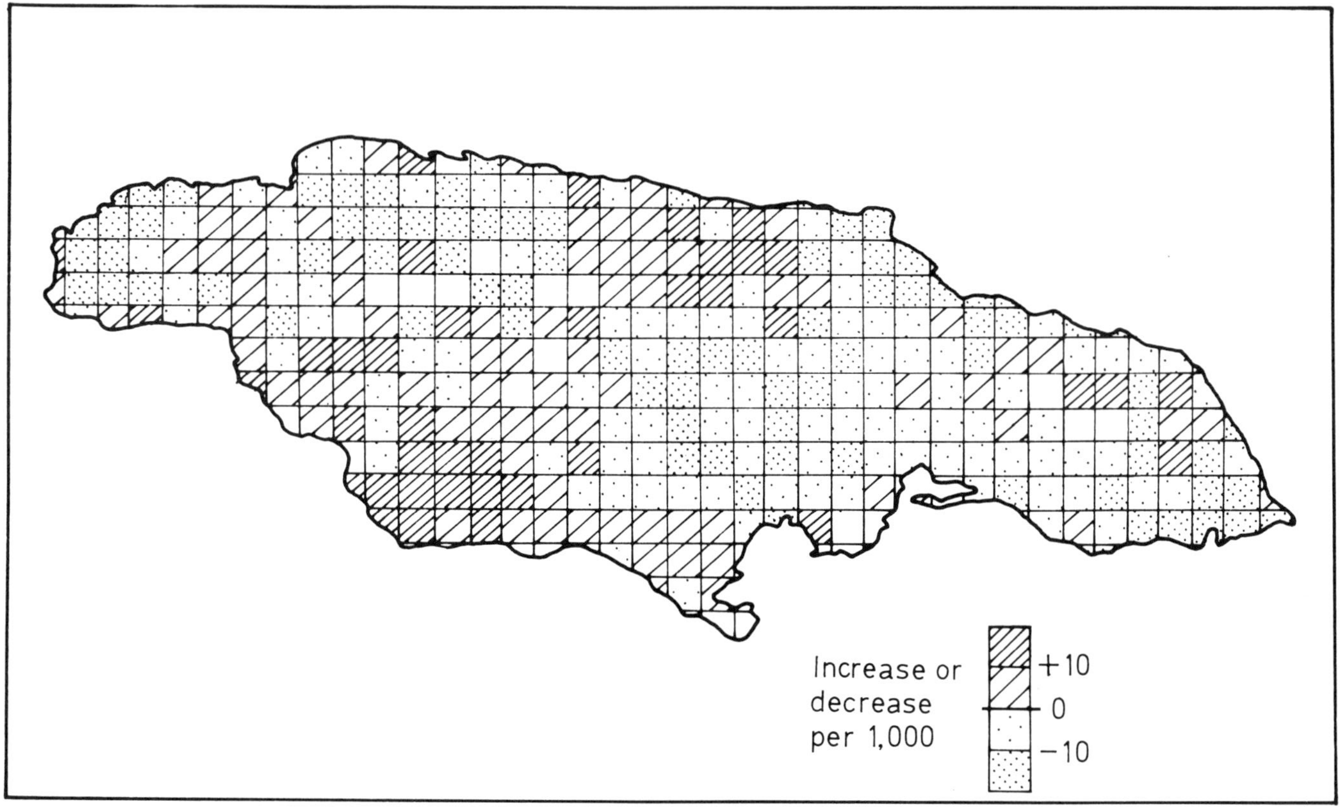

Figure 20. Natural increase of slaves, by quadrats, 1829–32. The blank quadrats were not populated.

Clarendon to St. Mary, and it localizes the areas of heavy decrease which straddled the borders of Westmoreland and Hanover, and of St. James and Trelawny. It is also important to note that the pattern was not a random one; that is, there was generally a consistent spatial gradation of rates of natural increase. From the core areas of positive natural increase in St. Elizabeth and St. Ann, the rates declined systematically into the core areas of heavy decrease.

In the period 1829–32 the towns showing positive natural increases were chiefly located in the western end of the island, though Spanish Town had a slight increase and the decrease in Kingston was quite low (Table 7). Thus it tended to be the largest towns which had the most notable natural increases. But the urban slave populations as a group clearly experienced a lower rate of natural decrease than the rural populations.

A first step in attempting to account for the temporal and spatial variations in natural increase is to weigh the relative importance of fertility and mortality. At the parish level in 1829–32 the coefficients of variation of the birth and death rates were 8.9 and 16.9 per cent, respectively. Similarly, at the quadrat level the coefficients of variation were 38.9 and 49.9 per cent. Mortality, then, was more important than fertility as a contributor to variations in the level of natural increase. Thus at the parish level 86.5 per cent of the variation in natural increase can be explained by the death rate ($r = -.93$) and only 32.5 per cent by births ($r = .57$); at the quadrat level the respective percentages were 60.8 and 18.5, and for the towns 82.8 and 47.6 (Tables A3.1–A3.3). Certainly the masters were wrong when they attempted to attribute the natural decrease of the slave population to preventive (fertility-depressing) checks. Mortality was fundamental.[20]

Mortality

Because of this relationship between natural increase and mortality, the downward trend in the rate of natural increase between 1817 and 1832 was matched by a similar upward trend in the death rate (Table 16). In contrast to the case with the trend in the rate of natural increase, however, it would be unwise to extrapolate the death rate back to 1807 on the basis of changes in the size of the total slave population; it has been argued from the age structure of the population in 1817 that 1807–10 was probably a period of relatively high fertility (and hence infant mortality),[21] but this must have been matched by high mortality among the recently arrived Africans who were still undergoing the process of 'seasoning'. There were also some aberrations from the general trends in natural increase and mortality between 1817 and 1832 in particular parishes. Vere, for example, achieved a natural increase in the period without showing any significant improvement in mortality.

In the period 1817–20 mortality was at a maximum in the eastern and

Table 16. *Crude death rates, 1817–32*

Parish	Registered deaths per 1,000				
	1817–20	1820–3	1823–6	1826–9	1829–32
Westmoreland	28.4	28.0	26.6	25.7	28.2
Hanover	28.1	26.6	27.6	25.2	29.4
St. James	27.1	28.2	29.0	27.3	32.3
Trelawny	24.4	28.8	29.6	26.4	29.7
St. Elizabeth	18.2	19.8	20.1	16.5	20.3
Manchester	19.2	19.4	15.5	15.8	19.4
St. Ann	23.0	23.3	22.5	21.5	21.5
Clarendon	23.2	30.7	25.1	22.8	28.5
Vere	24.0	23.9	22.3	24.9	24.3
St. Dorothy	21.4	23.3	19.5	21.5	29.5
St. Thomas-in-the-Vale	22.9	25.0	25.9	23.2	30.4
St. John	22.6	28.5	23.9	27.5	30.4
St. Catherine	19.8	20.5	18.8	17.2	25.4
St. Mary	29.5	27.3	27.8	31.9	32.1
St. Andrew	21.6	22.3	21.5	25.2	28.3
Port Royal	17.0	22.9	21.3	20.2	22.4
St. David	23.5	27.6	28.8	26.5	27.0
St. George	27.0	29.0	26.2	37.0	29.8
Portland	26.6	21.9	24.9	31.4	29.7
St. Thomas-in-the-East	27.9	31.1	30.4	36.1	37.2
Kingston	17.8	20.4	23.2	19.6	20.1
Total	24.3	25.9	25.1	25.6	28.0

Sources: T.71/683, Bundle 9 (1817–29); R.R.S. (1829–32).

western extremes of the island. Registered death rates in excess of 25 per 1,000 were recorded only in the far western parishes of Westmoreland, Hanover and St. James, and in the northeastern belt of parishes stretching from St. Mary to St. Thomas-in-the-East. Rates of less than 20 occurred in the urban parishes of Kingston and St. Catherine, and the coffee and pen parishes of Port Royal, Manchester and St. Elizabeth. By 1829–32 the pattern was less simple. The zones of heavy mortality spread into Trelawny in the west, and into the central parishes of St. Thomas-in-the-Vale, St. John, St. Dorothy and Clarendon. Only Manchester had a death rate of less than 20 per 1,000. At the quadrat level the core areas of natural increase were matched by centres of heavy mortality, focussed on St. Thomas-in-the-East, coastal St. Mary, the central interior parishes, and the northwestern parishes (Figure 21). Relatively low death rates spread from Vere to eastern Westmoreland in a continuous belt, and covered the greater part of St. Ann. Only in a few quadrats were natural decreases associated with death rates of less than 25 per 1,000, and most of these were in the coastal fringes of St. Elizabeth and Port Royal.

Male mortality was significantly heavier than female mortality, and the

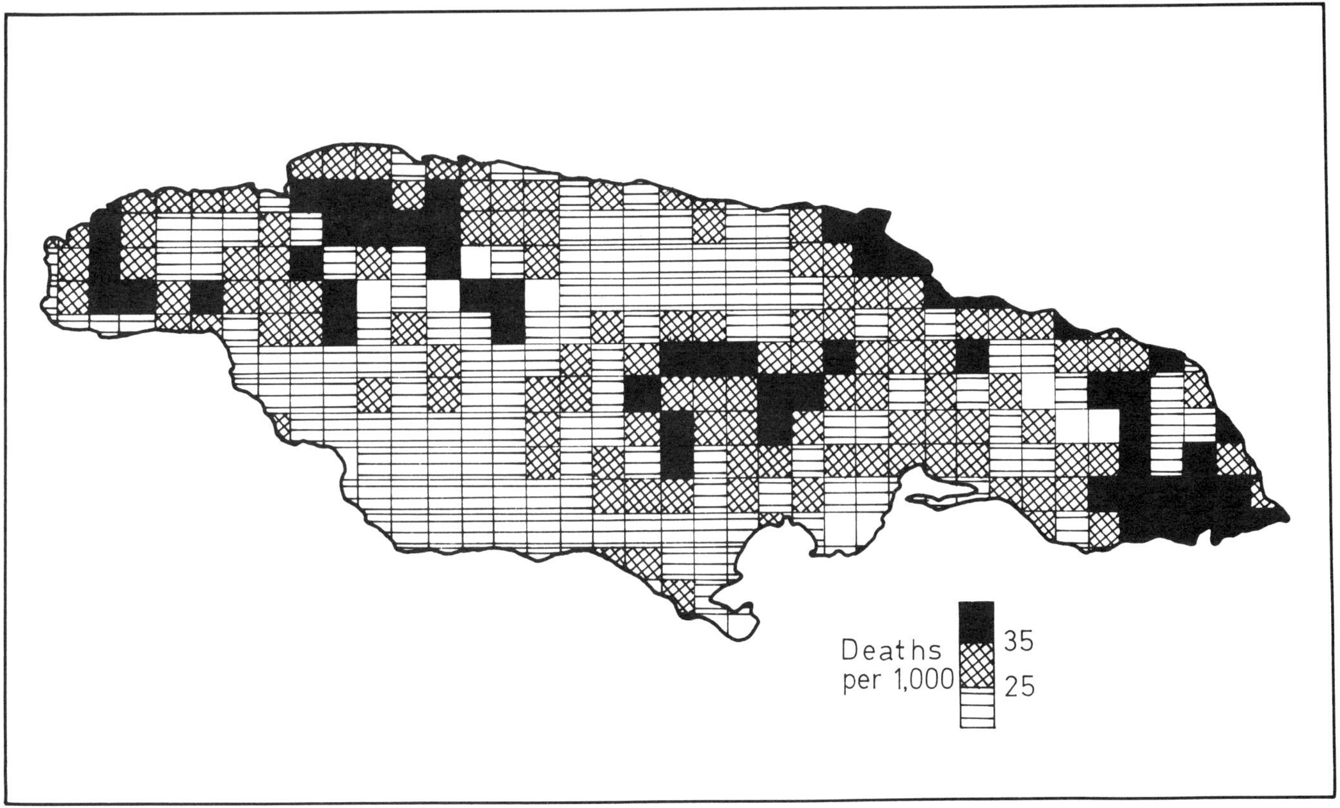

Figure 21. Mortality of slaves, by quadrats, 1829–32. The blank quadrats were not populated.

contrast between the sexes increased over the period 1817–32 (Table A3.10). Between 1817 and 1832 the male death rate increased from 25.9 to 31.4 per 1,000, but the female death rate rose only from 22.6 to 24.8. Thus, if the declining rate of natural increase is to be attributed to a deterioration in mortality, it must be related more particularly to a deterioration in male mortality. There were no aberrations from this trend in any of the parishes: in the period 1829–32 the coefficients of variation of the male and female death rates were 16.2 and 18.0 per cent, respectively. In the towns the gap between the sexes was even wider, the male and female death rates being 27.3 and 18.6 (Table 7); in a few towns the females suffered heavier rates than the males, but this may have resulted simply from the relatively small populations involved or from differences in age structure.

Differences in the mortality experience of males and females applied to both Africans and creoles. But the contrast between African and creole mortality levels was even greater than that between the sexes. Island level statistics are not available, but a sample of eight parishes from 1817 to 1820 demonstrates the pattern clearly (Table 17). In St. James the Africans experienced a death rate almost twice that of the creoles, and this ratio held for both males and females. Only in St. John were the African and creole death rates comparable, and only there did male creoles suffer a heavier mortality than female Africans. It would seem, then, that the African/creole ratio was more important than the sex ratio in determining mortality levels, but since the age structures of the African and creole sections were so distinct this conclusion has to be tested against the pattern of age-specific mortality.

The age-specific death rates for the eight parishes included in Table 17 show that a real difference between African and creole mortality levels did exist in some parishes but that in others the apparent difference can be attributed directly to variations in age structure (Table A3.13). It must be recalled that the Africans included in the mortality records for 1817–20 had all survived the 'seasoning' period successfully, so that the comparison is one between creoles and long-settled Africans. In none of the eight parishes was there any significant difference between African and creole mortality before about 35 years of age in the period 1817–20. In Port Royal, with the largest percentage African, African mortality exceeded creole mortality fairly consistently after 35 years of age, but this divergence was less clear in Manchester and not at all apparent in Kingston (Figure 22). In the most strongly creole of the parishes – Clarendon, Vere and St. John – African mortality was significantly greater than creole mortality only in the age-groups above 50 years (Figure 23). In St. James there was a very clear divergence between the rates after 35 years of age, but they then converged again from 65 years. A similar pattern occurred in Portland. Thus the apparent difference between the mortality levels of Africans and creoles was partly an illusion, applying only to some parishes (and within those parishes being confined to the 35–60 years age-groups).

Table 17. *African and creole mortality in eight parishes, 1817–20* (registered deaths per 1,000)

	Africans			Creoles		
Parish	Males	Females	Total	Males	Females	Total
St. James	42.1	37.2	39.7	23.7	19.8	21.6
Manchester	25.4	22.2	24.0	17.2	14.0	15.6
Clarendon	28.3	29.9	29.1	21.8	21.6	21.7
Vere	31.6	31.8	31.7	20.1	18.8	19.4
St. John	26.6	20.3	23.8	21.7	19.7	20.6
Portland	35.8	33.2	34.6	20.2	23.9	22.2
Port Royal	22.7	18.4	20.9	18.3	12.0	15.0
Kingston	24.8	16.7	20.5	15.3	14.3	14.8

Sources: T.71/680, Bundle 17; T.71/683, Bundle 9; R.R.S.

Excepting Kingston, the age-specific mortality profiles were very similar. Mortality in the first year of life has been separated from the 0–4 years age-group only for St. James (Figure 24), but it is clear – in spite of the understatement of infant mortality – that mortality dropped rapidly to a minimum of roughly 10 per 1,000 by 10–14 years of age. The death rate then increased steadily to about 50 per 1,000 by age 60, after which it rose steeply. In Kingston the profile was much flatter; mortality conformed to the general trend to about age 50, but then reached a plateau. It is also evident that male mortality was always greater than female in the first few years of life, maintained a rough equality to about 40 years, then increased more rapidly. In St. James the death rates for male and female Africans and creoles diverged only after 35–39 years of age, at which point male mortality consistently exceeded female; African and creole males suffered very similar rates, but African females experienced a heavier mortality than creole females (Figure 24).

The data contained in the Returns of Registrations of Slaves do not permit a systematic study of causes of death. The Act did not require the masters to specify cause of death and only a minority attempted to do so. Some of the causes cited merely highlight the masters' prejudices: 'a rank methodist fever', 'a methodist who died mad', 'a miserable victim to obi machination', 'fancied obeah', and 'neglecting himself', for example.[22] Even when cause of death was determined by a physician or surgeon, the limited medical knowledge of the period creates problems in interpretation. Some contemporary descriptive terms covered more than one disease: 'fever', for example, comprehended both malaria and yellow fever. Other terms have since acquired a much more specific meaning. Some disease attracted a variety of local names: leprosy, for example, was referred to in Jamaica as either joint evil, king's evil or cocobay. Again, symptoms were confused with diseases: 'diarrhœa' or 'looseness' when cited as causes of death were probably symptoms

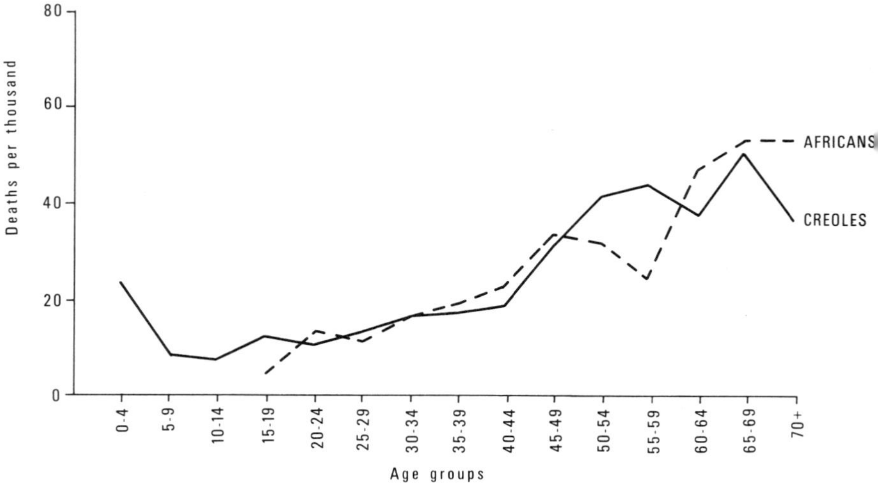

Figure 22. Age-specific mortality of the Kingston slave population, 1817–20.

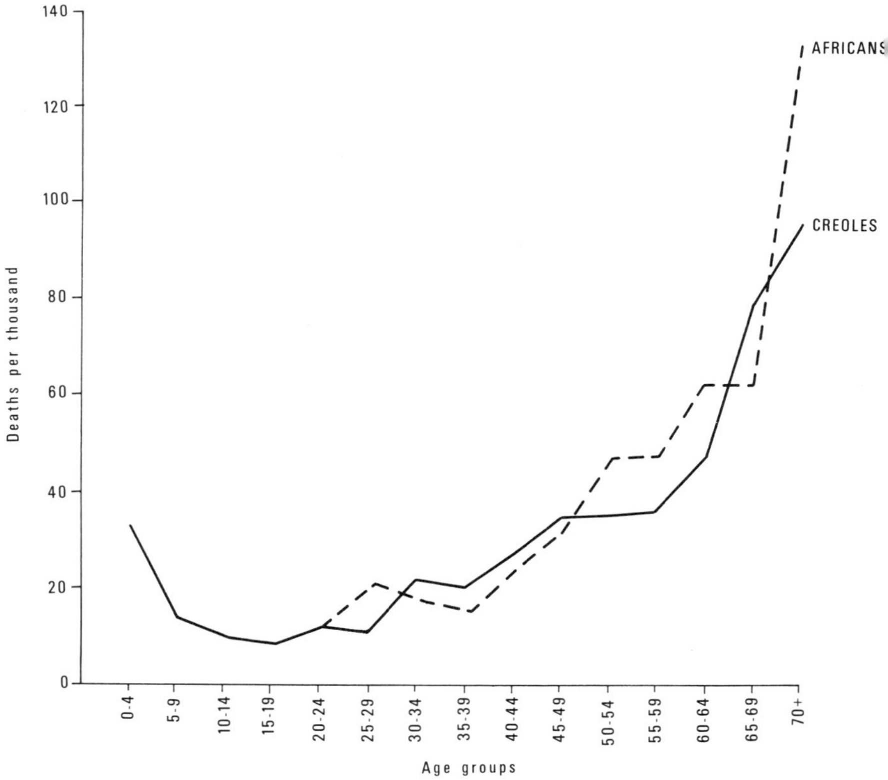

Figure 23. Age-specific mortality of the Clarendon slave population, 1817–20.

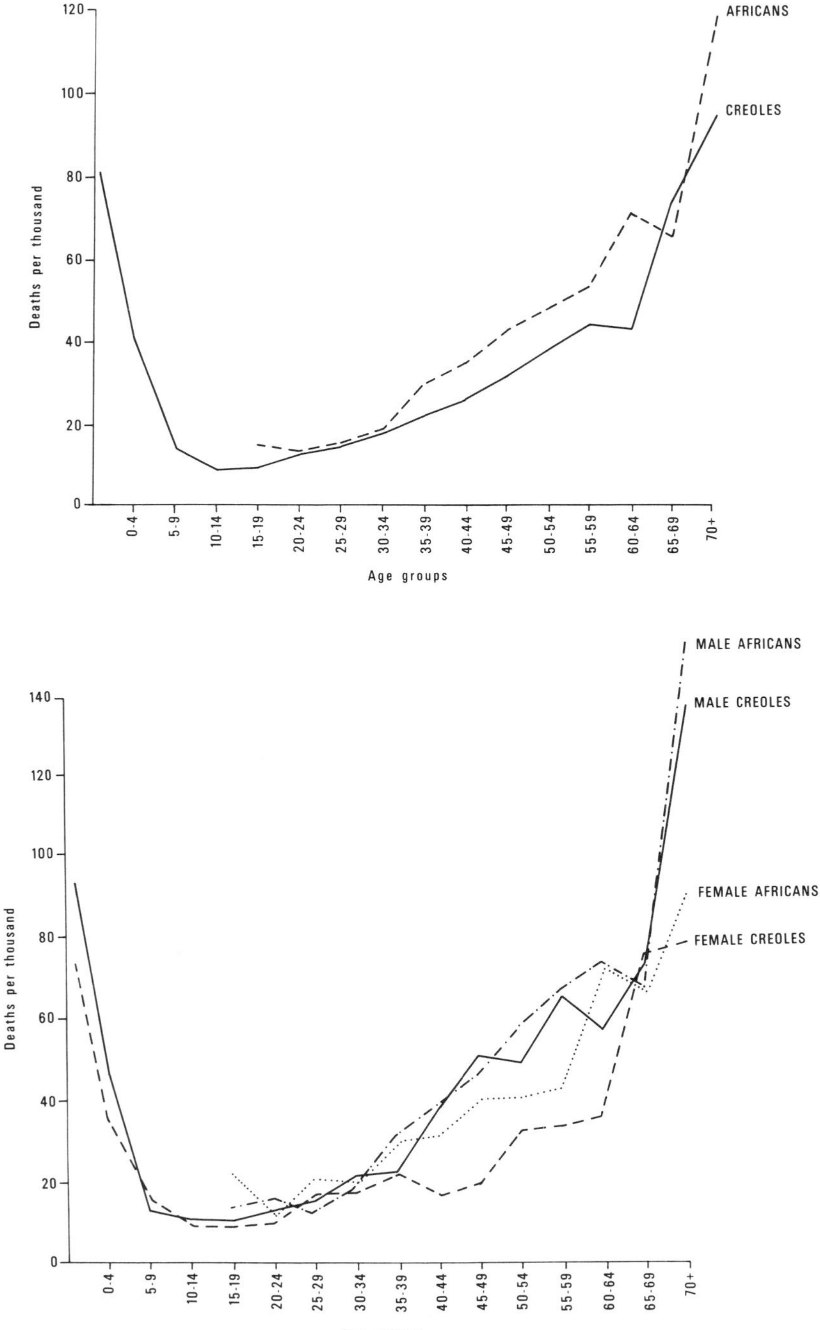

Figure 24. Age-specific mortality of the slave population of St. James, 1817–20.

of dysentery, for instance. Other causes, such as 'visitation of God' and 'suddenly', simply reflect the master's or physician's perplexity. Thus it is obvious that any attempt to classify the causes of death given in the returns is surrounded by pitfalls.

For the period 1817–20 the fullest listing of causes of death seems to be in the parish of St. James, though cause is noted for only 17 per cent of the deaths. The death rate for the 3,789 slaves in this sample was 31.4 per 1,000, compared to 27.1 for the parish as a whole. Thus the sample pattern must have been reasonably representative of conditions in the parish, except that accidental deaths had a propensity for being recorded whereas the causes of other deaths, even on the same slave-holding, might be omitted. A second sample has been assembled from the returns covering Old and New Montpelier Estates and Shettlewood Pen, in Hanover and St. James, for the period 1817–29. The total slave population on these properties was 958 in 1817 and 855 in 1829.[23] Thirdly, William Sells, member of the London Royal College of Surgeons and medical practitioner in Jamaica from 1803 to 1823, prepared a list of causes of death for 'part of Clarendon' in 1818. It covered one-quarter of the slaves in the parish, with a death rate of 27.9 per 1,000 compared to

Table 18. *Causes of death, St. James, 1817–20*

Cause	Total deaths	Males	Females	Slaves of colour	Africans	Age-groups 0–19	20–44	45+
Old age	53	27	26	—	43	—	—	53
Dropsy	39	24	15	1	21	6	21	12
Consumption	30	13	17	2	13	10	16	4
Dysentery	21	12	9	—	13	7	5	9
Fever	21	8	13	4	—	18	3	—
Fits	20	10	10	1	6	10	7	3
Weakly; debility	19	13	6	2	11	5	5	9
Pleurisy	14	12	2	—	12	—	6	8
Mal d'estomac	10	10	—	1	7	1	7	2
Joint evil; cocobay	10	9	1	—	6	2	4	4
Accidental	10	10	—	1	4	3	5	2
Locked jaw	9	3	6	1	—	7	1	1
Yaws	8	4	4	—	—	8	—	—
Swellings	7	2	5	—	3	4	2	1
Dirt eating	7	4	3	—	1	6	1	—
Worm fever	7	6	1	2	—	7	—	—
Venereal	5	1	4	—	2	1	2	2
Liver complaint	5	4	1	—	3	—	2	3
Inflammation of bowels	5	5	—	—	1	1	1	3
Other	57	31	26					
Total	357	208	149					

Source: R.R.S., Libers 37 and 40.

Table 19. *Causes of death, Old Montpelier, New Montpelier and Shettlewood, 1817–29*

Cause	Total deaths	Males	Females	Slaves of colour	Africans	Age-groups 0–19	20–44	45+
Weakness; debility	53	20	33	1	35	4	13	36
Dropsy	32	14	18	2	24	2	17	13
Dysentery	24	15	9	—	15	6	9	9
Fever	22	8	14	2	1	17	4	1
Old age	13	8	5	—	12	—	—	13
Fits, apoplexy	11	4	7	1	5	6	2	3
Convulsions; spasms	11	4	7	1	3	7	2	2
Bloated	9	2	7	—	3	5	1	3
Yaws	9	6	3	1	—	9	—	—
Pleurisy	7	5	2	—	5	—	4	3
Consumption	7	5	2	1	2	2	3	2
Visitation of God	7	3	4	—	4	2	1	4
Liver complaint	6	4	2	—	2	—	4	2
Tetanus; locked jaw	6	—	6	—	1	4	1	1
Invalid	5	2	3	—	5	—	2	3
Bowel complaint	5	2	3	—	2	1	1	3
Whooping cough	5	4	1	—	—	5	—	—
Other	56	29	27					
Total	288	135	153					

Source: R.R.S., Liber 27, f. 37; Liber 30, fos. 42 and 49; Liber 40, fos. 83–4; Liber 48, f. 163; Liber 66, fos. 159–60; Liber 75, f. 100; Liber 85, fos. 60–1. Liber 93, f. 33; Liber 96, f. 213; Liber 100, fos. 214–15.

23.2 for Clarendon during 1817–20.[24] Only causes accounting for five or more deaths have been detailed in Tables 18–20, but some of the causes classified as 'other' should no doubt be included in the specified categories.

The pattern presented in Tables 18–20 is grossly distorted by the understatement of infant mortality in the returns. If as many as 25 per cent of births went unrecorded because death occurred in the first few days of life, it follows that in the St. James sample roughly 90 deaths are missing, all attributable to infant mortality. The greatest cause of infant mortality was reported to be tetanus (locked jaw),[25] thus it should probably also be classified as the major cause of death overall, accounting for perhaps 20 per cent of total mortality. After tetanus came the ill-defined categories 'old age' and 'weakness', both of them affecting particularly African slaves over 45 years of age. Mortal diseases specific to the youthful section of the slave population were yaws, whooping cough, fever, worm fever, fits and convulsions. Some of these – such as whooping cough – occurred in epidemic form. In the case of yaws, it was said that many slaves in Jamaica used intentional inoculation, 'from an African opinion and custom in that country, that children should

Table 20. *Causes of death, part of Clarendon, 1818*

Cause	Total deaths
Aged and invalided	29
Cachexies (i.e., bad habit of body)	13
Fever	10
Worms	8
Died within the month	8
Consumption	7
Dropsy	6
Yaws	6
Accidental	6
Apoplexy and suddenly	5
Peripneumony and pleurisy	5
Other	38
Total	141

Source: William Sells, *Remarks on the Condition of the Slaves in the Island of Jamaica* (London, 1823), pp. 20–1.

undergo the disease at an early period of life'.[26] Deaths attributed to 'swellings', 'bloated' or 'dirt eating' also tended to affect the younger slaves most often. Since they were distinguished from dropsy and mal d'estomac, these causes of death probably comprehended the deficiency diseases and anemias resulting from malnutrition. Sells' list for Clarendon shows a heavier mortality from cachexies, fever and worms than in St. James or at Montpelier, and it is a general impression – based on the slight data available in the returns – that this may have applied throughout the eastern parishes. Geophagy (dirt eating) was said to prevail in wet rather than dry parishes, being common in St. Andrew but rare in the Port Royal mountains, for example.[27] It has generally been associated with ankylostomiasis (hookworm disease), but iron deficiency is an equally plausible explanation.[28]

Slaves in the 20–44 years age-group, who experienced the lowest mortality levels, died most often from dropsy, dysentery and consumption (the last probably concealing tuberculosis). Relative to the younger and older age-groups they also suffered particularly from pleurisy, leprosy, venereal disease and liver complaints (probably related to dysentery).[29] Dropsy and dysentery were in fact the major mortal diseases for which specific descriptions were given (excepting tetanus), and it is probable that they also overlapped those causes of death classified as inflammations and swellings. Dysentery was often of epidemic character.[30] Contemporary medical observers tended to overlook the importance of hygiene and living conditions in their epidemiological theories. Dysentery was related to 'obstructed perspiration' in alternations of temperature; it was confused with diarrhœa and hence the eating of 'unwholesome' food, such as pears and premature yams.[31] The contagious diseases – leprosy and venereal infections, for example – were relatively unimportant. Causes of death notable for their relative absence in the samples were smallpox (Jenner's plan of vaccination having been introduced to Jamaica in 1801), pneumonia, influenza and measles.[32] It was of great significance for the demographic history of Jamaica that the island escaped the cholera pandemic of 1826–37.[33]

African slaves appear to have died from pleurisy and leprosy more often than creoles, but in general creolization was an unimportant factor in cause-specific mortality after 1817. Although described as 'delicate and sickly inclined',[34] slaves of colour conformed closely to the disease-specific mortality pattern of the slave population as a whole, except perhaps for deaths from fever. But the view that fevers, which carried off the whites in great numbers, affected only mulattoes and house slaves was certainly incorrect.[35] Differences between the sexes generally reflected the African/creole ratio, though females seem to have suffered particularly from tetanus and males from leprosy. Accidental deaths are probably overstated in the sample lists, but it is certain that males were more affected than females; the diversity of their occupations meant that they were exposed to greater risks, especially in the manufacturing processes and transportation. Females, on the other hand, suffered from the risks associated with pregnancy and parturition. Few deaths were attributed to homicide or suicide.

Fertility

Relative to mortality, the pattern of fertility was uncomplicated. At the island level, the rate of *registered* births per 1,000 remained steady at about 23.0 between 1817 and 1820 (Table 21). It is probable that this rate did not vary significantly in the period after the abolition of the slave trade, excepting the years 1807–10. Some fragmentary evidence for the later eighteenth century also suggests a birth rate of about 23 per 1,000;[36] perhaps the secular trend should be pushed back even further.

A corollary of the absence of significant temporal variation in the level of fertility was the relative lack of spatial variation. In the period 1829–32, at the parish level, the standard deviation of the birth rate was only 2.1, compared to 4.7 for the death rate. In the towns the birth rate was 21.7 per 1,000, only 1.5 less than that in the parishes as a whole (Table 7). Between 1817 and 1832 there was a consistent increase in the birth rate in only three parishes – St. Elizabeth, Vere and St. Thomas-in-the-East – the death rate remaining fairly stable in the first two, but rising rapidly to a maximum in the case of St. Thomas-in-the-East. Six parishes showed a consistent decline in the birth rate: Clarendon, St. Thomas-in-the-Vale, St. John, St. Mary, Port Royal and St. George. This trend was associated with increases in mortality in all of these parishes, excepting an erratic movement in St. George. Only Port Royal

Table 21. *Crude birth rates, 1817–32*

Parish	Registered births per 1,000				
	1817–20	1820–3	1823–6	1826–9	1829–32
Westmoreland	21.0	19.9	21.5	20.6	23.0
Hanover	22.2	21.3	21.4	18.9	21.0
St. James	24.0	20.5	21.5	21.9	23.7
Trelawny	23.4	23.4	24.4	19.6	23.1
St. Elizabeth	24.0	24.3	25.1	25.5	27.7
Manchester	24.3	23.6	21.5	23.2	25.8
St. Ann	24.8	22.7	24.1	24.1	25.4
Clarendon	24.4	23.8	22.7	22.5	21.4
Vere	21.7	22.0	24.6	24.2	25.4
St. Dorothy	18.6	18.9	16.2	24.7	22.9
St. Thomas-in-the-Vale	25.0	24.5	21.7	19.9	20.8
St. John	25.7	23.0	22.4	22.2	21.3
St. Catherine	22.2	20.1	20.3	23.4	23.0
St. Mary	23.4	22.3	20.9	21.7	19.3
St. Andrew	25.2	25.9	25.5	23.1	23.7
Port Royal	28.1	27.7	26.7	25.0	24.5
St. David	26.4	23.8	23.9	20.1	22.9
St. George	25.9	24.3	23.5	21.4	21.9
Portland	24.1	23.3	22.0	24.2	25.0
St. Thomas-in-the-East	22.2	22.5	25.5	24.1	26.7
Kingston	20.8	22.4	23.4	20.9	18.3
Total	23.5	22.8	23.0	22.2	23.2

Sources: T.71/683, Bundle 9 (1817–29); R.R.S. (1829–32).

maintained a natural increase throughout the period in spite of its falling birth rate. The remaining parishes exhibited little variation in their levels of fertility over the period, following the trend for the island as a whole.

Because the data are relatively inaccessible, the pattern of age-specific fertility has been calculated for only a few holdings. At Old and New Montpelier and Shettlewood, in St. James and Hanover, the fertility of creole women was greater than that of Africans during the period 1817–32 (Table 22). But African and creole fertility were equivalent between 1817 and 1823; thereafter African fertility continued to decline, whereas creole fertility rose steadily. This divergence was a product of the changing age structures of the two populations within the fertile age-groups (Figure 18, above). In 1817, on these three properties, there were no African women under 25 years of age, in 1826 none under 30, and by 1829 none under 35. Thus it is difficult to use these data to test Patterson's argument that the young creole slaves were indifferent to child-rearing, whereas 'the habit of childbearing was too strongly rooted in the African woman for even the slave system to destroy it'.[37] Yet it is clear that at least among women over 25 years of age the creoles

Table 22. *African and creole age-specific fertility at Old Montpelier, New Montpelier and Shettlewood, 1817–32* (births per 1,000 woman-years)[a]

	1817–20	1820–3	1823–6	1826–9	1829–32	1817–32
AFRICANS						
Age-group						
25–29	51 (39)	95 (21)	— (3)	— (0)	— (0)	64 (63)
30–34	111 (81)	89 (45)	42 (24)	167 (12)	— (0)	99(162)
35–39	89(179)	84 (84)	83 (72)	31 (33)	83 (24)	82(329)
40–44	26 (78)	6(153)	21(147)	— (75)	— (36)	12(489)
General fertility rate	77(377)	49(303)	41(246)	25(120)	33 (60)	53(1106)
CREOLES						
Age-Group						
15–19	43(117)	16(126)	19(153)	51(177)	21(141)	32(714)
20–24	33 (60)	56 (72)	106(132)	133(105)	136(147)	105(516)
25–29	118 (93)	67 (90)	133 (45)	107 (84)	136(117)	112(429)
30–34	95 (63)	72 (69)	80 (75)	43 (69)	89 (45)	75(321)
35–39	125 (48)	88 (57)	72 (69)	63 (63)	43 (69)	75(306)
40–44	83 (12)	42 (24)	33 (60)	35 (57)	61 (66)	55(219)
General fertility rate	79(393)	52(438)	67(534)	74(555)	85(585)	72(2505)

[a] Woman-years given in parentheses.
Source: R.R.S., Liber 27, f. 37; Liber 30, fos. 42 and 49; Liber 40, fos. 83–4; Liber 48, f. 163; Liber 66, fos. 159–60; Liber 75, f. 100; Liber 85, fos. 60–1; Liber 93, f. 33; Liber 96, f. 213; Liber 100, fos. 214–15; Liber 129, f. 28 and f. 32; Liber 130, f. 170.

were slightly more fertile than the Africans. At Old Montpelier, the most thoroughly creolized of the properties, the creoles in all age-groups were most fertile throughout the period, whereas at Shettlewood a decline in African fertility was matched by a rapid increase in that of the creoles. But at New Montpelier, the estate with the greatest proportion of Africans, the fertility of the Africans exceeded that of the creoles throughout the period.[38]

If the evidence regarding African and creole fertility levels is confused, however, it is certain that creoles under 20 years were most infertile. Only slaves bearing children of colour demonstrated high fertility in this age-group.[39] This pattern conforms with that argued by Patterson. But following this initial infertility an early peak was reached, generally around 25 years of age, after which the decline in fertility was continuous. A further example, supporting this view, is provided by Bull Dead coffee plantation in Manchester, where all of the mothers during the period 1817–32 were creoles and the general fertility rate was twice that at Montpelier (Table 23). But at Bull Dead the concentration of high fertility into the 20–29 years age-groups was much greater than at Montpelier. Creole fertility in the 40–44 years age-group

Table 23. *Age-specific fertility at Bull Dead, Manchester, 1817–32*

Age-group	Births per 1,000 woman-years[a]	
15–19	73	(82)
20–24	250	(80)
25–29	214	(84)
30–34	127	(71)
35–39	111	(45)
40–44	45	(22)
General fertility rate	162	(384)

[a] Woman-years given in parentheses.
Source: R.R.S., Liber 19, f. 171; Liber 35, f. 220; Liber 37, f. 205; Liber 89, f. 201; Liber 99, f. 132; Liber 129, f. 172.

at Montpelier exceeded that in the 15–19 group, whereas at Bull Dead the reverse was true. In fact, excepting the low fertility of the 15–19 years age-group, the age-specific fertility profile for Bull Dead fits quite closely that of modern times.[40] At Montpelier, however, fertility approached modern levels only after 35 years of age. However generous the assumptions made regarding under-registration, the slaves were not a fertile population.

Explanations

In returning to the central theme – the reasons for the decline of the slave population after 1807 – it is clear that it will be necessary to account for the spatial and temporal variations in the rate of natural increase, as well as the absolute decrease. It is, therefore, important to distinguish several levels of explanation: the static and dynamic, and the internal and external. Some writers – both contemporary and modern – have used certain fixed factors to explain the failure of the slave population to maintain its numbers over the entire period of slavery, whereas others have used developmental models, particularly for the period after the abolition of the slave trade. Some trace the decrease to strictly demographic factors, internal to the development of the slave population, whereas others attribute it to externally determined factors acting on the slave population from outside. Of the internal, demographic explanations, the most influential centre on the sex ratio and age structure of the slaves. The external factors invoked are economic (the type and amount of labour exacted) and ecological. Many of the explanations advanced, of course, contain some combination of the static and dynamic, and internal and external factors, so it is necessary to attempt to isolate and measure the importance of the particular elements.

The sex ratio of the slaves has often been cited as the most fundamental of all the factors involved in the decrease of the population.[41] Burnley saw it as central to the debate between the masters and the humanitarians. When the masters' attempt to attribute the decrease to 'the national vices of the Negroes' proved untenable, he said,

> they seized upon the disparity of the sexes; and, as it is clear to the meanest capacity, that three men and one woman cannot replenish the earth as fast as an equality of the sexes; this proved strong ground, on which they firmly entrenched themselves. Their opponents, aware of the strength of this position, felt that their favourite theory of the cruelty of the master could never be satisfactorily established, unless the colonists were driven from it; long and bitter, consequently has been the warfare; profound have been the essays on puberty, procreation, and the term of child-bearing; registries have been dissected; figures heaped upon figures . . .[42]

While the slave trade had continued, slaves were imported in the ratio of three males to every two females, creating an insufficiency of mates for the male slaves.[43] The abolition of the slave trade, argued the masters, would lead inevitably to the depopulation of Jamaica.[44] Thus the humanitarians were quick to notice that the first registration of slaves in 1817 showed no disparity in the sexes, confirming their view that the decrease arose from maltreatment.[45]

At the parish level, the sex ratio of 1817 was not correlated significantly with the birth rate, death rate or rate of natural increase from 1817 to 1820. Transforming to logs, only the correlation with the birth rate becomes significant at the 99 per cent level of probability ($r = .54$). In the period 1829–32, when males were a minority in the slave population, the pattern was similar. At the quadrat level, there was a significant positive correlation between the sex ratio and the birth rate; at the parish level, the correlation was positive, but not significant. In the towns, on the other hand, the correlation with the birth rate was negative, though not significant. Only in the towns was there a significant correlation between natural increase and the sex ratio ($r = -.70$).[46]

Thus in the rural slave population fertility was stimulated, not depressed, by high sex ratios. This conclusion is not affected by the pattern of age-specific sex ratios, since high ratios were generally associated with especially high levels of masculinity in the most fertile age-groups (20–44 years).[47] In the parish of Vere, where the sex ratio was closest to an equality throughout the fertile ages, the birth rate was low. In most parishes there was also a rough equality in the 15–19 years age-group, which was relatively infertile; whereas in the relatively fertile 40–44 group the sex ratio tended to be at a maximum. In the towns, the significant correlation between the sex ratio and natural increase was a product of the former's connection with mortality, not fertility. At the quadrat level there was also a significant correlation with mortality. Thus it can be concluded that, in the period after the abolition of the slave trade, high sex ratios did not depress fertility as argued by the masters. But, because of the sex ratio's connection with the age structure of the population, high ratios did tend to raise mortality levels. It is certain that the sex ratio by itself, or changes in the sex ratio over the period, cannot account satisfactorily for the variations in the level of natural increase in the slave population.

The supposed effect of the sex ratio on reproduction was often linked to the ratio of African and creole slaves.[48] According to the masters, creole women generally shunned the Africans, while the creole men of property were able to lure away the African women they desired.[49] This was said to exacerbate the imbalance of the sexes, and lead to promiscuity, abortion and the spread of venereal disease. It was also thought that the Africans neglected their children, whereas the creoles nurtured them, valued cleanliness and were all married in the 'Jamaica style'.[50] But the principal way in which the African/creole ratio was thought to affect natural increase was through its relationship with the age structure. Thus Barclay argued that since the slave trade had brought a large number of adult Africans to Jamaica it would not be possible for the population to increase until the aged generations had died.[51]

Since the percentage of African-born slaves in 1817 has been established for a sample of nine parishes only, correlation coefficients have not been calculated. But the data suggest that the rate of natural increase and the birth rate during the period 1817–20 rose together with the percentage African, and that the level of mortality, on the other hand, tended to fall as the percentage African increased.[52] These tentative findings would appear to be contrary to the pattern argued by the masters, but they need to be viewed within a temporal context. For 1829–32, when it is necessary to use the percentage of deaths African as an index of the total proportion African, significant correlations with the vital rates are found only at the quadrat level and the coefficients are all small (Table A3.2). In contrast to the pattern suggested for 1817–20, there was a slight negative correlation between the percentage of deaths African and the rate of natural increase ($r = -.17$). This relationship must be explained by the positive correlation between African and total deaths ($r = .30$), since there was also a significant positive correlation between African deaths and the birth rate ($r = .16$). Hence it is difficult to show that a high ratio of Africans hindered reproduction, as was suggested in the discussion of the pattern of age-specific fertility.[53] But by 1829–32 natural increases were less likely to occur in areas with high percentages of male Africans because the latter had moved into a period in which they suffered heavy age-specific mortality. If it is true that the African section of the population was decreasing while the creole section was growing by natural increase, it is possible that high death rates could be associated with high percentages of aged Africans in areas which also had a growing group of creoles in the child-bearing ages. As with the sex ratio, it is obvious that the African/creole ratio by itself is incapable of explaining the pattern of natural increase in the slave population.

It will be necessary to discuss the importance of changes in age structure when considering dynamic explanations of the pattern of natural increase, later in this chapter.[54] Here it need only be noted that the only systematic measures available – the percentages under 6 years and over 70 years of age in 1834, by parishes – were not correlated significantly with the vital rates at the 99 per cent level, though most of the coefficients approached this level.[55] High percentages of young children were related to high birth rates and low death rates, and hence to natural increase. High percentages of old people were related to high death rates and rates of natural decrease, but the link with fertility was tenuous. These results are almost axiomatic, however. The important point is that these indicators of age structure are simply too crude to have any explanatory value.

In 1832 William Taylor, who had spent fifteen years in Jamaica, noticed the inadequacy of explanations based on the African/creole ratio and went on to tell a select committee of Parliament that it was a general feeling that increases generally occurred on coffee plantations and pens, and decreases on sugar estates.[56] The heavy mortality on sugar estates he attributed to night work, cane hole digging and the use of the whip. It is true that the work on coffee plantations was generally thought to be lighter, though some argued that during the picking season the labour was harder than on sugar estates.[57] The Rev. Samuel Stewart, noting that Manchester's slave population had increased while that of the island as a whole had decreased, explained this by saying that:

> The mortality in the lowlands from bilious fever is fully counterbalanced by the liability of the negro in these elevated situations to pulmonary and low nervous diseases. The increase must therefore be put to the credit of the climate and the comparative advantages of coffee over sugar cultivation, as regarded the production of these staple articles in slavery.[58]

Further, Edward Long claimed that slaves were most likely to reproduce where the labour was easiest: thus he considered that domestics had more children than those on pens, and the latter more than those on sugar estates.[59]

An immediate impression of the connection between population growth and the different types of land use can be gained by comparing the maps of natural increase (Figure 20) and of sugar and coffee production (Figures 2 and 3). But, for 1829–32, two major exceptions to the general rule appear: in Vere, a sugar parish, there was a natural increase, and in upper Port Royal, a coffee region, there was a decrease. Thus the correlation between the number of sugar estates in an area and the rate of natural increase was by no means perfect – only that at the quadrat level is significant ($r = -.34$). The prominence of sugar had no effect at all on fertility, but the correlations with the death rate were high both at the parish and quadrat levels ($r = .64$ and .38, respectively). But at the quadrat level the estimated number of pens and plantations during the period 1829–32 was more strongly correlated with fertility than mortality, and the link with natural increase, though positive, was slight ($r = .15$).

William Taylor recognized that Vere was an important aberration from his general rule. He said that 'in the parish of Vere, where there is little or no cane hole digging, I have always understood that the negroes increase rapidly; for the strength of negroes upon the estates in Vere is more than equal to the work upon the estates'.[60] He thought that the stiffness of the soil might be a factor; the fertility of the soil in Vere made almost continuous ratooning possible, hence the estates were smaller, while its dryness meant that the slaves' feet were relatively free of sores.[61] In Vere the slaves did not have provision grounds but were provided with Guinea corn and salt fish and pork, and they used their corn to raise poultry which they sold in Spanish Town or to hucksters who came from Kingston by boat.[62] They were said to be 'exceedingly well off'. In 1823 Williams noticed that there were many steam-driven mills in the parish, and that the works and buildings were on a larger scale than elsewhere.[63] These features of the parish are suggestive, but it also possessed other significant characteristics not noticed by contemporaries. The average slave-holding was larger than in any other parish, but the density of slaves per cultivated acre was the lowest in the island (probably a result of the extent of ratooning). Excepting Kingston, it had the lowest sex ratio in 1832, and the lowest percentage African, with perhaps the exception of Hanover. In 1817 the sex ratio approached an equality in the 0–54 years age-groups, and the age structure of the parish displayed a relatively mature pattern. Vere's death rate was not abnormally low, but the birth rate was above average. These factors suggest that Vere reached a balance between the sexes earlier than other sugar parishes and that this was the product of a growing creole population. The reasons for the natural decrease in the coffee regions of Port Royal by 1829–32 were essentially the converse of the demographic trends in Vere – the size of the African-male section of the slave population. These aberrations from the general economic-demographic rule obviously have to be accounted for in dynamic terms.

The relationship between crop type and natural increase is just as clear at the level of the individual slave-holding as at the regional level. Taking the 960 Accounts Produce properties which were classified into crop-combination types in Chapter 2, and relating them to the demographic data available in the Returns of Registrations of Slaves for 1829–32,[64] it appears that the only units to approach the extremely high rate of natural decrease on the sugar estates were the jobbing gangs (Table 24). The jobbing gangs were, of course, very often employed on the estates. Even when sugar was combined with pimento, which was generally associated with increases, the slaves

Table 24. *Demographic characteristics, by crop-combination types, 1829–32, (Accounts Produce properties)*

Crop combination	Males per 100 females	Births per 1,000	Deaths per 1,000	Natural increase	Births of colour (%)	African deaths (%)	Production per slave (£)
Sugar	92.0	22.7	35.1	−12.4	20.0	31.5	25.9
Coffee	101.2	25.1	23.3	+1.8	10.2	46.0	19.2
Coffee–labour	102.0	19.2	24.9	−5.7	9.2	38.9	13.5
Coffee–livestock	94.1	31.3	23.7	+7.6	19.2	47.8	19.7
Pimento	108.3	25.9	23.8	+2.1	15.0	25.0	25.6
Livestock	96.7	26.6	27.1	−0.5	17.2	32.3	17.8
Livestock–pimento	95.0	31.1	19.5	+11.6	16.9	20.3	21.5
Labour (jobbing)	102.4	24.9	33.1	−8.2	17.0	59.4	8.6
Livestock–labour	94.5	26.8	24.6	+2.2	12.4	41.0	10.9
Wharfage	138.7	15.8	18.0	−2.3	71.4	25.0	42.1
Sugar–pimento	92.1	27.9	29.3	−1.5	19.3	30.0	19.4
Coffee–pimento	102.3	31.1	19.8	+11.3	12.1	42.9	23.9
Livestock–dyewoods	91.6	33.2	29.1	+4.1	24.4	30.6	16.0
Pimento–livestock–labour	94.2	28.8	24.4	+4.4	6.5	41.0	11.2
Total	93.9	23.6	32.2	−8.6	17.9	33.6	23.4

Source: See Appendixes 1 and 2. For the number of properties and slaves included in each crop combination see Table 1, p. 00 above.

decreased. It follows that, in terms of the estimated distribution of the slave labour force around 1832 (Table 2), roughly 50 per cent of Jamaica's slaves were subject to this heavy rate of decrease – a rate three times greater than that for the slave population as a whole. The highest rates of natural increase, on the other hand, occurred where pimento was combined with the raising of livestock and the growing of coffee. Livestock production by itself showed a slight rate of decrease, but when combined with coffee, pimento, dyewoods or even jobbing, the slaves increased. Thus, although monocultural coffee plantations did not have a particularly high rate of increase around 1829–32, those contemporary observers who believed that pens and the minor staples were more conducive to increase than sugar were certainly correct.

It is more difficult to determine whether the association of natural increase with particular types of land and labour use was a product of the occupational demands of those units, of their disease environments, or of their other demographic characteristics. There were significant differences between the units in terms of the sex ratio and the percentage African, for example. But it is clear that the sugar estates had a low sex ratio and a relatively small percentage of Africans (Table 24), features not generally associated with high mortality; and within the sugar estates themselves there were no significant correlations between the death rate and the sex ratio or African/creole ratio

(Table A3.4). With the exception of the jobbing gangs, however, mortality on the sugar estates exceeded that on any other type of unit, by a wide margin. With the exception of wharves, which were predominantly male (the slaves generally having wives and provision grounds on neighbouring esates)[65] and coffee-labour combinations, the sugar estates also had the lowest birth rate in 1829–32. Although the level of masculinity was at a minimum on the sugar estates, this is not sufficient to explain the low level of fertility; within the sugar estates, variations in the sex ratio explain little of the variation in the birth rate ($r = -.14$), and the same applies to the African/creole ratio. It is possible that the low fertility and high mortality on the sugar estates reflected an aging population, though the sex ratio and percentage of deaths African tend to go against this view; but the age structure of the individual Accounts Produce properties needs to be established before this issue can be resolved satisfactorily. Unless other strictly demographic factors were involved, or it can be shown that sugar production took place in particularly unhealthy locations, it may be concluded that the natural decrease was related directly to the labour requirements of sugar.

The hardships of those slaves who belonged to jobbers were said to exceed even those suffered on sugar estates.[66] They were employed most often on the roads and on the sugar estates, where the heavy labour of cane hole digging was frequently the task. The jobbers' slaves were given the hard work the planters preferred not to give their own. Thus they died early, said Bickell, like 'over-wrought or over-driven horses'.[67] The death rate of jobbing slaves was only slightly less than that suffered on sugar estates, though part of this mortality can be explained by the fact that these slaves tended to be males and hence contained a high proportion of Africans (Table 24), there being a significant correlation between the death rate and the percentage of deaths African within the jobbing gangs (Table A3.4).

Variations between the different crop-combination types showing natural increases are more difficult to explain. Slaves employed in pimento combined with livestock or coffee increased more rapidly than those on monocultural pimento, coffee or livestock properties. The only significant correlation found in these groups is that between mortality and fertility on pimento properties (Table A3.4); the sex and African/creole ratios do not appear to be helpful. If the combinations including sugar and jobbing are excepted, it seems that increases tended to be greater where the units were most diversified; it is possible that slaves on such properties enjoyed a better diet and were less subject to seasonal labour requirements, but this could hardly be advanced as an adequate explanation. The planting and harvesting of crops, in contrast to the tending of stock and the cutting of timber, does not seem to have been a vital factor.

In order to clarify the general pattern it is useful to turn to the exceptions. Of the sugar estates included in the Accounts Produce sample 15 per cent (76 properties) showed natural increases during the period 1829–32, and 34 per cent of the coffee plantations (60 properties) had decreases. Thus, whereas the decline associated with sugar was rarely mitigated, the relative advantages of coffee were by no means general. The exceptional sugar estates were fairly evenly spread spatially, though very few natural increases occurred in the dense areas of St. John, St. Thomas-in-the-Vale, St. Mary and St. George. The concentration of exceptions in Vere has been discussed already, but it is worth noting that there were many estates in the parish with decreases. It does not appear that the pattern of exceptions was related to locality, though the band of relatively unmitigated decrease running from St. Mary to Portland was characterized by estate decline and abandonment, and the coastal strip was wetter than any of the other sugar regions. Turning to the demographic characteristics of the exceptional sugar estates, it is found that 41 of them had a lower sex ratio than the average for sugar estates; 57 had an above-average birth rate, whereas only 4 had an above-average death rate; and 45 had a smaller percentage of African deaths than normal. Although there may have been a tendency for the birth rate to be high where females were in the majority, these estates were not sufficiently atypical to explain their increases in terms of the sex ratio. The low level of mortality on these exceptional estates can be only partly explained by their high proportions of creoles. It is certain that many particular factors operated on the individual estates: sales and purchases of slaves, relationships with persons off the estates, the state of the provision grounds, the attitudes of the masters and the settledness of the agricultural regime.

Coffee plantations showing natural decreases were more localized than the exceptional sugar estates. Apart from a pocket of decreases in the May Day Mountains of Manchester, a recently settled and fertile coffee area,[68] the majority of the exceptional plantations were in the eastern mountain ridge. The latter was the oldest established coffee region and it was subject to much erosion and abandonment in the early nineteenth century;[69] but neither of these features predicate natural decrease. Of the 60 exceptional plantations, 57 had above-average death rates but only 34 had relatively large percentages of deaths African. A greater number of the exceptions are accounted for by variations in the sex ratio: thirty-three of them had more than 110 males per 100 females while eleven had less than 90. But, as in the case of sugar, it is certain that many local factors were involved.

A variation of the theory that the rate of natural increase was related to crop type was the argument that mortality was highest where the slave was worked the hardest or was most productive.[70] McMahon, for example, claimed that some attorneys arranged with overseers to force heavy crops in order to enhance their commissions and prestige, and that as a consequence the overseers exacted labour unmercifully.[71] The planters, on the other hand, contended that there was 'no symptom of that depravity, with which the planters and their creditors are branded, of trying to force immediate returns, without regard for the preservation of the capital, or the lives of the people'.[72] Long, writing in 1774, argued that if an estate produced more than one hogshead of sugar per slave few children could be expected to survive, because the mothers would have no time to care for them; yet if the ratio was half a hogshead per slave they would increase rapidly.[73] As a general rule, Long suggested that the ratio should be set at two hogsheads for every three slaves. He found only six parishes to be deficient of slaves by this rule, being, in increasing order of deficiency, Hanover, Westmoreland (with stiff, heavy soil), Vere (light soil), St. James, Clarendon and St. Thomas-in-the-East (soils of a middle grade).[74] By 1832 it is clear that Long's rule was not being followed. In that year the average production per slave on sugar estates was £25.9, this value being based on the assumption that a hogshead of sugar was worth £26.[75] It is true that output was expanded by the adoption of new cane varieties during the 1790s, but there was also a significant increase in the size of the average hogshead between 1774 and 1832.[76]

Long did not go on to relate his rule to the natural increase of the slave populations of the parishes, but the humanitarians did attempt such a correlation. In 1826 William Smith, the Socinian member of the Clapham Sect, told Parliament that in islands where the production of sugar was low per capita, such as Barbados and Anguilla, there were natural increases, but that the population decreased wherever production per slave reached eight hundredweights[77] (or roughly half a hogshead). A table was published in the following year showing the annual rate of change in the slave populations of the British West Indies and the amounts of sugar exported per slave. Difficulties in interpreting this table were recognized, but it was said that the results 'lead irresistibly to the conclusion of the comparatively deathful nature of sugar-cultivation, more especially in fertile soils'.[78] In this comparison Jamaica came out well, in contrast to Trinidad and Demerara, having the third highest rate of increase of the sugar colonies, after Barbados and Dominica.

It is difficult to demonstrate that the rate of natural increase did in fact vary according to the level of production per slave, since no direct measure of labour inputs is available. Taking the 960 Accounts Produce properties as a group, the variation in productivity can explain little of the variation in the rate of natural increase in 1829–32 ($r = -.21$), though the correlation is significant at the 99 per cent level and holds in the direction expected.[79] If the data are grouped by crop-combination types, natural increases seem to be associated with increasing production, with the important exception of sugar (Table 24). Taking the sugar estates alone, there are slight correlations between increasing productivity and high death rates and low birth rates, the link with fertility being the strongest (Table A3.4). Three other correlations of interest are significant at the 95 per cent level of probability: on pimento properties the death rate rose along with production ($r = .76$), and on livestock–pimento and livestock–labour units fertility fell as output increased (Table A3.4). But, on the remainder of the properties, production, fertility and mortality seem to have varied independently. But it is clear that the measure of production used here, the gross value of output per slave, is not a good index of the amount of labour exacted. Two extreme examples are the wharves where the labour input was subordinate to other services performed in relation to gross receipts, and the jobbing gangs in which no extraneous returns to capital or the fertility of the soil were involved. Slaves employed by wharfingers produced £42 per capita and those jobbed only £8; thus the heavy mortality experienced by the jobbing slaves is not weighted as would seem appropriate. Hence it is impossible to prove, with the available data, that the amount of labour exacted from the slaves affected the rate of natural increase.

The theory which related natural increase to slave-holding size was essentially a rationalization of the plantation system. The master who held a few slaves in town or jobbed them on the estates was said to be less able to provide for them than the planter who maintained a hospital and gave his slaves access to provision grounds.[80] But the available evidence does not support this theory. At the parish and town levels there are no significant correlations between slave-holding size and any of the vital rates for 1829–32. At the quadrat level, however, it seems that the largest holdings had the greatest natural decreases and were characterized by particularly heavy male mortality, whereas holdings of less than 20 slaves were associated with relatively high birth rates (Tables A3.1–A3.3). Each quadrat contained units of various sizes, but the dominance of particular size-groups can be estimated. In the quadrats in which holdings of less than 21 slaves made up 80 per cent of the total, the average birth rate was 23.2 per 1,000 and the death rate only 22.1; where more than 60 per cent of the holdings fell into the 21–100 range, the birth rate was 20.0 and the death rate 24.9; and where more than 20 per cent of the holdings were of more than 100 slaves, the figures were 23.3 and 32.3. The pattern of fertility seems somewhat capricious but mortality (and hence natural decrease) increased rapidly along with holding size. A more detailed picture emerges from an analysis of particular parishes for 1817–20 (Table A3.14). In general, mortality rose with increasing holding size to reach a peak in the 101–150 slaves group; it then fell, before rising again to another maximum in units of more than 350 slaves.

Further evidence of the relationship between slave-holding size and natural increase is provided by the Accounts Produce properties (Table 25). The pattern that emerges is very neat. None of the size-groups in this sample showed natural increases, but the rate of decrease rose steadily to a peak in the 251–300 group and then declined again. Mortality followed exactly the same trend. Fertility did not fit such a smooth curve, continuing to increase with holding size; the major break in this trend was in the 251–300 group where it fell to a near-minimum. Again, the sex ratio declined smoothly, reaching a minimum in the 251–300 group and then rising slightly. But the

Table 25. *Demographic characteristics, by slave-holding size groups, 1829–32 (Accounts Produce properties)*

Slaves per holding	Males per 100 females	Births per 1,000	Deaths per 1,000	Natural increase	Births of colour (%)	African deaths (%)	Production per slave (£)	Number of holdings
1–50	110.2	22.1	23.3	−1.2	9.6	46.8	22.1	91
51–100	99.9	22.4	27.0	−4.6	13.9	41.6	22.1	165
101–150	95.5	24.0	32.1	−8.1	16.4	38.4	21.9	185
151–200	94.9	23.3	32.9	−9.6	19.3	35.0	23.6	185
201–250	92.1	23.5	33.3	−9.8	18.6	28.9	24.9	135
251–300	91.4	23.1	33.7	−10.7	17.9	34.1	24.7	89
301–400	92.0	24.2	33.0	−8.8	20.2	31.3	23.1	82
401–500	93.1	24.5	32.5	−8.0	14.2	27.0	21.8	19
501–750	92.0	25.2	27.3	−2.0	17.6	32.1	23.0	9
Total	93.9	23.6	32.2	−8.6	17.9	33.6	23.4	960

Source: See Appendix 1.

correlations within the size-groups do not indicate that mortality can be explained in terms of the sex ratio (Table A3.5); and the general pattern of African deaths suggests that the lower the percentage the higher the death rate. Thus fertility and mortality were more closely tied to the sex ratio than to the African/creole ratio. The curves of natural decrease and mortality were also followed closely by the trend in production per slave, all of these curves reaching a peak in holdings of between 201 and 300 slaves. This may have approximated an optimum (sugar) holding size, in which the masters were able to maximize their control over the effective deployment of their slaves and capital equipment. Such control may have meant a maximization of the amount of labour exacted from the slaves, and hence a maximization of the physical brutality inherent in the slave system. But it should also be recalled that age structure varied with holding size, units in the 101–300 group generally having the most mature African slave populations. And the Accounts Produce sample of properties seems to have been unusual in having relatively low rates of natural decrease in the largest units.

The significance for natural increase of the direct physical brutality of the slave labour regime – the flogging of slaves, for example – cannot be tested with the available data. Whether close contact with a master or mistress in a small holding resulted in more or less brutality than contact with an overseer or driver on a large estate is uncertain.[81] In any case, the relationship between mortality and holding size described above is ambiguous. The data for cause of death are similarly unhelpful (Tables 18–20). For 1829–32 only one slave was reported to have died from a flogging ordered by the parish magistrates.[82] But 'debility' may have covered anything from constitutional frailty to malnutrition or continued brutal punishment, though it is clear that slaves between 20 and 44 years of age were not severely affected in this category. Deaths attributed to the 'visitation of God' might also include victims of gross brutality, but the range of ages seems too broad for this to be a general explanation. The masters' control of slave nutrition also appears to have been a relatively insignificant factor in natural increase. It has been argued that slaves dependent on imported food supplies disbursed by the master, as in Barbados, tended to suffer heavier mortality rates than those with their own provision grounds.[83] But it became clear soon after 1807 that the slave population of Barbados had achieved a natural increase, and in Jamaica the town slaves increased while those on the sugar estates decreased; within Jamaica the one sugar parish lacking a provision-ground system, Vere, was the only one to show a natural increase by 1834.

Behind all the structural factors involved in the decrease of the slave population, over which the masters felt they had some degree of control, there lurked always the Jamaica environment. The whites saw that while the slaves suffered heavy mortality their own losses were even more staggering. This mortality seemed endemic to the island. In the final stanza of his poem 'Jamaica', written in 1824, Jack Jingle asked

> And what awaits me now, sad Isle!
> The boon thou givest all thy sons
> An early grave.[84]

Yet the creole whites preferred to adopt a racial theory of African 'barbarism', and hence slavery, because they disliked the imputation of environmentally derived 'creole' manners and physique (even colour) being directed at them.[85] Thus they argued that white and black men were affected differently by tropical climates: whites suffered from the heat, and blacks from relative cold.[86] When it suited their purpose the planters used both heat and cold to explain the mortality of the slaves.

Before the germ theory of disease, etiology was generally discussed in atmospheric terms. 'Bad air' was a basic cause of disease.[87] The five signs of an unhealthy country listed by James Lind, in the late eighteenth century, all bear on this aspect of the environment.[88] The first sign was the sudden chilling of the air at sunset: 'It shows an unhealthy, swampy soil, the nature of which is such, that no sooner the sunbeams are withdrawn, than the vapour emitted from it renders the air raw, damp, and chilling, in the most sultry climates . . .' The second sign was thick noisome fogs, rising from valleys, and mud and slime. Thirdly, swarms of flies and gnats were related to stagnant air, especially in wooded regions. Fourthly, where butcher's meat was filled with maggots in a few hours, metals corroded quickly, and corpses became intolerably offensive in less than six hours, the place was unhealthy. The fifth sign was loose, white, sandy soil, which gave off pestiferous vapours, in connection with land-winds. Unhealthiness was universally related to areas in the lee of miasmatic swamps and marshes.[89] On the other hand, 'the most wholesome situations', wrote Quier of Lluidas Vale, 'are those on the sides of hills or mountains, where the soil is dry, and clear from woods and stagnating water; and where there are no morasses within three miles'.[90] In low places, dry situations distant from marshes and ventilated by a free air were thought the most healthy.

Quier, with many others,[91] believed that Jamaica had become more salubrious and temperate as the woods had been cleared. In order to combat the noxious atmosphere which developed whenever nature was left to itself,[92] the masters cleared the land around the slaves' huts and located them away from the drift of miasma. The masters also tried to turn nature against itself by making medicines from local plants, such as ginger, arrowroot, tamarind, lignumvitae and logwood.[93] Slaves suffering from stomach disorders, rheumatism and complaints of the liver could be sent to the mineral springs of the island. The physician at Milk River Bath reported in 1833 that he had cared for 'a very considerable number of the slave population, labouring under a variety of diseases – many of them of a very serious description, and for whose exclusive use there is a bath and lodging-house'.[94] The masters appointed medical practitioners to care for their slaves, but it was not until 1832 that a college of physicians and surgeons was set up in Jamaica; before this no proof of qualification was required, nor was there any school of medicine to teach the morbid anatomy and diseases peculiar to the tropics. In 1833 there were more than 200 legally authorized practitioners in the island, or roughly one to every 1,500 slaves.[95] Since those living in the towns must have directed their efforts to the free, white population, it is difficult to interpret the significance of the parochial distribution of the practitioners relative to the slave population. But the practitioner/slave ratio seems to have varied independently of the rate of natural increase in the slave population, which is perhaps not surprising in view of the medical practice of the period. The role of the slave 'doctor', nurse and midwife may well have been more important in the preservation of the lives of the slaves than the work of the legally authorized practitioner.

The masters often complained that the slaves refused to co-operate in the battle with the Grim Reaper. But the slaves probably had a different conception of etiology, seeing an intimate union between magic and medicine.[96] They believed that the deified souls of their departed ancestors and other spiritual beings were the controllers of disease, though diseases were often seen to be associated with particular environmental conditions and thus the spirits were given related names.[97] It was believed of children dying within nine days of birth that 'perrit tek dem'.[98] What the masters saw as a hand-to-hand contest with nature the slaves seem to have interpreted as a relationship with supernatural beings who mediated their will through the physical environment in a symbolic way.

Whereas the planters had no doubt about the impact of the environment on mortality, the humanitarians believed that they were merely trying to avoid the essential issue of ill-treatment. In 1804 Wilberforce told Parliament that in the United States of America the slaves were prolific,[99] and that

It being ascertained that such a rapid increase was obtained in America, he saw no reason to think why our West-India negroes might not keep up their numbers, but might positively increase to a great degree. The climate of America was so far from being more favourable, that the dews and exhalations with which it abounded were particularly unfavourable to the health of the negroes, accustomed to a dry and hot climate.

To a large extent the masters would have agreed with Wilberforce's view of the slaves' preferences. They argued that in general the blacks would rather live in the hot, lowland (sugar) areas than in the mountains of Jamaica.[100] They contended, however, that the insalubrity of Jamaica was not a simple question of temperature but of atmospheric changes and variations.[101] These atmospheric changes could affect the slaves in several ways. Thus the process of 'seasoning' followed for newly arrived Africans was also thought to be necessary in the movement of slaves from plantation to plantation within the island; heavy mortality was said to occur when slaves were 'removed to a climate which did not suit their constitution'.[102] Such cases were generally said to result from the removal of slaves from dry lowland areas to damp inland situations, where tetanus, catarrh, rheumatism and colds were prevalent.[103] Examples of such heavy mortality consequent on removal can certainly be found,[104] but it is doubtful that the adjustment to a new climate was the only factor involved.

It was widely believed that Jamaica suffered a 'sickly season' in the autumn, when the north wind set in.[105] According to Thomson, 'when the cold damp north winds first begin to prevail in the fall of the year, and during sudden alternations of temperature, from heavy showers suddenly lowering the previous heat, negroes are extremely subject to coughs and colds, in a more or less severe degree'.[106] Although the north wind set in from October, some believed that its effect on mortality was not felt fully until January.[107] There is no doubt that the sickly season affected the whites: the troops suffered their greatest mortality between October and January, when they fell most often to fevers;[108] and patients admitted to the Kingston Public Hospital, most of whom were white and resident in the town, suffered heavily from fevers and dysentery between November and February in the early 1830s.[109] For the slaves, the importance of the sickly season is less certain. At the interior estate of Worthy Park in St. John, where the north wind was said to cause annual attacks of intermittent fever, mortality was at a maximum in the last three months of the year in the period 1812–17, but in December, January and February in 1830–3.[110] At Old Montpelier in St. James, on the other hand, mortality was at a peak in June and July in 1817–20.[111] The morbidity figures for Rose Hall, a coastal sugar estate, reached a peak in the

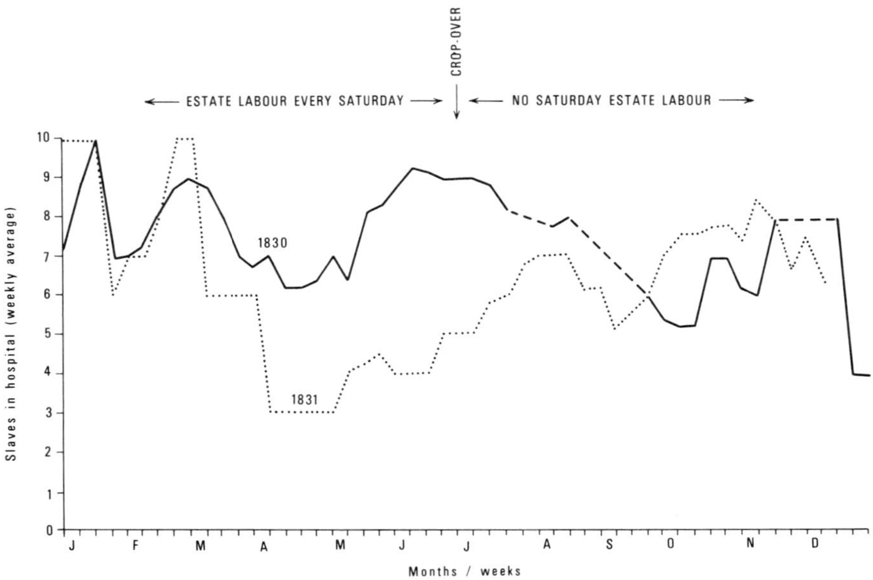

Figure 25. Slaves in hospital at Rose Hall, St. James, 1830 and 1831 (weekly averages).

first two months of the year in 1830 and 1831 (Figure 25). But in 1830 there was another peak in June and July, as at Old Montpelier, suggesting a link with the final weeks of the crop season and the heavy physical demands it entailed. In 1831, however, morbidity was at a minimum at Rose Hall during the crop season, then rose steadily during the months after crop-over when the slaves were not required to labour on the estate on Saturdays. The planters often argued that croptime was a healthy period for the slaves,[112] since they received extra rations of cane juice and molasses, but the available evidence is ambiguous. Yet it does seem that the seasonal pattern of mortality and morbidity was affected more by climatic variations than differences in the labour regime.

If climatic variations determined the seasonal pattern of mortality, they had considerably less influence on the absolute level of mortality experienced by the slaves. At a crude level it is clear that temperature, altitude and slope were not correlated significantly with mortality in 1829–32 (Table A3.2). But there were significant, if slight, positive correlations between the heaviness of the rainfall and male and total death rates ($r = .18$ and .16). The map of mortality at the quadrat level, similarly, does not suggest any relationships with the great areas of stagnant water, the breeding grounds of the malaria and yellow fever vectors (Figure 21); but it has already been shown that these were diseases which affected the whites much more than the slaves.

Thus, whereas the contrast between the mortality experience of Africans and Europeans in Jamaica might be explained by their relative immunities to the 'disease environment' they encountered,[113] the spatial and temporal variations in the mortality suffered by the slave population cannot be seen as a product of different disease environments. It has already been argued that few of the exceptional sugar estates which showed natural increases in 1829–32 can be accounted for in terms of locality or environment – though the wet north-eastern coastal strip was a zone of unmitigated *decrease*. Hence the fact that slaves living on sugar estates and coffee plantations encountered different environments was less important for their mortality experience than the economic-demographic characteristics peculiar to such units.

In the light of these fragmentary data it may be concluded that, apart from absolute wetness, environmental variations between places and between seasons did not play a very important role in the mortality experience of the slaves. If climate had a part, it was cloaked by other, more important, factors.

Finally, since it is clear that no one of the demographic, economic or ecological variables is capable of explaining the pattern of natural increase satisfactorily, an attempt must be made to weigh their relative importance and to discover the combination of factors providing the most efficient explanation of the pattern. A significant set of factors can be tested at the quadrat level for 1829–32, but here eight variables (the sex ratio, three slave-holding size groups, coloured births, African deaths, rainfall and sugar estates) can account for only 18 per cent of the variation in natural increase ($R = .43$). Three of these variables (African deaths, rainfall and sugar estates) explain as much as 17 per cent of the variation, yielding the following estimating equation:

$$Y_{13} = 10.23 - 0.17X_{21} - 1.58X_{39} - 0.04X_{49}$$

where Y_{13} is natural increase per 1,000 (1829–32), X_{21} is percentage deaths African, X_{39} is the number of sugar estates (in 1804), and X_{49} is mean annual rainfall. Thus, in Jamaica immediately before emancipation, slaves were least likely to experience natural increases when they lived on sugar estates in wet areas and when they were predominantly African; natural increases were most likely to occur where the slaves worked in relatively dry places, cultivated the minor staples or raised livestock, and were predominantly creole. Of these factors the most important was the economic, the number of sugar estates in a quadrat accounting for 11 per cent of the variation in natural increase.

Although this multiple regression analysis helps to separate the fundamental variables from the peripheral, the level of explanation achieved remains fairly low. One reason for this is that the analysis does not include some of the factors discussed earlier in this chapter and others are represented only indirectly. It excludes, for example, measures of the amount of labour exacted (such as production per slave) and of variations in nutritional levels. Age structure and crop type are represented only partially and indirectly. Thus the thesis that ill-treatment was the fundamental factor can only be said to be not proven, as a result of the problem of measurement. It is perhaps more important to notice that the variables isolated in the regression equation tended to pull against one another: sugar estates did not have the highest African/creole ratios, nor were they located in the wettest environments. This discordance helps account for the relatively low level of explanation achieved, but it also suggests that part of the problem may lie in the static nature of the analysis.

A dynamic model of economic-demographic development in the slave populations of the New World has been proposed by Curtin.[114] Although it is derived from observed differences between colonies, it may be applied to variations in the rate of natural increase within Jamaica relating to the stage of settlement. Curtin observes a 'curious paradox' in the relationship between the slave trade and demographic change:

> Where economic growth was most rapid, and slave imports were greatest, population decrease from an excess of deaths over births tended to be most severe. . . . On the other hand, colonies without notable economic growth over a few decades began to import fewer slaves. They could then begin to achieve more favourable rates of population growth.[115]

Thus in the sugar colonies 'demographic history tended to fall into a regular pattern over time'.[116] At first the ratio of slave imports to population would be high, producing an abnormal age/sex structure necessarily associated with a high rate of natural decrease. When the colony reached 'full production', argues Curtin, slave imports and population levelled off; as creoles increased in proportion to the African-born the deficit between deaths and births diminished and finally disappeared. Curtin sees the contrasts between the colonies of the British West Indies after the abolition of the slave trade as a good example of this process of development, Barbados reaching the point of natural increase soon after 1807 and Jamaica by the 1840s, whereas Guyana continued to suffer a heavy natural decrease. A similar model, applied strictly to Jamaica, has been argued by Craton who sees the basic factors in the emergence of natural increase as 'the equalization of the sex ratio' and 'the elimination of the African-born'.[117]

Curtin's model is attractive in its simplicity but is not completely satisfactory when applied to the sugar colonies of the British Caribbean or the regional variations within Jamaica.[118] It contains at least one important assumption which has not been tested adequately – the belief that the creole section of a slave population would grow naturally.[119] Thus for Curtin the observed natural decrease resulted from the continued importation of Africans who, because of their age/sex structure, contributed much to mortality but little to fertility, overwhelming the slow growth among the creoles. But whereas it can be shown, for example, that in the case of Jamaica, the sugar parish of Vere, with a natural increase by about 1825, had a high proportion of Africans, this pattern was shared by other sugar parishes which had heavy natural decreases. It is also evident that the parishes with the highest rates of natural increase, Manchester and Port Royal, had the largest African populations and were newly settled regions. But they produced coffee not sugar. Similarly, large percentages of Africans went together with relatively high rates of natural increase in the towns. Again, the declining sugar region of northeastern Jamaica experienced a heavy rate of natural decrease, in a population dominated by creoles. Studies of the age structure of particular slave-holdings are equally conflicting. Thus Craton's study of Worthy Park is essentially an argument for Curtin's model.[120] On other estates, such as Montpelier (Figure 18), it is clear that the creole section tended to be eroded in the same way as the African. So long as the planter believed that there was a cost advantage in purchasing African slaves rather than relying on creole increase, as he generally did until 1807, this is not surprising. The reasons for the continued erosion of the creole section after 1807 are less certain but, if creoles were less fertile than Africans, the initial impetus to fertility from the age/sex structure existing at the time of the abolition of the slave trade disappeared after 1810 until about 1825 when the creole population could begin to grow again.

For the British Caribbean as a whole, the evidence is more favourable to the broad outlines of Curtin's model of economic-demographic development. The heaviest rates of natural decrease occurred in the most recently settled colonies of Trinidad, Guyana and the ceded islands (Figure 26). In most of these colonies, however, there was an improvement in the rate of natural increase between 1817 and 1832 – in contrast to Jamaica – associated with a rapid decrease in the sex ratio and hence an increase in the creole section (Figure 27). The proportion of Africans in the slave populations of the British Caribbean in 1817 ranged from 55 per cent in the Demerara and Essequibo districts of Guyana to 7 per cent in Barbados.[121] (In Jamaica Africans made up 37 per cent of the slave population.) These differences in the size of the African-born section resulted in strong contrasts in age structure, Barbados having a youthful population around 1817 whereas Demerara was dominated by slaves in their thirties and the creole population could grow only slowly (Figure 28). Thus Barbados was able to maintain a positive natural increase throughout the period 1817–32, while the decrease in Demerara followed almost inevitably from the age structure of the slave population. With the exception of St. Lucia, the only colonies to achieve natural increases during this period were those established by the English in the early seventeenth century in the small islands of the eastern Caribbean; and within this group of old-established settlements only Nevis did not conform to the general demographic trend, following instead the pattern set by St. Christopher to about 1825 but then declining again, perhaps as a

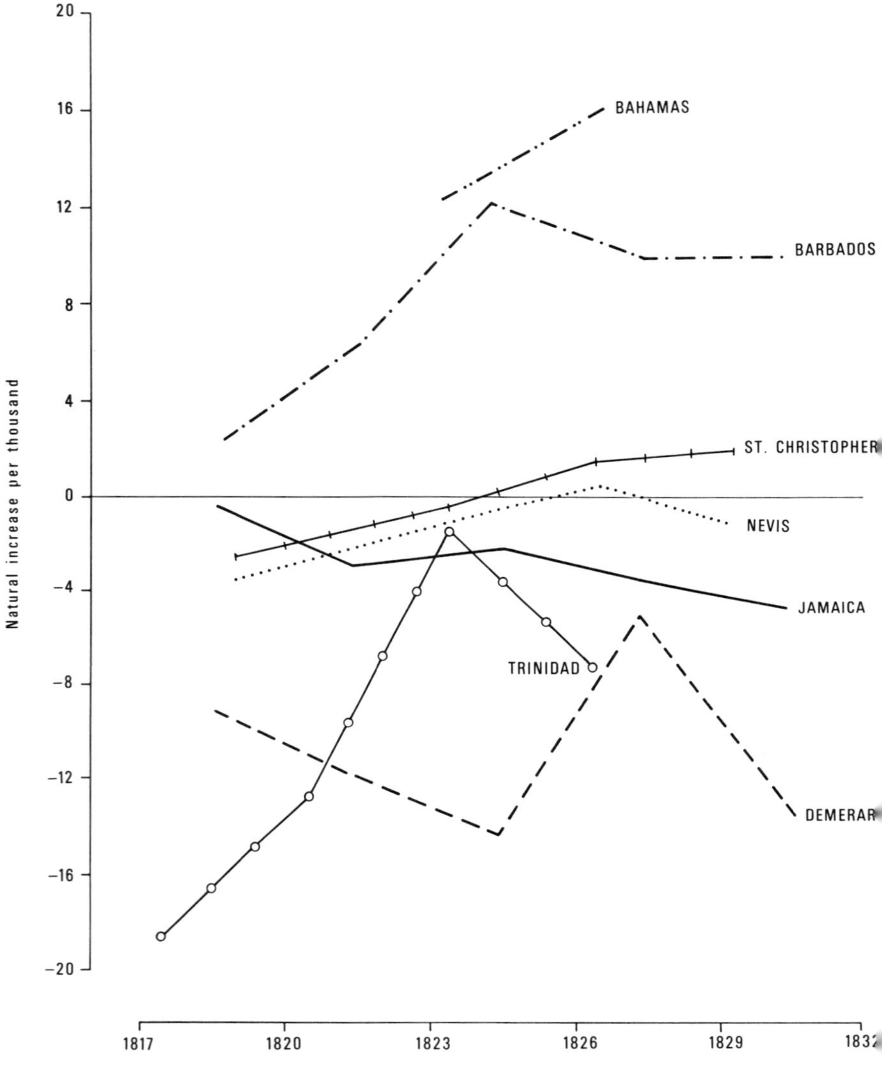

Figure 26. Rates of natural increase in the slave populations of seven British West Indian colonies, 1817–32.

result of the anomalous upward movement of the sex ratio (Figures 26 and 27).

It is obvious, then, that natural increases in the slave populations of the British Caribbean were related to the length of the period of settlement of the colonies. The tardiness of Jamaica in achieving a natural increase might be seen simply as a result of the scope for the continued expansion of settlement in the island. The parish of Vere, for example, might be looked on as analogous to Barbados, both places being long settled, strictly monocultural, lack-

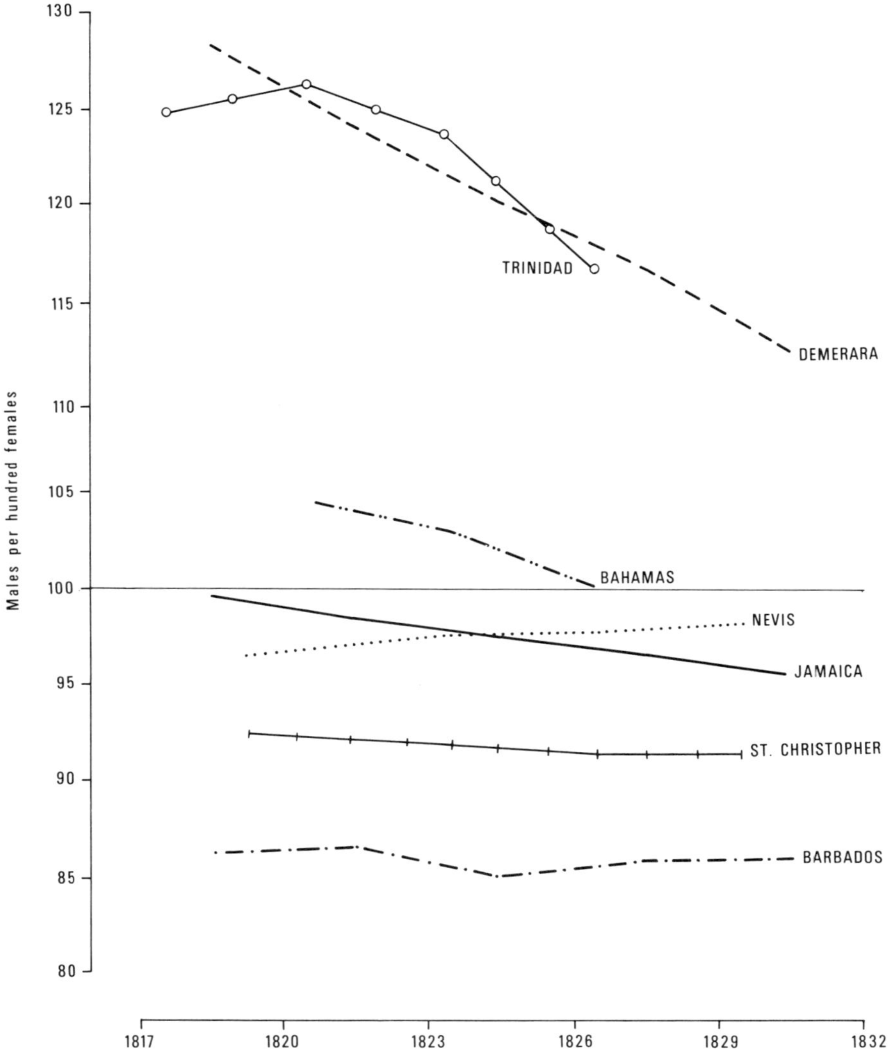

Figure 27. Sex ratios of the slave populations of seven British West Indian colonies, 1817–32.

ing a provision grounds system, and similar in topography. But the anomalies within Jamaica, noted above, are too numerous to be ignored – the fact that the areas which were most recently settled and had the largest proportion of Africans also showed the highest rates of natural increase, for instance. Thus the variations in the rate of natural increase within Jamaica cannot be taken merely to represent particular stages in the evolution of a single process of economic-demographic development. Although it seems certain that such a process (or processes) existed, it is also clear that its nature varied according

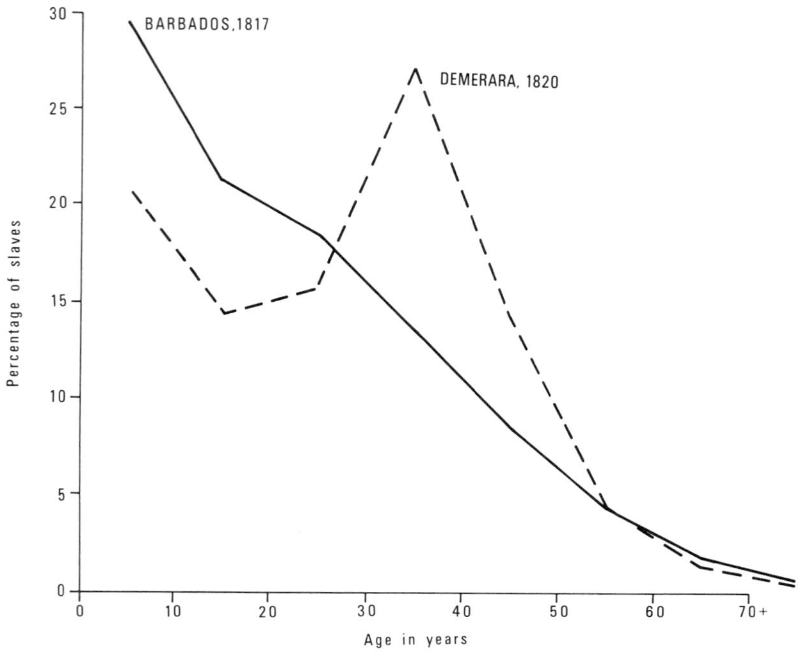

Figure 28. Age profiles of the slave populations of Barbados, 1817, and Demerara, 1820.

to the type of economic activity in which the slaves were employed and, less certainly, according to the 'disease environment' to which they were exposed. Wherever slaves were not engaged in the production of sugar, their chances of survival were greater. Thus in the Bahamas, where the economy depended on cotton, salt and wrecking, the rate of natural increase was high in spite of an apparently unfavourable sex ratio (Figures 26 and 27). Throughout the colonies, regardless of their stage of settlement, the urban slave populations increased significantly.[122] On the other hand, the ending of the slave trade did not always lead to a natural increase among the creole population; in Guyana the 'creoles' continued to decline until the end of the nineteenth century, probably for strictly epidemiological reasons.[123]

Variations in the rate of natural increase of the slave population of Jamaica, between the abolition of the slave trade and emancipation, depended on the type of economic activity in which the slaves were employed. But the precise reasons for this relationship are difficult to isolate because of the interconnection of the demographic and epidemiological factors associated with particular types of economic activity. Certainly no form of employment was strictly incompatible with the emergence of natural increase over time. At rates controlled by the various types of economic activity, the internal dynamic of the slave population did lead eventually to a position of increase.

CHAPTER 7

COLOUR, FAMILY AND FERTILITY

Colour

In discussing the fertility of the slave population in the previous chapter it was noted that because white, free coloured and free black fathers were necessarily ignored, an error intruded into the calculation of the birth rates. It was argued that this omission did not have a significant impact on the rates since the number of such fathers was generally small.[1] Between 1829 and 1832, however, 18.4 per cent of all registered slave births in Jamaica were coloured, and it is probable that more than half of these were fathered by whites (Table 26). Even if their numbers were not great, it seems that the free males were a particularly fecund group. It is necessary to account for this fecundity and to ask whether the women of colour among the slaves were similarly fertile.

In the United States of America all persons of African ancestry, of whatever proportion, were lumped together as 'Negro' both socially and legally.[2] In the Hispanic American colonies, on the other hand, the range of gradations of colour and racial mixture was almost infinite.[3] The British colonies in the Caribbean fell into an intermediate position between these two extremes. In Jamaica there were generally recognized to be four grades of colour between black and white,[4] and two between white and black, as shown in the diagram.

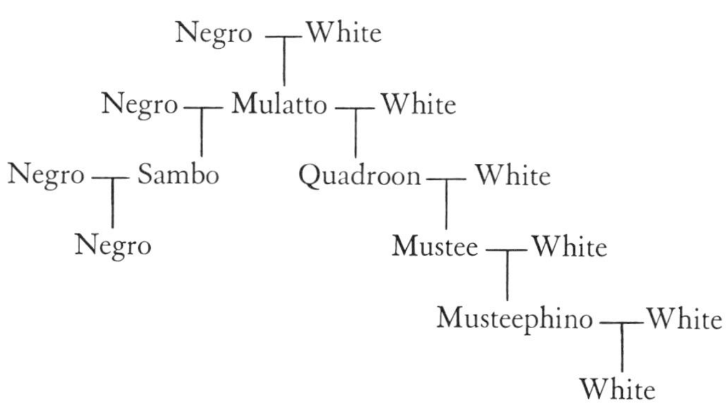

Since the scheme was structured by the whites it emphasized the gradations between black and white; in 1790 Moreton wrote that 'in my opinion, Mongrels, though thirty generations distant from blacks blood, cannot be real

Table 26. *Births and deaths of slaves of colour, 1829–32*

Parish	Percentage coloured				Percentage white paternity	
		Deaths				
	Births	Males	Females	Total	Births of colour	Total births
Westmoreland	23.6	9.6	8.7	9.2	55.8	13.2
Hanover	26.6	9.6	8.1	9.0	60.9	16.2
St. James	25.0	7.9	9.6	8.7	62.7	15.7
Trelawny	23.6	9.6	8.3	9.0	71.3	16.8
St. Elizabeth	16.6	9.2	9.3	9.2	40.4	6.7
Manchester	13.1	2.8	2.8	2.8	52.7	6.9
St. Ann	16.8	7.4	5.8	6.6	48.3	8.1
Clarendon	13.0	6.6	3.8	5.3	57.1	7.4
Vere	14.9	8.2	6.3	7.2	66.3	9.9
St. Dorothy	10.8	2.9	5.0	4.9	56.4	6.1
St. Thomas-in-the-Vale	16.6	6.5	7.5	6.9	64.8	10.8
St. John	14.9	5.5	7.9	6.7	67.9	10.1
St. Catherine	26.2	9.4	11.4	10.3	53.4	14.0
St. Mary	16.7	8.0	6.8	7.4	61.7	10.3
St. Andrew	15.3	5.5	5.9	5.7	54.5	8.3
Port Royal	12.5	5.0	2.5	3.9	73.3	9.2
St. David	12.3	5.0	5.3	5.1	73.0	9.0
St. George	13.1	4.4	5.8	5.0	46.2	6.1
Portland	15.0	7.1	4.8	6.0	49.6	7.4
St. Thomas-in-the-East	14.2	5.7	6.9	6.2	66.5	9.4
Kingston	34.8	11.8	11.8	11.8	49.9	17.4
Total	18.4	7.4	7.2	7.3	58.2	10.7

Source: R.R.S.

whites'.[5] But the slaves, though well aware of the implications of their place in the scale, do not seem to have used a more finely graded system, except that they may have observed the implicit distinctions in social status more closely than the whites on the side approaching blackness.[6] The whites commonly used two kinds of generalization: 'Negro' and 'slave' were synonymous (though by 1807 this was more often seen to be a falsity), and any slave of colour, regardless of his place in the scale, could be termed 'mulatto' or 'brown' or 'yellow'. The words Negro and black were interchangeable, except that the whites distinguished albinos and in the Returns of Registrations of Slaves for 1832 one slave was described as a 'yellow negro'.[7] When the precise classification of a slave of colour was uncertain he was sometimes called a 'mongrel'. Most of the masters took care to observe the gradations of the system but, to the extent that they generalized, figures derived from the Returns of Registrations of Slaves tend to understate the total size of the coloured slave population and to overstate the mulatto proportion of it.

In the returns for 1832 the most systematic data relating to colour are those for births and deaths (Table 26). Continued miscegenation need not necessarily have resulted in a growing coloured population, but in practice the process was probably cumulative. Thus it may be assumed that the percentage of births coloured was greater than the total percentage of slaves who were coloured. Some passed into the free community, but it is easy to dispose of the view that the whites generally freed their slave children:[8] in the period 1829–32, 4,041 coloured slave children were born (at least 2,000 of them having white fathers) but only 796 were manumized. Again, it can be assumed that the percentage of deaths coloured was less than the total. The precise relationship between births, deaths and total coloured is difficult to establish because complete returns are rare. But the pattern on ten estates in the period 1829–32 (Table 27) suggests that the total percentage tended to follow the percentages of births and deaths closely, and that it fell closer to the deaths than the births.[9] Only at Old Montpelier did the percentage of coloured deaths exceed the total coloured. The births represent the pattern of miscegenation within only three years, hence the relationship tends to be

Table 27. *Slaves of colour on ten properties, 1829–32 (percentages)*

Property	Total slaves coloured 1832	Births coloured 1829–32	Deaths coloured 1829–32
St. James			
Roehampton	7.5	25.0	0.0
Old Montpelier	8.1	10.7	11.7
Fairfield	6.3	14.3	4.3
Rose Hall	18.2	50.0	0.0
Hanover			
Paradise	22.2	57.1	21.4
Barbican	14.5	50.0	13.6
Point	17.3	39.4	16.7
Trelawny			
George's Valley	19.2	26.7	[a]
Manchester			
Albion	5.2	15.4	4.0
Maidstone	9.1	50.0	0.0

[a] Not known.

Sources: (1) R.R.S., Liber 129, f. 6; *P.P.*, 1832 (127), Lords, Vol. 1, p. 36; (2) R.R.S., Liber 129, f. 32; Old Montpelier Estate Account Book (Institute of Jamaica); (3) R.R.S., Liber 129, f. 47; (4) *Ibid.*, f. 40; J. Shore, *In Old St. James* (Kingston, 1911), p. 140; (5) R.R.S., Liber 130, f. 199; (6) *Ibid.*, f. 201; (7) *Ibid.*, f. 203; (8) R.R.S., Liber 134, f. 27; (9) R.R.S., Liber 129, f. 110; (10) *Ibid.*, f. 122.

more capricious. Assuming that the pattern displayed by the properties in Table 27 was normal, it may be estimated from the percentage of coloured deaths in the island as a whole that in 1832 about 10 per cent of the slaves were coloured.

This estimate can now be compared with those of Stewart, Eisner, Duncker and Brathwaite. Stewart, writing in 1823, believed that 'people of colour in a state of slavery' formed 'about a tenth part' of the total slave population (or 34,500).[10] This appears to be a good estimate, but recent writers on slavery have tended to reduce it significantly. Eisner calculated that in 1834 at least 23,000 slaves were coloured (7 per cent); she determined this figure by working back from the number of coloured people recorded in the 1844 census and subtracting a contemporary estimate of the free coloured population.[11] Duncker put the slave coloured population at only 15,362 in 1830 (5 per cent), but her handling of the statistics is unsatisfactory.[12] Brathwaite's discussion tends to push the proportion even lower, since he holds that the figure of 15,000 slaves coloured could be applied to 1823 as well as 1830.[13] But the alternative estimates seem to rest on less solid ground than that advanced above, since they depend heavily on contemporary estimates rather than on the analysis of systematic records. Flaws in the registration data used to derive the estimate of 10 per cent slave coloured in 1832 tend to make it a conservative one. By way of comparison, it may be noted that slaves of colour made up 7.7 per cent of the total slave population of the United States in 1850, and 10.4 per cent in 1860.[14]

Slaves of colour were concentrated into the urban areas of Jamaica. Kingston was most important absolutely, but some of the larger towns, especially in the west, had greater proportions of coloured slaves. In Lucea 56 per cent of births in the period 1829–32 were coloured, in Savanna la Mar 50 per cent, in Montego Bay 46 per cent, in Spanish Town 41 per cent, but in Kingston only 34 per cent. Slaves of colour were almost as numerous in all of the parishes of the western county of Cornwall, however, as in urban Kingston and St. Catherine (Table 26). In the remainder of the parishes the proportion was fairly uniform, though coloured slaves seem to have been least common in Manchester and Port Royal, the recently settled coffee parishes which were dominated by Africans.[15] When the distribution of coloured births during the period 1829–32 is considered at the quadrat level, some more definite areas of concentration appear: the far western tip of the island, the coastal fringe of St. James and Trelawny, and southern St. Elizabeth. Slaves of colour were least common in the inland regions of the eastern end of the island.

In addition to these variations in the spatial distribution of slaves of colour there were variations in the structure of the coloured group. Of the births, the largest group of coloured slaves comprised those classified as sambo, while the other gradations became less numerous the further they were removed from their black ancestors (Table 28). But of the deaths, the mulattoes easily

Table 28. *Births and deaths by colour, 1829–32*

Parish	Negro	Sambo	Mulatto	Quadroon	Mustee	Unknown	Total
Births							
Westmoreland	1,070	146	111	63	10	10	1,410
Hanover	989	140	138	57	23	9	1,356
St. James	1,218	151	165	67	22	4	1,627
Trelawny	1,355	120	142	125	31	0	1,773
St. Elizabeth	1,307	155	77	28	0	1	1,568
Manchester	1,243	89	87	12	0	8	1,439
St. Ann	1,595	166	115	32	8	5	1,921
Clarendon	949	61	51	25	5	4	1,095
Vere	509	30	39	14	6	25	623
St. Dorothy	321	17	18	4	0	0	360
St. Thomas-in-the-Vale	571	40	45	23	6	2	687
St. John	325	19	28	10	0	2	384
St. Catherine	432	55	44	17	2	7	557
St. Mary	1,130	87	90	41	9	13	1,370
St. Andrew	865	71	72	12	1	1	1,022
Port Royal	419	16	38	6	0	0	479
St. David	462	17	28	18	0	3	528
St. George	688	56	40	7	1	1	793
Portland	460	41	26	13	1	14	555
St. Thomas-in-the-East	1,596	88	97	66	12	0	1,859
Kingston	464	127	93	22	6	14	726
Total	17,968	1,689	1,547	662	143	123	22,132
Deaths							
Males	13,230	329	528	175	22	306	14,590
Females	10,998	275	378	163	31	265	12,110
Total	24,228	604	906	338	53	571	26,700

Source: R.R.S.

outweighed the sambo slaves. Whereas mulatto births exceeded sambo in half of the parishes, only in Kingston, St. Catherine and St. Thomas-in-the-Vale did sambo deaths exceed mulatto. This contrast was in part a result of the generation between mulatto and sambo. As the mulatto group grew in size as a result of white paternity, the males, who were the least likely to be manumized, were rarely able to find coloured mates and thus most commonly fathered sambo children.

Discussions of miscegenation in the slave societies of the British Caribbean tend to focus on the role of the whites, and especially on the sex ratio of the white group.[16] It is argued that those white men who could not find partners of their own colour, because of the preponderance of males in the white group, turned to the free coloured or the slave women.[17] In 1832, John Baillie, who had lived 27 years in Jamaica, admitted that he could not name a single overseer or bookkeeper who did not possess a mistress, and it was notorious that some attorneys kept a mistress on every estate in their charge and that they used to tour these estates indulging in orgies of fornication.[18] Often the life of the white bookkeeper was portrayed as a melancholy affair; he had to keep watch at night and got little rest:

> A respite very short to sleep or to wake,
> And to play with a yellow, or a black snake.[19]

The slave, on the other hand, could not refuse the advances of the whites:

> Me fum'd when me no condescend;
> Me fum'd too if me do it;
> Me no have no one for 'tand my friend,
> So me am forc'd to do it.[20]

The size of the slave coloured population, then, might be expected to increase along with the ratio of whites to slaves.

In order to test the role of the white/slave ratio it is necessary to estimate the size and distribution of the white population. At the first census, in 1844, there were 15,776 whites in Jamaica.[21] Thus Eisner's estimate of 15,000 in 1834 appears rather too low, while contemporary estimates of 30–35,000 between 1807 and 1830 do not seem to be supported by the fragmentary detailed parish data.[22] All that is required here, however, is a picture of the scatter of the whites and, as there is no evidence of a great redistribution of whites between 1832 and 1844, it is reasonable to use the census figures (which provide the first systematic breakdown by parish) for comparison with the slave coloured population during the period 1829–32 at the parish level.[23] At the quadrat level no reliable data are available, so a rough rule has been applied: one white has been attributed to each holding with less than 21 slaves, 1.5 to those with 21–100 slaves, and two to those with more than 100 slaves.[24] This gives a total of 8,243 whites in the rural quadrats. Assuming that the distribution of the urban whites between Kingston and the outports did not change radically between 1832 and 1844, and that the ratio of slaves to whites was roughly the same in Kingston and the other towns, it can be estimated that there were 8,500 urban whites in 1832. Adding the rural and urban estimates gives a rounded total of 16,750 whites in 1832, which approximates to the 1844 total and thus justifies the method of calculating the distribution of the rural whites; the total itself is not important, merely serving to validate the estimate of the rural white/slave ratio.

At the parish level, coloured births were correlated significantly with the white/slave ratio ($r = .63$).[25] But the correlations with coloured deaths are not significant at the 99 per cent level of probability. Hence, although it is true that slave births of colour became more common as the number of whites increased in proportion to the slave population, the relationship does not provide an entirely satisfactory explanation of the size of the slave coloured population.

At the quadrat level, small, but significant, correlations are found between the rural white/slave ratio and the percentage of coloured births and deaths in 1829–32. In contrast to the pattern at the parish level, however, these correlations are negative; coloured births ($r = -.14$) and deaths ($r = -.26$) increased in inverse proportion to the number of whites per slave. But these coefficients are too small to permit generalization, and exclude the urban pattern.

The hypothesis underlying the preceding analysis is a crude one, that the size of the slave coloured population was a function of the number of white males who could force themselves upon the slave women. Several vital factors are ignored in this approach to the question. It excludes white transients (such as seamen and the touring attorney), it omits the sex ratio of the whites and their internal forms of family life, it ignores the large group of slave and free coloured, and it leaves out of account the potential availability of slave women. The importance of such complicating factors can be shown by examining the coloured children fathered by whites. (Here it is assumed that only those classified as sambo did not have white fathers, though in fact mulattoes could be the progeny of two mulattoes or a quadroon and a sambo.) At the parish level, a negative correlation, significant at the 95 per cent level of probability, is found between the percentage of coloured births resulting from white paternity and the white/slave ratio ($r = -.50$); thus the greater the number of whites relative to the slaves, the fewer of the coloured births did they father.

In 1844 the white sex ratio stood at 143.1 males per 100 females, ranging from 107.5 in Kingston to 291.8 in Vere.[26] It is probable that the ratios were higher in the period of slavery,[27] but the fragmentary data available suggest that the general pattern of contrasts between parishes was similar to that in 1844. Comparing these sex ratios with the percentages of births and deaths of slaves of colour during 1829–32 (Table 26) suggests that there was no significant relationship between the two. If anything, the percentage of slave coloured decreased as the white sex ratio rose. This impression is confirmed by plotting the percentage of total slave births fathered by whites against the white sex ratio (Table 26). Although this relationship between the apparent availability of white women and the fathering of large numbers of slave children by whites might suggest that it conceals a contrast between rural and urban white family patterns, it must be noted that the percentages of total slave births fathered by whites in Hanover, St. James and Trelawny were exceeded only by Kingston. Thus it is clear that the white sex ratio can explain no more of the variation in the size of the slave coloured population, at the parish level, than can the white/slave ratio.

Of the alternative explanations, the most promising is the sex ratio of the slaves. At the parish level there are strong correlations between the slave sex ratio and births of colour ($r = -.77$) and coloured deaths ($r = -.78$) in the period 1829–32. The greater the excess of slave women the larger the

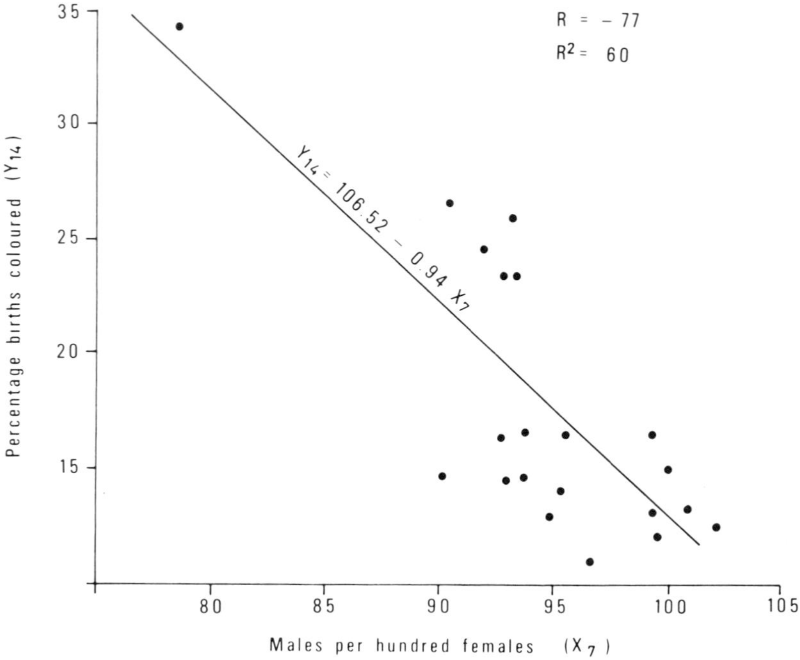

Figure 29. Regression of slave sex ratio (1832) on percentage of slave births coloured (1829–32).

slave coloured population. Of the variation in coloured births, 60 per cent can be accounted for by the slave sex ratio (Figure 29), compared to only 39 per cent by the white/slave ratio. The link is even stronger if the sex ratio of 1817 is considered: the correlation with coloured births in the period 1829–32 was —.78 and with deaths —.85. This pattern may have become stronger after 1807, and especially after 1820, as the sexes approached an equality; but the regional inequalities probably existed even before 1807. Within the towns and in the Accounts Produce sample of properties the relationship worked in the same direction, but the correlations were not significant.[28] At the quadrat level the link was inverted, though once again the correlations were not significant.[29]

Several reasons for the link between colour and the slave sex ratio can be advanced.[30] A simple one is that where the slave women could less readily find slave mates they were more amenable to the advances of the whites and free coloureds. Where females formed the largest majority, in the towns, white and free coloured males were also present in considerable proportions; but the size of the slave coloured populations continued to reflect the relative femininity of the towns. The contrast between the towns and the rural parishes becomes even greater if the age-specific sex ratios of the slaves are considered (Figure 13). But in the towns the sex ratio of the whites was better balanced than it was in the country, hence the high percentages of sambo births in Kingston and St. Catherine. Here the free coloured males, who were handicapped in the competition for free coloured females by the status of the whites, mated with black slaves. There were also said to be large settlements of free coloured in St. Elizabeth and the Portland district of Vere,[31] and the 'free blacks and browns' were said to be 'much in the habit of skulking around the negro houses and grounds'.[32] It has been noted already that whites fathered the smallest proportion of coloured slaves in St. Elizabeth.

Of the types of economic enterprise identified from the Accounts Produce properties in 1832, coloured births were most common amongst the slaves employed on wharves (71 per cent, see Table 24). The wharves also had the most masculine population of all the groups; the slave males, however, seem to have had partners on neighbouring plantations where they could find provision grounds,[33] and the wharves were the centre of a large transient white group. Afer the wharves, the largest slave coloured populations were found on sugar estates, and the smallest on coffee and pimento properties. On sugar estates masculinity was comparatively low (92 males per 100 females), whereas on pimento properties it was high (108) and on coffee plantations the sexes were evenly balanced (101). But these contrasts are also suggestive of different types of social relations. At the quadrat level there were significant correlations between sugar estates and coloured births ($r = .22$) and deaths ($r = .34$). At the parish level, these correlations remain positive but are not significant. On the coffee plantations the percentage of Africans was much higher than it was on sugar estates, and by 1829–32 the Africans were unlikely to contribute to births of colour. A relationship can also be identified between pens, which were associated with resident proprietorship,[34] and a low proportion of slave births fathered by whites ($r = -.57$); this link is the corollary of the role of the free coloured in these parishes.

Although married white men had sexual relations with slaves,[35] the resident, settled paterfamilias was less likely to do so than the bachelor, transient bookkeeper or overseer living on a large isolated sugar estate. According to Kelly, few of the white mercantile class kept mistresses by 1830, though the estate overseers continued in this tradition.[36] The relationship can be tested by examining the link between colour and slave-holding size, since size was closely tied to absenteeism. At the parish level, holding-size was negatively correlated with coloured births ($r = -.62$) and deaths ($r = -.54$), because of the heavy weighting from the small units of Kingston. When this urban bias is removed, at the quadrat level, the correlations with size are positive but small. A much clearer pattern is found in the Accounts Produce properties; these show a fairly steady increase in coloured births with increasing size (Table 25). Miscegenation seems to have been at a minimum on holdings of between 21 and 100 slaves, the units falling between the urban and large-scale plantation patterns.

To summarize in a schematic way, the slaves were most often coloured in the towns, where they mixed both with the white and free coloured populations; to an only slightly lesser extent the slaves bore children of colour on large sugar estates (where the slave sex ratio approximated that of the towns), the fathers most often being whites; miscegenation involving slaves was at a minimum on the medium-sized plantations producing coffee and pimento where the masters tended to be resident, though in some of the major pen areas the slaves formed liaisons with the free coloured population.

In spite of the complications, the size of the slave coloured population of Jamaica about 1832 can be explained fairly satisfactorily. At the parish level, seven of the relevant factors taken together can account for 87 per cent of the variation in coloured births,[37] but three of them can explain as much as 83 per cent ($R = .91$), giving the following estimating equation:

$$Y_{14} = 87.80 - 0.68X_7 - 0.28X_{27} + 0.07X_{38}$$

where Y_{14} is the percentage of births coloured during 1829–32, X_7 is the slave sex ratio in 1832, X_{27} is the number of slaves per white, and X_{38} is the number of sugar estates in 1834. Of these factors the most basic were the slave sex ratio and the white/slave ratio.[38] Thus the ending of the slave trade must have meant a fairly rapid increase in the size of the slave coloured population, because of the decline in the sex ratio as well as the cutting-off of African (black) increments to the population.[39] Its rate of growth is uncertain but, around 1834, slaves of colour (on sugar estates at least) were concentrated into the younger age-groups and, even allowing for manumission, it follows that the slave coloured population was expanding significantly.

The dynamics of the process of miscegenation, which may seem submerged in the preceding structural analysis, can best be understood by examining the life histories of particular slave groups. Genealogies can be extracted from the Returns of Registrations of Slaves, in a partial fashion, by tracing links through the maternal line. Nothing is known about the fathers, but their colour can be inferred. Such partial genealogies have been reconstructed for five slave-holdings: Barbican and Paradise, sugar estates located near Lucea in Hanover;[40] Old and New Montpelier sugar estates in St. James; and Shettlewood livestock pen in Hanover.[41] For the first two properties the genealogies include only slaves alive in 1832, whereas the others cover the period 1817–32. Slave coloured births ranged from 7 per cent at New Montpelier to 57 per cent at Paradise. The properties also varied in their size, rates of natural increase and isolation from towns.

Examples of the partial genealogies reconstructed are shown in Figure 30. For Barbican and Paradise each of the male (Δ) and female (O) symbols represents an individual slave alive in 1832. The examples from the Montpeliers and Shettlewood are more detailed, including all kin living between 1817 and 1832, and the households in which they lived in 1825; occupa-

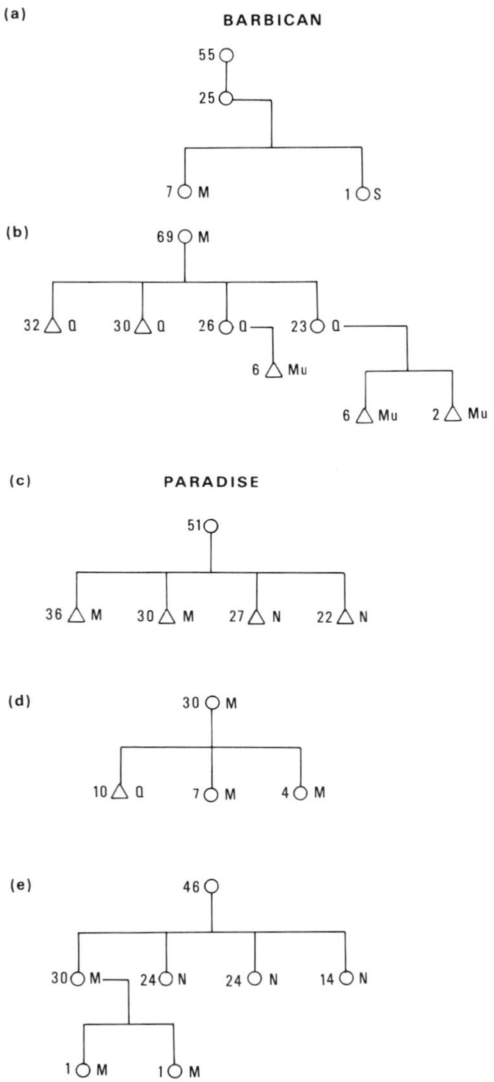

Figure 30. Genealogies of various slaves attached to Barbican, Paradise, Old Montpelier, New Montpelier and Shettlewood. Each male (Δ) and female (O) symbol represents an individual slave. The number to the left of the symbol gives age. The letter to the right gives colour, if the slave was not black (S = sambo; M = mulatto; Q = quadroon; Mu = mustee). For Barbican and Paradise, ages apply to 1832; for the other examples, they apply to 1825. Numbers below symbols give the list-number of the household in which the slave lived, in 1825, for Old and New Montpelier, and Shettlewood (see text). Occupation, in 1825, is given below the symbol for Old Montpelier. Dates under symbols indicate year of birth (if 1825–32) or death (1817–25).

(f)

OLD MONTPELIER

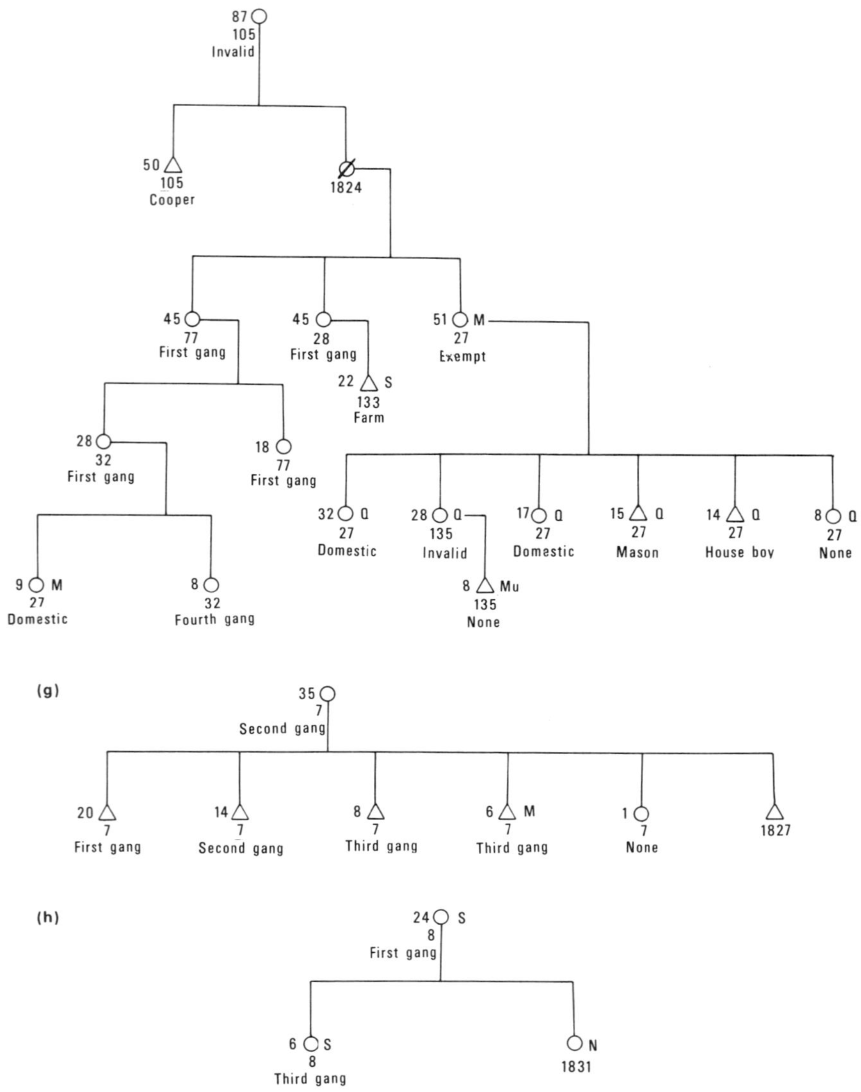

Figure 30. Genealogies of various slaves attached to Barbican, Paradise, Old Montpelier, New Montpelier and Shettlewood. Each male (Δ) and female (O) symbol represents an individual slave. The number to the left of the symbol gives age. The letter to the right gives colour, if the slave was not black (S = sambo; M = mulatto; Q = quadroon; Mu = mustee). For Barbican and Paradise, ages apply to 1832; for the other examples, they apply to 1825. Numbers below symbols give the list-number of the household in which the slave lived, in 1825, for Old and New Montpelier, and Shettlewood (see text). Occupation, in 1825, is given below the symbol for Old Montpelier. Dates under symbols indicate year of birth (if 1825–32) or death (1817–25). (Continued)

(i) NEW MONTPELIER

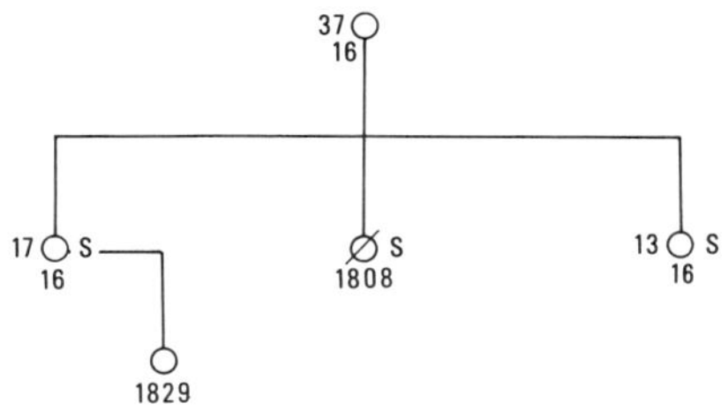

(j) SHETTLEWOOD

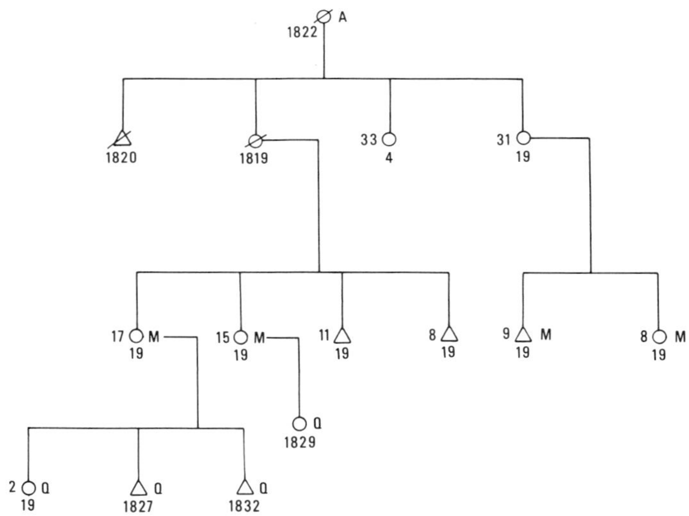

Figure 30. Genealogies of various slaves attached to Barbican, Paradise, Old Montpelier, New Montpelier and Shettlewood. Each male (Δ) and female (O) symbol represents an individual slave. The number to the left of the symbol gives age. The letter to the right gives colour, if the slave was not black (S = sambo; M = mulatto; Q = quadroon; Mu = mustee). For Barbican and Paradise, ages apply to 1832; for the other examples, they apply to 1825. Numbers below symbols give the list-number of the household in which the slave lived, in 1825, for Old and New Montpelier, and Shettlewood (see text). Occupation, in 1825, is given below the symbol for Old Montpelier. Dates under symbols indicate year of birth (if 1825–32) or death (1817–25). (Continued)

tions are known only for Old Montpelier. The completely black genealogies reconstructed were generally three times as numerous as those containing slaves of colour, except that at Paradise there were ten of each. Taking only those genealogies which included more than two generations, the proportion containing slaves of colour increased to one-half on all the properties except Old Montpelier (one-fifth) and New Montpelier (one-quarter). But if allowance is made for connections through the paternal line, it is probable that by 1834 the majority of slaves were in some way kin to coloured people.

Contemporary opinions regarding the process of miscegenation are largely confirmed by the sample genealogies. It was very rare for a slave woman to bear children darker than herself. Paradoxically, the chances of her doing so decreased as her colour approached whiteness. The quadroon women had all of their children by white men. Only one example of a mulatto woman having a child by a black man is found; and she had earlier had a quadroon child (by a white).[42] It was more common for sambo women to have black children, by black men (Figure 30, h and i). A similar pattern emerges if the chances of a woman bearing a child of her own colour are considered. No quadroon woman had children as dark as herself. But some mulatto women had mulatto children, and some sambo women mothered samboes (Figure 30, d, e, h). Most of the children of black women, on the other hand, were black. For the slave male, the pattern was reversed. The lighter his colour the less likely he was to father children lighter than himself or even of his own colour. A classical example of the process of selective mating, systematically producing 'clearer' children of higher caste, is found in genealogy (f) of Figure 30. Smaller cross-sections of the same process appear in several of the other partial genealogies. The slaves gradually moved from field labour to employment about the great house and, if the process had continued, the children of these mothers would have become legally white and free within one or two generations.

These contrasts in the pattern of miscegenation for slave men and women at different positions along the scale of colour gradations are also evident in the life cycles of individual slave women. Quadroon women, obviously, had all of their children by white men. Mulatto, sambo and black women, however, sometimes had children by men of different colours at different stages of their lives. For all of these women the movement was from white towards black fathers. Some mulatto women had all of their children by whites, having up to seven registered births over periods of up to 25 years; some continued to bear quadroons even after they passed the age of 40 years (Figure 30, b and f). It is difficult to say whether such cases represent stable unions, but mulatto women were said to lose their attractiveness (to whites) after 25 years of age,[43] so it seems unlikely that they would find new white mates when they became mature. None of the sambo or black slave women, on the other hand, appear to have had long-term relationships with whites. But a few cases can be found of black women having long-term unions with mulatto men (Figure 30, i). When mulatto women lost their white mates (generally in their early twenties) they turned to other mulattoes, or perhaps quadroons or mustees; the latter cannot be documented because there were no accepted designations for the children of such unions. Some of the black women passed from white men to mulattoes but the majority turned to black men. There were also contrasts between African and creole blacks. No case of an African woman bearing a coloured child occurred on the five sample properties. With the exception of Shettlewood Pen, it was also unusual for the daughters of Africans to have children by whites. It may be that the family structure of the Africans – which, it will be argued below, was most often nuclear or polygynous – operated against racial mixing, but the Africans were also older and less physically attractive to the whites than the creoles.[44]

In some ways the black slave woman was less constricted by the colour-caste system than the coloured woman was.[45] Lewis recounted that Psyche, a black creole of Cornwall Estate in Westmoreland, had been one of the wives of Nicholas, a mulatto, but had quarrelled with him after bearing a black child, and left him for a white bookkeeper.[46] But in fact it was very rare for a black woman to bear black children and then coloured ones (Figure 30, g). This has important implications for the understanding of the pattern of miscegenation. Either the white males' 'right of control over the bodies of black women'[47] was not exercised without regard to slave family structure and the reactions of the women, or the slave women aborted pregnancies resulting from rape by the whites. The latter alternative is an interesting one, but it leaves unexplained why abortion was not resorted to by those black women who did not already have black children. If the former is plausible, it would appear that the process of miscegenation followed rules known and obeyed by the whites as well as the slaves and that direct physical compulsion was perhaps unimportant relative to the psychosocial imperatives.[48] These rules were only in part a reflection of the somatic preferences of the whites. But the rules could be followed much more readily in the years after 1807, as the female and creole sections of the slave population grew and slaves of colour became increasingly numerous.

Colour and fertility

When they discussed what they saw as the fundamental preventive (fertility-depressing) checks to the growth of the slave population, the whites were silent on their own direct contribution to the fertility of the population and the role of the slave women of colour. But it seems that there was in fact a positive connection between miscegenation and the level of fertility in the slave population.

At the quadrat and town levels, there were positive correlations between the percentage of slave births coloured and the total birth rate during 1829–32.

Table 29. *Colour-specific fertility at Old Montpelier, New Montpelier and Shettlewood, 1817–32,* (Births per 1,000 woman-years)[a]

Age-group	Colour of mother: Sambo	Mulatto	Quadroon	Total coloured	Black creoles	All women: Creoles	Africans
15–19	67	135	63	103 (68)	23(646)	32(714)	— (0)
20–24	71	208	0	128 (47)	102(469)	105(516)	— (0)
25–29	0	214	0	113 (53)	112(376)	112(429)	64 (63)
30–34	0	306	0	125 (32)	72(289)	75(321)	99(162)
35–39	0	100	0	42 (24)	78(282)	75(306)	82(392)
40–44	0	250	—	91 (11)	53(208)	55(219)	12(489)
General fertility rate	27	190	22	106(235)	70(2270)	72(2505)	53(1106)

[a] Woman-years given in parentheses.
Source: See Table 22, p. 117, above.

But the correlation was significant at the 99 per cent level of probability only for the quadrats, and the connection was not strong ($r = .27$). At the parish level, the correlation was negative but not significant. The positive connection is seen more clearly in colour-specific fertility rates. These have been calculated for Old and New Montpelier sugar estates and Shettlewood Pen, 1817–32, for which the age-specific fertility rates have already been discussed (Table 22). The fertility of slave women of colour – samboes, mulattoes and quadroons – was significantly higher than that of black creole women, on this group of properties (Table 29). The contrast with African women was even greater. Only in the 35–39 years age-group did the fertility of black women exceed that of coloured women. But the strongest contrast occurred in the 15–19 years age-group where the coloureds were almost five times as fertile as the blacks. Thereafter the difference in the fertility of the two groups was much less impressive. Of the women of colour the most fertile were always the mulattoes. Thus fertility did not increase with increasing whiteness; this was the corollary of the fact that the quadroons were the least fertile of all the women, including the blacks, and that they were the most exclusive in looking for white fathers for their children.

A similar pattern emerges from the distribution of births of colour. In the 15–19 years age-group 50 per cent of all slave births were coloured, at Old and New Montpelier and Shettlewood; whites fathered almost 40 per cent of all births to mothers in this age-group (Table 30). Thereafter the percentage of coloured births dropped to a much lower level, decreasing with age. Quadroon births were much more numerous than mulatto or sambo, and this accounts for the high fertility of the mulatto mothers. But some of the mulatto women lost their white mates as they aged, yet maintained a high

Table 30. *Births of colour at Old Montpelier, New Montpelier and Shettlewood, 1817–32*

	Number of births						
Mother's age-group	Sambo	Mulatto	Quadroon	Mustee	Total coloured	Black	Percentage of births coloured
15–19	3	2	5	1	11	11	50.0
20–24	3	—	4	—	7	47	12.9
25–29	2	2	6	—	10	42	19.2
30–34	—	1	2	—	3	37	7.5
35–39	—	2	1	—	3	52	5.4
40–44	—	1	1	—	2	16	11.1
Total	8	8	19	1	36	205	14.9

Source: See Table 22, p. 117, above.

level of fertility throughout their lives. Quadroon women (and samboes) were much less successful at doing this.

The reasons for the high fertility of the slave coloured women are not certain. It may be that the coloured woman could see positions of relative status for her children within the slave system and their eventual escape from it. The slave of colour did not necessarily have to pass through every stage between blackness and whiteness before attaining freedom; his chances of manumission were always greater than the black's.[49] And the coloured child's mother, even if she was black, could have some hope of manumission for herself as well as her child. More immediately, she too could look for relative advantages within the slave system if she had children for white men. Hence the exclusivism of the women of mulatto and lighter grades of colour. For the black and sambo women these hopes were all much more distant. Even if the black woman mated with a free coloured man, the chances of his being able to pay for the manumission of her children or herself were relatively remote, and he could do little to alter her material welfare within the slave system. Thus, because of the essential economic impotence of the slave, the normal relationship between social status and fertility was reversed. The slave woman of colour and status was therefore more prepared to expose herself to the risk of pregnancy than was the black woman.[50]

If it is true that the coloured slave woman was more willing to expose herself to the risk of pregnancy when her child would be of a lighter colour than herself, the level of fertility still depended on the frequency of intercourse with white or coloured men. This was probably not a limiting factor, however, since it seems that the white males were at least as fertile as the blacks within the slave population. It has been estimated that 10.7 per cent of all slave births were fathered by whites between 1829 and 1832 (Table 26). (They were more fertile than whites in the United States, where whites fathered between 0.5 and 8.0 per cent of slave births in the 1850s.[51]) It is more difficult to estimate the size of the white male population of Jamaica[52] but it probably fell between 10,000 and 20,000, thus comprising from 5.7 to 10.8 per cent of the total male population (including slaves, free coloureds and free blacks). Hence the fertility of the slave coloured women was not likely to be reduced by their having intercourse with whites rather than blacks. This might be explained in part by the possibility that after 1807 the white males were even more heavily concentrated into the most fertile age-groups than the blacks. Once again there were differences between the urban and rural patterns. In Kingston, for example, whites probably made up 25 per cent of the total male population yet fathered only 17 per cent of slave births. Whites were similarly infertile in the settled pen parishes where slave fertility was high. But there is no doubt that the whites made a significant direct contribution to the fertility of the slaves or that the whites' coloured daughters were more fertile than their black sisters.

Family

Whereas the whites ignored the role of miscegenation in slave fertility, they were at pains to demonstrate that the family structure of the slaves was a major preventive check to the growth of the population. They believed that the slaves were essentially promiscuous and/or polygamous, and that this inevitably depressed fertility. The masters attributed this condition to 'African debauchery', while the humanitarians traced it to the brutality of the slave system.[53] But, apart from the dispute over causes, there was little disagreement about the nature of slave family structure. The contemporary consensus has found its way into the modern interpretation because of this apparent uniformity, independent of its roots in the myth of primitive promiscuity. Thus, for Patterson, 'the family was unthinkable to the vast majority of the population' of Jamaica and 'the nuclear family could hardly exist within the context of slavery'.[54] In general, the view of the slave family which emerges is one of 'matrifocal' residential units dominated by mothers and grandmothers, in which the father or husband's place was always insecure.[55] The only significant challenge to this view comes from Brathwaite, who rather obliquely comments that perhaps 'the slaves' sense of family was not always as disorganized as some contemporary and modern accounts suggest'.[56]

All of these interpretations of slave family structure are based on the contemporary literary sources, rather than on the analysis of actual slave families.[57] Unfortunately, the detailed data necessary for the study of slave families are rarely available.[58] Here an attempt will be made to study only a small sample of properties, for which the documentation of household composition appears to be unique: Old and New Montpelier sugar estates, and Shettlewood pen, to which reference has been made frequently in earlier sections.[59]

As well as various lists of the slaves on the estate, the Account Book for Old Montpelier also contains a 'Report of the state and condition of Old Montpelier negro houses and provision grounds and the number of stock possessed by each family', dated 1 August 1825.[60] The first column of this report is titled 'Names with their families and dependants, if any' and consists of groups of names, the number of individuals in each group being totalled in the margin. The second column is headed 'Condition of houses' and links to each of the groups in the first column a description of one or more houses. These groups and their associated houses can be confidently identified as households or rather 'housefuls'. (The 'household' denotes only the co-resident family, whereas 'houseful' includes all persons resident in the house or premises.[61]) Then follow detailed statements of the livestock, gardens and provision grounds belonging to each group, a list of the provisions planted, and remarks on the 'state of culture' of the grounds. Only 47 groups are listed in the report, but it is clear that pages have been lost from the Account Book. In 1832 the owner of the properties, Lord Seaford, presented to the House of Lords 'a report made to me, on my application, by the gentleman managing my estates', dated 1 August 1825.[62] This was a continuation of the Old Montpelier report found in the Account Book, together with similar data for New Montpelier and Shettlewood. These reports contain no information about kinship. But links through the maternal line can be traced by relating the names in the reports to the data available in the Returns of Registrations of Slaves 1817–32.[63]

These three sets of data have been collated and analysed using methods analogous to family reconstitution.[64] A problem generally encountered in family reconstitution studies is that of the identification of individuals, but here slaves could not enter or leave the population without record of the fact. Names did change, however. In July 1816 almost all of the slaves at Old Montpelier, five-sixths of those at New Montpelier and half of those at Shettlewood were baptized, thus receiving 'christian' names and surnames before the first registration of 1817.[65] Yet the old names recurred. The registration data can be checked internally, since they give information regarding sex, age, colour and so on. But the 1825 report is not subject to such checks, and here an Old Montpelier list for 1828 giving old and christian names together is particularly valuable.[66] Three household members could not be identified at Old Montpelier, fifteen at New Montpelier, and two at Shettlewood. Consequently, several single-member housefuls and one of six have had to be excluded from some aspects of the analysis.

The limitations of the data are fairly clearly defined. They say nothing about paternity. Even links through the maternal line are discoverable only if the mother was living (on the same property as her child) in 1817 or the child was born in the period 1817–32. The report of 1825 provides only a static picture of the residential pattern, thus it cannot be used, except indirectly, to measure the stability of the family system. Fertility for the period 1817–32 can be related to household structure only as it was in 1825. But Seaford's purpose in producing this report was to impress the opponents of slavery with the material welfare of his slaves, not to make any statement on family structure. Thus the data are relatively neutral. Seaford was described as a 'humane, well-intentioned' absentee proprietor, but he was also the 'acknowledged head' of the West India interest.[67] In 1797 he brought in a motion which placed in the hands of the colonial legislatures the encouragement of 'a reform in the manners and morality of the negroes' which would end polygamy, a family system he thought unfavourable to population growth.[68] But this was more a delaying tactic than evidence of genuine interest in amelioration. In 1831 he asked the Moravians to instruct his slaves, but they declined since they expected the Anglicans to erect a church nearby.[69] Seaford's benevolence seems to have extended little beyond permitting the slaves to run livestock on the estate pastures.[70]

Old and New Montpelier estates were in St. James, in the valley of the Great River about twelve miles from Montego Bay; Shettlewood pen adjoined, being on the western side of the river, in Hanover. Old Montpelier was settled about 1745 and the New Works in 1775. The properties covered 10,000 acres in St. James and 2,000 in Hanover, roughly 1,000 acres being planted in canes in the 1820s.[71] On Old and New Montpelier, 7,632 acres were in woodland and ruinate, supplying timber for staves and fuel. The estates produced nothing for sale other than sugar and rum, though their old, meagre livestock were sent to Shettlewood pen for fattening. A butchery at Shettlewood supplied neighbouring estates with fresh beef, and the pen also bred planters' steers and mules for sale.[72] In 1825 the 864 slaves on the three properties occupied 51 acres of gardens, in which their houses were located, and had the use of 589 acres of provision grounds.[73] But 42 of the slaves lived at 'Farm', a part of the estate 'which is cultivated for the supply of the estates with vegetables and ground provisions; where a range of cottages has likewise been built for the convalescent negroes or others whose health may require rest or particular attention'.[74] In 1825 Farm supplied Old Montpelier with large quantities of yams, cocos and plantains. Many of the slaves working or recuperating there suffered from complaints such as elephantiasis, leprosy and ulcers, but there were at least two or three healthy families whose chief function was the production of provisions. Farm was supervised by a white overseer; and on the estates there was a constant turnover of overseers serving under William Miller, the attorney for the entire period 1817–32. At the end of 1825 seven whites lived at Old Montpelier. Free coloured people lived on and around the properties, and from time to time large numbers of jobbing slaves were hired to work on the estates, but the holdings were relatively isolated.

The limitations of the 1825 report, noted above, make it difficult to classify the households/housefuls satisfactorily. An attempt to do so is shown in Table 31. In addition to the 252 units classified, there were 25 houses at Farm, most consisting of single individuals. The latter have been excluded from the general analysis because of the temporary character of the establishment at Farm. A total of 50 slaves, 42 of them at Farm, could not be included in the classification.

The modal houseful comprised a male, a woman and her children (Type 1). This was followed by Types 4 (a male and a female) and 2 (a woman, her children and others). More than half of the housefuls contained consanguines (identifiable through the maternal line). The picture changes somewhat if the houseful types are analysed in terms of the number of individuals they accounted for. Almost 75 per cent of the slaves lived in units containing consanguines (Types 1–3 and 6–9). Half of them lived in housefuls of Types 1 and 2, the latter being in many cases essentially a sub-type of Type 1. Thus although less than 25 per cent of the slaves lived exclusively with identifiable kin, almost 50 per cent lived in units approximating the elementary family. This has important implications for the understanding of slave family structure. It suggests that the woman-and-children household was far from dominant, whatever the importance of the mother–child link.

Table 31. *Composition of housefuls at Old Montpelier, New Montpelier and Shettlewood, 1825*

	Number		Percentage		Mean
Houseful type	Slaves	Units	Slaves	Units	size
1. Man, woman, her children	204	50	25.2	19.8	4.1
2. Woman, her children, others	199	35	24.5	13.9	5.7
3. Woman, her children	95	29	11.7	11.5	3.3
4. Male, female	76	39	9.3	15.5	2.0
5. Males, females	93	28	11.4	11.1	3.3
6. Male, woman, her children, her grandchildren	24	4	2.9	1.6	6.0
7. Woman, her children, her grandchildren	19	4	2.3	1.6	4.8
8. Woman, her children, her nephews, her nieces (and their children)	15	2	1.8	0.8	7.5
9. Siblings, others	22	6	2.7	2.4	3.7
10. Male	25	25	3.1	9.9	1.0
11. Female	19	19	2.3	7.5	1.0
12. Males	14	7	1.7	2.8	2.0
13. Females	9	4	1.1	1.6	2.3
Total	814	252	100.0	100.0	3.2

Source: See text.

Table 32. *Distribution of Africans and slaves of colour between the houseful types of Old Montpelier, New Montpelier and Shettlewood, 1825*

Houseful type	Africans			Slaves of colour		
	No.	% total	% excluding children	Mulatto	Quadroon	Sambo
1	66	33.2	67.3	2	—	2
2	56	28.1	47.5	3	2	7
3	21	22.1	67.7	3	7	1
4	45	46.8		—	—	1
5	41	45.1		—	—	—
6	4	16.0	50.0	—	—	—
7	3	15.0	75.0	1	1	1
8	—	—	—	6	6	—
9	3	13.6	—	—	—	—
10	17	73.9		—	—	2
11	14	82.3		—	—	—
12	6	42.8		—	—	—
13	4	44.4		1	—	—
Total	280			16	16	14

Source: See text.

Of the three properties, the elementary family household was most important at New Montpelier, the estate that was the most recently settled, suffered the greatest stresses in terms of the movement of slaves, had the highest proportion of Africans and the heaviest mortality. The implications of this pattern must be sought in the composition of the housefuls. The distribution of Africans among the houseful types was similar to that for the total population (Table 32). In absolute numbers, the concentration of Africans into Type 1 units at New Montpelier was greater than that for any of the houseful types on the other two properties. Thus when Africans formed households, other than single-member units, they most often established those of Type 1, whereas creoles participated in the more complex Type 2. This might suggest that the Africans attempted to maintain nuclear family households, while the creoles, dislocated by the experience of slavery, were unable to do so; or it may simply mean that the ramifications of creole kinship were so much greater.

The distribution of slaves of colour contrasted strongly with that of Africans (Table 32). Those with white fathers (mulattoes and quadroons) lived almost exclusively in households dominated by mothers, grandmothers and aunts. There was no place for slave mates in such households. But the residential pattern of those slave women who seem to have had long-term relationships with white men is uncertain. By contrast, sambo children (whose mothers were almost all black) generally lived in households containing po-

Table 33. *Occupational composition of the houseful types at Old Montpelier, 1825*

	Field gangs		Drivers		Trades and skills		Domestics		Minor field		No task	
Houseful type	Males	Females	Males	Females	Males	Females	Males	Females	Males	Females	Males	Females
1	16	19	2	—	5	1	1	1	9	7	6	5
2	18	34	1	—	11	3	—	7	10	6	3	17
3	8	10	—	—	—	—	4	3	1	1	5	5
4	12	16	1	—	5	—	—	1	7	6	—	1
5	6	14	—	—	7	—	—	2	1	3	—	2
6	2	8	—	—	2	—	—	1	1	—	—	3
8	—	—	—	—	1	—	1	3	—	—	—	2
9	3	3	—	—	—	—	—	—	1	—	—	—
10	4	—	—	—	3	—	—	—	5	—	2	—
11	—	5	—	—	—	1	—	3	—	2	—	2
12	4	—	—	—	3	—	—	—	1	1	1	—
13	—	3	—	1	—	—	—	—	—	—	—	1
Total	73	112	4	1	37	5	6	21	36	26	17	38

Source: See text.

tential male mates (black men) but always lacking potential fathers (mulattoes).

A general consideration of the age structure of the houseful types is not very useful since it conceals too many other variables. Almost all of the types contained the whole spectrum of ages, especially those consisting of consanguines. Slaves living alone tended to be relatively old, most being Africans over 40 years of age. Those living with siblings were generally young adults. As the slave aged, the major shift was from housefuls based on consanguines (especially the mother-and-children type) to those containing males and females who were not identifiable kin. But this pattern was confused by the connection between age and the African/creole ratio.

At Old Montpelier, at least, there was a relationship between the occupations of the slaves and the types of households/housefuls in which they lived (Table 33). The major determinants of occupation, in turn, were sex, age and colour. The majority of the females worked in the field, whereas males were employed in a much wider range of occupations, especially in the trades. Almost all of the male slaves of colour at Old Montpelier were put to trades, though they did not dominate the group. Female slaves of colour, however, made up almost all of those who were domestics or washerwomen. Thus only aged or invalid black females could expect to escape labour in the field, and it was more difficult for women to attain positions of status or relative independence.[75] At Old Montpelier, field slaves were to be found in all of the houseful types, except Type 8 (in which the slaves were all coloured domestics or tradesmen). In general, field slaves comprised about half of the occupants of each type. But male field slaves were always outnumbered by females, except when they lived in all-male units. Slaves with authority in the field, the drivers, most often lived in housefuls containing women and children rather than non-kin. Tradesmen followed a similar pattern, but more often lived alone or with males and females who were not identifiable kin. Domestics tended to live in units dominated by women (Figure 30, f). Since they were often older, slaves employed in minor field tasks frequently lived as solitaries (especially the watchmen) or with non-kin.

Since sex, country, colour, age and occupation were not separate but interdependent characteristics, some broad patterns can be seen in the composition of the slave households/housefuls. The Africans, the aging section of the population, formed either elementary families or lived as solitaries. Most of those living alone were over 40 years of age and the men, who were generally employed as watchmen, could not easily find a place in the wider household system. Some of the latter were not provided with gardens or provision grounds, but were 'fed from the overseer's store'.[76] (One old watchman, in St. Ann, was given food by the children of his shipmates.[77]) Slaves of colour, with their privileged occupations and blood allying them to the great house and the whites, formed households in which slave men had no part and which were tightly organized around the maternal connection. Creole blacks, the majority of the population and of the field labour force, were widely distributed among the houseful types but were a dominant element in Types 2 (mothers, their children and others) and 4, 5, 12 and 13 (groups of males and females who cannot be identified as kin). The ramifications of kinship among the creoles were important organizing factors which could not be matched by the Africans' common experiences of regional origin or of being shipmates.[78]

Houseful Type 1 has so far been defined strictly as comprising a male, a woman and her children. More needs to be known about the male before it can be considered a nuclear family household. In only three cases can the male and woman be identified certainly as mates. In 1825, three weeks after the household report was made, Charles Rose (Ellis) and Ann Ellis 1st of Old Montpelier were married by an Anglican priest.[79] They were creole blacks, Charles Rose (aged 34 years) being a mason and Ann Ellis (31 years) working in the first gang. Ann Ellis' two children lived with them, immediately before the marriage, in a 'good stone house, shingled' with a new kitchen. They possessed two cows, a steer and a bull calf, ten hogs and four chickens, and had the use of six acres of provision grounds in which were planted yams, cocos, corn and plantains. On the same day in 1825 Charles Beckford married Becky Richards of New Montpelier; they too were creole blacks, aged 26 and 37 years respectively. Becky Richards' daughter, aged 15 years, lived with them. Their house was of wattle and thatch and the only livestock they had were hogs and chickens; they had one acre of provision grounds. In 1827 Richard Trail and Elizabeth Miller of Shettlewood were married.[80] Like the other couples, they were creole blacks, but were younger (24 and 23 years respectively). In 1825 they had lived together, with Elizabeth Miller's two children, who were both surnamed Trail suggesting that they were also Richard Trail's children. Their house was wattled and thatched but in bad condition; they had a cow and three acres planted in yams, cocos and plantains. At Old and New Montpelier the mothers of the married couples had all died by 1825 but the mothers of Richard Trail and Elizabeth Miller, both Africans, lived with their other children. Thus while marriage was confined to black creoles who already lived together, with the woman's children, it included a wide range of ages and, probably, of statuses within the slave hierarchy.

The identification of mates in the remaining housefuls must rest on less solid evidence. The two most obvious indicators are the age difference of the potential mates and the ordering of individuals within the houseful lists. All of the males and women in houseful Type 1 were older than 20 years and most were over 40 years of age. At Old Montpelier twelve of them were separated by less than ten years, seven by more than ten years, but only three by more than twenty years. At New Montpelier thirteen were separated by less than ten years, eleven by more than ten, and only two by more than twenty. At Shettlewood none of the six potential mates were separated by more than eleven years. Thus the evidence from age suggests that most of the men and women living in houseful Type 1 were mates.

The evidence provided by the ordering of names in the lists is tantalizing but inconsistent. For Old Montpelier the lists are ordered in a manner suggestive of status within the houseful. With one exception, all of the Type 1 housefuls in which the male and woman were separated by less than ten years in age are arranged thus: male, woman, her children (listed by age). At Shettlewood the form was, with two exceptions, slightly different: woman, male, the woman's children. At New Montpelier the houseful members were divided by sex: male, the woman's male children, woman, her daughters. Thus it is difficult to use these data to determine male or female headship. But only five of the fifty Type 1 housefuls were arranged so that the male was placed at the end of the list, and most of these involved men and women more than 20 years apart in age. Probably 90 per cent of the males and women in this type, then, were mates.

Mates can also be sought in houseful Types 2, 4, 5, 6 and 9. Of the four Type 6 housefuls (male, woman, her children and grandchildren) only two seem to be extensions of Type 1. The males in the other two units were in their twenties, whereas the women were in their fifties and seventies; they were most probably collaterals. Using the same principles, it seems that roughly half of the housefuls of Types 2 and 9 contained mates. For Type 4 (male and female) the only evidence available is that of age, and on this basis

Table 34. *Ages of male and female co-residents in houseful Type 4 at Old Montpelier, New Montpelier and Shettlewood, 1825*

Age of male	Age of female co-resident								Total males
	0–9	10–19	20–29	30–39	40–49	50–59	60–69	70+	
0–9	—	—	—	—	—	—	—	—	—
10–19	—	—	1	—	—	—	—	—	1
20–29	—	1	1	3	—	1	1	—	7
30–39	—	—	2	5	1	—	—	—	8
40–49	1	1	—	4	3	2	—	—	11
50–59	—	—	—	—	6	2	—	—	8
60–69	—	—	—	—	—	1	—	—	1
70+	—	—	—	—	—	—	1	1	2
Total females	1	2	4	12	10	6	2	1	

Source: See text.

it appears that about 75 per cent of the pairs may have been mates (Table 34). In Type 5 (males and females) additional evidence can be found in the ordering of the lists, and this suggests a similar proportion to that found for Type 4; but the possible complexities are much greater.

In general, probably 100 of the 252 housefuls at Old and New Montpelier and Shettlewood contained mates. Almost half of these housefuls comprehended only the mates and the woman's children. It is impossible to estimate the number of women who did not live together with their mates, but it must have been at least 30. Some of their mates had died, but others lived in separate houses or on other properties. There is concrete evidence of the latter. In 1825 James Lewis of Shettlewood cut the throat of his 'wife', Ann Thomas of Old Montpelier, and then killed himself.[81] They were aged 30 and 24 years, respectively. Both were the children of African mothers, who were living in 1825, and both seem to have lived all their lives on their particular properties.

Beyond the anecdotal evidence, the best estimates of the extent of the residential separation of mates can be found in the records of the Moravian church. The Moravian missionaries kept detailed records of slaves married and baptized by them, and of the 'partners' of slaves received into the congregation.[82] Unfortunately, they were not active in the area of Montpelier, but concentrated their efforts in the coffee and pen parishes of Manchester and St. Elizabeth.[83] Between 1827 and 1834 the Moravians at Carmel and Fairfield performed 189 marriages of slaves,[84] and of these 54 (28 per cent) involved partners living on separate properties. Of the separated marriage partners, twenty-six were only a mile apart, but eight of them were more than three miles distant. The Moravian data concerning the partners of their unmarried church members are more difficult to analyse, but it appears that

Table 35. *Ages of 'partners' belonging to Fairfield Moravian Church, 1824*

Age of male	Age of female partner 15–19	20–24	25–29	30–34	35–39	40–44	45–49	50–54	55–59	Total males
15–19	1	—	—	—	—	—	—	—	—	1
20–24	1	—	—	—	1	—	—	—	—	2
25–29	—	—	2	—	—	—	—	—	—	2
30–34	—	—	3	7	4	3	—	—	—	17
35–39	—	—	—	3	1	1	—	—	—	5
40–44	—	—	—	3	3	—	1	—	—	7
45–49	—	—	—	2	2	2	—	1	3	10
50–54	—	—	—	—	—	1	—	—	1	2
55–59	—	—	—	—	1	1	—	1	—	3
Total females	2	—	5	15	12	8	1	2	4	

Source: 'List of the Members of the Congregation at Fairfield arranged according to the estates on which they reside, October 12th, 1824' (Moravian Church Archives, Malvern, Jamaica); R.R.S. (for ages).

roughly the same proportions were separated as in the case of marriages. Very few of the partners were separated by more than two miles (Figure 31). It is also important to note that in many cases all of the slaves on a particular property with partners elsewhere tended to be exclusively male or exclusively female. At Chevely Plantation, for example, fourteen men but no women had separated partners, whereas at Mount Prospect seventeen woman but no men found mates outside the property. This may be seen as a response to the sexual imbalance on particular properties, rather than a devaluation of the principle of co-residence.[85] By linking the names in the Moravian records to the Returns of Registrations of Slaves, it is possible to establish the demographic characteristics of the partners and marriage mates.[86] Of those identified successfully, the great majority were Africans, in contrast to the pattern at Montpelier. But the pattern of age differences for the Moravian partners (Table 35) does suggest that the principles used to identify mates in the Montpelier data are valid. The level of residential separation of mates belonging to the Moravian church should, however, be seen as a lower limit.[87]

The residential separation of mates was also a feature of polygamous family organization, for which there is some evidence in the 1825 report on Montpelier and Shettlewood. Five men, but no women, were listed for two houses, all of them at Old Montpelier. In the second house for which they were listed their names appear at the end of the list, in parentheses. George Ellis, a creole carpenter aged 54 years, lived with the mother of Ann Thomas (mentioned above), her three children and the son of Ann Thomas. His second house comprised Bessy Ellis, an African nurse, her five children, and an aged invalid woman. Like George Ellis, most of the other men attributed

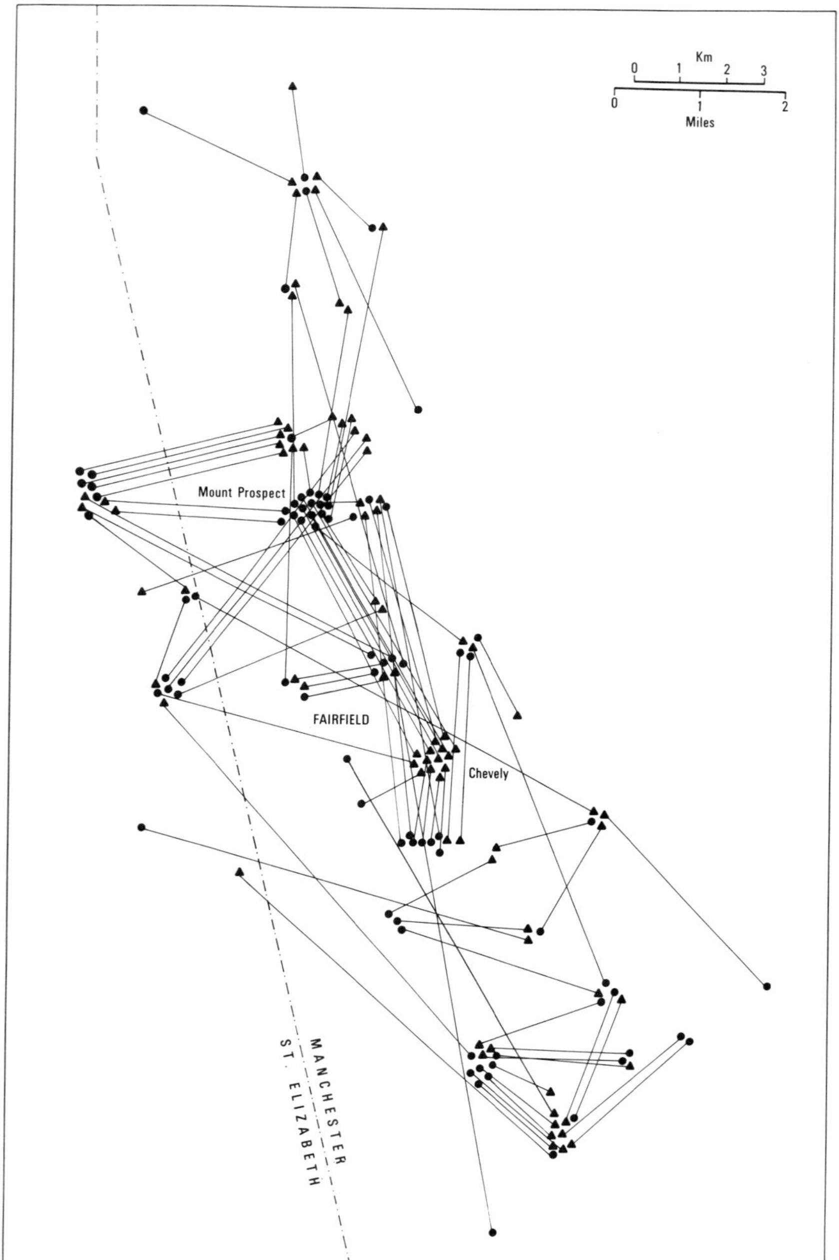

Figure 31. Slave 'partners' belonging to Fairfield Moravian Church, Manchester, 1824. Linked male (Δ) and female (O) symbols represent partners.

to two houses held positions of some authority on the estate. The head driver, David Richards 2nd, a black creole aged 49 years, lived in one house with an invalid creole woman aged 47, and a mulatto woman and her (but not his) quadroon daughter. In his second house the only occupant was a black creole woman aged 37, who worked in the first gang. William Squires, an African aged 50 years who was in the first gang and acted as stillerman, lived with an African woman aged 45 years; in his second house lived an invalid African aged 41 years and her two children. Similarly, William Richards 1st was an African aged 49 years who worked in the first gang and as a boiler; an African woman lived in each of his houses, one aged 45 and the other 43 years, and both working in the first gang. Finally, James Hedley, a 34-year-old creole of the first gang, lived with a creole woman aged 39 years who worked alongside him; in his second house lived another creole woman, aged 45 years, and her daughter.

Although the available evidence does not make it possible to identify these men as polygynists with certainty, it is probable that they were.[88] Their positions within the slave hierarchy fit closely the contemporary testimony on polygamy. In every case the houses were occupied only by women and their children, excluding the possibility of co-resident mates other than the potential polygynists. It must also be noticed that, with the exception of David Richards, the houses were always adjacent in the list which, it will be argued below, signified spatial contiguity. Creole polygynists were as numerous as the Africans but, unlike the monogamous mates, the polygamous households at Old Montpelier were generally exclusively African or exclusively creole.

Polygynists living with several women in a single house are more difficult to identify, but they can be looked for in houseful Types 2 and 5. About one-third of these 63 units comprised a man and more than one woman (and their children) but in terms of their age structure only a minority of them could have been mates.

There is no evidence of the 'grandmother family' at Montpelier and Shettlewood; that is, no households were discovered consisting of a woman and her grandchildren, the mother of the children living elsewhere. Even when their mothers were dead it was very rare for grandchildren to live with their grandmothers. Similarly, in the absence of their mothers, it was very rare for children to live with their paternal kin. With the most generous assumptions it is certain that less than ten housefuls (of Types 4, 5 and 12) could have consisted of fathers and their children or grandchildren.

At least 70 slaves were moved to Shettlewood from the eastern end of the island between March 1816 and 1817,[89] and in 1819 the 53 survivors of the seasoning period went to New Montpelier. It seems that mothers were not separated from children in this move, and that siblings whose mothers died between 1817 and 1819 were kept together. By the time of the 1825 report 33 of these slaves survived at New Montpelier, distributed between fourteen houses; another five lived at Farm. Five Africans and one creole (whose mother had died) moved singly into housefuls made up of New Montpelier slaves. All of these housefuls were of Type 5, indefinable groups of males and females, except that an African, Moses Richards, established a household with a New Montpelier African and her three children (aged fourteen, five and two years). But the remaining 27 Shettlewood slaves lived in eight houses which contained no New Montpelier slaves. All but one of the children continued to live with their mothers. There is little evidence in the composition of these housefuls that the movement of the slaves disrupted the relationships of mates or mothers and children. But the Shettlewood slaves probably found it difficult to integrate themselves into the New Montpelier household system. Only Africans, who moved in with other Africans, had any success in this respect. The women mothered very few children after going to New Montpelier, so that no child born between 1819 and 1825 was alive in the latter year. This pattern began to change only at the end of the 1820s when the girls who had come from Shettlewood reached maturity.

To summarize, it is fair to conclude that the slaves can be placed in three major categories relative to their place in family and household organization. Firstly, there were the slaves who had no family but lived with friends or as solitaries. Most of them were male Africans but many creoles entered this category as they grew old. Around 1825 roughly 30 per cent of the slaves at Montpelier and Shettlewood fell into this group, compared to 50 per cent in Trinidad and 20 per cent in Barbados about 1807.[90] Thus the lack of family links was largely a product of the slave trade itself, and as the creole section grew this category declined in importance. Secondly, the great majority of the 70 per cent of the slaves who did possess family links lived in simple family households, most of them nuclear units. Although creoles were important in this category, it was also the most common form of family organization for the Africans. The third category was dominated by creoles and consisted of varieties of extended family households. But this category was relatively unimportant, since the nuclear family household maintained its dominance along with the growth of the creole section. The importance of these results is that they contradict the received interpretation that the matrifocal family was dominant during the period of slavery. They present a challenge to those who have argued, like Patterson, that 'the nuclear family could hardly exist within the context of slavery', or, with Smith, that 'normally the children resided with their mother, and the parents lived apart, singly or with different mates'.[91]

So far the housefuls/households at Montpelier and Shettlewood have been defined essentially in terms of the co-resident kin occupying a single house. There are some exceptions, however, ten of the groups of 'families and dependants' occupying two or three houses. Most of the latter were Type 2 housefuls, containing coloured and skilled slaves; they generally had the use of relatively large areas of provision grounds and possessed considerable numbers of livestock. It is evident that these slaves had more than one house not because of their numbers but because of their privileged occupations and relative prosperity; many groups of similar size had to live in a single house. It is probable that these multiple-house units formed compounds or 'yards', with the houses set out around a central open area. Support for this view comes from a description of Hope Estate in the parish of St. Andrew, published in 1818. After noting that each house was fenced off from the others, the writer observed:

But those [slaves], who are entrusted with duties of responsibility or skill, have better houses. In some instances whole families reside within one enclosure: They have separate houses, but only one gate. In the centre of this family village, the house of the principal among them is generally placed, and is in general very superior to the others.[92]

As well as these multiple-house units, the evidence in the 1825 report for separate houses is also suggestive of yard formation. The manner in which this report was compiled is unknown, but since the overseer had to make a visual inspection of the houses and grounds, the listing probably follows some sort of route from house to house. Thus it is likely that houses listed next to one another were spatially adjacent as well.

At Old Montpelier thirty slaves did not live with their mothers, but thirteen of them lived in the house listed next to their mothers' and another three were only one house further removed. At Shettlewood three slaves lived next to their mothers, six one house removed, and seven further away. But at New Montpelier only one slave was listed next to his mother, while six lived further away. In general, 50 per cent of the slaves who did not live with their mothers were no further away than one or two houses. It is also clear that at New Montpelier fewer children moved away from their mothers; but when they did they moved much farther. Among the children not living with their mothers the differences between the sexes are of interest (Table 36). Sons most often stayed close to their mothers, with the exception

Table 36. *Residential pattern of children not living with their mothers, Old Montpelier, New Montpelier and Shettlewood, 1825*

	Old Montpelier		New Montpelier		Shettlewood	
Child's residence	Males	Females	Males	Females	Males	Females
Living in next house	9	4	—	1	2	1
Living in next house but one	1	2	—	—	4	2
Living further away	5	9	4	2	2	5
Total	15	15	4	3	8	8

Source: See text.

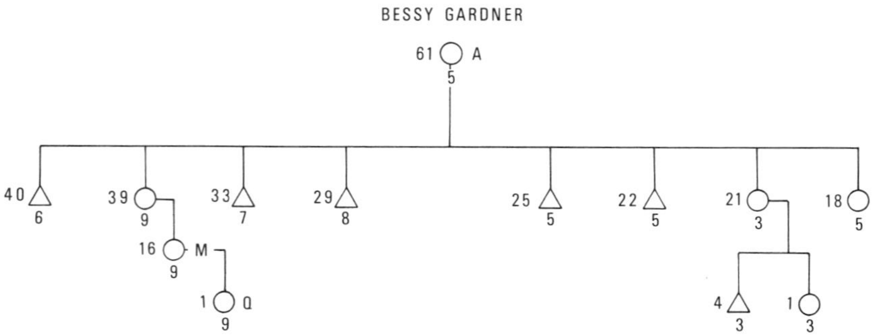

Figure 32. Bessy Gardner's connection, Shettlewood, 1825. (See the notes to Figure 30, pp. 149–51.)

of those at New Montpelier, while daughters tended to move away. In part these contrasts were complementary, since it appears that the sons who stayed near their mothers were establishing households with other women's daughters. Daughters either moved away from their mothers to live near the mothers of their mates or, less often, lived with their children in the same house as their mother. Only one woman whose mother was living in 1825 had moved to a house lacking a possible mate.

This pattern of movement applied not only to individual sons and daughters, but also to sets of siblings, and this resulted in groups of households, probably organized into yards, related by blood to a single woman. A clear example of this occurred in the houses numbered 5 to 9 at Shettlewood (Figure 32). In house 5 lived Bessy Gardner, an African aged 61 years, and her two youngest sons and daughter. Her eldest son lived alone in house 6. House 7 was occupied by her second son and a woman who was pregnant at the time of the household report (and whose mother, an African, lived with an African man in house 23). In house 8 was her third son and an apparently unrelated man and woman (aged 20 and 22 years). Bessy Gardner's eldest daughter lived in house 9 with her mulatto daughter and quadroon granddaughter. Her other daughter, Elizabeth Miller, had moved away (though not very far, perhaps) to house 3, where she lived with her two children and the man she married in 1827.

Colour also played a role in the formation of linked household groups. At Old Montpelier all of the mulatto slaves and twelve of the fourteen quadroons lived in three adjacent houses. Since most of them were domestics, and because of their exclusivism in looking for white mates, it is probable that they were located close to the great house. The movement of slaves, too, was a factor in the creation of spatially linked household groups. Of the thirty-three Shettlewood slaves living at New Montpelier in 1825, nineteen lived in houses 29 to 33. These houses comprehended almost all who had retained the mother–child residential link. The one Shettlewood man to establish a household with a New Montpelier woman lived in house 31, so it seems that he brought her into the Shettlewood knot of houses. A simple explanation of the unity of the Shettlewood slaves at New Montpelier is that they moved into houses built for them in 1819 at a single site. In 1825 all of these houses were described as 'good; stone, shingled'. Houses 34, 36 and 37 were similarly described but by 1825 were occupied by slaves who had lived on the estate since 1817 at least. Perhaps the spatial separation was a cause, as well as a measure, of their isolation within the New Montpelier population.

The fundamental problem here is one of defining the physical limits of the premises occupied by co-resident groups of slaves. If the fence around a group of houses was more important in the slaves' concept of household than the walls of the houses, it follows that units defined above as nuclear, mother–child or solitary households should really be classified as extended, polygynous or multiple family households. Probably the houses on these properties were not strictly set in straight lines, as on some other estates.[93] But the role of the yard in domestic functions (the other aspect of 'household') is less certain. The most important of these functions were the provision and preparation of food, and the care of children. Since the 1825 report linked separate families to discrete houses, livestock and rights to gardens and provision grounds, it would seem that the slaves regarded these things as separate rights and possessions rather than common property. Within the slave system the care of children was often controlled by the masters, rather than being a potential function of the yard. Thus it appears that domestic functions do not provide a safe basis for deciding the relative significance of co-residence within houses as against yards. But it is clear that relatively few slaves could have lived in simple family households which were grouped into extended or polygynous yards.

This picture of slave family and household structure at Old Montpelier, New Montpelier and Shettlewood is based on a static cross-sectional analysis of the evidence. It must now be asked whether it conceals a degree of chaos resulting from the developmental cycle of the domestic group.[94] Patterson, for example, sees the mating system of the slaves passing through five phases, the fourth of which involved 'an ordinary monogamous union' when women reached middle or late middle age.[95] Thus the dominance of the nuclear family household at Montpelier might be seen simply as a reflection of the abnormal age structure of the period following the abolition of the slave trade. An indirect approach to this problem is to determine how the women in each age-group were distributed between the houseful types (Table 37). This does suggest that the nuclear family household (Type 1) was the dominant residential unit for women only between the ages of 35 and 49 years. Part of the reason for this, however, was not that they lived alone with their children before settling with a man, but that they lived in childless co-residential unions or in extended family households. The latter suggests that the age pattern was affected by the African/creole ratio. Thus the dominance of extended types in the age-groups below 35 years was simply a product of

Table 37. *Distribution of women, by age, between the major houseful types, Old Montpelier, New Montpelier and Shettlewood, 1825*

Age of woman	Type 1 Man, woman, her children	Type 2 Woman, her children, others	Type 3 Woman, her children	Type 4 Male, female	Type 5 Males, females	Type 11 Female	Total (all houseful types)
15–19	9	18	7	1	5	—	48
20–24	5	10	3	3	10	2	40
25–29	3	4	4	1	1	—	17
30–34	3	8	3	5	8	—	31
35–39	10	5	4	7	5	4	38
40–44	21	12	10	8	5	1	60
45–49	9	5	5	2	3	2	28
50–54	3	5	1	6	3	3	25
55–59	1	3	1	—	—	—	5
60–64	—	5	3	2	3	4	18
Totals	64	75	41	35	43	16	310

Source: See text.

the weight of the creole section in those groups. With the exception of the 25–29 years group, there is nothing to suggest that the mother-and-children household type dominated either in the early years of child-bearing or after the menopause.

It is possible only to speculate on the stability of unions at Montpelier and Shettlewood. The evidence found in the surnames of children living in nuclear family households does suggest that some of the mates had long-term relationships. Yet there were few cases of consistency in the surnames given to a woman's children. This is not necessarily proof of instability, since children were rarely given surnames before their tenth year and very often these names reflect those of the whites on the estates (even when they were not the fathers). But where children had the same surname as the potential mate in the household they were generally younger than those with other surnames, which is certainly suggestive of instability.

So long as their mothers lived, however, very few slaves moved to separate houses, and most of those who did move were over 20 years of age. In 1825 the majority of them lived with their mates and children (houseful Types 1 and 2), or simply with their mates (Type 4). Very few of them lived alone, and it has been noted already that only one woman lived with her children, apart from her mother and without a mate. In so far as daughters whose mothers were alive formed relationships with men, they continued to live in their mothers' houses until they conceived or gave birth to children. One pro-slavery observer claimed that 'the negroes having families do all they can to retain their children in them; and they retain them sometimes to the age of 40 years, and even after. The consequence is, they do not form regular marriages, or such connections as are prolific'.[96] On the other hand, very few women lived with their mothers after bearing children, and most of these were slaves of colour who did not form unions within the slave population (Figure 30, j). The rarity of women living without a mate is suggestive of a more stable pattern of unions than Patterson recognizes,[97] unless it can be argued that women parting with co-resident mates either quickly engaged new ones or returned promptly to their mother's household. It seems improbable that new unions would have been based on co-residence in the first instance. But the second possibility would fit neatly if, as seems often to have been the case, the women had moved into households established by sons close to their living mothers.

The problem of stability is an intractable one in the context of the data available for Montpelier and Shettlewood. It must also be emphasized that generalization from this case study to Jamaica as a whole after the abolition of the slave trade would be dangerous. In particular, it is probable that in the towns the slave family and household was more often female-headed, as a result of miscegenation, the low sex ratio and the size of the slave-holdings. But the urban population was small, so that this should be seen as no more than a possible exception to the dominant agricultural pattern. Confidence in the results obtained for Montpelier and Shettlewood is strengthened considerably by the similar patterns found in studies of Trinidad in the early nineteenth century, Martinique in the late eighteenth century and *ante bellum* America.[98] The slave family can no longer be characterized as matrifocal and promiscuous, and its instability deserves serious reconsideration.

Family and fertility

If the masters and the missionaries were mistaken about the structure of the slave family and household, their views concerning the connection between family form and fertility seem to have come close to the truth. Once again, the only data available to test this connection are those for Old and New Montpelier and Shettlewood, 1817–32. The extent of under-registration of births on these properties has been discussed already,[99] and the general age-specific fertility rates for Africans and creoles are presented in Table 22. Broad age-specific fertility rates for each of the houseful types containing women are now given in Table 38. A basic difficulty in this analysis is that the houseful type of each woman is known only for 1825. To meet this problem the rates have been divided into two periods, 1817–25 and 1825–32, but it is clear that some births will have been attributed to the wrong houseful type. For example, a woman living with her children in 1825 might have borne all of them between 1817 and 1825 while living with a mate, the man having

Table 38. *Age-specific fertility rates by type of houseful, Old Montpelier, New Montpelier and Shettlewood, 1817–25 and 1825–32*[a]

Houseful type	Births per 1,000 woman-years[b] 15–24 age-group	25–34 age-group	35–44 age-group	15–44 age-group
1817–25				
1	89 (67)	307 (75)	93(214)	138(356)
2	77(109)	106(113)	92(130)	91(352)
3	22 (46)	200 (65)	99(101)	113(212)
4	— (42)	15 (65)	—(100)	5(207)
5	— (90)	— (94)	— (76)	—(260)
6	222 (9)	— (8)	87 (23)	100 (40)
7	118 (17)	— (0)	83 (12)	103 (29)
8	200 (5)	— (13)	167 (6)	83 (24)
9	— (17)	— (21)	— (2)	— (40)
11	— (16)	37 (27)	— (17)	17 (60)
13	— (20)	56 (18)	— (3)	24 (41)
1825–32				
1	66(157)	— (46)	45(111)	48(314)
2	107(197)	135 (89)	12 (85)	92(371)
3	44 (68)	200 (35)	136 (44)	109(147)
4	130 (23)	108 (37)	— (68)	55(128)
5	16 (63)	103 (58)	27 (74)	46(195)
6	167 (24)	333 (3)	77 (13)	150 (40)
7	31 (29)	111 (9)	— (4)	48 (42)
8	167 (18)	— (3)	— (4)	120 (25)
9	30 (33)	105 (19)	— (14)	45 (66)
11	— (3)	250 (12)	29 (35)	80 (50)
13	167 (6)	— (9)	— (5)	50 (20)

[a] The periods are divided at 30 June 1825.
[b] Woman-years given in parentheses.
Source: See text.

died in, say, 1824. More importantly, the female children living in such a household frequently moved into the child-bearing age-groups after 1825, and it is probable that if they had children they then lived in households containing a mate. In general, it seems that the rates for 1817–25 are more reliable indicators than those for the later period. In houseful Type 1, for instance, the 'women' had 48 children from 1817 to 1825 and the 'children' only one, whereas from 1825 to 1832 the 'women' mothered only seven children and the 'children' nine. Thus the inclusion of children in the calculation of woman-years does not depress greatly the fertility of the women during the period 1817–25, but does so considerably for 1825–32.

Concentrating on the period from 1817 to 1825, then, the most fertile women were those who lived with a mate and their children (houseful Type 1), followed by those who lived in units lacking mates (Types 3 and 7).

The pattern remains the same if Types 1 and 4 are amalgamated and compared with Types 3, 11 and 13 combined.[100] Thus the co-residence of a mate was conducive, though not essential, to relatively high fertility. Housefuls of Type 2 (a woman, her children and others) were not as fertile since they frequently included invalids and unconnected individuals. The very low fertility of women living alone, with other women, with a man, with groups of men and women, or with siblings, may be seen as a corollary of the strong tendency for children to live with their mothers. But the women living in such units demonstrated a significant increase in fertility after 1825, suggesting that they moved into, or created by bearing children, different houseful types. The relatively low fertility of women living apart from their mates may be explained in terms of reduced coital frequency, and this factor probably also affected some of the women living in houseful Type 2. In summary, the most fertile women were those who lived with a mate, followed by those living exclusively with their offspring, while the least fertile were those living with adults who were not identifiable kin.

Excepting those houseful types which accounted for only a few births (Types 6–8), the most fertile age-group was always the 25–34 years group. Within this age-group the highest fertility (0.307 births per woman-year) occurred among women in houseful Type 1, followed by those in Types 3 (0.200) and 2 (0.106). At the property level, however, housefuls of Type 1 were the most fertile only at New Montpelier, where they were dominated by Africans. At Old Montpelier Type 3 housefuls were more fertile than Type 1, since the latter had a more mature age-structure, reducing the fertility of the women's category and incorporating a larger proportion of female children over 15 years. The pattern at Shettlewood was somewhat aberrant, probably because of the small numbers involved; but if Types 1 and 2 are seen to overlap, the divergence is minor.

The results of this analysis suggest, first, that the planters' belief that fertility might be increased by the formation and maintenance of stable monogamous unions was not unrealistic. The missionaries' emphasis on marriage, however, seems to have had little relation to fertility. And, although the evidence is slight, polygyny seems not to have reduced the fertility of women living in such households, contrary to the view of both planter and missionary.[101] At Old Montpelier, where the evidence of polygyny is strongest, the sexes were evenly balanced so that it could hardly have exacerbated the shortage of women complained of in earlier periods. It is possible that, as some of the masters contended, fertility was reduced by the prolonged residence of children with their parents; certainly daughters rarely moved away before bearing children, and they were particularly infertile during adolescence, though few men remained with their parents after their twentieth birthday. But this pattern of fertility does not necessarily mean that the relatively stable monogamy of middle age was preceded by early casual mating.

CHAPTER 8

MANUMISSIONS, RUNAWAYS AND CONVICTS

Although virtually unaffected by migration, the slave population of Jamaica between the abolition of the slave trade and emancipation was not strictly 'closed'.[1] It has been established, in the previous chapter, that white, free coloured and free black men made a significant contribution to the fertility of the slave population. But the population also experienced losses from causes other than mortality and migration. Slaves left the population when they reached the point of legal whiteness but there is no record of their numbers, which seem unlikely to have been significant. Between 1829 and 1832, however, 1,362 slaves were manumitted, 446 ran away and 124 were transported. Another 255 were removed from their masters, though remaining slaves, by being committed to the workhouse. This total of 1,932 slaves seems a minor loss when contrasted with the 26,700 deaths in the triennium, but the causes of these minor losses were fairly selective so that they had a significant impact on the structure of the population.

Colour, sex and birth-place as measures of the slave's status within the system gained concrete expression in the variable incidence of manumission. In the period 1829–32 only 41 per cent of the slaves manumitted were males (Table 39).[2] In the previous triennium, 1826–29, only 32 per cent had been males.[3] But the percentage of the slaves manumitted who were males increased steadily as they moved from blackness to whiteness. Of the black slaves manumitted from 1829 to 1832 only 38 per cent were males, but 47 per cent of the quadroons were males, and 55 per cent of the mustees. This pattern was related to the fact that the chances of manumission increased as the slaves approached whiteness. Compared to total births during the period 1829–32 (Table 28), only 3 per cent of the blacks were manumitted and 9 per cent of the samboes, but 23 per cent of the mulattoes and mustees, and 30 per cent of the quadroons. Thus there was a significant positive correlation between manumissions and births of colour at the parish level ($r = .79$) and with coloured deaths ($r = .72$).[4] Yet, although it would appear that a slave's chances of manumission were greater if his father was white, at the parish level there was a negative correlation between manumissions and the percentage of slave coloured having white fathers ($r = -.34$). In Kingston and St. Catherine the black slaves manumitted were actually more numerous than the coloured, and the same held true for the males of Clarendon and St. Andrew, and the females of St. Elizabeth, St. David, St. Dorothy, Port Royal and St. George. A similar problem arises in looking at the African/

Table 39. *Manumissions, 1829–32*

Parish	Colour					Africans	Males	Total
	Black	Sambo	Mulatto	Quadroon	Mustee			
Westmoreland	16	8	29	12	3	1	32	71
Hanover	15	14	16	9	3	2	30	59
St. James	24	7	30	23	2	3	36	86
Trelawny	13	13	22	27	3	5	29	78
St. Elizabeth	50	23	23	3	—	15	49	99
Manchester	9	5	16	—	—	1	17	30
St. Ann	22	14	29	16	1	4	36	84
Clarendon	28	3	15	10	1	5	24	58
Vere	8	1	10	4	3	1	10	30
St. Dorothy	11	1	2	1	1	1	8	16
St. Thomas-in-the-Vale	30	5	21	5	6	6	33	68
St. John	5	4	4	4	—	2	7	18
St. Catherine	55	7	8	8	4	10	34	83
St. Mary	12	4	23	29	6	3	27	74
St. Andrew	37	12	14	9	—	11	29	72
Port Royal	10	2	4	2	—	3	5	22
St. David	5	—	7	—	—	—	5	12
St. George	10	2	6	3	—	4	11	21
Portland	10	—	15	4	—	—	11	36
St. Thomas-in-the-East	19	2	15	12	—	5	16	48
Kingston	177	29	50	20	—	44	109	297
Total males	212	68	152	94	18	50	558	
Total females	354	88	207	107	15	76	804	
Total	566	156	359	201	33	126	558	1,362

Source: R.R.S.

creole ratio of manumissions. Although only 9 per cent of the slaves manumitted were Africans, at the parish level there was no significant correlation between manumissions and the percentage of deaths African ($r = -.09$).

It seems that although sex, colour and birth-place were related to the pattern of manumission, there is a need to re-examine the causes of this pattern. The variable correlating most strongly with manumissions was the percentage of slaves living in towns ($r = .89$), but it was in the most urbanized parishes that black manumissions outweighed coloured. Since the towns had high percentages of females and coloured slaves, it might seem that it is only by chance that the manumitted slaves tended to be female and coloured. On the other hand, there may have been two patterns, one rural and the other urban. In the rural areas, where non-predial slaves were generally recruited from the coloured creoles, manumission may have conformed closely to the traditional pattern: the chances of a slave gaining his freedom increasing with his whiteness. There is no doubt that the latter also applied in the towns: in Kingston 58 per cent of the slaves fathered by whites were manumitted during the period 1829–32, compared to only 25 per cent for the island as a whole. But in Kingston 60 per cent of the total slaves manumitted were blacks, compared to only 42 per cent for the island as a whole. In the towns, the entire slave population was non-predial, hence domestic and quasi-independent slaves able to accumulate cash were recruited from the entire range of colour and creolization.[5]

It is possible that the pattern was changing, as after 1826 the number of manumissions paid for began to exceed those granted gratuitously.[6] In general, the masters seem to have manumitted a decreasing number of slaves in the years after 1807, except perhaps for the last few years of slavery.[7] Relatively, the number of slaves who purchased their freedom or whose manumission was paid for by others increased over the period. Another hint that black slaves with an opportunity to purchase their freedom did so comes from variations in age at manumission. In Westmoreland, for example, black male slaves were manumitted at an average age of 42 years and females 36 years, samboes at 32 and 22, mulattoes at 15 and 20, quadroons at 14 and 15, and mustee males at 2 years.[8] Black slaves probably had to purchase their freedom, whereas the children of white men were more likely to be released gratuitously.[9]

Although the evidence is limited, it is reasonable to conclude that the slaves released by manumission differed according to whether they purchased their freedom or were manumitted by a benefactor. Most of the latter probably belonged to the coloured slave elite on rural estates. Those slaves who purchased their own freedom were predominantly black town-dwellers, because the nature of their occupations and their relative independence enabled them to acquire cash, and because the urban, skilled slave saw more to be gained from freedom than did his rural counterpart.[10] In fact the black predial slave could see relatively little benefit from manumission so long as slavery remained the foundation of Jamaican society. By the time of emancipation, manumission was essentially an urban phenomenon, and its relationship with colour, sex and birth-place was a function of the urban pattern rather than simply a direct result of these factors or of white paternity.

In contrast to those manumitted, the slaves who ran away from their masters were predominantly black and male, and were very often Africans (Table 40). But, in common with those manumitted, a large proportion of them were town slaves.

Before discussing the reasons for this pattern of running away, it is necessary to make certain strictures on the statistics in Table 40. In the first place, there is difficulty in defining a 'runaway' slave. Some slaves absented themselves for a few days or weeks, at quite frequent intervals, in order to visit family or friends; the master was unlikely to advertise such slaves as runaways or to suspect that they would not return eventually of their own

Table 40. *Runaways, 1824, 1832 and 1834*

Parish	Totals 1824	Totals 1832	Totals 1834	1832 Slaves of colour	1832 Africans	1832 Females	1832 Mean age
Westmoreland	178	6	121	1	2	1	51
Hanover	112	22		1	10	5	49
St. James	139	17	82	2	2	2	41
Trelawny	139	17		1	5	7	44
St. Elizabeth	171	24		2	6	5	47
Manchester	224	10		1	4	1	44
St. Ann	237	40		6	5	15	46
Clarendon	223	13		1	7	4	48
Vere	111	8		1	3	3	45
St. Dorothy	49	6		—	2	3	36
St. Thomas-in-the-Vale	111	16	69	—	5	7	42
St. John	83	18		—	3	6	?
St. Catherine	60	22	69	3	8	7	48
St. Mary	205	51	156	4	7	16	48
St. Andrew	69	38	38	3	11	9	40
Port Royal	27	10	37	1	3	5	42
St. David	45	13	49	—	6	5	49
St. George	82	5	69	—	3	—	44
Portland	46	5	42	2	1	1	?
St. Thomas-in-the-East	90	5		—	1	2	?
Kingston	—	100	160	8	19	48	32
Total	2,373	446	(892)	37	113	152	44

Sources: J.H.A.V., 1824, pp. 189, 247; R.R.S. (1832); T.71/851 (1834).

accord.[11] Other slaves ran away for much longer periods of time, presumably with the intention of escaping permanently from slavery, and did not return to their masters unless captured. In listing runaway slaves, then, the masters generally noted both of these types in their plantation books, but omitted the former quite often when making their Returns of Registrations of Slaves. Thus in June 1832 only 446 slaves were returned as being runaways (Table 40). Official island returns, however, put the number at 2,555 in 1818, and (excluding Kingston) 2,373 in 1824.[12] In 1834 the valuers appointed by the assistant commissioners of compensation noted the number of runaways in only eleven of the twenty-one parishes (comprising 46 per cent of the slave population); but for those parishes they found 892 runaways which, if the parishes were representative, suggests a total of 1,960 for the island as a whole.[13] Hence it appears that the 446 runaway slaves included in the registration returns for 1832 were probably only the long-term runaways, and it is likely that their characteristics differed from the short-term runaways. A further problem is that after a time the masters struck the long-term runaways from their lists, presuming them dead or permanently lost. Thus the number of slaves reported by the masters as being runaway at any particular date would be less than the presumed total runaway population of the island.

These difficulties make it impossible to estimate the number of slaves who ran away in any particular year. It is possible only to calculate the number of slaves who had run away over a period but were still regarded by the masters as properly a part of the effective slave population. In these terms, there were roughly 2,000 runaways in 1834, or 0.6 per cent of the total slave population.[14] Comparison with the statistics for 1818 and 1824 suggests that the runaway proportion of the slave population had decreased over the period following the abolition of the slave trade. This decline can be explained by the decreasing proportion of male Africans in the population, the slaves most likely to run away. The high average age of the long-term runaways listed in the Returns of Registrations of Slaves for 1832 is evidence of this trend (Table 40).[15] But it also appears that town slaves were becoming increasingly important as runaways; Kingston accounted for 22 per cent of the long-term runaways registered in 1832, and 8 per cent in 1834, whereas only 4 per cent of the total slave population lived in the town. There is also some evidence of a similar growth in the urban and peri-urban parishes of St. Catherine and St. Andrew. Town slaves had opportunities to escape from the island by ship and to pass themselves off as free men, especially if they possessed skills permitting them a relative freedom of movement. But the town slave was less well placed to escape to the hills to establish provision settlements, the traditional mode of the rural slave and the 'new negro'.[16] As with manumission, the urban slave saw greater opportunities for establishing himself successfully as a free man within the context of a slave society. By 1832 most of the long-term runaways were black, but the propensity of coloured slaves to run away was only slightly less than their weight in the total population. Most of the coloured runaways were town slaves, and they were significantly younger than their black, rural counterparts.

Some of the complexities of the pattern of running away in the rural slave population can be illustrated by considering a particular plantation. In 1832 New Forest Plantation in Manchester comprised 4,000 acres and carried 320 head of livestock. There were 90 male and 106 female slaves on the plantation, the total having increased from 158 in 1817. The number of African-born slaves decreased from 37 to 22 between 1817 and 1832; only two of the slaves were coloured at the latter date.[17] Between 1828 and 1832 at least 24 of the New Forest slaves ran away and they stayed away for an average of six months, the range being four days to three years.[18] Thus over these five years the plantation lost 143 man-months of potential slave labour, or 28.6 months per annum – 1.25 per cent of the total slave labour time available. Altogether roughly 12 per cent of the slaves ran away at some time during the period, but three of them ran away twice and one three times, though these absences were generally short. Although the majority of the slaves were females, they accounted for only 20 per cent of the runaways. All of the female runaways worked in the field gangs, with the exception of Elizabeth Jones who was attached to the great house and returned after almost six months 'with a letter'. The occupations of the male runaways were more varied, including only six field labourers. Five of them were penkeepers, two masons, two carpenters and two watchmen. The head carpenter ran away for four months and the head penkeeper for eighteen. Some of the runaways were said to be old or sickly, though most were described as 'able'. It is important to notice that six of the runaway slaves were hired from other properties, and most of these stayed away for relatively short periods but were more likely to run away more than once. Dublin, for example, was a hired slave employed in the second gang; he ran away first in August 1829, but was brought in two months later by the Maroons; in February 1830 he left the plantation for four months and on his return was forgiven; less than a month later he ran away for another six weeks, being brought out of the Mandeville workhouse and forgiven.[19] Other runaways were treated much less tolerantly. For instance, George Palmer, a sheep boy, was punished when he returned of his own accord after an absence of only four days. Two of the New Forest runaways were tried and transported after absences of three years and nine months, and one was sentenced to the workhouse after running away for three months.

Whereas running away was essentially a universal response to servile status *per se,* it is important to notice that, if the hired slaves are excluded, almost one-third of the runaways at New Forest were skilled or held positions of privilege and authority on the plantation.[20] Similarly, at the parish level there were significant correlations between running away and the size of the non-predial slave population ($r = .79$), the percentage of births coloured ($r = .61$) and manumissions ($r = .88$). Together with the growing importance of the towns, this evidence suggests that, increasingly, as emancipation approached runaways were not the lowliest slaves, those furthest removed from white society, but rather those possessing the skills and accomplishments which enabled them to merge into the free population.

Yet most of the runaway slaves failed to merge successfully and permanently into free society or to isolate themselves, and many suffered for their attempts. The commonest punishments were transportation and committal to the workhouse. Between 1829 and 1832, 124 slaves were transported to Cuba or the hulks in England, at the island's expense.[21] But the planters felt that these places of terror were inadequate and that they really needed 'a sort of Botany Bay' for incorrigibles.[22] Not all of the slaves transported were convicted of running away; from 1829 to 1832 some 35 slaves were transported for their part in the rebellion of 1831,[23] though it is difficult to explain why so many came from St. Elizabeth (Table 41). Others were transported for theft. In 1807, for example, the slave Jasper broke into the

Table 41. *Slaves transported and committed to workhouses, 1829–32*

Parish	Transportations				Committals to workhouses			
	Total	Females	Africans	Slaves of colour	Total	Females	Africans	Slaves of colour
Westmoreland	11	2	4	1	12	3	3	—
Hanover	4	1	—	—	6	—	2	—
St. James	10	—	2	—	10	1	3	1
Trelawny	6	—	—	1	19	2	2	2
St. Elizabeth	40	3	5	3	6	1	1	—
Manchester	5	—	3	—	12	1	5	—
St. Ann	—	—	—	—	35	3	5	1
Clarendon	2	—	—	—	15	—	5	1
Vere	9	2	3	1	—	—	—	—
St. Dorothy	4	—	—	—	5	—	—	1
St. Thomas-in-the-Vale	4	—	—	1	14	2	6	—
St. John	6	2	2	—	2	—	—	—
St. Catherine	—	—	—	—	16	1	1	—
St. Mary	3	—	1	1	30	6	5	—
St. Andrew	1	1	—	—	17	1	6	1
Port Royal	4	1	2	—	4	1	2	—
St. David	—	—	—	—	5	—	2	—
St. George	—	—	—	—	14	4	6	—
Portland	4	—	2	—	2	—	1	—
St. Thomas-in-the-East	9	—	—	5	23	2	8	1
Kingston	2	1	—	1	8	1	—	—
Total	124	13	24	14	255	29	62	8

Source: R.R.S.

distilling-house of Fonthill Estate, St. Ann, at night, and stole a calabash of rum, for which he was transported;[24] and in 1825 a slave was transported from Trelawny for stealing from a slave-house on a neighbouring estate.[25] Even more than the runaways, those transported were predominantly male and black, but fewer of them were Africans. Slaves of colour were rarely transported, and most of those sent out during the period 1829–32 were probably rebels; the conspiracy at Manchioneal accounts for some of the five mulattoes transported from St. Thomas-in-the-East.

Of the slaves committed to the workhouse from 1829 to 1832 only 11 per cent were females and 3 per cent coloured, but at least 25 per cent of them were Africans (Table 41). In 1794 some 76 per cent had been Africans and in 1813 57 per cent.[26] A good number of these slaves were runaways, and this probably accounts for the decreasing proportion of Africans. Even free blacks and free people of colour who lacked proof of their freedom and were found wandering were committed if they had the 'appearance of a slave'.[27] In addition to the runaways, slaves were convicted for depredations on the planters' property, and the severity of punishments seems not to have varied greatly whether the property was slave or otherwise. In Westmoreland, for example, Cato of Delve was committed to the workhouse for three months for the manslaughter of a slave, while another was given the same period plus 39 lashes each month for being found with fresh beef in his possession.[28] In St. Ann a slave who stole four pails of rum was sentenced to six months hard labour and received 39 lashes in the public market on the Sunday after going into the workhouse and again on the Sunday before his discharge; another slave who beat a woman to death received the same sentence plus three months.[29] Many parishes jobbed their convict slaves on the public roads, and the slaves thus continued to be a source of revenue to the parish and, indirectly, the planter.[30]

Manumission, running away, transportation and committal to the workhouse did not have a very considerable impact on the size of the slave population of Jamaica but affected its structure significantly. Those slaves committed to workhouses did not in fact leave the slave population, and their labour was withdrawn only temporarily and partially from their masters. In terms of annual losses, manumission was most important, accounting for about 500 slaves each year by the 1820s. The annual loss to the slave population from running away is more difficult to establish, but it was certainly less than 500 by 1834. It is probable that the proportion of slaves running away decreased in the period after 1807, along with the decline in the African section of the population, so that this form of escape from slavery must have been more important than manumission until about 1817. Losses to the slave population from transportation were relatively minor, amounting to less than 50 per annum. Since manumission and running away increasingly became urban phenomena, their impact on the size of the town slave populations was significant and may partially account for the decline of the numbers in Kingston. The reduction of the number of slaves with white fathers through manumission had the most obvious effect on the structure of the slave population. Although manumission, running away and transportation were also selective in terms of sex, age and birthplace, their impact on these aspects of the structure of the total slave population was insignificant.

PART III

DEMOGRAPHIC CHANGE AND ECONOMIC DECLINE

CHAPTER 9

ORGANIZATION OF SLAVE LABOUR

The slave master was determined, above all, to allocate the labour-time of his slaves as profitably as possible. The idea that slave economies were maintained, in the face of their essential unprofitability, for considerations of social status, appears to have little validity.[1] Similarly, the contention that slavery was an inherently inefficient system of labour organization, in which the master gained benefits chiefly from the pleasure of conspicuous consumption, is not well founded.[2] In fact the masters seem to have exploited the labour of their slaves quite efficiently. The master's claim to property rights in human capital – slaves – pushed outwards the supply curve of labour, so that he commanded a labour input greater than that which would be offered voluntarily on a free market. Thus the master exploited the slave's labour in this sense as well as providing the slave with a return to his labour below the value of his marginal revenue product.[3]

In the eighteenth century the Jamaica planter could control the size and composition of his slave labour force through selective purchase from the slave-ships. After 1807 this became impossible, and the immobility of the slave population meant that regional inequalities in the distribution of the labour force emerged which could not be overcome through the island slave market.[4] As well as reducing the absolute size of the slave labour force, the abolition of the slave trade also reduced the elasticity of the backward-bending supply curve of labour, making it increasingly expensive for the master to respond to changes in the demand for labour. Thus, although it has been shown that the slave population of Jamaica was not strictly 'closed' after 1807, the master could not readily increase (or decrease) the size of his slave labour force, in the short-run, or control its composition. He could attempt to extract the maximum amount of labour-time from the maximum number of slaves on his property, by manipulating the organization of tasks to keep the slaves fully occupied throughout the year and through the use of physical coercion and various incentives.[5] But the planters had employed these techniques of labour–profit maximization long before the abolition of the slave trade; the abolition meant that more than ever the master confronted a fixed labour force, changes in the structure of which he was largely powerless to control.

The significance of this fixity in the location and composition of the slave labour force lay in the fact that it resulted in functional inequalities. The master saw the allocation of slaves to particular tasks as being determined by their sex, age, colour, birthplace and state of health, so that he was forced to make a compromise between the demand for labour on his property and the characteristics of the available slave population. By the late eighteenth century, certain general principles regarding the manipulation of slave labour had emerged, but they were strained by the demographic changes which took place between 1807 and 1834. These general principles, illustrated by examples from particular holdings, will be discussed in this chapter, as a prelude to an examination of their impact on the level of productivity in the slave labour force.

Occupational allocation

In his *Instructions for the Management of a Plantation in Barbados, and for the Treatment of Negroes &c.*, published in 1786, the planter Edwin Lascelles wrote:

> One of the most important parts of management is a judicious division of negroes into gangs. The application of their labour to works suited to their strength and ability requires the strictest attention. A manager, immediately after his entrance upon a plantation, ought to examine individually the state and condition of every negro; and then to assort them in such a manner, that they may never be employed upon any work to which their powers are not equal.[6]

For Jamaica, a neat summary of the general principles involved in the allocation of slaves to occupations, on sugar estates, was provided by Roughley.[7] The first or great gang, he said, should be 'composed of a mixture of able men and women . . . drafted and recruited from all the other gangs, as they come of an age to endure severe labour'. The second gang was to be made up of those 'who are thought to be of rather weakly habits, mothers of sucking children, youths drafted from the children's gang, from twelve to eighteen years of age, and elderly people that are sufficiently strong for field-work'. The third or weeding gang was to comprise all the healthy children between the ages of five and twelve years. It was unhealthy for the slave child to remained unemployed for long, said Roughley; idle habits should not be allowed to take root. The cattle and mule-boys should never be chosen from the Africans or youths between twelve and twenty years of age: 'Take then the tractable, docile youth, of creole birth, for most of them know how both to lead and yoke cattle, and ride and tackle mules'. Watchmen, placed along the estate line and in the provision grounds to guard against cattle and thieves, were to come from those no longer capable of field labour:

> As some slaves begin to decline by inevitable old age, infirmity, or disability to stand the more heavy laborious, field work, they should be allotted to those kinds of occupations which do not bear hard upon them. Something they should always have to do, to keep their minds employed, and their bodies in easy activity.

Finally, the house slaves 'should always be composed of the people of colour belonging to the property, or cleanly, well-affected slaves to white people', neat, civil, quiet, sober, upright, and 'not addicted to steal away to the negro-houses'.

In addition to these general rules of Roughley, it was widely held that slaves of colour should not be employed in field labour and that they should be given preference in the training of tradesmen, 'the flower of the slave population'.[8] They were also given preference in the appointment of headmen, except that the 'drivers' of the field slaves were generally black.[9] The resulting hierarchy of supervisory roles and occupational statuses contained within it the elements of coercion and the incentives fundamental to the maximization of the slaves' labour output. Yet this functional differentiation was not without its pitfalls; as the Barbados Agricultural Society observed in 1812:

One of the causes of depression among our slaves and of the consequent diseases is derived from a source the least likely perhaps to attract the notice of a superficial observer. We mean the inequality among them. They should be placed as nearly as possible on an equality and be taught to think as highly as possible of themselves as human beings in such a state can. They should be guarded from the oppression of their brother slaves who happen of necessity to be placed over them and by being encouraged to realize a comfortable peculium of their own, feel themselves to have an interest at stake and a regard for home.[10]

But the supervisory slaves did not allocate their fellows to occupations; they simply regulated the rate of labour and the day-to-day performance of tasks. They did, however, have opportunities to show favour – to their kin, for example. As William Miller, one of the great northside attorneys of Jamaica, explained in 1833:

On all estates arrangements are made at the commencement of crop, and each particular class of labourers has its separate duty apportioned. The arrangement is generally left among the head people who study their own convenience in placing their families in immediate connection upon the same watch or spell with themselves; but it is always subject to the approval of the manager.[11]

The general principles of occupational allocation discussed thus far applied strictly to sugar estates. But, although the tasks of slaves on other types of units were varied, the basic principles of allocation were similar.[12] The degree of occupational differentiation tended to decrease along with holding size, and slaves often had greater opportunities for relatively independent activity outside the sugar estates. Task work was also more common, especially on coffee and pimento plantations. A more significant contrast is that since domestic functions were particularly in demand in the towns the direct connection between the size of the female slave coloured population and the domestic group did not hold. But, essentially, the masters always allocated slaves to occupations on the basis of their sex, age, colour, birthplace and health.

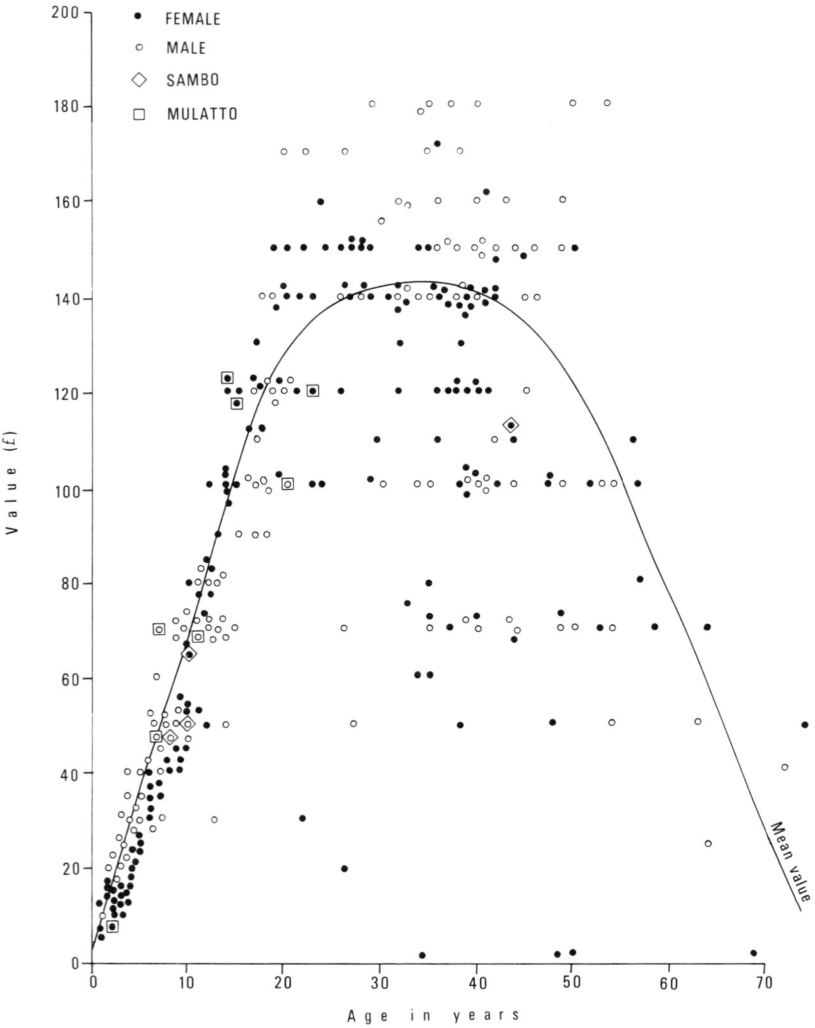

Figure 33. Age-value profile of slaves, Shrewsbury Estate, Portland, 1817.

Of all the demographic characteristics considered by the masters in allocating slaves to occupations, age was the most fundamental. Whether a slave was male or female, African or creole, or black or coloured simply placed limits on the basic pattern of allocation determined by age. As a corollary, the masters valued their slaves, as property and human capital, largely on the basis of age. It has been shown by Fogel and Engerman that in the United States the age-price profiles of slaves followed closely the curve of net earnings by age,[13] thus an examination of age-value profiles throws considerable light on the returns masters expected from slaves at different

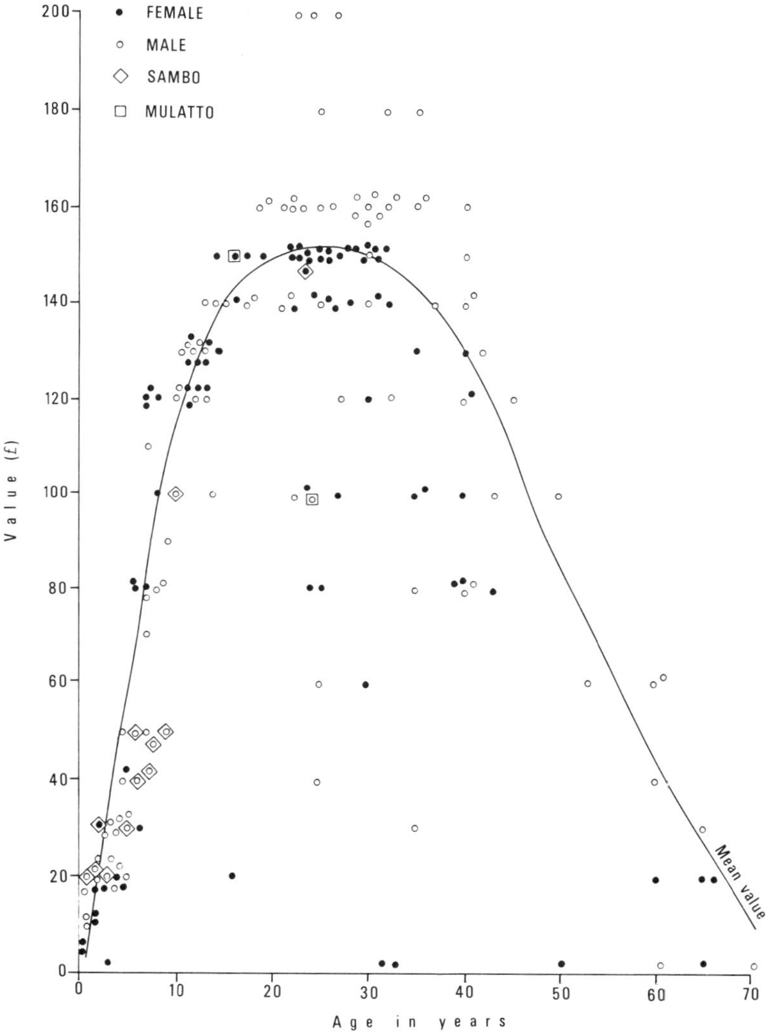

Figure 34. Age-value profile of slaves, Cape Clear Pen, St. Mary, 1817.

points in their life cycles. For Jamaica, it is possible to find the value placed on each slave belonging to a particular slave-holding when the master's property was inventoried at his death, and the demographic characteristics of the slaves so valued can be filled out from the Returns of Registrations of Slaves, for the years around 1817. Two examples of the resulting age–value profiles are shown in Figures 33 and 34. Shrewsbury was a monocultural sugar estate located in Portland, with 329 slaves in 1817.[14] Cape Clear Pen in St. Mary raised planters' stock, sold beef to neighbouring sugar estates, and jobbed some of its 189 slaves on them.[15]

In spite of their economic contrasts, the age–value profiles of the slaves on these two properties were very similar. There was a considerable scatter of values, especially between the ages of 20 and 45 years when some slaves possessed highly valued skills while others were prematurely debilitated, but the average value followed a smooth curve. The slave's value rose steeply until about age fifteen, then levelled off to reach a peak at roughly 30 years. It then fell sharply after about 40–45 years, though the rate of decline seems to have slowed slightly after about 60 years of age. The only significant contrast between the age–value profiles of the two properties was that the pen's curve was skewed relative to that of the sugar estate. Thus the slaves at Cape Clear reached their peak value earlier than those at Shrewsbury, and also fell off more quickly. The reason for this contrast probably lay in the fact that there was a higher ratio of skilled slaves on sugar estates, who remained apprentices into their twenties but maintained high values into their later years as well. It is more difficult to explain why the average peak value at Cape Clear exceeded that at Shrewsbury; but it is obvious that penkeepers expected net average earnings from slaves in their prime equal to those obtained on sugar estates.

Divergences from the age–value profiles of these slave populations, resulting from differences in sex, colour and country, were relatively minor. Health was, of course, a much more variable factor. Males were valued more highly than females in the earliest years of life, but the sexes then seem to have reached a rough equality during adolescence. After age twenty males were once again valued more highly, but the difference was small, generally only £10 or less than 7 per cent of the total value. On average, the males aged 20–40 years at Cape Clear Pen were valued at £139 while the females were put at £124; this difference may be explained largely in terms of the skills of the males. After 40 years of age the gap between the sexes narrowed even further. Colour also tended to depress the values placed on slaves, but only in an inconsistent and marginal fashion. Finally, it does appear that creoles were valued more highly than Africans, around 1817 (Figure 35). The planters generally agreed that this was the case, though at the same time arguing that the cost of breeding slaves exceeded that of importing them.[16] Once more, this contrast was closely related to the acquired skills of the two groups. It is probable that there was a closing of the gap between the values placed on creoles and Africans in the years after 1807, as all of the Africans were fully seasoned by 1817. Similarly, there may have been a convergence of values for males and females as the reproductive function of the latter increased in importance.

Although the patterns revealed in the age–value profiles are of great interest, they are themselves reflections of the basic principles involved in occupational allocation. To follow the operation of these principles in practice it is necessary to look at some specific examples of their application on Jamaican estates.

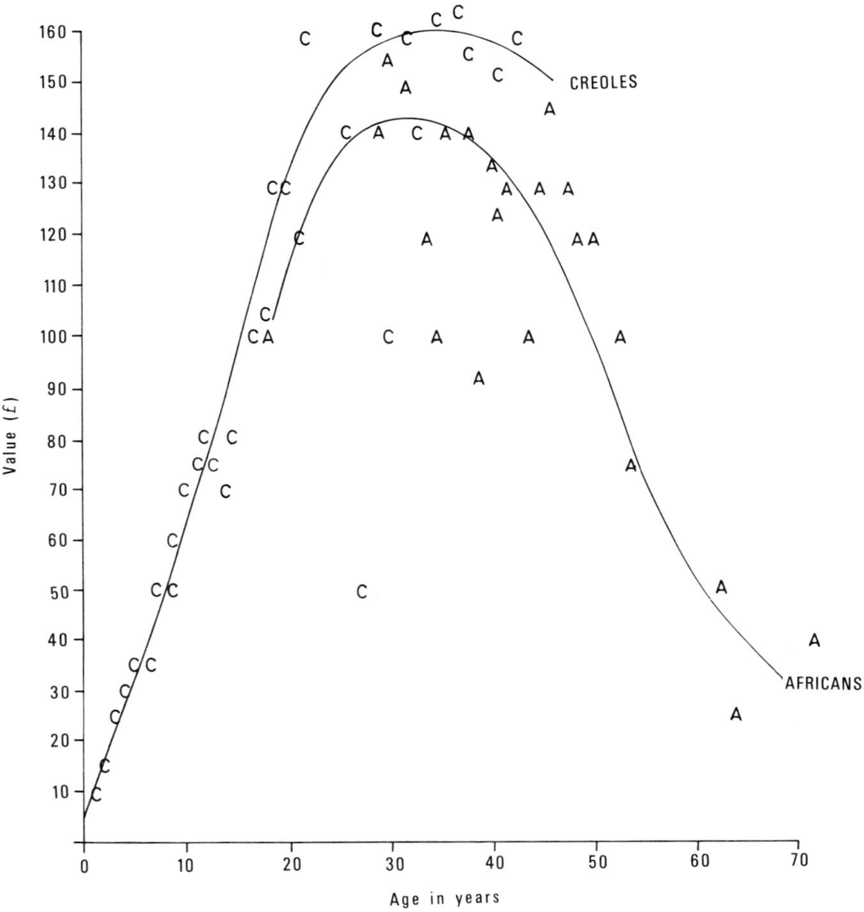

Figure 35. Mean values of African and creole male slaves, by age, Shrewsbury Estate, 1817.

Rose Hall Estate, St. James Rose Hall was a small coastal sugar estate, with only 111 slaves in 1832. It was in the hands of receivers. Although it was small, the average production per slave in 1832 was almost £52, twice the average for sugar estates. There were 60 female slaves and 51 males. But, despite a low level of fertility, the rate of natural increase (—12.0 per 1,000) was not abnormal. The age distribution of the slave population was more evenly balanced than on many sugar estates, and 43 per cent of the slaves were in the vital 20–44 years age-group in 1832. But this group was dominated by women. Twenty of the slaves were coloured (18 per cent) and eighteen were Africans (16 per cent), thus the estate had a higher proportion of creoles and slaves of colour than was normal for sugar estates.[17]

The point which emerges most clearly from the pattern of occupational

Table 42. *Occupational allocation at Rose Hall, 1832*

Occupation	Total	Slaves of colour	Africans	Sick, weakly, disabled	Bad, indolent, runaway	Age: Mean	Age: Range
Males							
Field	6	—	—	—	2	23	13–31
Drivers	2	—	—	—	—	37	35–39
Distillers/boilers	3	—	1	1	—	34	27–54
Fishermen	1	—	—	—	1	32	—
Cartmen	3	—	—	—	1	27	21–31
Masons	1	—	1	1	1	56	—
Carpenters	2	—	—	1	—	49	44–54
Coopers	4	1	—	2	1	38	25–54
Blacksmiths	1	—	—	—	—	37	—
Domestics	5	4	1	1	1	20	9–54
Pen	9	—	1	—	4	19	6–44
Watchmen	6	—	3	6	1	56	42–64
Hogmeat Gang	2	1	—	—	—	5	4–5
Not working	6	4	—	—	—	2	1–6
Total	51	10	7	12	12		
Females							
Field	29	2	3	7	7	34	12–54
Driveress	1	—	1	1	—	54	—
Grasscutters	7	—	5	7	1	57	54–59
Attending small stock	2	1	—	1	—	15	13–17
Attending children	2	—	2	1	—	58	54–62
Hogmeat gang	8	2	—	—	—	6	4–9
Hospital	2	—	—	1	—	33	23–44
Domestics	6	3	—	—	—	25	13–42
Not working	3	2	—	—	—	3	1–4
Total	60	10	11	18	8		

Source: Rose Hall Journal, 1817–32, Vol. 2 (Jamaica Archives, Spanish Town); Joseph Shore and John Stewart, *In Old St. James* (Kingston, 1911), pp. 140–51.

allocation at Rose Hall in 1832 (Table 42) is that the range of possibilities was much more limited for women than men and that as a result half of them were employed in the field, whereas only one in eight of the males was a predial.[18] Thus women remained in the field longer than the men, and two sambo women were recruited to field labour. All of the male predials were described as healthy, but seven of the women were 'weakly', two suffering from venereal disease and two from whitlow (paronychia, a swelling about the finger nails). Only one of the male slaves of colour was employed other than as a tradesman or domestic – a mulatto boy, five years old, who collected grass for the pigs and poultry. Of the women of colour, however, only three were domestics while five were attached to agricultural tasks. African males also had better chances of being occupied as tradesmen or in other non-predial tasks than did the women. Apart from the infirm women

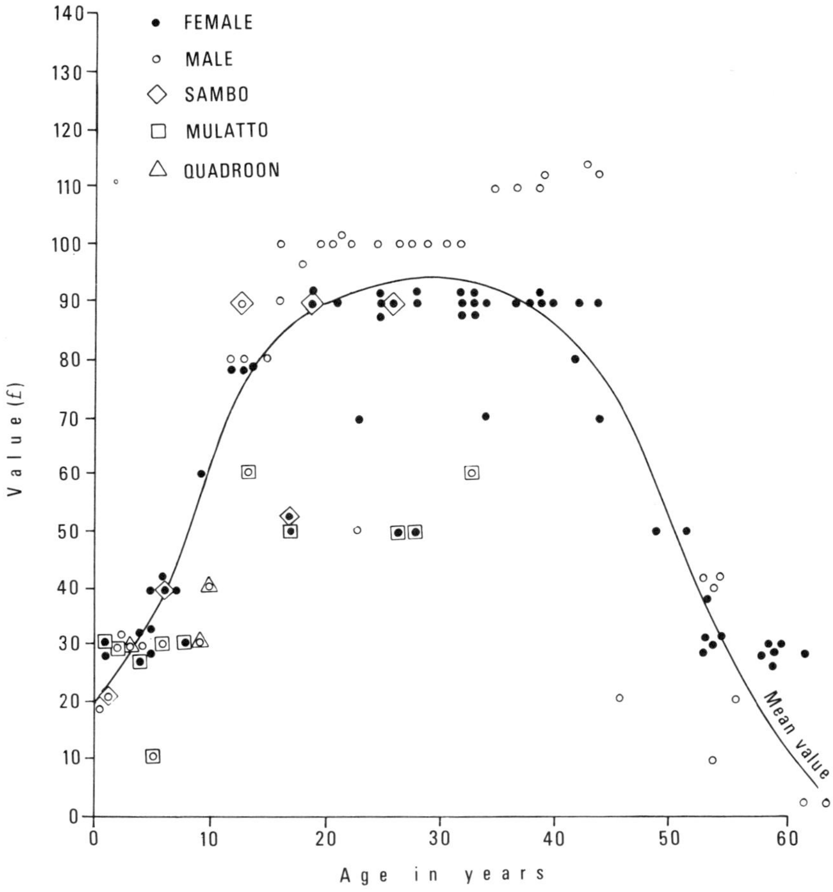

Figure 36. Age-value profile of slaves, Rose Hall Estate, St. James, 1832.

in the field gangs and the tradesmen, all of the weakly slaves were employed as watchmen or grasscutters; this condition was closely related to aging. All of the women said to be of a 'bad' or 'indolent' disposition were placed in the field gangs, but males with such reputations were employed in much more independent occupations; the head cooper, for example, was described as a 'drunkard', but the estate could hardly afford to relegate him to the field.

Within the limits imposed by sex, colour and health, the most fundamental determinant of occupational allocation at Rose Hall was age. The range of ages within each group was limited, except in the case of the field slaves (the gangs not being distinguished) and the tradesmen and domestics who were bound by colour and skills acquired over the years. The age–value profile of the slave population at Rose Hall in 1832 (Figure 36) was similar to that established for Shrewsbury and Cape Clear around 1817, though the peak values at Rose Hall were significantly lower. Compared to the pattern at Shrewsbury, the values at Rose Hall were similar to the age of about 15 years but then levelled off to form a plateau until 44 years, and fell more rapidly in the older age-groups. Women never reached the values attained by skilled men, but the differential was rarely greater than £10 in the years of peak value. Females seem to have been valued more highly than males when young and old; infant mortality was higher for males than females, and among the aged it seems that a grasscutter was valued more highly than a watchman. Coloured slaves, especially those with white fathers, were valued less highly than blacks; the relatively large proportion of slaves of colour at Rose Hall meant that many of them could not be employed in the highly valued skilled occupations.

Occupational allocations did not remain fixed throughout the year, of course, but shifts seem to have been confined largely to the able, predial group.[19] At Rose Hall the principal variation was in the number of slaves from the first gang employed in odd jobs.[20] The first gang normally comprised 35 slaves, but on 14 February 1832, for instance, it was reduced to 24 and the second gang increased to 17, the first being employed breaking stones for the lime kiln and the second cutting copperwood (presumably for the kiln). The next day the first gang was cutting the wood, and the second filling the kiln; then both were cutting wood. Until the end of February the first gang continued to cut wood, but the second was moved to trashing the canes. In March, when preparations were made for the crop, the field gangs were reduced to a total of 21 slaves and no grasscutters were employed. The relieved slaves worked in the boiling-house, still-house, mill-house and yard; some 22 slaves were hired from Grange Pen, most of them to cut canes and work in the mill. On some days in July the slaves in the mill and still-house were recruited to the field gangs to cut canes or to plant new fields, and the latter distribution continued after the completion of the crop on 13 July. Thus there were some predials who left the fields to perform skilled tasks during crop, but they were all black men of about 30 years of age; although the coopers and masons were employed in the field during September, it is not certain that the mulatto cooper was included. The limits of flexibility were fairly narrow.

Maryland Plantation, St. Andrew This coffee plantation was situated near Irish Town, at about 2,500 feet above sea-level, on the road leading north out of Kingston. It was owned by Sir Edward Hyde East, son of one of the ancient Jamaica planting families, who was born in the island but left it to be called to the bar in 1786, to support the West India interest in Parliament, and to be declared bankrupt in 1831.[21] The plantation was managed by an attorney and an overseer. Although it produced coffee, there was a natural decrease in the slave population of the plantation, and in 1832 average production per slave was a low £13.[22]

Table 43. *Occupational allocation at Maryland, 1822, by age-group*

Occupation		0–9	10–19	20–29	30–39	40–49	50+	Total
Field								
Males:	Black	18	21	14	11	8	6	78
	Coloured	—	1	—	—	—	—	1
Females:	Black	11	17	11	19	14	6	78
	Coloured	—	—	—	—	—	—	—
Watchmen/Pen								
Males:	Black	—	2	1	—	4	15	22
	Coloured	—	—	—	—	—	—	—
Females:	Black	—	1	—	1	—	6	8
	Coloured	—	—	—	—	—	—	—
Tradesmen								
Males:	Black	—	2	6	6	2	2	18
	Coloured	—	—	—	2	2	—	4
Hospital								
Females:	Black	—	—	—	—	3	3	6
	Coloured	—	—	—	—	—	—	—
House								
Males:	Black	—	2	—	—	1	—	3
	Coloured	1	—	—	—	—	—	1
Females:	Black	—	—	—	2	3	1	6
	Coloured	3	2	—	—	—	—	5
Invalids								
Males:	Black	—	—	1	—	—	9	10
	Coloured	—	—	1	—	—	—	1
Females:	Black	—	—	—	2	4	22	28
	Coloured	—	—	—	—	—	—	—
TOTAL[a]		33	48	34	43	41	70	269

[a] Excluding 62 children, less than 6 years of age, not working.
Source: Maryland Estate Book, 1 January 1822.

In 1822, the year for which occupational data are available, there were 331 slaves at Maryland, 170 males and 161 females.[23] Of the total, 41 per cent were less than 20 years of age, 31 per cent were between 20 and 44 years, and 28 per cent were over 44 years; only in the last group did the women outnumber the men. The occupational pattern at Maryland is shown in a simplified form in Table 43. All of the coloured females were domestics and the males tradesmen, with the exception of a sambo boy of twelve years who was in the field. At Maryland the slaves were not classified into gangs in the list of 1822, but a head driver, second driver, third driver and children's driver (all men, unusually) were noted, so it is probable that the pattern of organization was in fact similar to that on sugar estates. As at Rose Hall, the women were kept in the field longer than the men, and in the 20–59 years age-group only nine of the women (excluding invalids) were not employed in the field whereas twenty men were not. The 'weakly' males were removed

Table 44. *Occupational allocation at Irwin, 1821*

Occupation	Total	Slaves of colour	Africans	Age	
				Mean	Range
Males					
First gang	37	—	—	35	20–55
Second gang	16	—	—	14	10–21
Third gang	12	—	—	9	5–12
Drivers	3	—	—	35	28–49
Masons	3	—	—	35	28–46
Carpenters	5	2	—	31	11–45
Coopers	5	—	1	31	22–49
Blacksmiths	2	—	—	29	25–32
Domestics	8	6	—	21	13–36
Attending Stock	8	1	—	29	13–64
Watchmen	16	—	1	54	39–84
Hospital	1	—	—	23	—
Invalids	3	—	—	61	44–70
Not working	16	1	—	2	0–5
Total	135	10	2		
Females					
First gang	46	—	1	30	14–51
Second gang	23	—	—	23	11–64
Third gang	7	—	—	21	6–54
Domestics	12	5	—	28	8–49
Grasscutters	15	—	—	48	39–64
Midwives	2	—	—	49	46–52
Hospital	2	—	—	50	49–50
Invalids	11	—	—	61	39–82
Not working	6	—	—	4	2–6
Total	124	5	1		

Source: List of Slaves and Stock on Irwin Estate, 28 December 1821.

from the field to tend the cattle, sheep and hogs or to watch the lines much earlier than the women were given the task of attending the poultry, except when they were diseased or disabled. The recruitment of black women to domestic work stopped as soon as female slaves of colour were born on the plantation, but blacks were regularly apprenticed to the trades. Carpenters were apprenticed at approximately five-year intervals, but when mulattoes were on the plantation it seems that they were often apprenticed along with a black slave; it is difficult to account for this, unless the planter feared the coloured slave would be manumitted or be especially susceptible to disease. With the exception of the hospital doctor, all of the Africans were predials.

Irwin Estate, St. James In 1832, with 231 slaves, a natural increase of —12.9 per 1,000 and an average production of £26.1 per slave, Irwin was the archetypal sugar estate.[24] But at the end of 1821, the year for which occupational data are available, there were 259 slaves on the estate and the males maintained a majority; 34 per cent were less than 20 years old, 42 per cent between 20 and 44 years, and 24 per cent older than 44 years.[25] Females were in a majority in the first and second gangs, but much less so than seems to have been the case by 1832 (Table 44). There was very little overlap in the age-groups included in the three gangs, and few slaves were kept in the first gang after reaching the age of 45 years. All of the female slaves of colour, and a majority of the males, were domestics. But one sambo boy of thirteen years attended the livestock, along with black boys of similar age, even though blacks of fifteen and sixteen were working as domestics.

The allocation of occupations at Irwin followed very closely the principles laid down by Roughley. A clearer understanding of the operation of these principles can be obtained by examining the attorney or overseer's reallocation of tasks for 1822. Following the list of slaves for 1821 there is another, undated, list of certain slaves showing their age (in 1822), colour, state of health and occupation; many of the occupations appearing here are pencilled in by the names in the list of 1821. Using these two lists it is possible to follow the planter's reorganization of the slave labour force and to see which factors he thought important in allocation. These data are summarized in Table 45. The first point to note is that slaves of colour were taken into the protection of the house when old enough to be given domestic tasks; the females remained there throughout their lives, but most of the males were

Table 45. *Changes in occupation at Irwin, 1821–2*

Name	Colour	Age in 1821	Condition	Occupation in 1821	Occupation in 1822
Males					
William	Quadroon	4	Healthy	Not working	Domestic
Jack	Mulatto	15	Healthy	Domestic	Mason
John	Mulatto	16	Healthy	Domestic	Mason
George	Mulatto	34	Weakly	Domestic	Tailor
James	Mulatto	36	Healthy	Domestic	Mt. Fairfield
Jack	Sambo	13	Healthy	Attending stock	Domestic
William	Black	10	Healthy	Third gang	Domestic
Titus	Black	11	?	Second gang	Third gang
Howie	Black	12	?	Second gang	Third gang
Toby	Black	12	?	Second gang	Third gang
Winton	Black	13	?	Second gang	Third gang
Joe	Black	13	Weakly	Second gang	Attending sheep
Patrick	Black	14	?	Second gang	Third gang
Robin	Black	21	?	Second gang	Hogmeat gang
Hughie	Black	21	?	First gang	Third driver
Chester	Black	39	Weakly	First gang	Watchman
Sam	Black	31	Healthy	First gang	Watchman
Harris	Black	44	Weakly	Invalid	Watchman
Trim	Black	44	?	Watchman	Second gang
Billy	Black	46	Weakly	First gang	Watchman
Howe	Black	54	Healthy	First gang	Watchman

Table 45. *Changes in occupation at Irwin, 1821–2* (*Continued*)

Name	Colour	Age in 1821	Condition	Occupation in 1821	Occupation in 1822
Females					
Susan	Mulatto	12	Healthy	Domestic	Mt. Fairfield
Pepper	Black	11	?	Second gang	Third gang
Phoebe	Black	11	?	Second gang	Third gang
Margery	Black	12	?	Second gang	Third gang
Nevis	Black	12	?	Second gang	Third gang
Thisbe	Black	12	?	Second gang	Third gang
Venus	Black	12	?	Second gang	First gang
Clemmie	Black	12	Weakly	Second gang	Attending fowls
July	Black	13	?	Second gang	First gang
Marina	Black	13	?	Second gang	First gang
Sophy	Black	13	?	Second gang	First gang
Deborah	Black	15	?	Second gang	First gang
Elinda	Black	31	Weakly	Second gang	Carpenter's cook
Juba	Black	32	?	First gang	Second gang
Calia	Black	34	Weakly	First gang	Nurse
Daphne	Black	42	?	First gang	First gang cook
Esther	Black	43	?	First gang	Second gang
Kate	Black	44	?	First gang	Second gang
Poll	Black	46	?	First gang	Second gang
Cynthia	Black	46	?	Second gang	Grasscutter
Nelly	Black	46	Healthy	Midwife	Indulged
Linda	Black	47	?	First gang	Second gang
Rachel	Black	47	?	First gang	Second gang
Tulip	Black	48	?	First gang	Second gang
Nancy	Black	49	?	First gang	Second gang
Sophy	Black	49	Healthy	First gang	Washerwoman
Jenny	Black	49	?	Second gang	Grasscutter
Peggy	Black	49	?	Second gang	Second gang cook
Wannica	Black	49	?	Grasscutter	Second gang
Juba	Black	54	Weakly	Grasscutter	Boiling oil
Patience	Black	58	Weakly	Invalid	Picking cotton
Fidelia	Black	59	?	Second gang cook	Grasscutter
Joan	Black	62	?	Invalid	Grasscutter
Bess	Black	64	Healthy	Grasscutter	Attending fowls

Source: List of Slaves and Stock on Irwin Estate, 1820 to 1827.

apprenticed to trades when they were about sixteen years old. (The designation 'Mt. Fairfield' refers to the estate's pen, and probably domestic work.) Some coloured males remained in the house longer and a few, it seems, were taught crafts at later ages. It will be noticed that Jack, the sambo boy who had been attending the livestock, was brought into the house; he was said to be 'ill disposed', so his period outside may have constituted a punishment.[26] No males were moved into the first gang in 1822 but five girls, aged 12–15 years, were shifted to it from the second gang. Movements out of the first gang involved weakly men who became watchmen and women over 30 years who went to lighter duties or the second gang. It is hard to explain why the seven males and five females of 11–21 years were moved 'down' from the second gang to the third, unless they were sick. No slaves left the third gang except William, who went to the house; he was one of the two black slaves at Irwin to have a Christian name (Cargil Mowat) as well as an old name. The other, Soby Askey, a 34-year-old black, whose occupation in 1821 is unknown, was described as healthy and 'indulged' in 1822. When a slave became sick his task was lightened, but when he recovered he was reallocated to something heavier even if aged or weak, as in the cases of Trim and Wannica. In sum, the allocation of tasks depended on the interplay of age and health, within the limits set by sex and colour.

This pattern of occupational reallocation at Irwin from 1821 to 1822 may be compared with that at Old Montpelier from 1828 to 1829, where the general distribution of tasks has been described already.[27] As at Irwin, there was a gulf between the ages of 20 and 45 years when occupational changes were very rare; this was reflected in the plateaux of the age-value profiles. At Old Montpelier only one slave in this age-group changed occupation in 1828–9, a healthy creole cook who was moved into the first gang. In general, there was a regular progression through the field gangs until the age of 20 years when the slave lodged in the first gang, though the males were occasionally taken from the second gang to be apprenticed to trades. The range of ages for entry to a particular gang was quite narrow. By the age of 45 years the slaves who survived at Old Montpelier were frequently described as 'weakly', and as the master's expectation of a return from their labour declined they passed from field to farm, to watchman, to invalid.

Demographic change and labour organization

These examples of the allocation of slaves to occupations suggest that the masters saw definite limits to the flexibility of the slave labour force. Such limits were set, first of all, by the immutable characteristics of sex and colour, and by the inexorable life cycle of the slave. The master could not control these aspects of the composition of his labour force, except by selective sale, purchase and manumission. He also saw the slaves' health and disposition as important in the allocation of occupations but, although he did have a degree of control over these factors, he generally claimed or felt a powerlessness to affect them. The master could more readily determine the absolute size of his slave-holding but the abolition of the slave trade made this increasingly expensive. Similarly, changes in the structure of the slave population consequent on the abolition placed stresses on the master's fixed principles of labour organiization, which he saw as affecting adversely the profitability of his enterprise.

Late in 1833, Joseph Gordon, attorney for estates in the twelve eastern parishes of Jamaica, told the Assembly that 'there are upon no estate more negroes than are considered necessary for the cultivation of that property, and it is necessary that all should remain together to carry it on'.[28] In the light of the high rates of natural decrease established in Chapter 6 this is not surprising. But where there were natural increases, as in Vere, it was said that 'the strength of the negroes upon the estates . . . is more than equal to the work upon the estates'.[29] If the natural increase went together with an immature age structure, as in the coffee parishes, however, the planters continued to complain of a shortage of labour.[30] For example, the attorney of Hermitage Plantation in St. Elizabeth told its absentee owner in 1822 that the property needed ten or fifteen extra slaves,

> but there is great difficulty now in purchasing any negroes since the abolition of the slave trade. If there are any negroes for sale many applications are prior made to obtain a preference of purchase, and cash or a good bill of exchange given down for the payment and a gang of negroes would average round old and young included on a valuation from £110 to £140 per head according to the appearance and abilities.[31]

The movement of slave prices in Jamaica between 1807 and 1834 has not been studied rigorously but there is reason to question the view that they rose 'steeply' after 1807.[32] The evidence collected from the inventories suggests that valuations maintained a peak of about £140 at age 30 from 1807 to the early 1820s, then decreased significantly as emancipation loomed.[33] What the planters were really complaining of was the contrast between the cost of purchasing a 'new' African from the slave-ships (with the attendant risk of early death) and the price of a creole. This contrast may be seen by comparing the age–value profile of the Westmoreland jobbing gang of 38 slaves belonging to Martin Wagstaffe in 1808 with that of the 49 slaves owned by Lauchlan McLean, a Kingston shipwright, in 1831 (Figures 37 and 38).[34] The peak value had dropped from £140 to £100 but, more importantly, whereas only four of Wagstaffe's slaves were put at less than £80 as many as 34 of McLean's were so valued. Twenty of Wagstaffe's slaves were 'new negroes', all valued at between £100 and £300. The peak value of £100 for McLean's shipwright slaves in 1831 is similar to that found for Rose Hall sugar estate in 1832. It seems that values fell even further after 1832, as at Whim Estate, in St. Dorothy, in early 1833 the peak value was only £70 for males and £50 for females (Figure 39).[35] There only the head carpenter was put at more than £80. The age–value profile also became decreasingly steep in the early and late years of life (as at Rose Hall), so that by 1833 slaves did not reach values of more than £25 before they were ten years old, whereas around 1817 they had reached £50. Thus, although the working of the Jamaica slave market requires much closer analysis before definitive answers can be obtained, it appears that slave prices reached a peak about 1807, remained fairly constant into the early 1820s, then fell rapidly as emancipation threatened and the plantation economy suffered a definite decline.

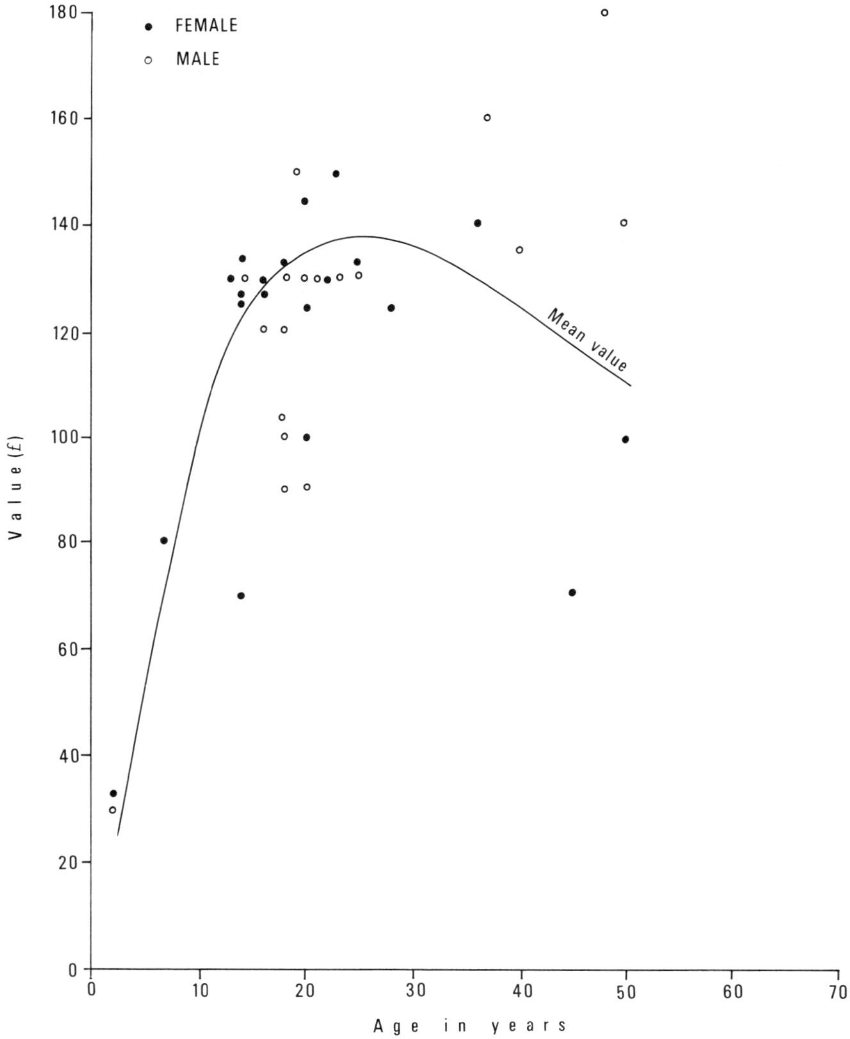

Figure 37. Age-value profile of slaves belonging to Martin Wagstaffe, Westmoreland, 1808.

The dearth of slaves lamented by the planters had a cumulative effect on estate output. During crop it was necessary to maintain a large force in the field by day in order to plant new canes. Thus it was said that 'On estates which are weak-handed, it is not possible to put in the spring plant and go on with the manufacture of produce at one and the same time. Any of those duties omitted during that period, would lessen the produce of the ensuing crop.'[36] This seems to have been the case on Georgia Estate in St. Thomas-in-the-East where the shortness of the crop in 1833 was attributed to having put in a late spring plant, and this in spite of two purchases of slaves in

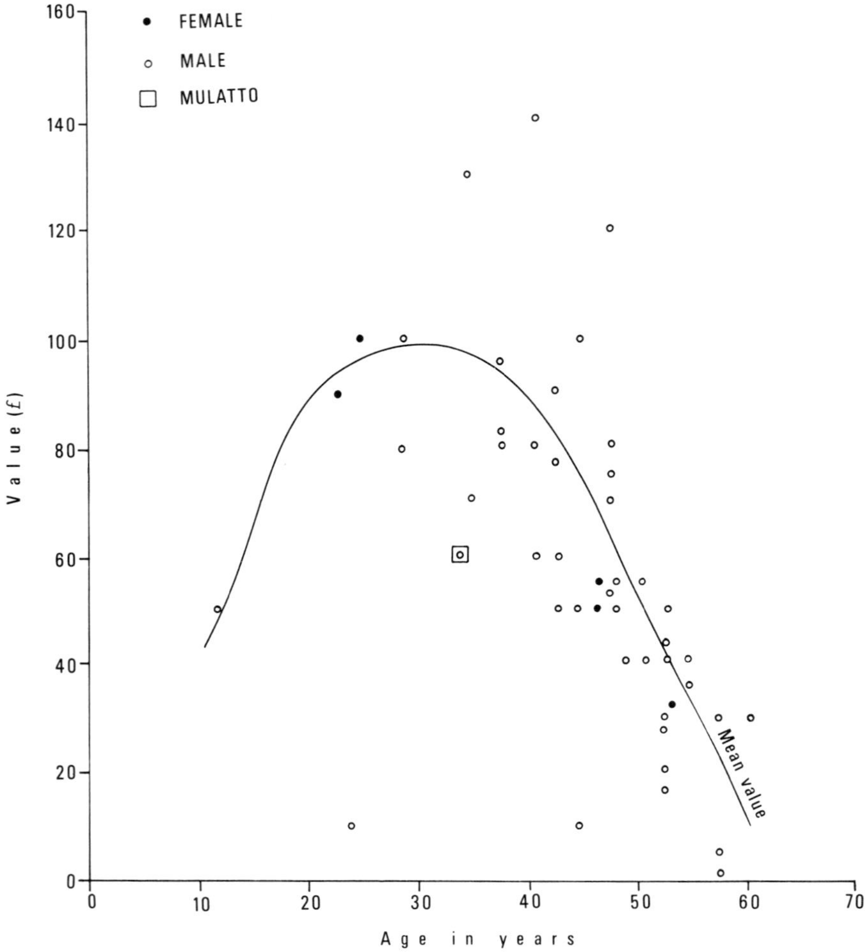

Figure 38. Age-value profile of slaves belonging to Lauchlan McLean, Kingston, 1831.

1826.[37] Similar problems occurred on coffee plantations. To return to Hermitage, it happened in 1819 that nearly all of the coffee ripened at the same time,

> and our strength being weak, and no jobbing gang to be hired to assist, even at offering so high a price as 3/2 for the picking every barrel of coffee in its green state, I am apprehensive we shall have much of it fallen off the trees before we can pick it, which will make the labour very tedious in picking it off the ground, and perhaps if any heavy rains come on it may be lost in part . . .[38]

Thus the seasonal variations in labour needs could be solved only in part by hiring jobbing gangs. The alternative was to maintain sufficient slaves to

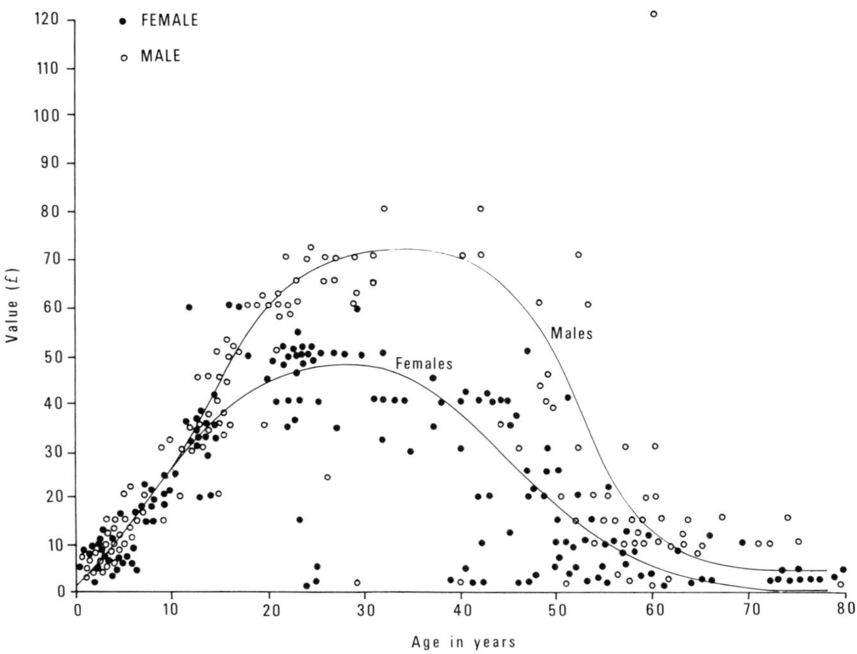

Figure 39. Age-value profile of slaves, Whim Estate, St. Dorothy, 1833.

meet the requirements of the crop, but then profitable employment had to be found for them in the dead season.

It was no comfort to the planter to know that the level of output per slave was being maintained if at the same time his gross receipts were falling. He also had invested in fixed assets: buildings, machinery, aqueducts, wains, barbecues and so on. Hence he saw his costs as constant, independent of the size of the crop, and production was kept up even if prices fell. For a particular estate there was thus a need to maintain a certain level of output in order to make it viable.[39] Similarly, the planters held that the expenses of a small sugar plantation were in many ways equal to those on large estates; hence the planter stretched his credit to its limits so that 'his estate can be brought up to a certain scale', and, argued the Jamaica Assembly in 1804, 'far from being, in all cases, a symptom of prosperity, extending plantations is not unfrequently a paroxysm of despair'.[40] When a planter said that his holding was 'weakhanded' he was thinking in these terms. He had to support every slave, whether productive or not. According to the masters, this put them in a difficult position, as their ruin loomed, for:

> However desperate the situation of the planter may be, he never ceases to struggle for the maintenance of his negroes. Without them his stock, his buildings, his

land, are of no value; and it never occurs to him to check the approaches of poverty by encroaching on the necessaries and comforts of his people.[41]

Productivity depended not only on numbers but also on the structure of the slave population. It should be obvious from the discussion of the principles underlying occupational allocation and the shape of the age–value profiles that the most important of the structural factors was age. The slave's most productive years, when he was required to perform the heaviest labour and was valued most highly, were those between 20 and 45. In 1826 Barclay claimed that there was in Jamaica an excess of slaves under the age of 20 and over 40 years.[42] He estimated that it would take fifteen years for this situation to be rectified. It had been predicted by the Jamaica Assembly in 1804, when it argued that the abolition of the slave trade would lead inevitably to the destruction of the burgeoning coffee industry; it held that

no care or attention to the welfare and increase of the negroes can prevent these consequences. They may increase in number, but the effective labourers must diminish; the coffee-plantations, having been settled, or at least carried to their present state of prosperity, within the last twelve years, are cultivated by Africans, almost all purchased within that period, and yet in the prime of life. A planter with an hundred such negroes may probably work eighty of the number. Twenty years hence, supposing his people to increase, by births beyond the deaths, to one hundred and twenty, he will not be able to work more than from thirty to forty able hands; the rest will consist of invalids, the aged past labour, and children not yet fit for it. Should fifty additional labourers be purchased, the work of the one hundred and seventy will be more than the first hundred could perform; the produce and return to the proprietor will be much less . . .[43]

Although – not surprisingly – the Assembly overstated its case, this prediction of the effects of abolition on the composition of the slave labour force was not far from the reality. The Assembly's estimate was directed at 1824 but the only systematic age data available are for 1817. Taking the 15–39 years age-group as the core of the 'able hands', then, it appears that this group made up 50 per cent of the slave population of Port Royal in 1817 and 45 per cent in Manchester, the two recently settled coffee parishes with natural increases.[44] If the Assembly's assumption of a participation rate of 80 per cent is accepted, these estimates fall to 45 and 36 per cent in Port Royal and Manchester, respectively. Thus, although the effective labour force, (the able hands) did not fall as low as the Assembly's predicted 25–33 per cent of the total slave population, it did approach this proportion.

Unlike the African purchased from the slave-ship, the creole slave had to be supported for many years before the master could look for a return. Even before birth a child constituted a drain on the plantation's work force. By the 1820s planters exempted women from regular field work as soon as they reported missing their menses, and from all forms of labour when four months pregnant, according to Thomson.[45] After the woman was delivered of her child, and if it survived, she remained in the second gang as long as

Table 46. *Barham's estimate of the cost of rearing a slave to age fourteen, in 1823*

	Sterling
1. Loss of mother's labour (allowance being made for cases where child born dead or dies immediately)	£10
2. Medical attendance, with insurance on mother's life	£5
3. Interest on items (1) and (2) for 14 years	£15
4. Maintenance for 14 years, @ 2 per cent interest (beyond value of any labour)	£40
5. Insurance on life of child to 14 years	£10
Total	£80

Source: J. F. Barham, *Considerations on the Abolition of Negro Slavery, and the Means of Practically Effecting It* (London, 1823), p. 79.

she was giving it suck, and this could be for up to two years.[46] Thus the need to maintain the slave population involved the effective removal from the major field gangs of some of the most able slaves for relatively long periods. Barham in 1823 and Hibbert in 1830 both calculated that earnings from a slave's labour did not exceed the cost of his maintenance until he reached the age of fourteen years.[47] Barham put the total cost of rearing a slave to fourteen years at £80 sterling and Hibbert at £120 sterling, though the latter admitted that his estimate might appear high. The components of Barham's estimate are shown in Table 46. The inventory valuation of slaves at Shrewsbury and Cape Clear in 1817 (Figures 33–35) shows an average value of around £120 currency at age fourteen, which comes close to Barham's cost estimate (£112 currency) and suggests that his was the more realistic calculation.

The planter would willingly sell his old, 'worthless' slaves but there was no market.[48] Laws were also passed to prevent the gratuitous manumission of old, infirm, diseased and disabled slaves; after 1816 some responsible free person was required to give a bond for every slave manumitted in case he became a charge on the parish.[49] Thus the death of an aged slave caused little sorrow in the planter's heart. In 1820, for instance, the attorney of Hermitage Plantation wrote to England saying: 'I am sorry to inform you we have a few days ago lost an old invalid woman named Nancy. She has been doing little or nothing for the property for some time past, and her loss is not much felt in consequence.'[50] So long as the slave lived, however, an attempt was made to exploit his available strength. Many slaves were valued positively into their sixties but, as the proportion of aged slaves increased in the years after 1807, the masters felt them to be a growing burden since the tasks to which they could be allocated productively were limited.

The abolition of the slave trade also affected the masters' preference for males over females. They believed males to be stronger and more flexible in the range of occupations to which they could be put.[51] Although they were expected to perform the same tasks as males in the field, females were not thought capable of the same rate of labour; when cane holing was the task a male and a female were generally placed together to work two sections jointly, according to Barclay.[52] But since females came to dominate the field gangs this cannot always have been practised. As the sex ratio fell after 1807, and favoured females by 1820, it would seem probable that the planters found increasing numbers of females in their field labour force. This trend is not as easily established as might be expected. At Worthy Park Estate, for example, 65 per cent of the field labour force was female in 1832, whereas in 1789 it had been 71 per cent and in 1793 only 54 per cent.[53] Thus it seems that the demand for male labour outside the field had always been great enough to make male predials a minority, even after large numbers had been purchased from the slave-ships. But the proportion of the total slave population employed in the field at Worthy Park increased between 1790 and 1832, to reach 64 per cent at the latter date, and this trend does suggest an increasing concentration of females in the field labour force.[54] By 1832 71 per cent of the 185 females on the estate were field labourers but only 55 per cent of the 130 males were so employed.[55] As well as finding an increased proportion of females in their field gangs, the masters found it necessary to indulge those who became pregnant once they had to depend on natural increase for the maintenance of the slave labour force. This they saw as further depressing productivity, at least in the short run.

Colour has long been recognized as a vital factor in determining occupation and status,[56] but the connection with potential productivity has not been made. Often it has been seen only as a source of social status distinctions within occupational groups, and the number employed as, say, domestics is interpreted as a function of the status goals of the masters rather than of the size of the slave coloured population.[57] The masters, however, had strong convictions about the capacities for labour of people of colour. The greater the infusion of white blood, the weaker the slave was thought to be. Thus 'on a sugar estate one black is considered as more than equal to two mulattoes', wrote Lewis; quadroons were 'rather delicate and sickly inclined'; mulatto children of mulatto parentage were 'weak and effeminate'; and the musteephino was 'pallid and sickly-looking'.[58] The customary allocation of males to skilled trades and females to domestic work was at least as much a reflection of the masters' perception of the physical capacities of the slave of colour as of any considerations of status. Thus, when in 1832 John Baillie, the owner of Roehampton, was asked how many domestics there were on his estate, he found it almost tautological to reply: 'There are upon my estate twenty-six brown people, eight of them females; and those are all considered domestics, for people of colour are never put into the field.'[59]

The evidence is clear that the masters found burdensome the growth of the slave coloured population after 1807. In 1814 Sir Simon Taylor, trustee for Haughton Court Estate, located near the port of Lucea in Hanover, petitioned the Assembly as follows:

the several slaves, whose names and degrees are mentioned in the schedule annexed, part of the slaves upon Haughton-Court plantation, being slaves of colour, several of them quadroons, and in appearance not different from white persons, altogether unfit for field labour, and cannot in any other manner be employed to advantage on the said plantation, it would be for the interest of the petitioner, and all others interested in the said plantation, to exchange them for negro slaves . . .[60]

Taylor was forced to petition the Assembly in this manner because of legal impediments to the manumission of slaves by owners with only a limited interest. The House assented to his request.[61] A similar case came up in 1819 on Grange Pen and Knollis Plantation[62] and another in 1821 on York and Gale's Valley Estates, Trelawny.[63] The petition in the latter case was rather more extensive in scope; the trustees asked that the estate's 'mulatto, quadroon, mestee, and other slaves of colour should be sold or manumised for valuable considerations, and the clear monies produced thereby, after paying such expences as should be incurred, should be laid out in the purchase of negro slaves'.[64] The final case of this sort appeared in 1832 when the trustees of Braziletto and Hillside Plantations in Vere stated that they were in possession of several slaves of colour, 'altogether unfit for field labour' and otherwise redundant, and that

it would be greatly for the benefit of all persons interested if the said slaves of colour were manumised for any equivalent in negro slaves or money, which the reputed parents of most of the said slaves are anxious to do, and the money that may be received as such equivalent laid out . . . in the purchase of negro slaves, or the said negro slaves given as an equivalent, and placed upon the said plantation and hereditaments, for the better cultivation and improvement thereof . . .[65]

Between 1829 and 1832 four samboes, two mulattoes and one quadroon were born at Braziletto and Hillside, and the estates had a natural increase of eight per thousand.[66] But even here it seems that the accumulated slave coloured population was large enough to be a burden; perhaps slaves of colour became redundant more quickly where the total population was growing.

These cases are known only because of legal intricacies, which were largely removed by 1824,[67] but there is other evidence to show that the redundancy of slaves of colour was general. In 1833 the attorney of Georgia Estate noted pithily that 'from the great number of coloured persons on the property it is a great drawback on the field labour'.[68] There one-half of the births and one-third of the deaths were coloured, during the period 1829–32.[69] It was a general practice to require substitutes whenever slaves were manumitted.[70] In 1820 a Mr. Bonthorne wished to release his mulatto daughter from Hermitage Plantation but the attorney, William Adlam, proposed that he should exchange her 'for a good young negroe man or woman to be sold to the H in lieu of her, for we are very weak handed on the property'. Adlam valued the slave at between £140 and £160 but said that should Bonthorne offer £140 'I think the heirs may agree to take that sum as mixtures are not so valuable on properties as negroes for the females are seldom employed otherwise than as house domestics.'[71] Similarly, the 'increase' list of Worthy Park for 1816 noted: 'Martin, a negro boy 12 years of age, received for Thomas James, a quadroon, 5 yrs. old, manumitted by Charles James.'[72] In 1817 a mustee female aged three was manumitted and replaced by a black female aged twelve; a quadroon male of six was replaced by a black male of thirteen, and another quadroon female of twenty by a black female aged thirty years.[73] Since the replacements were all older than the slaves of colour manumitted, it would seem that the estate drove a hard bargain in this process. But, whereas no slaves of colour were employed as field or factory labourers at Worthy Park in the late eighteenth century, when they made up less than 5 per cent of the population,[74] by 1832, when they had expanded to 9 per cent of the dwindling population, this rule had been broken. In 1832 three of the mulatto males and one of the two samboes were employed in the field, though none of them in the first gang. Female slaves of colour continued to monopolize the domestic occupations but one mulatto was in the first gang and six of the seven samboes worked in the field.[75] In general, it appears that those slaves with white fathers continued to receive preferential treatment, while sambo slaves were put to field work, especially if they were females. At Old Montpelier in 1825, for example, all seven of the male samboes were employed in the trades or in supervisory roles, but two of the three sambo females were put into the first gang.[76] All of the mulattoes, quadroons and mustees on the estate were allocated to occupations fitting the traditional pattern.

For the masters, the growth of the slave coloured population meant both a weakening of the strength of a plantation's labour force and the emergence of a functional imbalance in its occupational composition. For the slaves, the growth of the coloured group meant that an increasing number of them had expectations of positions of status within the system, but, as a result of the abolition of the slave trade, they saw the chances of their fulfilment being attenuated. Thus the sambo daughter of a mulatto mother could no longer hope to escape the rigours of field labour, for example. Sometimes, before the abolition of the slave trade, the mothers of children by white men had been able to obtain positions of privilege for their black sons and daughters as well; this became increasingly unlikely as emancipation approached.

Sex, age and colour were characteristics of the slave population over which the master had only limited control. He could, however, do something to influence the health and 'disposition' of his slaves. Hard work was not counterpoised to health in the planter's mind, since he held that 'the laborious are in general the most healthy part of mankind'.[77] But the impact of sickness on productivity is obvious. It has been argued that the West Indian planter preferred to underfeed and overwork his slaves, and then look for replacements.[78] The abolition of the slave trade removed the assumption essential to this attitude, and there is some evidence that the masters permitted the slaves more time to work their provision grounds in the early nineteenth century. In any case, it has been noted already that the relationship between the decline of the slave population and the extent of the master's control over the slaves' food supply is a very uncertain one.[79] Essentially, because of his environmental theory of etiology, the master had but little hope that his best efforts to improve the health of his slaves would prove effectual.

The view that slavery was an inefficient system of labour organization has been based very largely on a particular interpretation of the slave's attitude to work, what the masters called his 'disposition'. Thus Pitman, in 1926, asserted that 'the costliness of slave labour inhered, of course, in such tendencies as stupidity, slacking, illness, real or feigned, thieving, lack of interest, and occasionally, malicious sabotage and running away'.[80] And Ragatz: 'the West Indian negro had all the characteristics of his race. He stole, he lied, he was simple, suspicious, inefficient, irresponsible, lazy . . . '[81] The Jamaica planters would have concurred with these descriptions of the 'Negro character' but they had by no means such a narrow view of the costliness of the slave system. Yet they were agreed that the disposition of slaves should be taken into account in occupational allocation.[82] It was good news whenever an attorney or overseer could report that the slaves in his charge were 'healthy and well disposed' or 'well disposed, effective, good working people'.[83] The masters made a distinction between African and creole slaves, the latter being described as more amenable to control and less likely to run away.[84] Yet at Rose Hall in 1832, for example, only one African was included among the twelve slaves whose disposition was described as 'bad', 'indolent' or 'drunkard'.[85] It has been shown already that, although Africans continued to run away in large numbers, an urban, creole pattern of running away emerged after 1807.[86] Thus the planters' expectation that the slaves would become increasingly 'well disposed' as the process of creolization accelerated seems to have had little foundation.

After 1807 the structure of the slave population of Jamaica changed in a manner contrary to the planters' ideal. It became less 'effective' and less 'flexible'. Not only was the number of slaves in the most productive age-groups decreasing absolutely and relatively, but the slaves in these groups were also increasingly female and coloured.

CHAPTER 10

LEVELS OF PRODUCTIVITY

Although the evidence marshalled in the previous chapter suggests that the demographic changes consequent on the abolition of the slave trade affected significantly the organization of the Jamaican slave labour force, it is more difficult to demonstrate that these changes depressed the productivity of the slaves. In spite of this difficulty, it is important to attempt to test this relationship since it is basic to deciding whether the slave system was a cause of economic decline.[1] Most historians have, of course, emphasized the role of other, external factors in the economic decline of the British West Indies and the abolition of slavery – the American Revolution, competition from new sugar producers, British fiscal legislation, mercantilism, humanitarianism and the shifting balance of power within the British economic and political systems, for example.[2] But, within this wider framework, the nature of the slave system has been seen as a crucial factor in the British West Indian sugar industry's lack of 'competitive efficiency'. To it is traced the conservatism of the masters in field and factory technology, and the supposed economic ill-effects of absenteeism.[3] In general, historians have seen the link connecting the demography of slavery and the decline of the plantation economy as a fairly simple one. It has been argued that in some – perhaps most – of the British West Indian colonies slavery so permeated society that the slave population became very dense, functionally unbalanced, and hence a burden on the masters who maintained the system simply for considerations of social status.[4] The demographic-economic changes which occurred in Jamaica in the early nineteenth century were, obviously, much more complicated than this.

Secular trends

All the measures of productivity which can be derived from the available data are fairly crude since they have to be based on marketed output rather than total production levels. To begin with the long-term trends, an impression of the pattern can be obtained by relating the flow of export commodities to the size of the total slave population in the years between 1800 and 1834. Systematic data for the entire period are available only for the six major export staples – sugar, rum, molasses, coffee, pimento and ginger – but these constituted 90 per cent of the total value of Jamaican exports around 1832 and maintained a similar level throughout the period.[5] The average value of these items for five-year periods, at 1832 prices, are shown in Table 47.[6] Of the export items excluded from this table the most important were dyewoods, timber and hides, but only the dyewoods (valued at £62,435 in 1833/4) surpassed ginger. The six export staples included accounted for at least 80 per cent of the total gross receipts derived by the masters from the labour of their slaves.[7] Over the period 1800–4 the gross value of output in these six items (at 1832 prices) fell by 10.7 per cent. But output had risen to a peak in 1805–9 and maintained a high level until 1820–4. In sugar the fall was 15.5 per cent. Over the same period the total slave population decreased by only 7.1 per cent, following a curve of growth and decline similar to that for gross output.[8]

Production per slave maintained a fairly consistent level between 1800 and 1834, falling by only 3.8 per cent over the entire period (Table 47). Thus productivity declined less rapidly than the slave population and even more slowly than gross output. It also followed a trend similar to that for both of these movements, rising steeply to a peak in 1805–9 then falling away gradually until about 1830 when the rate of decline increased. This general trend

Table 47. *Average export crop production and slave labour productivity, 1800–34*

	Annual average value of exports (£ currency, 1832 prices)						
Period	Sugar	Rum	Molasses	Coffee	Pimento	Ginger	Total
1800–4	2,351,149	618,549	1,647	818,551	52,626	11,172	3,853,694
1805–9	2,564,307	738,889	1,789	1,209,942	68,265	17,448	4,600,640
1810–14	2,111,870	650,932	976	1,077,466	60,936	18,128	3,920,308
1815–19	2,322,436	657,810	1,036	884,140	85,965	41,266	3,992,653
1820–4	2,251,355	555,646	1,637	954,433	82,812	21,478	3,867,361
1825–9	1,944,692	498,598	1,495	999,801	109,926	81,114	3,635,626
1830–4	1,985,984	483,831	1,904	748,624	145,890	74,195	3,440,428

Period	Average slave population	Average production per slave (£ currency)	Average London sugar price (s sterling per cwt.)	Average value of sugar at current prices (£ currency)
1800–4	337,137	11.43	53.2	6,013,515
1805–9	349,362	13.17	43.6	5,375,182
1810–14	350,643	11.18	54.8	5,563,965
1815–19	345,252	11.56	53.0	5,917,747
1820–4	338,000	11.44	32.6	3,528,565
1825–9	322,421	11.28	33.8	3,160,124
1830–4	313,000	10.99	27.2	2,597,056

Source: See text and note 6 to Chapter 10.

is not readily explained in terms of the demographic changes discussed in the previous chapter. In fact it runs counter to the expected pattern in terms of the changing age structure of the slave population and hence to the potential labour force participation rates. It also runs counter to the trend expected to result from the supposed sex and colour differentials in productivity. Thus when the master complained of economic distress he was wrong, it seems, to attribute any more than a marginal amount of it to a decline in the productivity of his slaves. The data used here do not take into account the changing cost structure of the slave labour force but, if the planter had to spend more to support aged slaves and to care for mothers and their children, these slaves and their fellows covered this cost by keeping up the *average* level of output. Since the masters no longer had the opportunity of purchasing slaves from the slave-ships, their expenditure on the provision of a labour force was significantly reduced. If they allowed their slaves more time to work provision grounds and gardens this seems to have had but little impact on the absolute level of output of the slaves when labouring for the masters.

The relatively slow rate of decline in slave labour productivity between 1800 and 1834 cannot be accounted for in terms of improvements in agricultural practices or manufacturing technology. The introduction of the Otaheite cane after 1790 greatly increased the output of sugar but it had already completely replaced the creole variety by about 1800.[9] Little success was achieved in attempts to introduce the plough, and there were very few steam-mills in Jamaica before 1834, most of them no more efficient than the average water-mill.[10] But the level of total output was, to a certain extent, supported by diversification within the plantation economy: pimento and ginger production expanded considerably, and the coffee industry did not lose its impetus until about 1830.

The sugar planters, the most vocal of the slave masters, rightly saw themselves as suffering the most significant cuts in profits and productivity. And the planter, especially the absentee, was never comforted by the fact that the level of productivity of his slaves might be increasing, if at the same time he saw his real income declining. This was in fact his situation. The average price of British West Indian muscovado on the London market fell by almost 50 per cent between 1800 and 1834 (Table 47). The value of Jamaican sugar production at current prices fell by 56.8 per cent over the same period and, if it is assumed that 50 per cent of the slave population was directly employed in the industry throughout the period, it follows that the current value of sugar output per slave fell from £35.68 in 1800–4 to £16.60 by 1830–4.[11] Thus the planter, preoccupied with present problems, saw his income falling away and imputed part of this decline to changes in his slave labour force.

Consequently, the planters failed to notice that the effective slave labour force of Jamaica as a whole increased, or at least maintained, its level of productivity between 1800 and 1834. The important point, of course, is that this trend in the level of productivity runs counter to the view that the slave system proved itself inherently inefficient as a strategy of labour organization in the early nineteenth century. Certainly the sugar plantation economy of Jamaica entered a period of decline after 1820, but it was a decline resulting from adverse external market factors, not from stresses within the slave labour system.

Demographic-economic relations around 1832

These tentative conclusions are necessarily based on a fairly gross analysis of the data for the years 1800 to 1834. If the level of productivity of the Jamaican slave population did in fact increase or remain constant, contrary to the trend expected to follow from the principles of slave labour organization discussed in Chapter 9, it must be asked why this was so. How were the masters able to extract an increasing level of output from the slaves in order to keep pace with the demographic changes they saw as inevitably depressing productivity?

A partial answer to this question may be sought through an analysis of the Accounts Produce sample of properties for 1832, which permits a closer linking of the economic and demographic factors than the gross island-level statistics allow. The slaves on these 960 properties accounted for slightly more than 50 per cent of the total population. A rough estimate of production per slave can be obtained by simply dividing the total value of (marketed) output by the number of slaves on these properties: £23.36 per slave (Table 24, above). This figure may be compared with Eisner's first measure of productivity for 1832: £25.33.[12] Eisner's measure is higher than that found for the Accounts Produce properties because it is based on a global estimate of gross domestic product (ground provisions produced for domestic consumption making up 27.7 per cent of gross domestic product in 1832); but Eisner also includes in her calculation the free section of the population (10 per cent of the total in 1834), so that the two estimates are similar.

The demographic characteristics of the slaves attached to the Accounts Produce properties in 1832 can be established by relating the properties to the Returns of Registrations of Slaves for 1829–32. Six demographic factors can be isolated in this way: the sex ratio, birth rate, death rate, rate of natural increase, percentage of births coloured and percentage of deaths African. Thus some of the factors discussed in Chapter 9 cannot be quantified directly, the most significant gap in the data being a measure of the age structure of the slave populations on the properties, which is reflected only uncertainly in the levels of fertility and mortality and the percentage of deaths African. None of the six demographic characteristics identified correlated strongly with the level of production per slave around 1832 (Table 48). But there was a significant correlation between production per slave and natural increase

Table 48. *Productivity and demographic characteristics, Accounts Produce properties, 1829–32: correlation coefficients*[a]

		X_7	X_9	X_{12}	X_{13}	X_{14}	X_{21}	X_{51}
Males per 100 females	X_7	1.00						
Births per 1,000	X_9	—.11	1.00					
Deaths per 1,000	X_{12}	*—.20*	—.09	1.00				
Natural increase	X_{13}	.11	*.56*	*—.87*	1.00			
Percentage births coloured	X_{14}	—.10	.00	.07	—.06	1.00		
Percentage deaths African	X_{21}	.09	—.10	.05	—.09	—.11	1.00	
Production per slave	X_{51}	—.06	*—.18*	*.14*	*—.21*	.07	.02	1.00

[a] The italic coefficients are significant at the 99 per cent level of probability.
Source: See text.

(r = —.21); the less the slaves were able to maintain their numbers the more they produced for the masters. It must be noted, however, that whereas mortality was more important than fertility in determining the rate of natural increase, there was a slightly higher correlation between fertility and production than between mortality and production. This suggests that a large number of unproductive children – and consequently pregnant women and mothers with infants at the breast – was a greater drain on the average productivity of a property than an aged population. But the total population is, of course, a crude measure of the potential labour force; it is difficult to determine how far the presence of a large proportion of infants affected the productivity of those in the most productive age-groups, the 'able hands'.

On the 960 Accounts Produce properties as a whole, the six demographic characteristics taken together can account for only 6 per cent of the variation in production per slave. Fertility and mortality by themselves can explain almost as much (R = .22), yielding the following estimating equation:

$$Y_{51} = 25.49 - 0.25X_9 + 0.11X_{12}$$

where Y_{51} is production per slave (1832), X_9 is births per 1,000 (1829–32), and X_{12} is deaths per 1,000 (1829–32). The sex ratio, African/creole ratio and percentage coloured have no significant impact on the level of average production. Thus it seems that the attempt to account for variations in the level of slave productivity in terms of demographic factors has failed. But it is obvious that there were many factors other than the strictly demographic which affected productivity, and if these can be isolated the importance of the demographic factors may be seen more clearly. Before attempting this, however, it is necessary to notice the relevance of this general conclusion (the suggestion that demographic factors were relatively unimportant in determining levels of productivity) to the apparent paradox, considered in the first section of this chapter, of a fairly steady level of productivity in the major export staples between 1800 and 1834. This paradox might be resolved by suggesting that the labour component in productivity was relatively insignificant. But this is certainly opposed to the views of the masters, so the complicating factors deserve much closer attention.

Productivity did not vary randomly on the different types of properties. It ranged from £8.6 in jobbing gangs to £42.1 in wharves (Table 24, above). In jobbing, the labour (and hence demographic) component was almost total, whereas on the wharves there was a high return to services and fixed assets, with a relatively small labour input. Between these two extremes lay the agricultural units in which there was a variable environmental and locational factor. The highest returns per slave occurred on sugar estates (£25.9), followed by pimento (£25.6), pimento–livestock (£21.5), coffee–livestock (£19.7), coffee (£19.2), livestock (£17.8), coffee–labour (£13.5) and livestock–labour (£10.9) pens and plantations. Since these values are dependent on current (1832) prices it is possible that some of these contrasts are illusory. Pimento production was probably more labour-intensive than coffee or livestock, but sugar was more capital-intensive than these types of land use.[13]

These two kinds of distortion – variations in inputs other than labour and variations due to estimates based on prices – can most easily be removed by grouping the properties into land use types and repeating the correlation and regression analysis for each type separately (See Table A3.4, and Table 49).

Table 49. *Multiple regressions on production per slave: crop-combination groups, 1829–32*

		Sugar	Coffee	Coffee–labour	Coffee–livestock	Pimento
Constant	a	26.20	20.53	16.71	18.85	57.19
Males per 100 females	X_7	.03	.00	—.07	—.09	—.33
Births per 1,000	X_9	—.29	—.09	.19	.31	—.65
Deaths per 1,000	X_{12}	.09	—.07	.09	—.27	.71
Percentage births coloured	X_{14}	.02	—.02	—.13	.01	.13
Percentage deaths African	X_{21}	.01	.10	—.02	.11	.13
	R^2	.05	.06	.19	.47	.64
	R	.22	.25	.44	.69	.80

		Pimento–livestock	Livestock	Livestock–labour	Labour	Total
Constant	a	84.71	19.65	—.73	8.07	27.43
Males per 100 females	X_7	—.24	.00	.15	.01	—.02
Births per 1,000	X_9	—1.31	—.15	—.67	—.10	—.26
Deaths per 1,000	X_{12}	—.12	.04	—.03	.05	.10
Percentage births coloured	X_{14}	.49	.10	.39	—.04	.05
Percentage deaths African	X_{21}	—.19	—.01	.31	.02	.00
	R^2	.65	.09	.44	.24	.06
	R	.81	.30	.66	.49	.24

This standardizes the pricing procedures and removes at least some of the variation in material inputs, though it does not account for variations in the quality of the material inputs. But it is important to recognize that this process of grouping also removes some of the demographic factor, since there were significant variations in the structure of the slave populations on the different types of properties (Table 24, above). It could, for example, be argued that the high productivity of slaves attached to wharves was a function of their very high rate of masculinity, low birth and death rates, and low percentage of deaths African, suggesting a concentration in the 'prime' age-groups. The demographic structure of most of the other types of land and labour use was not as sharply defined as this, but the process of grouping does submerge some of the detail, affecting adversely its ability to explain the economic-demographic relationship satisfactorily.

On the sugar estates, the demographic factor explains less of the variation in production per slave than it does for all of the Accounts Produce properties taken together (Table 49). As with the total group, the birth and death rates can explain as much of the variation as the five demographic characteristics taken together.[14] Once again, there was a stronger correlation between the level of productivity and the birth rate ($r = -.19$) than the death rate ($r = .12$). Sugar estates occupied a variety of sites, so it may be asked whether the ecological factor was not more important than the demographic in determining the level of production. Not enough is known about the soil, slope and climate of the lands planted in cane on each of the particular Accounts Produce properties to allow the fine analysis required to test this relationship rigorously, but some broad trends can be identified from the map of productivity rates (Figure 2, above). Three regions of low productivity stand out: Portland, the Liguanea Plain (St. Andrew) and the valley of the Great River (Hanover/St. James). The last region was the centre of the rebellion of 1831 and it was undoubtedly affected by the devastation of the estates there, though on some of the estates which were burned the production of the slaves was above average.[15] On the Liguanea Plain low productivity may well have been a result of the dryness of the area and the transition of some of the estates to the supply of pasturage and provisions for Kingston. On the coast of Portland and the Long Bay area of St. Thomas-in-the-East the problem was one of excessive precipitation, since it received more than 100 inches per year. An alternative explanation of the low productivity of Portland may lie in the fact that settlers had been encouraged to take up land in the parish at the end of the eighteenth century, for 'strategic' reasons,[16] perhaps pushing sugar into regions of only marginal suitability. Regions of high productivity are more difficult to delimit. In most parts of the island production varied locally, but a few areas merit mention: littoral St. Mary, the Seville area west of St. Ann's Bay, Falmouth's hinterland, St. Thomas-in-the-Vale and Lluidas Vale, and the Plantain Garden River. These were principally areas of alluvial soil but high productivity was obtained on other land types as well.

A comparison can also be made between the productivity of planting and ratooning estates.[17] At the island level the effect of these two systems is not apparent; production per slave was high in both Vere and the interior vales, for example. But the yields obtained at Roehampton and Latium Estates in St. James in 1831 show that plants were considerably more productive than ratoons, and that the yield of the latter tended to decrease the longer they were left in the ground.[18] At Latium, plants yielded 1.4 hogsheads of sugar per acre but fourth ratoons only half a hogshead. Roehampton, with a large proportion of its land in plants, was thus able to achieve a higher yield per acre than Latium. In 1831 there were 350 slaves at Roehampton and 450 at Latium; production per slave was 0.81 and 0.79 hogsheads, respectively, a much closer rate than might be expected from the yields per acre. Both of the estates used jobbing gangs to plant about half of their new canes. It seems that the labour involved in planting cancelled out the higher yield.

On coffee plantations the demographic factor accounted for 6 per cent of the variation in production per slave, only slightly more than on sugar estates. As in the case of sugar, fertility tended to depress the rate of productivity but, in contrast to sugar, mortality also depressed it (Table A3.4). The African/creole ratio, however, was able to explain nearly as much of the variation in productivity as the five demographic variables take together ($r = .22$). This suggests that production per slave was highest where Africans dominated the population but had not passed into the age-groups of heaviest mortality. It has been shown that there was a great concentration of Africans in the coffee parishes: Manchester (52 per cent of deaths 1829–32), St. George, Port Royal and St. David (all 47 per cent).[19] This contrast in the African/creole ratios of the eastern and western coffee regions was reflected in the level of productivity. In Port Royal no plantation had an average production per slave greater than £30, whereas in Manchester seventeen reached this level (Figure 3, above). The higher ratio of Africans in Manchester can be explained in terms of the recent settlement of the parish but it must also be asked whether environmental factors contributed to the contrasting levels of productivity. Coffee was grown in loose soil on steep slopes subject to erosion. In 1816 it was claimed that erosion had already begun in St. Mary, St. George, St. Andrew and St. Thomas-in-the-East; this process had been accelerated by the great storm of October 1815 which washed away the works and houses on many large plantations in Port Royal and St. David.[20] The process of erosion and abandonment continued throughout the first half of the nineteenth century.[21] Thus it is difficult to distinguish between the contribution to productivity of the relatively youthful male African population of Manchester and the virginity of the soil and slopes of the parish. Since the difference in the African/creole ratio of the eastern and western parishes was slight, it would seem that the ecological factor was uppermost.

Of all the types of land use, the demographic factor was more important on those properties producing pimento. The five variables taken together account for 64 per cent of the variation in production per slave, and the death rate and sex ratio alone account for 62 per cent (Table 49). The pimento plantations were all concentrated into a small area so their physical environments were fairly homogeneous, though those with the highest productivity were closest to the coast; perhaps there was a cartage factor here, but it is more probable that the interior plantations were affected by pimento leaf rust disease which is prevalent in regions more than 1,000 feet above sea level and affects yields significantly.

Pimento, as a monoculture, was labour-intensive, needing only to be harvested. Very often this work was allocated on a task basis.[22] Thus it is not surprising that the demographic factor explains more of the variation in productivity in pimento than in any of the other monocultures. On the pens which produced only livestock the demographic variables could account for only 9 per cent of the variation in production per slave. These pens were widely scattered but productivity does not seem to have been regionalized. Labour-intensity also breaks down as a measure of the role of the demographic factor in the case of the jobbing gangs, the purest example of all. Here the demographic variables account for only 24 per cent of the variation in production per slave, though it seems that fertility and mortality worked in the directions found on sugar estates, and colour also depressed productivity. More than any other type of unit, however, the productivity of the jobbing gang depended on external forces – the demand for labour on estates and plantations, and the enterprise of the jobber in finding work for his slaves. Thus it tended to be greater in the upland areas where the demand for cane hole digging was wider.

On the monocultural properties, then, the demographic factor was important where labour was a major input (pimento and jobbing), but statistically insignificant where other material inputs were greater (sugar, coffee and livestock). On the mixed two-crop properties the demographic factor explains a much greater amount of the variation in productivity. It is not easy to account for this contrast. Diversification did not necessarily mean a more efficient use of labour measurable in terms of output per slave. In fact productivity was generally lower on the two-crop properties than on the monocultures, with the exception of jobbing (Table 24, above). The two-crop properties were considerably larger than the monocultures and all except coffee–labour had natural increases during the period 1829–32; it was this growing slave population which accounted for low productivity and also perhaps for diversification. On the pimento–livestock properties the demographic factor accounted for 65 per cent of the variation in output per slave (which fell between pure pimento and pure livestock production), and here the rate of natural increase was higher than on any other land use type (11.6 per 1,000). On coffee–livestock properties the demographic variables taken together accounted for 47 per cent of the variation in productivity, and on livestock–labour units 44 per cent. But the samples of two-crop properties are generally too small to produce significant correlations, so that the economic-demographic relationships tend to appear inconsistent.

By grouping the Accounts Produce properties into crop types it has been possible to minimize the role of material inputs in determining the level of productivity, yet the relative importance of the demographic variables remains similar to that found for all the properties taken together. The basic factors seem to have been mortality and fertility; the more the slaves were able to maintain and augment their numbers the lower their productivity. But, in contrast to the pattern of natural increase, fertility was more important in determining the level of productivity than mortality. The only exception was the case of coffee, where high fertility and mortality both depressed output; this may be explained by the positive correlation between production per slave and the percentage of deaths African ($r = .22$), an index of the number of aged slaves on an estate. It is probable that these characteristics should be interpreted as reflections of the unknown age distribution. Although production per slave generally increased along with masculinity, the effects of colour and the African/creole ratio were capricious and usually insignificant.

A fundamental factor affecting the level of productivity was the relationship between the number of slaves on a property and the work to be done. It is difficult to define the latter concept, but it has been noted already that the size of the available labour force influenced the type of land and labour use combination designed by the planter.[23] If the Accounts Produce properties are sorted into groups by slave-holding size it is found that production per slave was at a maximum in the 201–250 group (Table 25, above). In 1832 the average sugar estate had on it 223 slaves. Slave-holdings of this size seem to have approached an optimum in the exploitation of labour, with the highest rate of mortality; but they also had very low sex ratios and small proportions of Africans. They also approached an optimum in the exploitation of the capital equipment employed in sugar production. In the eighteenth century many writers saw a plantation of 200 slaves as a minimum or optimum-sized unit,[24] and Pares has argued that the technology of sugar made an estate of 300–350 slaves, with 300 acres in cane, a unit of maximum size.[25] The planters were well aware of this optimality and spoke of their efforts to bring estates up to 'a certain scale' as a response to low labour- and capital-productivity.[26] But dividing the Accounts Produce properties into groups by size produces no highly significant correlations between output per slave and the five demographic variables (Table A3.5; Table 50). Only in the 401–500 group did these variables account for more than 20 per cent of the variation in productivity, and in the 201–250 group they accounted for

Table 50. *Multiple regressions on production per slave: slave-holding size-groups, 1829–32*

		1–50	51–100	101–150	151–200
Constant	a	33.36	25.60	26.48	21.80
Males per 100 females	X_7	—.04	—.06	—.01	.00
Births per 1,000	X_9	—.25	—.19	—.29	—.32
Deaths per 1,000	X_{12}	.00	.09	.08	.25
Percentage births coloured	X_{14}	—.06	.06	.13	.10
Percentage deaths African	X_{21}	.03	.09	—.05	—.02
	R^2	.05	.06	.12	.19
	R	.22	.24	.35	.44

		201–250	251–300	301–400	401–500
Constant	a	26.41	29.37	25.70	37.65
Males per 100 females	X_7	.04	.15	.02	.02
Birth per 1,000	X_9	—.28	—.21	—.25	—.45
Deaths per 1,000	X_{12}	.16	.15	.04	.04
Percentage births coloured	X_{14}	—.03	.06	—.01	—.36
Percentage deaths African	X_{21}	—.06	.00	.01	—.10
	R^2	.06	.11	.06	.26
	R	.24	.33	.24	.51

only 6 per cent, suggesting that the optimality of this group resulted as much from the efficient utilization of capital equipment as from the maximization of labour output. Only in the 101–250 groups were there any significant simple correlations between productivity and the demographic factors, and the most important of these showed that high productivity went along with low fertility and high mortality, as was suggested by the analysis at the crop-combination level. The only other significant correlations were with colour in the 101–200 groups and these, surprisingly, were positive.

In sum, then, the hypothesis that the demographic structure of the Jamaican slave labour force was a basic determinant of its productivity is not readily proven from the available quantitative data. Three reasons for this failure may be suggested. The hypothesis may be wrong, or it may be cloaked by complicating factors, or the difficulty in verifying it may be a result of purely methodological problems. To begin with the last proposition, it must be emphasized that the Accounts Produce provide no information relating to costs, hence the measure of production per slave is a crude one. It includes only marketed output. If, for example, a planter employed some of his slaves in producing food crops, or pasturing livestock, or making lime, instead of purchasing these items, the productivity of his slaves would seem less than those whose master purchased these things and allocated all of his slaves' time to the raising of export staples. Similarly, if a planter hired a jobbing gang to dig cane holes instead of employing his own slaves, the level of production per slave would be augmented artificially; and if an estate and pen were joint owned the latter might send jobbing gangs to the estate without recording this as income. Beyond this problem is the fundamental difficulty of valuing production and measuring the inputs of effort and skill. Certainly the monetary values used here (since they are the only systematic measure available) can be misleading.

The problem of external, complicating factors hardly needs emphasis. But it has been demonstrated that it is not easy to account for all of the spatial variations in productivity levels in terms of locational, environmental factors. Thus John Baillie, in 1832, told a select committee that some estates with 700 slaves made only as much sugar as others with 400. When asked: 'Do you refer to profit or gross proceeds?' he replied 'Gross proceeds or produce. In consequence of the situation of the property there are so many contingencies, such as variety in soil, climate, and so on.'[27] As well as these factors, production was affected by the skill of the tradesmen and managers, the efficiency of the mill equipment and the solvency of the proprietor, which determined the estate's ability to purchase working stock, tools and so on.

The slave masters of Jamaica claimed that the abolition of the slave trade initiated a process of demographic change which inevitably depressed the productivity of the slave labour force, and that this placed them in a dilemma. Before 1807, replacements – male, mature and black – could be purchased to fill the gaps or to augment the labour force. Now the masters had to decide whether to maintain production and wipe out their slaves, their capital, in a few short years or to maintain their slave population and walk the tightrope between solvency and ruin. Publicly, the masters took the long-sighted view. As early as 1815 the Jamaica Assembly could assert that

> There is strong reason to believe, that even before the sexes shall be completely equalized, there will be a natural increase in the numbers, but not in the effective strength, of the slaves. . . . Although the labourers will be augmented, the produce of the island must decline, there being no symptom of that depravity, with which the planters and their creditors are branded, of trying to force immediate returns, without regard for the preservation of the capital, or the lives of the people.[28]

In fact it appears that, although total production and the value of that production declined between 1807 and 1834, this decline was not matched by a decrease in the *average* level of productivity of the slave population (Table 47, above).[29] Thus the masters managed to extract an increased output from the 'effective' labourers, even if they were unable to maintain the absolute level of production throughout the period. Where they were most successful in doing this the slaves tended to have relatively low fertility rates and, to a lesser extent, high mortality. In part, this relationship was a reflection of the age distribution. In part, too, it reflected the masters' desire to 'force immediate returns' in the face of declining incomes. But variations in the sex ratio seem not to have affected the level of productivity and, if anything, a large coloured population on a property seems to have increased production rather than depressing it.

Although the Jamaica planters' cries of economic distress were genuine, at least by the later 1820s, it does not follow that their distress resulted from the slave system or the demographic changes consequent on abolition other than the simple absolute decline in the slave population. In fact the masters seem to have managed to increase the productivity of the slave labour force after 1807, so that their desire to retain slavery was not opposed to their economic welfare or based on abstract considerations of social status. As an economic system for the organization of labour, there is nothing to suggest that slavery fell of its own weight, in Jamaica. One reason for this, and for the maintenance of the level of productivity, was that the masters shifted the slave labour force to regions and tasks where returns could be maximized.

Stress and change in the use of land and labour

Change in the pattern of land and labour use was a response to many factors other than the strictly demographic but it may be assumed that, where productivity was marginal as a result of physical or locational disadvantages, demographic change would have the most immediate impact. Of all the reactions to the changing structure of the slave population, the most obvious was the abandonment of estates. In 1816 Lewis claimed that many estates had been thrown up merely from a shortage of slaves, and that some planters were moving their slaves to a single property in order to maintain a working unit.[30] Thus it may be that slaves were concentrated increasingly into units approximating the optimum size, contributing to the maintenance of a relatively high level of productivity. But, whereas the sugar estates were able to keep up yields through the application of manure, it was believed that the coffee plantations on the steep slopes in the eastern parishes became useless after erosion began, being replaced only by a sour grass. Thus the planters opposed attempts to attach the slaves to the soil and argued that the solution to the problem was to send the slaves from the abandoned coffee plantations to the coastal sugar estates deficient in strength.[31] Between 1805 and 1815 some 56 coffee plantations in St. George were abandoned or sold and 2,707 slaves from them were removed or sold to other properties; in St. Andrew 22 plantations were thrown up and 1,543 slaves sold or removed.[32] This process continued into the 1830s. The movement of slaves from coffee to sugar production meant that the slave labour force was reallocated to uses which maximized returns to the master. The contraction of settlement in the coffee regions, away from the areas of marginal returns, also meant that the coffee plantations which survived tended to be those with the highest productivity levels.

It is difficult to identify the sugar estates which were abandoned in Jamaica in the early nineteenth century, but an estimate can be made by subtracting the number of properties with more than 100 slaves in 1832 from the number of sugar estates shown on Robertson's map of 1804, for each quadrat. Mapping these abandoned estates shows that some of them were on the margins of the sugar areas of 1832, notably in Portland, St. Elizabeth, Westmoreland and backland Trelawny, where productivity was relatively low. But abandonment occurred chiefly within the sugar areas, so it was not simply a reaction to environmental disadvantages. Two major regions in which abandonment was rare stand out: Vere and St. Mary. In Vere it is known that the slaves maintained their numbers, so that labour shortage was unlikely to be a significant problem; but in St. Mary the rate of natural increase was lower than in any other parish for the greater part of the period before emancipation, and it can only be suggested that the slave population was augmented by purchases from the deserted inland coffee plantations.[33] In both of these parishes productivity was generally high. At the quadrat level, abandonment was correlated significantly with mortality ($r = .21$) and hence natural increase ($r = -.22$).[34] But since high mortality also went along with high productivity levels, it is difficult to argue that the inability of the slave population to increase naturally was an important factor in economic distress.

Rather than abandon their estates, many planters attempted to find alternative activities, which demanded less labour, in order to maintain gross receipts. Thus as sugar and coffee production gradually fell away there was a sharp increase in the output of pimento and ginger between 1800 and 1834 (Table 47, above). Most of this increase in the production of minor staples occurred on sugar estates and pens, rather than on independent holdings. Cases of the exploitation of dyewoods, timber and provisions by properties in distress have been noted already.[35] A more immediate source of income could be found in the livestock on estates, but its sale was generally a prelude to abandonment.[36] In St. Andrew some estates were shifting from sugar to livestock production around 1832.[37] Papine, for example, sold fat cattle, meat, sheep, Guinea corn and fruit around 1829, though in 1832 it sold only sugar, rum and old livestock;[38] between 1829 and 1832, 100 of the 700 slaves at Papine were moved to sugar estates in Vere and Clarendon.[39] Opponents of slavery argued that if emancipation meant the end of sugar the estates could be converted to pens, but the planters were quick to point out that the pens were dependent on the estate market and that they already bred more livestock than the estates required.[40] In fact the number of taxable livestock in the island decreased fairly steadily between 1817 and 1832,[41] a decline which reflected the diminution of the slave population. On a limited number of properties, however, it seems that land use diversification may have resulted from a growing slave population rather than a diminishing one.

The decrease in the absolute size of the slave population also put pressure on the principles involved in the traditional allocation of slaves to occupations. It has been noted already that some slaves of colour (generally samboes) were being forced into the field gangs, along with increasing proportions of females and aging slaves.[42] Similarly, the movement of slaves from Kingston into the rural parishes suggests that many slaves used to town life and occupations were being put to agricultural tasks. The pressure on occupations of status came to seem considerable. Thus in 1817 Lewis reported that a slave requested that his son, who was employed as a house boy, be put to a trade rather than to field labour, but Lewis explained that 'my own shops are not only full at present, but loaded with future engagements'.[43] He went on to say that since abolition it was impossible to fill places so he could not send the boy to Savanna la Mar to learn a trade, such as tailoring. Another planter, in 1832, stated that a group of free people had settled at Cavaliers in St. Andrew, 'not being able to get employment in town, for the trades were overstocked there'.[44] At the same time, the prices paid for the hire of town slaves fell after about 1820, making it increasingly difficult for those permitted to practice self-hire to satisfy the demands of their masters.[45] Thus the maintenance of productivity levels in the major export staples was achieved, in part, by a rationalization of the occupational structure of the Jamaican slave population, a reduction in its functional imbalance, which cut off some of the opportunities slaves had seen for positions of relative status and independent activity within the slave system.

CHAPTER 11

OVERSEER DAY DONE?

On 27 December 1831 the greatest of the Jamaica slave rebellions was initiated by the firing of Kensington Estate on the headwaters of the Orange River, near Maroon Town, in St. James. In the next two weeks it spread into the neighbouring parishes of Hanover, Westmoreland, St. Elizabeth, Manchester and Trelawny, while smaller outbreaks of violence occurred in some of the eastern parishes. Roughly 20,000 slaves are said to have been involved in the rebellion; at least 200 were killed during it and another 312 were later executed, two-thirds of them in St. James and Hanover. Fourteen whites were killed and property valued at £1,132,440 was destroyed.[1]

Not only was this rebellion the most extensive in Jamaica's history but its aims also differed from those which preceded it. In the seventeenth and eighteenth centuries the Maroon Wars were typical of attempts to escape from slave society and the plantation economy, and to live independently of it.[2] These revolts were generally led by Africans, and often by particular ethnic groups amongst the African slaves. In 1831, however, it was not the Africans who took the lead but the creoles, especially those who had achieved some degree of status within slave society and saw the possibilities of complete liberty. As argued by Schuler, 'If anything, a "creolization" of slave protest had taken place, and slaves seemed anxious to find a better place for themselves *within* the traditional plantation society . . .'[3] There was an immediate sense in which the slaves believed that the masters were withholding the freedom bestowed on them by the British Parliament, but there was also a deeper kind of stress which stemmed from the abolition of the slave trade, the consequent demographic cycle and the pressure it applied to the traditional principles of occupational allocation.

In order to test this proposition it is necessary to examine the pattern and personnel of the rebellion. In February 1832 the governor told the Assembly that all of the leaders of the rebellion seemed to have been men in 'confidential' positions on the estates.[4] In May, Hamilton Brown, colonel of the St. Ann militia and rabid supporter of the anti-nonconformist Colonial Church Union, commented that 'it was the head people and the most indulged servants who were ringleaders during the rebellion'.[5] John Baillie, whose estate (Roehampton) was burnt, told Parliament in the same month that he had offered some of his slaves an opportunity to purchase their freedom but all had refused even though they had sufficient property to pay for it:

so much so that there was one man, who has been executed the other day in the rebellion, that I suppose was worth six, seven, or eight hundred pounds; he had cattle running upon my estate, and other property. . . . He was originally a mason, and made a great deal of money in that way. I found him so confidential a man, as I conceived, that I took him from his profession as a mason and made him my head driver; he continued so for some time; he got rather lame and infirm, though he was a man of only forty-eight years of age. I then made him the ranger; his business was to ride round the estate; he had a mule and a servant boy to attend him and hold his mule; . . . In the last return which I received he is put down exempt from labour; this was up to May 1831; he was one of the ringleaders in the rebellion.[6]

The slave had been named after his master, and in 1832 he was 59 years old; he was an African.[7]

At Old Montpelier, as at Roehampton, the slaves were given special privileges in the possession of livestock but it, too, was burnt.[8] Two men were shot during the rebellion at Old Montpelier, and three were transported for their role in it; all of them were black and creole.[9] One of those shot, James Richards, was aged 44 years and worked as a mason; in 1825 he had lived with a woman (then aged 21); in 1828 when the overseer reported on the 'disposition' of the slaves he noted that James Richards was 'plausible and doubtful'. The other slave shot, Giles Miller, was 27 years old and 'seemingly well disposed'; he was in the first gang, and in 1825 had lived with an African woman aged 51, her two daughters (one of whom may have been his mate) and one grand-daughter. Of the three Old Montpelier slaves transported, Charles Morris was a mason aged 34, 'seemingly well disposed' (in 1828); in 1825 he lived with his African mother and an African man (perhaps his father). Charles Tharpe, aged 28, was made driver of the first gang in 1826; in 1825 he lived with his mother, his siblings, an African man (Gillian Tharpe), and another woman. Dublin Malcolm, the third and youngest of the transportees, was aged 22 in 1832; in 1825 he had lived with his mother, his two brothers and a man aged 52 who worked as a mason; in 1828 Dublin Malcolm was moved into the first gang, and was described as 'frequently runaway'. Thus it seems that the masters early recognized certain qualities in those slaves who were to become rebels. Although the rebels had all grown up within the slave system, some of them had gained positions of status whereas others had not, whatever their expectations following the success of their fathers or siblings in doing so. Similarly, at Shettlewood, the pen linked to Old Montpelier estate, the four men hanged for rebellion were all creoles, aged between 29 and 40 years. One of them, Richard Trail, had been married in the Established Church in 1827. All of them had sisters with mulatto children.

At Manchioneal Bay, in St. Thomas-in-the-East, 'a very serious plot' was detected. According to the attorney John Mackenzie, 'it was of a very extensive character, and but for the immediate marching of a body of troops, the

Table 51. *St. James rebels, 1831–2*

	Males		Females	
	Number	Mean age	Number	Mean age
Shot in the rebellion				
Blacks	74	38	6	28
Samboes	—	—	—	—
Mulattoes	2	46	—	—
Africans	24	43	1	—
Creoles	52	37	5	28
Total	76	39	6	28
Executed				
Blacks	72	37	1	44
Samboes	1	20	—	—
Mulattoes	3	24	—	—
Africans	19	49	—	—
Creoles	57	31	1	44
Total	76	36	1	44

Source: R.R.S., Libers 127 and 129.

whole of the whites would have been butchered that night'.[10] Here it seems that the slaves of colour played an important part in the rebellion. Only one slave was shot during the martial law, a black aged 24 years, but two other blacks were shot by order of courts martial. A mulatto aged 45 years and a sambo aged 37 were hanged, and a mulatto of 21 was transported. All of these slaves were males and creoles.[11]

In St. James, the centre of the rebellion, slaves of colour seem to have played only a minor role (Table 51). The number of slaves shot during the rebellion was a much more arbitrary measure of involvement than those executed.[12] Some children were killed in the fighting but the youngest slave to be executed (by order of courts martial or civil) was eighteen years old. The average age of African slaves shot was lower than for those executed, whereas for the creoles the situation was reversed. Thus it seems that there was a hard core of older African slaves who planned revolt, while the creole plotters were relatively young (averaging about 30 years, the age when the masters valued them most highly). It seems that Africans were not as well represented among the plotters as might be expected from their total weight in the population, taking their age structure into account. At least two male Africans in St. James committed suicide during the rebellion, one aged 60 and the other 40 years. In addition, a quadroon aged 38 'cut his throat' and a mulatto aged 18 committed 'suicide'. But the most obvious feature of Table 51 is that the active participants in the rebellion were almost exclusively male, and this pattern was repeated in the other parishes.[13]

A complete understanding of the nature of the rebellion would depend on much fuller data relating to occupation and kinship than are available, for those who were shot by the rebels while protecting their masters' property as well as for the activists. But it does seem that the focus of the rebellion was found among slaves who had attained positions which they wished to enhance, or had failed to reach positions gained by their forebears because of the changing balance of colour and creolization, or wished better for their children within the plantation hierarchy. The chief centres of rebellion were in areas where the proportion of creole, coloured and non-predial slaves was high. They were also monocultural sugar areas where the system of colour and status was most highly developed, and where the heavy rate of natural decrease was placing stress on the system. It was essentially a rural rebellion, though the towns also possessed some of these features in high degree. In the towns, however, slaves more often achieved a quasi-independence or bought their freedom, whereas the rural slaves could see few advantages in such freedom within the fixed structure of a slave society. And the declining population of Kingston (where there was a surplus of skilled tradesmen), together with the total decrease in the island, meant that the town's role as a safety-valve was diminished.

The fundamental goal of the rebellion was liberty. The slaves certainly did not expect to resolve their expectations within a slave society. What they planned to do in terms of the reconstruction of the economy and society is less certain, however. But it does seem that they hoped to capture the masters' possessions, not simply to destroy them, and some of the rebels' acts suggest an attempt to obtain liberties within the plantation society.[14] The whites, on the other hand, struck at the privileges the slaves had already established. The militia was instructed to retaliate wherever the rebels burnt estates by burning their houses, killing their hogs, poultry and horned cattle, and destroying their provision grounds.[15]

The slave plantation economy of Jamaica had recovered from rebellions before, but that of 1831 struck at the foundations of the economic institutions of the island in a year when the metropolitan sugar price reached the bottom of a trough. The London sugar price of 1831 was lower than it had been for almost a hundred years, having fallen rapidly from the peak of 1814. Between 1793 and 1829 more than sixty West Indian merchants and brokers were declared insolvent, but in 1831 ten were so declared.[16] Thus the planters had to cope both with a depression in the market and, in some cases, the destruction of their works. In addition to the impoverishment which the planters claimed the rebellion caused, it brought a more general feeling of insecurity 'for property and life' which the planters wanted resolved.[17]

In the political arena in which the legislative decision to abolish slavery was made, the British Parliament, the rebellion strengthened the hand of the humanitarians and their supporters. It came at a time when the active Quaker-led Agency Committee was stirring up public opinion and when the Reform of Parliament had almost halved the representation of the West India interest.[18] Whereas the resident proprietors were agreed, publicly, that emancipation would result in further rebellion,[19] at least some absentees favoured emancipation by the middle of 1832. According to Thomas Babington Macaulay, writing in August 1832, 'Lord Harewood, Lord St. Vincent, and Lord Howard de Walden, the son-in-law of Lord Seaford, have all . . . declared themselves decidedly for emancipation as necessary to the safety of their own property.'[20] All of these absentees had estates in Jamaica, and Seaford's Montpelier had been a centre of rebellion. By the middle of 1833 the agent for Jamaica and the delegates sent to England to represent the colonial cause had been instructed to co-operate in achieving emancipation so long as the vital question of compensation to the slave masters was resolved in their favour.[21] Thus the Jamaica Assembly's formal protest against the Emancipation Act of 1833 was confined to constitutional issues and the question of compensation.[22]

In 1814, with the price of sugar at its peak, William Wilberforce had been asked 'whether he had any plan in contemplation for the entire oblivion of slavery all over the world?' He replied: 'The object of the friends of the abolition of the slave trade had been in the first place to stop all supplies of slaves from Africa, and then they hoped that the amelioration of the state of the slaves in the West Indies would follow as a matter of course.'[23] This view, common to the Saints, derived from the fallacy that slavery was 'created and sustained' by the slave trade.[24] Hence their surprise that slavery did not fade away after 1807. Yet, although emancipation did not follow abolition 'as a matter of course', there was more truth in Wilberforce's expectation than he later appreciated. The abolition of the slave trade initiated a secular decline in the absolute size of the slave population of Jamaica which reduced its total output. But the rate of decline in population and output was fairly slow until about 1820, when it began to accelerate. This acceleration coincided with the collapse of the metropolitan sugar price, so that the planters saw a rapid and sustained diminution in their gross receipts. Further, the abolition of the slave trade resulted in a top- and bottom-heavy age structure which significantly reduced the effective slave labour force. It also reduced the masculinity of the population, forcing an increasing proportion of women into the field, women whom the planter hoped would bear children to maintain the number of slaves on his property. At the same time the slave coloured population increased – no longer being controlled by the constant injection of Africans (blacks) – and this the planter saw as limiting the flexibility of his labour force. Consequently, as well as a decline in total output after 1820, there was a decline in the average productivity of the slave population.

For the slaves, the changing demographic pattern produced an increasing number who had expectations of status within the plantation system and who appreciated the advantages of total freedom. The principles of occupational allocation followed by the masters were based on their perception of the work-capacity of individuals, not on questions of status; but these customary rules inevitably came to be perceived by the slaves in status terms. Thus, although the masters showed some willingness to readjust the principles to fit the changing demographic situation (and by so doing seem to have managed to keep up productivity levels), this readjustment meant that the slaves' expectations for themselves and their families, within slave society, were realized less frequently. The slave's chances of working in a skilled or domestic task, especially in a town where a semi-independent existence might be achieved, were reduced relative to the number of slaves who thought themselves 'qualified', particularly for the growing group of coloured slaves and creoles (who knew the rules). The resulting stress was a basic cause of the rebellion of 1831, which in turn increased the ever-present fear in the hearts of the whites, an economic and corporeal fear that urged them to grasp the immediate sop of compensation. Certainly the Jamaica planters would not have abandoned slavery in 1833 if left to themselves, for they continued (probably correctly) to see it as the most profitable system of labour organization available to them. But the British Parliament, acting in a much broader economic and political context, determined not to act without the co-operation of the colonial proprietors. Their co-operation was induced to a large measure by the consequences of the demographic changes which followed from the abolition of the slave trade.

APPENDIXES

APPENDIX 1

WEIGHTS, MEASURES AND VALUES, 1832

Chapter 5 contains a general discussion of the methods used to classify the Accounts Produce properties for 1832. Here the standard weights, measures and values employed are presented, together with some notes on their derivation.

Some items listed in the Accounts Produce have been excluded from the analysis: items not produced within the calendar year, and items not produced on the properties. Money received in legal judgements and prize money won at horse races has been omitted. Money received from the sale of slaves, from manumissions, from compensation for slaves committed to the workhouse or transported, and from condemnation certificates of slaves executed, has also been excluded because it was recorded very rarely (and hence erratically) in the Accounts Produce. Finally, money derived from supplying rations, labour, cartage, grass or lodgings to the militia during the rebellion has been excluded, since this income was abnormal and highly localized. Only in a very few cases were receipts from any of these items considerable.

The standard weights, measures and monetary values used in this study are given in Table A1.1. These are the median values. Where the data are extensive the range has also been shown. The estimated standard units are derived from the data contained in the Accounts Produce for 1832; where additional sources have been used, and where the method of calculation requires explanation, comments have been made below the table. The values of each unit of weight or volume have been calculated, as far as possible, directly from the data relating to that specific unit. Thus, for instance, the value per lb. of sugar contained in a hogshead is less than that sold by the lb.

All of the values are expressed in Jamaica currency. (£1.4 currency equals £1 sterling.)

Table A1.1. *Standard weights, measures and monetary values*

	Lbs.			Value		
	Median	Min.	Max.	Median	Min.	Max.
Sugar[a]						
Hogsheads	2,000	1,344	2,308	£26	—	—
Tierces	1,300	600	1,450	£17	—	—
Barrels	250	130	336	£3 5s	—	—
Casks	1,300	—	—	£17	—	—
Bags	150	—	—	£2 4s		
Pounds	—	—	—	3½d	3¼d	5½d

Table A1.1. *Standard weights, measures and monetary values* (*Continued*)

	Gallons			Value		
	Median	Min.	Max.	Median	Min.	Max.
Rum[b]						
Puncheons	115	83	123	£14	—	—
Hogsheads	57.5	40	85	£7	—	—
Casks	40	25	79	£5	—	—
Gallons	—	—	—	2s 6d	2s 0d	3s 8d
Molasses						
Puncheons	110	86	114	£6	—	—
Casks	72	—	—	£3 5s	—	—
Gallons	—	—	—	1s 2d	1s 1d	1s 4d

	Lbs.			Value		
	Median	Min.	Max.	Median	Min.	Max.
Coffee[c]						
Puncheons	2,550	—	—	£114	—	—
Tierces	850	736	890	£38	—	—
Casks	800	—	—	£36	—	—
Bags	430	135	443	£19	—	—
Barrels	165	—	—	£7 10s	—	—
Pounds	—	—	—	1s 0d	6d	1s 4d
Pounds (triage)	—	—	—	6d	—	—
Pimento[d]						
Tierces	—	—	—	£9	—	—
Bags	115	100	139	£3 8s	—	—
Casks	200	—	—	£6	—	—
Barrels	58	—	—	£1 14s	—	—
Pounds	—	—	—	7d	5d	8d
Ginger[e]						
Tierces	490	—	—	£22	—	—
Casks	—	—	—	£15	£12	£18
Bags	70	—	—	£2 12s	—	—
Pounds	—	—	—	9d	—	—
Tamarind						
Kegs	300	—	—	£10	—	—
Pounds	—	—	—	8d	—	—
Arrowroot						
Pounds	—	—	—	10d	—	—

Lime	
Temper lime	30s per hogshead
White, building lime	13s 4d per hogshead
Dyewoods	
Chipped	£5 per ton
In the tree	£2 per ton
Ground provisions	
Unspecified	10s per cwt.
Yams and cocos	10s per 100 lbs.
Plantains	7s 6d per 100 lbs.
Corn	9s per bushel
Grass	5½d per bundle

Table A1.1. *Standard weights, measures and monetary values (Continued)*

Unworked timber	
Lumber	£30 per 1,000 feet
Mahogany	£15 per log
Yacca	£15 per log
Lancewood spars	6s 8d each
Deals	£12 per 1,000 feet
Staves	£20 per 1,000
Shingles	£4 per 1,000
Worked Timber	
Hogsheads (empty)	22s 6d each
Tierces (empty)	20s each
Puncheons (empty)	40s each
Casks (empty)	8s 4d each
Spokes	50s per 100
Wood hoops	20s per bundle; £14 per 1,000

	Value		
	Median	Min.	Max.
Livestock			
Fat cattle (per head)	£17	£13	£24
Fat stock	£14	£8 10s	£19
Fat steers	£18	£14 10s	£22
Fat heifers	£18	£17 10s	£19 10s
Fat cows	£14	£12	£20
Fat sheep	£9	—	—
Beef (per lb.)	10d	9½d	10d
Mutton (per lb.)	1s 8d	10d	1s 8d
Spays (per head)	£6	£6	£7
Spayed heifers	£10	£5	£19
Young spayed heifers	£16	—	—
Steers	£15	£7	£22 10s
Young steers	£18	—	—
Cows	£10	£6	£19
Calves	£4	£2 10s	£6
Open heifers	£12	£6	£20
'Cattle'	£14	£6 10s	£20
Meagre cattle	£7 10s	£7	£7 10s
Lean cattle	£8	£7 10s	£9
Meagre stock	£6	£6	£7
Lean stock	£7 10s	£7 10s	£8 10s
'Stock'	£7 10s	£7	£8
Bulls	£30	£20	£40
Bull calves	£35	—	—
Planters' steers	£17	£17	£18
Planters' stock	£17	£16 10s	£18
Old stock	£8	£7 10s	£9
Old cattle	£8	£5 10s	£10
Old steers	£8	£7	£8 10s
Sheep	£9	—	—
Wethers	£2 10s	£2	£3
Rams	£3 10s	—	—
Fat stags	£22	—	—
Horses	£40	£20	£76
Old horses	£6	—	—
Geldings	£60	—	—

Table A1.1. *Standard weights, measures and monetary values (Continued)*

	Value		
	Median	Min.	Max.
Livestock (Continued)			
Fillies	£50	£20	£50
Colts	£16	—	—
Ponies	£25	—	—
Mares	£25	£25	£33
Mules	£30	£25	£35
Old mules	£10	—	—
Asses	£8	£7	£8
Poultry	1s	9d	1s
Hides (each)	10s	—	—
Labour (jobbing)			
'Negro labour' (per day)	2s 3d	1s 3d	3s 4d
Great gang (per day)	2s 1d	—	—
Cane holing (per day)	2s 6d	2s 1d	2s 11d
Second gang (per day)	1s 8d	1s 6d	1s 8d
Cleaning canes (per day)	1s 3d	—	—
Road (per day)	2s 1d	2s 1d	2s 6d
Tradesmen (per day)	5s	—	—
Plumbers (per day)	5s	—	—
Masons (per day)	3s 9d	3s 1d	5s
(per year)	£30	—	—
Blacksmiths (per day)	5s	—	—
(per year)	£30	£20	£35
Carpenters (per day)	5s	3s 4d	5s
(per year)	£22	£20	£25
Coopers (per day)	3s 9d	—	—
(per year)	£30	£25	£35
Domestics (per year)	£15	—	—
Boys (per year)	£12	—	—
Men (per year)	£22	£16	£45
Women (per year)	£18	£10	£21
Cane hole digging (per acre)	£7 10s	£6 10s	£8 10s
Picking pimento (per barrel)	6s 8d	—	—

[a] *Sugar:*

Hogsheads. In the Accounts Produce for 1832 three planters assumed standard weights for hogsheads: two used 1,500 lbs. and one 2,000 lbs. Another planter described hogsheads of 'from 14 to 16 hundred' as 'heavy hogsheads'.[1] To estimate the standard size in Jamaica around 1832 it is necessary first to examine mean sizes and then the range of variations. For some estates the Accounts Produce list the total weight and number of hogsheads shipped. A sample of ten such estates suggests a normal distribution of weights about a mean of 2,051 lbs.[2] To test the validity of this assumption it is necessary to consider the distribution of weights for individual hogsheads. Such data are available for Windsor Lodge, Hopewell and Spot Valley,[3] and are plotted in Figure A1.1. They show graphically that hogshead-weight was normally distributed, so that the mean of roughly 2,000 lbs. may be used as an approximation to the median weight. But the data for Spot Valley also show that the same estate could use hogsheads of different median sizes in different years: in 1827 and 1828 the median weight was 1,680 lbs., in 1829 and 1830 it was 1,932 lbs., in 1831 it fell to something between these extremes, and in 1832 it returned to 1,932 lbs. (the mean being 1,933 lbs.). These variations reflect changes in the availability of hogshead types where the planter did not raise all he used each year. They point up clearly the pitfalls involved in comparing estates and time-series based on hogshead numbers. *Tierces.* The rule that three tierces of sugar equalled two hogsheads[4] is

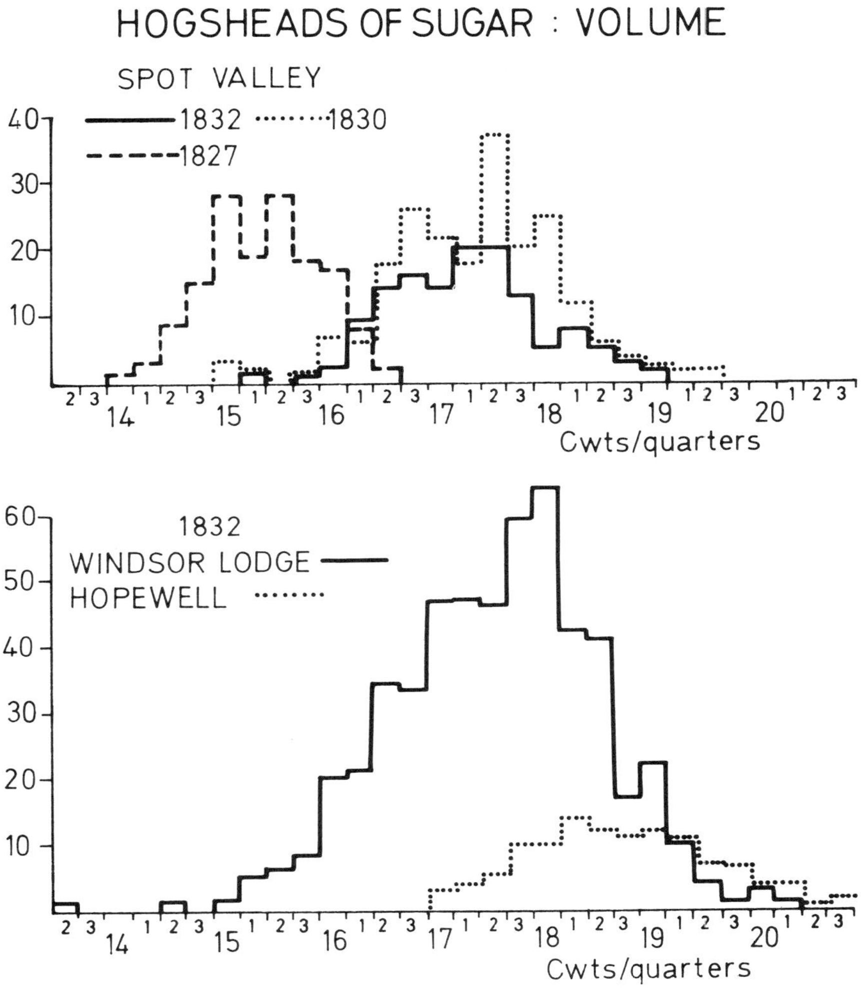

Figure A1.1 Weight of hogsheads of sugar, 1827–32.

applicable to 1832. *Casks*. The weight attributed to this unit is based on the volumetric relations of hogsheads and casks of rum. Some data for 1796 suggest that casks may have held more than tierces.[5] *Bags*. This weight is derived from the weight/volume ratios found for bags of coffee and pimento, relative to sugar. *Value*. In 1832 the average price paid for sugar exported to Great Britain (exclusive of the duty of 24s sterling) was 27s 8d sterling per cwt.,[6] or 38s 9d currency. But what is required here is an f.o.b. estimate of value, and in any case not all of the sugar produced was exported. The ruling or median price in Jamaica was about 3½d per lb., or 32s 8d per cwt. This results in a standard value of £29 3s 5d per hogshead, which approximates the averages found in the Accounts Produce.[7] But this value is based on gross weights, so it is necessary to make a reduction for tare and drainage. For ten shipments of sugar by Spot Valley and Windsor Lodge tare and drainage consistently accounted for about 10 per cent of the gross weight.[8] This loss is greater than that reported for Grenada in the late eighteenth century; but the figure of 6.5 per cent given by Hall[9] is only for 'leakage' so may not include tare. Here all of the value for sugar have been reduced by 10 per cent, giving a rounded £26 per hogshead. Bags, however, weighed only about 6 lbs. so no adjustment has been made for tare. The hogshead itself was worth £1, but since it is not known when the

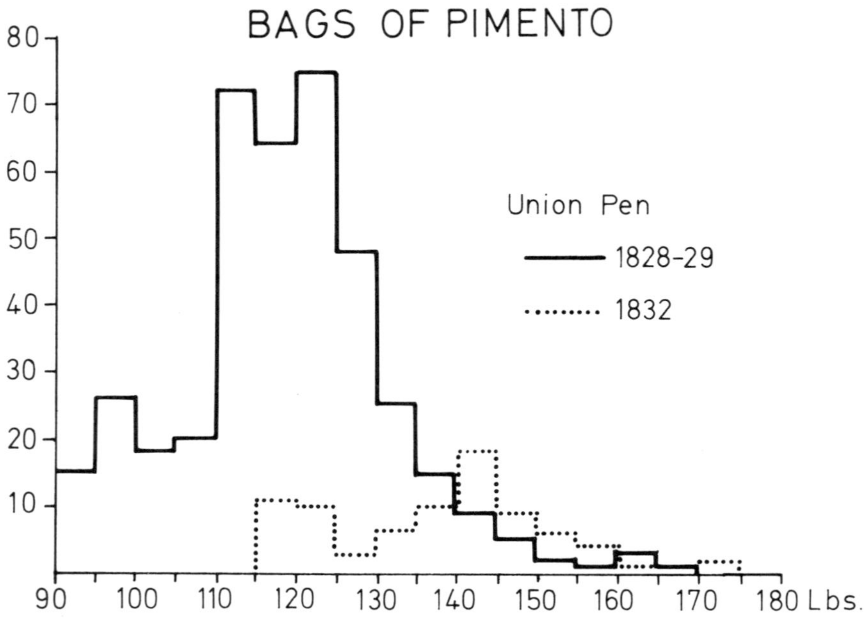

Figure A1.2 Weight of bags of pimento, 1828–32.

hogsheads were made on the estates their value has been excluded; some local purchasers found their own hogsheads.

[b] *Rum:*

Puncheons were twice the size of hogsheads. For 150 puncheons listed individually in the Accounts Produce for 1832 the mean volume was 114.2 gallons and the median fell between 114 and 115. *Value.* Rum sold in Britain fetched from 2s 10d to 3s sterling per gallon, the average price being 2s 11d.[10] Within Jamaica (where it was subject to an excise duty of 6d per gallon) it fetched from 2s to 2s 8d per gallon. No reduction for tare is necessary for rum or molasses.

[c] *Coffee:*

Puncheons, casks and barrels. The weights of these, when filled with coffee, are derived from the measures found for sugar, rum and molasses, relative to the weight/volume ratio of tierces of coffee and sugar. *Tierces* were the most commonly used units for coffee. Compared to sugar, the range of weights was narrow. *Value.* Coffee varied considerably in quality, so that the range of prices was greater than that for sugar. Triage (the broken, burnt refuse left after the third grading) was generally sold for 6d per lb.,[11] but it may be that triage was not always specified as such. The prices used here are based on Jamaica sales. The average price of coffee exported to Britain in 1832 was 9¾d sterling per lb.[12] Although coffee did not lose weight by leakage, the tare was as considerable as for sugar. Thus the gross weights have been reduced by 10 per cent.

[d] *Pimento:*

Bags were most common. Three planters used 100 lbs. as a standard measure in 1832.[13] Data for the variation in size of individual bags are available for Union Pen, St. Ann,[14] and are shown in Figure A1.2. *Value.* Prices varied according to whether bags were found by the purchaser or the seller. An empty bag was worth from 2s 6d to 3s 9d. No tare has been subtracted. The prices used are based on island sales.

[e] *Ginger:*

Bags. The weight used for this unit is that given by Edwards for 1768.[15]

Table A1.2. *Total value of output on Accounts Produce properties, 1832*

	Gross receipts (£ currency)	Percentage of total receipts
Sugar	2,399,878	61.27
Rum	573,168	14.63
Molasses	15,047	0.38
Coffee	468,938	11.97
Pimento	76,836	1.96
Ginger	2,535	0.06
Tamarind	17	0.00
Lime	399	0.01
Dyewoods	9,348	0.23
Ground provisions and corn	7,198	0.18
Grass	2,130	0.05
Unworked timber	8,069	0.20
Worked timber	1,333	0.03
Working livestock[a]	100,264	2.55
Old and killing livestock[b]	117,425	2.99
Other livestock[c]	12,963	0.33
Hides and skins	203	0.00
Pasturage and rent of land	20,800	0.53
Cartage and boatage	13,506	0.34
Wharfage	11,942	0.30
Daily rate labour: field and road	60,449	1.54
Daily rate labour: tradesmen and domestics	7,081	0.18
Yearly rate labour	7,831	0.19
Sundries[d]	6,081	0.15
Total	3,916,794	100.00

[a] Planters' steers, planters' stock, steers, spayed heifers, mules, asses.

[b] All 'fat' stock, cows, open heifers, sheep, calves, stags, and all 'old', 'lean' and 'meagre' stock.

[c] Bulls, horses, poultry; offals; covering mares or asses.

[d] Arrowroot, surveying cane pieces, horse shoeing, coconuts, milk, grinding coffee, spaying heifers, cutting mules, fish, lodging houses and unspecified accounts.

APPENDIX 2

CROP COMBINATIONS, 1832

The following is a complete list of the crop combinations derived from classifying the 960 Accounts Produce properties for 1832, according to the method described in Chapter 2 above. The number of slaves located on each type has been calculated from the Returns of Registrations of Slaves for 1832.

Table A2.1. *Crop combinations on Accounts Produce properties, 1832*

	Number of properties	Number of slaves
Monocultures		
Sugar	527	117,670
Coffee	176	22,562
Livestock	56	5,529
Labour (jobbing)	25	1,338
Pimento	15	1,287
Wharfage	6	148
Rent (of land for pasturage or cultivation)	4	55
Sundries (see Appendix 1)	4	139
Cartage	2	105
Ginger	1	5
Two-crop combinations		
Livestock–labour	34	4,205
Coffee–labour	15	1,513
Coffee–livestock	11	1,885
Livestock–pimento	11	1,263
Sugar–pimento	4	682
Coffee–pimento	4	354
Livestock–dyewoods	4	412
Labour–rent	4	334
Pimento–labour	3	228
Sugar–livestock	3	637
Sugar–coffee	3	889
Livestock–cartage	3	357
Coffee–ginger	1	98
Unworked timber–livestock	1	111
Unworked timber–coffee	1	92
Livestock–grass	1	307
Sugar–unworked timber	1	94
Sugar–rent	1	148
Coffee–sundries	1	7
Rent–pimento	1	85
Sugar–sundries	1	134
Sundries–provisions	1	40

Table A2.1. *Crop combinations on Accounts Produce properties, 1832 (Cont.)*

	Number of properties	Number of slaves
Three-crop combinations		
Pimento–livestock–labour	4	532
Unworked timber–livestock–labour	3	176
Coffee–livestock–labour	2	217
Livestock–labour-cartage	2	170
Dyewoods–livestock–wharfage	1	91
Dyewoods–livestock–labour	1	446
Sugar–livestock–labour	1	561
Pimento–livestock–dyewoods	1	46
Coffee-pimento-labour	1	44
Dyewoods–livestock–cartage	1	41
Rent–livestock–labour	1	87
Livestock–labour–sundries	1	446
Sugar–rent–labour	1	112
Labour–rent–pimento	1	12
Grass–livestock–rent	1	69
Four-crop combinations		
Provisions–livestock–labour–cartage	1	26
Livestock–unworked timber–rent–labour	1	290
Labour–coffee–rent–livestock	1	95
Five-crop combinations		
Coffee–pimento–cartage–livestock–labour	1	129
Coffee–pimento–unworked timber–livestock–labour	1	104
Dyewoods–unworked timber–cartage–livestock–labour	1	68
Grass–livestock–rent–labour–cartage	1	107
Six-crop combinations		
Sugar–coffee–pimento–dyewoods–livestock–labour	1	547
Provisions–coffee–pimento–livestock–unworked timber–labour	1	153
Livestock–sundries–rent–provisions–worked timber–labour	1	203
Coffee–labour–livestock–rent–pimento–provisions	1	105
Wharfage–livestock–sundries–unworked timber–labour–lime	1	154
Sugar–cartage–unworked timber–wharfage–provisions–rent	1	114
Total	960	167,858

Sources: A.P., Libers 72–4; R.R.S., Libers 115, 116, 119, 120, 124–41.

APPENDIX 3

STATISTICAL TABLES

DEFINITIONS OF VARIABLES CORRELATED IN TABLES A3.1–A3.5

X_1 Slaves per square mile, 1832. *Source:* The number of slaves is derived from the R.R.S., Libers 115, 116, 119, 120, 124–41, as are all of the demographic data used here, unless stated otherwise. For the method of allocation to quadrats and towns, see Chapter 5 above.

X_2 Total slave population (for towns), 1832.

X_3 Mean slaves per holding, 1832.

X_4 Percentage holdings with less than 21 slaves, 1832.

X_5 Percentage holdings with 21–100 slaves, 1832.

X_6 Percentage holdings with more than 100 slaves, 1832.

X_7 Males per 100 females (slaves), 1832.

X_8 Males per 100 females (slaves), 1817. *Source: J.H.A.V.*, 1817, p. 39.

X_9 Births per 1,000 slaves, 1829–32 (annual average).

X_{10} Male deaths per 1,000 (slaves), 1829–32.

X_{11} Female deaths per 1,000 (slaves), 1829–32.

X_{12} Deaths per 1,000 slaves, 1829–32.

X_{13} Natural increase per 1,000 slaves, 1829–32. (For the definition of births, deaths and natural increase, see Chapter 5 above.)

X_{14} Percentage births coloured (slaves), 1829–32.

X_{15} Percentage male deaths coloured (slaves), 1829–32.

X_{16} Percentage female deaths coloured (slaves), 1829–32.

X_{17} Percentage total deaths coloured (slaves), 1829–32.

X_{18} Percentage coloured births (slaves) with white fathers, 1829–32. (That is, mulattoes, quadroons and mustees.)

X_{19} Percentage of male deaths African (slaves), 1829–32.

X_{20} Percentage of female deaths African (slaves), 1829–32.

X_{21} Percentage of total deaths African (slaves), 1829–32.

X_{22} Percentage slaves less than 6 years of age, 1834. *Source: J.H.A.V.*, 1834, p. 317.

X_{23} Percentage of slaves 'aged', 1838. *Source:* R. M. Martin, *History of the Colonies of the British Empire* (London, 1843), p. 8.

X_{24} Slave population in 1832 as a percentage of that in 1817. *Source:* 1817 from *J.H.A.V.*, 1817, p. 39.

X_{25} Apprentices in 1838 as a percentage of slaves in 1832. *Source:* Martin, *op. cit.*, p. 8.

X_{26} White population, 1832. (Estimated, at the quadrat level, by attributing one to each holding with less than 21 slaves, 1.5 to those with 21–100 slaves, and two to those with more than 100 slaves.)

X_{27} Slaves per white, 1832. *Source:* Jamaica Census, 1844, for the number of whites per parish.
X_{28} Manumissions, 1829–32.
X_{29} Runaways, 1829–32.
X_{30} Net purchases of slaves, 1829–32.
X_{31} Miles to coast.
X_{32} Miles to nearest urban port, 1832.
X_{33} Miles from town to nearest town, 1832.
X_{34} Slave population of nearest town, 1832.
X_{35} Population potential, Kingston, 1832. (Population potential is defined as:

$$V_c = \frac{1}{r} \cdot Dds$$

where V_c is the aggregate accessibility at a given point (Kingston), D is the density of population over an infinitesimal area ds (quadrat), and r is the distance from ds to c. See J. Q. Stewart and W. Warntz, 'Macrogeography and Social Science', *Geographical Review,* Vol. 48 (1958), pp. 167–84.)

X_{36} Population potential, urban ports, 1832. (As for X_{35} but c being the nearest port in each case.)
X_{37} Slaves per cultivated square mile, 1832. (Using the cultivated acres reported by James Robertson on his Jamaica map of 1804.)
X_{38} Number of sugar estates, 1834. *Source:* Douglas Hall, *Free Jamaica* (New Haven, 1959), p. 82.
X_{39} Number of sugar estates, 1804. *Source:* James Robertson's map of Jamaica.
X_{40} Number of sugar estates 'abandoned', 1804–32. (X_{39} minus the number of holdings with more than 100 slaves in 1832.)
X_{41} Head of taxable livestock per slave, 1832. (Livestock as returned in March 1832, *Jamaica Almanack,* 1833.)
X_{42} Number of pens and plantations, 1832. (The number of holdings with more than 100 slaves in 1832 minus X_{39}.)
X_{43} Percentage of slaves urban, 1832.
X_{44} Percentage of slaves non-predial, 1834. *Source:* T.71/851 (Public Record Office, London) and Martin, *op. cit.,* p. 8.
X_{45} Mean slope of land. (Derived by Wentworth's formula:

$$\tan\left(\frac{n}{G} \cdot \frac{VI}{3661}\right)$$

where n is the number of grid/contour crossings (on the Jamaica 1:50,000 topographic map), G is the aggregate length of the grid lines in miles, and VI is the contour interval in feet (250). See G. H. Dury, *Map Interpretation* (London, 1960), p. 176.

X_{46} Relative relief. (The difference in feet between the highest and lowest points in the quadrat.)
X_{47} Maximum altitude.
X_{48} Dissection ratio. (X_{47} divided by X_{46}.)
X_{49} Rainfall (modern averages).
X_{50} Miles of road per square mile, 1804. *Source:* Robertson's map of 1804.

X_{51} Gross receipts produced per slave, 1832. (Derived from the A.P. for 1832; see Chapter 10 and Appendix 1.)

The coefficients in italic in Tables A3.1–A3.5 are significant at the 99 per cent level of probability.

SOURCES FOR TABLES A3.11–A3.14

The data relating to age structure in 1817 and age at death 1817–20 are taken from the following sources:

	1817	*1817–20*
St. James	R.R.S., Libers 30, 31	R.R.S., Libers 37, 40
St. Elizabeth	R.R.S., Libers 10, 12, 23	R.R.S., Liber 34
Manchester	R. R. S., Libers 11, 19; T.71/65	R.R.S., Libers 35, 37
Clarendon	T.71/680, Bundle 17	R.R.S., Libers 53, 55
Vere	T.71/683, Bundle 9	R.R.S., Liber 18
St. John	R.R.S., Libers 19, 20	R.R.S., Liber 55
Port Royal	T.71/683, Bundle 9	R.R.S., Libers 9, 17
Portland	R.R.S., Liber 20	R.R.S., Liber 16
Kingston	R.R.S., Libers 3, 11, 12, 14, 16, 18, 24	R.R.S., Libers 3, 14, 15, 33, 36, 38b, 39, 41, 45, 49

The T.71 data for Clarendon, Vere and Port Royal, which consist of summary sheets covered with pen strokes, do not specify that they relate to 1817 (or even to age), but this may be deduced from the organization of the material and the total populations. There are some differences between the number of deaths extracted from the R.R.S. and the totals recorded in T.71/683, Bundle 9, but the difference is generally less than 20. In the case of St. Elizabeth, the R.R.S. total is 313 deficient, so that these data have been excluded from Tables A3.13 and A3.14. There are also variations in the percentage of slaves whose age at death during the period 1817–20 is unknown, as follows:

	Africans	*Creoles*
St. James	0.5	0.3
Manchester	5.6	8.6
Clarendon	6.3	2.3
Vere	0.0	0.0
St. John	10.1	4.6
Port Royal	18.6	11.0
Portland	0.3	0.9
Kingston	4.7	10.2

The age-specific death rates in Table A3.13 have been inflated by these proportions to make them comparable; it is unlikely that the non-recording of age at death was age-specific, since it generally applied throughout a particular return, rather than selectively. The size-groups to which deaths are attributed are those in which the slaves lived in 1817, though this is difficult to control where there was considerable sale and movement of slaves.

Table A3.1. *Correlation coefficients: parishes*

		X_1	X_3	X_4	X_5	X_6	X_7	X_8	X_9	X_{10}	X_{11}	X_{12}	X_{13}	X_{14}	X_{15}	X_{16}	X_{17}	X_{18}	X_{19}	X_{20}	X_{21}	X_{22}	X_{23}	X_{24}	X_{25}	X_{27}	X_{28}	X_{29}	X_{30}	X_{37}	X_{38}	X_{41}	X_{43}	X_{44}
Slaves per square mile	X_1	1.00																																
Slaves per holding	X_3	−.52	1.00																															
% holdings under 21 slaves	X_4	.59	−.85	1.00																														
% holdings 21–100 slaves	X_5	−.51	.50	−.87	1.00																													
% holdings over 100 slaves	X_6	−.48	.98	−.80	.41	1.00																												
Males per 100 females, 1832	X_7	−.71	.43	−.73	.82	.36	1.00																											
Males per 100 females, 1817	X_8	−.53	.54	−.74	.73	.49	.85	1.00																										
Births per 1,000	X_9	−.46	.23	−.35	.37	.20	.49	.38	1.00																									
Male deaths per 1,000	X_{10}	−.15	.26	−.14	−.01	.26	−.07	.06	−.31	1.00																								
Female deaths per 1,000	X_{11}	−.39	.31	−.15	−.02	.29	.01	.03	−.14	.89	1.00																							
Total deaths per 1,000	X_{12}	−.29	.28	−.13	−.03	.28	−.02	.05	−.23	.96	.97	1.00																						
Natural increase per 1,000	X_{13}	.08	−.15	−.02	.17	−.16	.20	.10	.57	−.93	−.88	−.93	1.00																					
% births coloured	X_{14}	.62	−.62	.74	−.70	−.54	−.77	−.78	−.40	−.04	−.14	−.09	−.07	1.00																				
% male deaths coloured	X_{15}	.45	−.44	.63	−.70	−.34	−.75	−.77	−.28	−.11	−.14	−.12	.00	.85	1.00																			
% female deaths coloured	X_{16}	.44	−.57	.75	−.70	−.55	−.70	−.81	−.35	.05	.01	.05	−.17	.83	.78	1.00																		
% total deaths coloured	X_{17}	.48	−.54	.75	−.76	−.47	−.78	−.85	−.35	−.04	−.06	−.04	−.10	.89	.93	.94	1.00																	
% births with white fathers	X_{18}	−.19	.50	−.27	−.02	.53	.06	.14	−.11	.35	.43	.40	−.38	−.13	−.15	−.17	−.18	1.00																
% male deaths African	X_{19}	.15	.19	−.37	.48	.12	.45	.54	−.06	−.07	−.27	−.19	.14	−.30	−.56	−.42	−.53	.12	1.00															
% female deaths African	X_{20}	.13	.05	−.23	.33	.03	.40	.55	.21	−.29	−.43	−.37	.40	−.15	−.39	−.42	−.45	.01	.80	1.00														
% total deaths African	X_{21}	.15	.14	−.33	.43	.08	.46	.58	.06	−.17	−.35	−.28	.25	−.26	−.54	−.45	−.53	.07	.96	.93	1.00													
% under 6 years, 1834	X_{22}	.01	−.01	−.02	.08	−.06	.19	.01	.41	−.41	−.26	−.35	.45	−.02	−.02	−.01	−.05	−.24	.08	.33	.20	1.00												
% 'aged', 1838	X_{23}	−.47	.36	−.26	.09	.38	.09	.13	−.11	.38	.41	.41	−.39	−.12	.08	−.04	.01	−.05	−.23	−.15	−.21	−.13	1.00											
1832 slaves as % of 1817	X_{24}	−.52	.51	−.66	.64	.44	.60	.53	.56	−.39	−.28	−.35	.51	−.58	−.58	−.54	−.59	−.01	.24	.30	.29	.28	.00	1.00										
1838 slaves as % of 1832	X_{25}	.06	−.15	.19	−.10	−.24	−.03	−.26	.04	−.45	−.34	−.38	.34	−.10	−.05	.30	.16	−.05	.03	.01	.04	.34	−.37	.37	1.00									
Slaves per white	X_{27}	−.50	.76	−.62	.33	.75	.32	.51	.08	.42	.50	.47	−.37	−.63	−.44	−.46	−.49	.50	−.02	−.09	−.06	−.15	.37	.31	−.18	1.00								
Manumissions	X_{28}	.88	−.63	.66	−.53	−.58	−.75	−.68	−.38	−.16	−.39	−.30	.11	−.79	.70	.66	.72	−.34	−.08	−.08	−.09	−.04	−.36	−.58	.01	−.67	1.00							
Runaways	X_{29}	.83	−.50	.49	−.38	−.45	−.57	−.51	−.50	−.15	−.40	−.28	.05	.61	.53	.49	.54	−.25	.03	−.03	.00	.01	−.38	−.49	.11	−.52	.88	1.00						
Net purchase of slaves	X_{30}	−.01	.25	.04	−.24	.22	−.23	−.30	−.10	.31	−.41	.39	−.36	.09	.15	.38	.32	.14	−.26	−.29	−.27	.23	.40	−.03	.33	.26	−.06	−.03	1.00					
Agricultural slave density	X_{37}	.99	−.52	.56	−.45	−.50	−.66	−.48	−.41	−.20	−.44	−.35	.14	.57	.40	.41	.44	−.24	.20	.19	.21	.02	−.47	−.46	.07	−.50	.87	.81	−.12	1.00				
Sugar estates, 1834	X_{38}	−.26	.26	−.09	−.10	.28	−.15	−.05	.01	.60	.65	.64	−.53	.24	.31	.20	.26	.23	−.34	−.26	−.34	−.07	.43	−.24	−.40	.27	−.07	−.21	.30	−.32	1.00			
Livestock per slave	X_{41}	−.33	−.52	−.09	.22	−.09	.20	−.05	.36	−.49	−.36	−.42	.49	−.05	.12	.14	.16	−.57	−.33	−.21	−.28	.27	.19	.42	.33	−.16	−.07	−.14	.16	−.30	−.05	1.00		
% slaves urban	X_{43}	.96	−.63	.70	−.60	−.58	−.73	−.65	−.42	−.19	−.39	−.31	.10	.72	.53	.54	.58	−.22	.08	.12	.10	.06	−.43	−.58	.11	−.63	.89	.77	−.04	.95	−.26	−.27	1.00	
% slaves non-predial	X_{44}	.92	−.68	.71	−.57	−.64	−.67	−.65	−.39	−.20	−.41	−.32	.13	.71	.52	.58	.59	−.29	.08	.09	.09	.05	−.44	−.60	.13	−.69	.90	.79	−.06	.91	−.31	−.20	.98	1.00

Table A3.2. *Correlation coefficients: quadrats*

		X_1	X_3	X_4	X_5	X_6	X_7	X_9	X_{10}	X_{11}	X_{12}	X_{13}	X_{14}	X_{17}	X_{21}	X_{26}	X_{27}	X_{30}	X_{31}	X_{32}	X_{35}	X_{36}	X_{39}	X_{40}	X_{42}	X_{45}	X_{46}	X_{47}	X_{48}	X_{49}	X_{50}
Slaves per square mile	X_1	1.00																													
Slaves per holding	X_3	*.47*	1.00																												
% holdings under 21 slaves	X_4	*−.19*	*−.52*	1.00																											
% holdings 21–100 slaves	X_5	−.04	.03	*−.35*	1.00																										
% holdings over 100 slaves	X_6	*.51*	*.92*	*−.49*	*−.17*	1.00																									
Males per 100 females, 1832	X_7	.01	.02	*.31*	.11	.00	1.00																								
Births per 1,000	X_9	.12	.09	*.31*	*.16*	.05	*.40*	1.00																							
Male deaths per 1,000	X_{10}	*.25*	*.35*	−.02	.12	*.31*	.09	*.26*	1.00																						
Female deaths per 1,000	X_{11}	.06	.12	.06	.09	.09	*.68*	*.16*	.10	1.00																					
Total deaths per 1,000	X_{12}	*.23*	*.33*	.03	*.16*	*.28*	*.22*	*.23*	*.82*	*.50*	1.00																				
Natural increase per 1,000	X_{13}	*−.14*	*−.25*	*.17*	−.05	*−.23*	.05	*.43*	*−.60*	*−.36*	*−.78*	1.00																			
% births coloured	X_{14}	.06	.10	*.18*	.01	.08	*.16*	*.27*	*.43*	.00	*.35*	*−.16*	1.00																		
% deaths coloured	X_{17}	*.17*	*.21*	.00	.07	*.19*	.03	*.21*	*.15*	.03	.13	.01	*.36*	1.00																	
% deaths African	X_{21}	.06	.07	*.15*	*.19*	.06	.10	*.16*	*.25*	.03	*.30*	*−.17*	*.24*	−.09	1.00																
White population	X_{26}	*.36*	−.08	*.27*	.05	*−.08*	.09	*.23*	*.14*	.00	.11	.05	.13	*.19*	*.15*	1.00															
Slaves per white	X_{27}	*.49*	*.98*	*−.45*	.06	*.87*	.04	*.14*	*.38*	*.14*	*.37*	*−.25*	*.14*	*.26*	.10	−.02	1.00														
Net purchase of slaves	X_{30}	*.14*	.09	.01	.03	.07	.03	−.04	.09	.01	.07	−.09	.09	.10	.04	*.34*	.11	1.00													
Miles to coast	X_{31}	*−.27*	−.13	−.05	*.14*	*−.16*	.02	−.03	−.04	.07	−.02	.00	−.07	−.12	.02	−.07	*−.14*	−.01	1.00												
Miles to urban port	X_{32}	*−.29*	*−.16*	.00	*.12*	*−.18*	.02	.02	*−.18*	−.03	*−.16*	*.16*	*−.15*	*−.22*	.03	*−.15*	*−.18*	−.04	*.69*	1.00											
Population potential, Kingston	X_{35}	*.33*	.13	.00	.04	.11	.04	.08	*.18*	.05	*.17*	−.10	−.03	.05	.10	*.58*	*.18*	*.25*	−.11	*−.16*	1.00										
Population potential, ports	X_{36}	*.35*	*.21*	−.07	.00	*.20*	.00	.01	*.23*	.10	*.24*	*−.22*	.10	*.14*	.02	*.27*	*.24*	*.16*	*−.28*	*−.41*	*.19*	1.00									
Sugar estates, 1804	X_{39}	*.50*	*.47*	*−.18*	−.04	*.46*	−.02	.03	*.37*	*.17*	*.38*	*−.34*	*.22*	*.34*	−.05	*.32*	*.51*	*.18*	*−.23*	*−.37*	*.23*	*.50*	1.00								
Abandoned estates, 1804–32	X_{40}	*.18*	.11	−.03	.06	.11	−.01	−.04	*.20*	.10	*.21*	*−.22*	.13	*.21*	−.03	*.20*	.13	.12	−.10	*−.21*	.11	*.29*	*.68*	1.00							
Pens and plantations, 1832	X_{42}	*.14*	.03	.00	.06	.08	.05	*.16*	−.01	−.06	−.05	*.15*	−.11	−.07	*.17*	*.37*	.06	.04	*.15*	*.27*	*.42*	−.06	*−.25*	*−.26*	1.00						
Mean slope	X_{45}	−.09	−.10	−.11	.13	−.13	−.04	−.03	.02	.02	.03	−.04	−.07	*−.19*	.03	.03	−.10	−.06	*.39*	.11	*.17*	−.10	−.13	−.02	*.17*	1.00					
Relative relief	X_{46}	−.02	−.07	−.05	.10	−.11	−.03	.06	.01	−.05	−.02	.05	−.10	−.12	.07	.13	−.06	.00	*.17*	*.16*	*.24*	−.08	*−.15*	−.08	*.38*	*.59*	1.00				
Maximum altitude	X_{47}	*−.13*	−.10	−.12	*.27*	*−.16*	.00	.04	.04	−.03	−.01	.04	−.12	*−.18*	.11	.01	−.09	−.04	*.36*	*.25*	.11	−.13	*−.21*	−.11	*.23*	*.53*	*.45*	1.00			
Dissection ratio	X_{48}	−.06	−.01	−.07	*.18*	−.06	.01	.02	.08	−.02	.03	−.02	−.05	−.08	.09	−.06	−.01	−.02	.12	.07	−.04	−.04	−.06	−.04	−.01	.04	−.08	*.78*	1.00		
Average rainfall	X_{49}	.03	−.02	−.03	.05	−.02	.10	.08	*.18*	.10	*.16*	−.10	.10	−.08	.00	−.07	−.03	−.10	.09	*−.14*	−.09	.00	−.02	.03	−.06	.04	*.35*	*.27*	.02	1.00	
Road miles per square mile	X_{50}	*.54*	*.23*	.06	−.12	*.28*	.04	.01	.12	.09	*.14*	*−.14*	.05	*.27*	−.07	*.25*	*.24*	.12	*−.38*	*−.30*	*.23*	*.27*	*.39*	*.23*	−.07	*−.29*	*−.18*	*−.26*	−.06	*−.24*	1.00

Table A3.3. *Correlation coefficients: towns*

		X_2	X_3	X_7	X_9	X_{10}	X_{11}	X_{12}	X_{13}	X_{14}	X_{17}	X_{21}	X_{30}	X_{33}	X_{34}
Slave population	X_2	1.00													
Slaves per holding	X_3	—.04	1.00												
Males per 100 females, 1832	X_7	—.16	.30	1.00											
Births per 1,000	X_9	—.05	—.08	—.28	1.00										
Male deaths per 1,000	X_{10}	—.03	—.09	*.59*	—.41	1.00									
Female deaths per 1,000	X_{11}	—.03	—.40	*.67*	—.11	*.55*	1.00								
Total deaths per 1,000	X_{12}	—.04	.12	*.75*	—.33	*.93*	*.82*	1.00							
Natural increase per 1,000	X_{13}	.01	—.12	*—.70*	*.69*	*—.89*	*—.67*	*—.91*	1.00						
% births coloured	X_{14}	.24	.03	—.28	.13	—.15	—.10	—.17	.19	1.00					
% deaths coloured	X_{17}	.12	.07	—.10	.23	—.07	.00	—.05	.14	*.61*	1.00				
% deaths African	X_{21}	—.05	—.23	—.24	—.23	.16	—.21	—.01	—.09	—.04	—.20	1.00			
Net purchases of slaves	X_{30}	—.08	.16	—.13	—.06	—.04	.02	—.03	.00	.45	.24	—.10	1.00		
Miles to nearest town	X_{33}	—.02	.16	.25	—.15	.15	.30	.24	—.25	.32	.15	—.28	*.54*	1.00	
Slave population of nearest town	X_{34}	.08	.00	—.11	—.04	.02	—.06	—.02	—.01	.24	.14	—.16	*.50*	.02	1.00

Table A3.4. *Correlation coefficients: crop-combination groups*

Sugar (527 properties)

		X_7	X_9	X_{12}	X_{14}	X_{21}	X_{51}
Males per 100 females	X_7	1.00					
Births per 1,000	X_9	*—.14*	1.00				
Deaths per 1,000	X_{12}	—.02	—.05	1.00			
% births coloured	X_{14}	*—.11*	—.02	—.04	1.00		
% deaths African	X_{21}	*.19*	*—.15*	.09	*—.17*	1.00	
Production per slave	X_{51}	.07	*—.19*	*.12*	.02	.05	1.00

Coffee (176 properties)

		X_7	X_9	X_{12}	X_{14}	X_{21}	X_{51}
Males per 100 females	X_7	1.00					
Births per 1,000	X_9	*—.28*	1.00				
Deaths per 1,000	X_{12}	*—.16*	.09	1.00			
% births coloured	X_{14}	—.09	—.04	.11	1.00		
% deaths African	X_{21}	—.03	*—.12*	—.04	—.04	1.00	
Production per slave	X_{51}	.02	—.10	—.09	—.04	*.22*	1.00

Coffee–labour (15 properties)

		X_7	X_9	X_{12}	X_{14}	X_{21}	X_{51}
Males per 100 females	X_7	1.00					
Births per 1,000	X_9	.09	1.00				
Deaths per 1,000	X_{12}	.25	—.14	1.00			
% births coloured	X_{14}	—.21	.41	.37	1.00		
% deaths African	X_{21}	.32	—.11	.28	.01	1.00	
Production per slave	X_{51}	—.30	.22	—.02	.12	—.21	1.00

Coffee–livestock (11 properties)

		X_7	X_9	X_{12}	X_{14}	X_{21}	X_{51}
Males per 100 females	X_7	1.00					
Births per 1,000	X_9	—.41	1.00				
Deaths per 1,000	X_{12}	—.03	—.17	1.00			
% births coloured	X_{14}	—.19	.17	—.37	1.00		
% deaths African	X_{21}	.46	—.46	—.13	—.16	1.00	
Production per slave	X_{51}	—.19	.35	—.55	.23	.16	1.00

Pimento (15 properties)

		X_7	X_9	X_{12}	X_{14}	X_{21}	X_{51}
Males per 100 females	X_7	1.00					
Births per 1,000	X_9	—.40	1.00				
Deaths per 1,000	X_{12}	.05	*—.68*	1.00			
% births coloured	X_{14}	.16	.23	—.05	1.00		
% deaths African	X_{21}	.23	—.15	.48	—.27	1.00	
Production per slave	X_{51}	—.15	—.51	*.76*	—.12	.34	1.00

Livestock (56 properties)

		X_7	X_9	X_{12}	X_{14}	X_{21}	X_{51}
Males per 100 females	X_7	1.00					
Births per 1,000	X_9	—.22	1.00				
Deaths per 1,000	X_{12}	—.10	—.15	1.00			
% births coloured	X_{14}	—.17	.01	.14	1.00		
% deaths African	X_{21}	.25	*—.48*	.11	.10	1.00	
Production per slave	X_{51}	.00	—.20	.13	.21	.11	1.00

Table A3.4. *Correlation coefficients: crop-combination groups (Continued)*

Livestock–pimento (11 properties)

		X_7	X_9	X_{12}	X_{14}	X_{21}	X_{51}
Males per 100 females	X_7	1.00					
Births per 1,000	X_9	—.33	1.00				
Deaths per 1,000	X_{12}	.05	—.26	1.00			
% births coloured	X_{14}	.00	.00	.46	1.00		
% deaths African	X_{21}	—.50	.14	.23	.22	1.00	
Production per slave	X_{51}	.18	—.70	.21	.29	—.24	1.00

Livestock–labour (34 properties)

		X_7	X_9	X_{12}	X_{14}	X_{21}	X_{51}
Males per 100 females	X_7	1.00					
Births per 1,000	X_9	—.02	1.00				
Deaths per 1,000	X_{12}	.05	.00	1.00			
% births coloured	X_{14}	—.19	.15	—.02	1.00		
% deaths African	X_{21}	—.02	.08	.17	—.10	1.00	
Production per slave	X_{51}	.13	—.40	.06	.15	.39	1.00

Labour (25 properties)

		X_7	X_9	X_{12}	X_{14}	X_{21}	X_{51}
Males per 100 females	X_7	1.00					
Births per 1,000	X_9	.02	1.00				
Deaths per 1,000	X_{12}	—.26	.14	1.00			
% births coloured	X_{14}	—.07	.11	—.05	1.00		
% deaths African	X_{21}	—.24	.23	.52	.02	1.00	
Production per slave	X_{51}	.08	—.26	.25	—.24	.18	1.00

Table A3.5. *Correlation coefficients: slave holding size-groups*

1–50 Slaves (91 holdings)

		X_7	X_9	X_{12}	X_{14}	X_{21}	X_{51}
Males per 100 females	X_7	1.00					
Births per 1,000	X_9	—.03	1.00				
Deaths per 1,000	X_{12}	—.31	—.15	1.00			
% births coloured	X_{14}	—.02	.03	—.02	1.00		
% deaths African	X_{21}	—.06	—.11	.30	.00	1.00	
Production per slave	X_{51}	—.11	—.17	.07	—.06	.07	1.00

51–100 Slaves (165 holdings)

		X_7	X_9	X_{12}	X_{14}	X_{21}	X_{51}
Males per 100 females	X_7	1.00					
Births per 1,000	X_9	—.13	1.00				
Deaths per 1,000	X_{12}	—.11	—.14	1.00			
% births coloured	X_{14}	—.10	.16	.03	1.00		
% deaths African	X_{21}	.27	—.13	.06	—.03	1.00	
Production per slave	X_{51}	—.07	—.13	.12	.05	.15	1.00

101–150 Slaves (185 holdings)

		X_7	X_9	X_{12}	X_{14}	X_{21}	X_{51}
Males per 100 females	X_7	1.00					
Births per 1,000	X_9	*—.19*	1.00				
Deaths per 1,000	X_{12}	.00	—.08	1.00			
% births coloured	X_{14}	*—.15*	*—.13*	.02	1.00		
% deaths African	X_{21}	*.14*	—.07	—.01	*—.11*	1.00	
Production per slave	X_{51}	—.01	*—.24*	*.14*	*.23*	—.10	1.00

151–200 Slaves (185 holdings)

		X_7	X_9	X_{12}	X_{14}	X_{21}	X_{51}
Males per 100 females	X_7	1.00					
Births per 1,000	X_9	—.10	1.00				
Deaths per 1,000	X_{12}	*—.12*	—.05	1.00			
% births coloured	X_{14}	—.02	—.06	.09	1.00		
% deaths African	X_{21}	*.12*	—.04	—.01	*—.17*	1.00	
Production per slave	X_{51}	—.03	*—.25*	*.34*	*.19*	—.05	1.00

201–250 Slaves (135 holdings)

		X_7	X_9	X_{12}	X_{14}	X_{21}	X_{51}
Males per 100 females	X_7	1.00					
Births per 1,000	X_9	—.04	1.00				
Deaths per 1,000	X_{12}	—.03	—.08	1.00			
% births coloured	X_{14}	*—.23*	*—.22*	*.16*	1.00		
% deaths African	X_{21}	.10	*—.12*	*—.14*	*—.12*	1.00	
Production per slave	X_{51}	.05	*—.17*	*.15*	.02	—.09	1.00

251–300 Slaves (89 holdings)

		X_7	X_9	X_{12}	X_{14}	X_{21}	X_{51}
Males per 100 females	X_7	1.00					
Births per 1,000	X_9	.00	1.00				
Deaths per 1,000	X_{12}	—.07	—.20	1.00			
% births coloured	X_{14}	.17	—.15	.00	1.00		
% deaths African	X_{21}	.10	.05	—.03	*—.30*	1.00	
Production per slave	X_{51}	.19	—.19	.19	.13	—.02	1.00

Table A3.5. *Correlation coefficients: slave holding size-groups (Continued)*

301–400 Slaves (82 holdings)

		X_7	X_9	X_{12}	X_{14}	X_{21}	X_{51}
Males per 100 females	X_7	1.00					
Births per 1,000	X_9	—.07	1.00				
Deaths per 1,000	X_{12}	—.15	—.19	1.00			
% births coloured	X_{14}	—.21	.10	.00	1.00		
% deaths African	X_{21}	.05	—.17	—.06	—.24	1.00	
Production per slave	X_{51}	.04	—.23	.09	—.05	.06	1.00

401–500 Slaves (19 holdings)

		X_7	X_9	X_{12}	X_{14}	X_{21}	X_{51}
Males per 100 females	X_7	1.00					
Births per 1,000	X_9	—.26	1.00				
Deaths per 1,000	X_{12}	.08	—.15	1.00			
% births coloured	X_{14}	—.05	—.18	.22	1.00		
% deaths African	X_{21}	.25	—.44	—.45	—.29	1.00	
Production per slave	X_{51}	.12	—.26	.15	—.31	.05	1.00

501–750 Slaves (9 holdings)

		X_7	X_9	X_{12}	X_{14}	X_{21}	X_{51}
Males per100 females	X_7	1.00					
Births per 1,000	X_9	.28	1.00				
Deaths per 1,000	X_{12}	—.02	.70	1.00			
% births coloured	X_{14}	—.06	.01	—.18	1.00		
% deaths African	X_{21}	.06	—.01	.08	—.59	1.00	
Production per slave	X_{51}	.09	.45	.63	—.20	—.01	1.00

Table A3.6. *Parish populations: slaves returned for poll tax, 1800–17*[a]

Parish	1800	1805	1810	1815	1817
Westmoreland	20,864	21,068	21,275	20,540	21,017
Hanover	23,054	22,604	23,348	21,996	22,848
St. James	25,296	24,071	21,121	22,909	23,739
Trelawny	27,827	28,480	27,743	27,248	27,754
St. Elizabeth	18,362	20,335	21,850	22,924	18,232
Manchester[b]	—	—	—	—	14,384
St. Ann	21,055	23,158	23,666	23,675	23,604
Clarendon	20,068	20,552	20,978	19,534	17,950
Vere	10,537	10,272	14,637	15,331	7,929
St. Dorothy	5,017	4,829	5,034	4,885	4,812
St. Thomas-in-the-Vale	11,478	11,831	12,695	11,665	11,835
St. John	6,628	6,889	6,832	6,080	6,053
St. Catherine	8,223	8,150	6,489	7,565	7,891
St. Mary	24,846	25,988	25,410	24,773	25,395
St. Andrew	14,234	16,074	14,199	14,493	14,964
Port Royal	4,640	6,005	7,749	6,818	6,831
St. David	5,184	6,071	7,130	7,588	7,409
St. George	11,672	11,506	13,408	13,203	12,748
Portland	8,375	8,072	7,538	7,882	7,534
St. Thomas-in-the-East	27,583	25,836	26,734	25,517	24,996
Kingston	5,996	6,984	5,847	6,499	8,157
Total	300,939	308,775	313,683	311,125	316,082

Year	Island totals	Year	Island totals	Year	Island totals
1800	300,939	1806	312,341	1812	319,912
1801	307,094	1807	319,351	1813	318,424
1802	307,199	1808	323,827	1814	314,982
1803	308,668	1809	323,714	1815	311,125
1804	308,542	1810	313,683	1816	314,038
1805	308,775	1811	326,830	1817	316,082

[a] The poll tax givings-in were for March 28 in each year.
[b] The parish of Manchester was created from St. Elizabeth, Clarendon and Vere in 1814, but its returns were not separated until 1817.
Sources: J.H.A.V., 1801, p. 247; 1802, p. 182; 1803, p. 217; 1804, p. 212; 1805, p. 205; 1806, p. 257; 1807, p. 210; 1809, p. 98; 1810, p. 238; 1811, p. 125; 1812, p. 152; 1813, p. 140; 1814, p. 169; 1816, p. 204; 1817, p. 39; *Jamaica Almanack*, 1816.

Table A3.7. *Parish populations: slaves and apprentices, 1817–38*[a]

Parish	1817	1820	1823	1826	1829	1832	1834	1838
Westmoreland	22,659	22,366	22,284	22,137	20,820	20,131	20,003	19,971
Hanover	23,779	24,092	22,759	23,801	22,161	20,889	20,505	20,552
St. James	25,641	26,840	25,034	23,247	23,422	22,329	21,843	21,904
Trelawny	28,497	28,774	27,305	26,493	25,964	25,186	25,062	25,042
St. Elizabeth	20,143	20,045	19,565	18,719	19,531	18,211	19,673	19,858
Manchester	15,077	16,595	19,053	19,768	18,302	18,905	18,662	18,774
St. Ann	24,814	25,236	25,363	26,377	24,977	24,789	24,822	25,128
Clarendon	19,397	19,086	18,381	17,729	17,538	16,662	15,996	15,905
Vere	8,056	8,090	7,945	8,232	8,134	8,213	8,275	8,377
St. Dorothy	5,305	5,527	5,571	5,391	5,233	5,240	5,354	5,383
St. Thomas-in-the-Vale	12,241	12,122	11,879	12,952	11,350	10,695	10,352	10,368
St. John	6,133	5,944	6,050	6,042	6,108	5,894	6,164	6,176
St. Catherine	9,679	9,111	8,927	8,567	7,984	8,143	8,474	8,525
St. Mary	26,826	25,587	26,501	25,019	24,168	23,241	22,737	22,736
St. Andrew	15,830	15,213	15,022	14,907	14,736	14,056	13,586	13,785
Port Royal	7,217	7,256	6,749	6,628	6,652	6,392	6,128	6,264
St. David	7,758	8,061	7,939	8,018	7,714	7,640	7,594	7,608
St. George	13,640	13,214	12,801	12,775	12,276	11,899	11,747	11,760
Portland	8,184	8,205	9,224	7,859	7,569	7,234	6,869	6,875
St. Thomas-in-the-East	26,422	26,422	25,785	24,556	23,945	22,406	22,790	22,799
Kingston	17,954	16,615	13,553	11,966	13,837	12,552	12,531	12,578
Total	345,252	342,382	336,253	331,119	322,421	310,707	309,167	310,368

[a] The populations 1817–32 are as at 28 June; 1834 as at 1 August; 1838 as at 9 February. For 1817–32 the populations relate to the registered slave populations. The 1834 figures are those collected by the valuers appointed by the Compensation Commission. For 1838 the population is made up of apprentices, children 'under age', and 'aged'. The 1832 populations given in the table are from the records of the Slave Register Office and differ from those calculated from the R.R.S. (see Chapter 5 for discussion). For 1820 to 1826 the parish populations have been estimated by multiplying the slaves given-in for poll tax by a ratio of R.R.S. to poll tax. For 1817 and 1832 both the R.R.S. and poll tax parish totals are known; for 1817–32 the R.R.S. and poll tax island totals are known. An island-level curve of R.R.S./poll tax ratios was calculated and this curve applied to the variable parish ratios of 1817 and 1832. This methods provides island totals nearer to the R.R.S. than a straight-line interpolation; but it results in a slight over-estimation (2,019 in 1820 and 62 in 1826). The totals in the table are from *P.P.*, 1833, XXVI (539), p. 474, so that the estimated parish totals do not tally. An incomplete list of parish totals for 1820 is found in *J.H.A.V.*, 1820, p. 122.

Sources: 1817: J.H.A.V., 1817, p. 39; *1820, 1823, 1826:* estimated from the poll tax givings-in (*Jamaica Almanacks*); *1829, 1832:* T.71/683, Bundle 9; *1834:* Robert M. Martin, *History of the Colonies of the British Empire* (London, 1834), p. 9; *1838: ibid.*, p. 8.

Table A3.8. *Registered slave births by parish, 1817–32*

Parish	1817–20	1820–3	1823–6	1826–9	1829–32
Westmoreland	1,420	1,335	1,433	1,325	1,410
Hanover	1,592	1,497	1,494	1,304	1,356
St. James	1,891	1,593	1,554	1,532	1,627
Trelawny	2,009	1,968	1,967	1,542	1,773
St. Elizabeth	1,446	1,446	1,442	1,464	1,568
Manchester	1,155	1,259	1,254	1,294	1,439
St. Ann	1,863	1,721	1,867	1,856	1,921
Clarendon	1,406	1,339	1,235	1,188	1,097
Vere	526	529	598	595	623
St. Dorothy	302	315	266	394	360
St. Thomas-in-the-Vale	913	883	808	726	687
St. John	465	414	407	404	384
St. Catherine	626	544	533	581	561
St. Mary	1,843	1,745	1,618	1,601	1,370
St. Andrew	1,174	1,175	1,146	1,026	1,022
Port Royal	611	582	536	497	479
St. David	627	570	572	474	528
St. George	1,044	950	901	805	793
Portland	593	609	563	559	555
St. Thomas-in-the-East	1,763	1,761	1,923	1,751	1,859
Kingston	1,077	1,014	909	810	726
Total	24,346	23,249	23,026	21,728	22,138

Sources: T.71/683, Bundle 9 (1817–29); R.R.S. (1829–32).

Table A3.9. *Registered slave deaths by parish, 1817–32*

Parish	1817–20	1820–3	1823–6	1826–9	1829–32
Westmoreland	1,917	1,878	1,769	1,655	1,734
Hanover	2,018	1,868	1,928	1,736	2,030
St. James	2,133	2,192	2,099	1,912	2,398
Trelawny	2,096	2,421	2,392	2,078	2,290
St. Elizabeth	1,096	1,179	1,152	948	1,173
Manchester	916	1,035	905	902	1,084
St. Ann	1,728	1,771	1,749	1,654	1,606
Clarendon	1,340	1,726	1,361	1,519	1,480
Vere	582	574	542	611	595
St. Dorothy	348	388	321	342	463
St. Thomas-in-the-Vale	837	900	965	846	1,006
St. John	410	512	434	501	548
St. Catherine	557	554	494	426	615
St. Mary	2,318	2,134	2,148	2,353	2,288
St. Andrew	1,004	1,012	966	1,122	1,231
Port Royal	370	482	427	403	438
St. David	558	662	690	624	622
St. George	1,089	1,131	1,006	1,392	1,082
Portland	653	572	637	726	660
St. Thomas-in-the-East	2,209	2,438	2,296	2,629	2,589
Kingston	925	922	889	758	798
Total	25,104	26,351	25,170	25,137	26,730

Sources: T.71/683, Bundle 9; R.R.S. (1829–32).

Table A3.10. *Crude slave death rates by sex and parish, 1817–20, 1826–9 and 1829–32*[a] *(registered deaths per 1,000)*

Parish	1817–20 Males	1817–20 Females	1826–9 Males	1826–9 Females	1829–32 Males	1829–32 Females
Westmoreland	30.6	25.9	28.6	24.5	30.1	25.5
Hanover	30.0	26.6	28.1	24.2	32.5	26.5
St. James	30.8	24.8	29.7	24.9	34.1	30.6
Trelawny	26.3	22.8	30.2	23.4	32.8	26.8
St. Elizabeth	19.1	17.2	17.3	15.1	21.5	17.6
Manchester	22.7	17.5	17.5	15.3	21.5	16.7
St. Ann	24.9	21.5	25.0	19.1	23.5	19.8
Clarendon	23.3	22.7	30.1	27.7	31.1	26.5
Vere	24.8	23.4	28.4	22.0	25.9	22.8
St. Dorothy	23.7	19.9	26.7	17.1	31.6	27.4
St. Thomas-in-the-Vale	23.5	22.1	26.6	23.2	35.0	26.1
St. John	23.8	20.8	29.2	25.6	31.6	29.3
St. Catherine	21.3	17.4	21.0	14.7	27.7	23.1
St. Mary	30.0	27.6	33.9	31.1	36.9	27.8
St. Andrew	22.1	20.2	28.3	22.4	32.3	24.7
Port Royal	19.3	14.6	23.7	16.7	24.7	20.3
St. David	25.0	22.8	29.0	24.8	29.5	24.6
St. George	27.5	25.6	39.0	36.6	33.6	26.1
Portland	26.6	26.6	35.5	28.7	32.2	27.4
St. Thomas-in-the-East	30.1	25.6	39.0	34.2	41.0	32.8
Kingston	20.3	14.7	21.3	15.9	25.5	15.9
Total	25.9	22.6	28.3	23.8	31.4	24.8

[a] The rates for 1817–20 are based on the numbers of each sex living in 1817; those for 1826–9 on 1829; and those for 1829–32 on the 1829–32 means.
Sources: Calculated from *J.H.A.V.*, 1817, p. 39; T.71/683, Bundle 9; R.R.S.

Table A3.11. *Slave age structure in nine parishes, 1817*

	Africans			Creoles			
Age-group	Males	Fe-males	Total	Males	Fe-males	Total	Total
St. James							
0–4	—	—	—	1,191	1,261	2,452	2,452
5–9	—	—	—	1,219	1,220	2,439	2,439
10–14	1	5	6	1,199	1,132	2,331	2,337
15–19	49	15	64	937	955	1,892	1,956
20–24	213	148	361	822	865	1,687	2,048
25–29	471	364	835	631	745	1,376	2,211
30–34	637	574	1,211	472	599	1,071	2,282
35–39	742	719	1,461	438	520	958	2,419
40–44	671	579	1,250	287	373	660	1,910
45–49	490	445	935	190	274	464	1,399
50–54	435	459	894	153	205	358	1,252
55–59	251	291	542	71	119	190	732
60–64	237	274	511	60	83	143	654
65–69	124	147	271	23	40	63	334
70+	171	212	383	27	64	91	474
Unknown	1	—	1	—	—	—	1
Total	4,493	4,232	8,725	7,720	8,455	16,175	24,900
St. Elizabeth							
0–4	—	—	—	1,083	1,132	2,215	2,215
5–9	—	—	—	1,086	1,145	2,231	2,231
10–14	—	2	2	968	884	1,852	1,854
15–19	42	17	59	760	687	1,447	1,506
20–24	235	171	406	538	655	1,193	1,599
25–29	502	403	905	463	544	1,007	1,912
30–34	622	546	1,168	420	418	838	2,006
35–39	635	480	1,115	359	357	716	1,831
40–44	452	372	824	233	295	528	1,352
45–49	301	219	520	165	210	375	895
50–54	248	245	493	182	191	373	866
55–59	134	120	254	97	119	216	470
60–64	160	141	301	86	133	219	520
65–69	68	57	125	48	73	121	246
70+	106	107	213	79	154	233	446
Unknown	—	1	1	9	11	20	21
Total	3,505	2,881	6,386	6,576	7,008	13,584	19,970

Table A3.11. *Slave age structure in nine parishes, 1817 (Continued)*

	Africans			Creoles			
Age-group	Males	Fe-males	Total	Males	Fe-males	Total	Total
Manchester							
0–4	—	—	—	918	894	1,812	1,812
5–9	—	—	—	860	871	1,731	1,731
10–14	3	—	3	633	578	1,211	1,214
15–19	53	29	82	359	406	765	847
20–24	326	263	589	269	316	585	1,174
25–29	814	617	1,431	206	280	486	1,917
30–34	877	637	1,514	161	204	365	1,879
35–39	788	584	1,372	110	118	228	1,600
40–44	582	331	913	70	105	175	1,088
45–49	284	249	533	42	55	97	630
50–54	257	200	457	40	57	97	554
55–59	107	79	186	11	19	30	216
60–64	105	118	223	22	31	53	276
65–69	27	20	47	9	8	17	64
70+	37	45	82	7	21	28	110
Unknown	12	6	18	—	—	—	18
Total	4,272	3,178	7,450	3,717	3,963	7,680	15,130
Clarendon							
0–4	—	—	—	1,059	1,112	2,171	2,171
5–9	—	—	—	960	1,018	1,978	1,978
10–14	—	—	—	874	812	1,686	1,686
15–19	28	18	46	689	612	1,301	1,347
20–24	122	124	246	520	662	1,182	1,428
25–29	367	302	669	558	624	1,182	1,851
30–34	605	563	1,168	377	425	802	1,970
35–39	604	480	1,084	304	413	717	1,801
40–44	544	409	953	262	279	541	1,494
45–49	399	257	656	160	232	392	1,048
50–54	336	270	606	181	254	435	1,041
55–59	135	127	262	85	166	251	513
60–64	131	118	249	96	178	274	523
65–69	46	45	91	28	71	99	190
70+	59	82	141	59	136	195	336
Unknown	—	—	—	—	—	—	—
Total	3,376	2,795	6,171	6,212	6,994	13,206	19,377

Table A3.11. *Slave age structure in nine parishes, 1817 (Continued)*

Age-group	Africans			Creoles			Total
	Males	Fe-males	Total	Males	Fe-males	Total	Total
Vere							
0–4	—	—	—	381	438	819	819
5–9	—	—	—	354	414	768	768
10–14	—	—	—	355	389	744	744
15–19	3	4	7	318	299	617	624
20–24	62	51	113	274	280	554	667
25–29	161	95	256	261	290	551	807
30–34	207	179	386	194	237	431	817
35–39	259	185	444	188	203	391	835
40–44	223	186	409	140	181	321	730
45–49	143	107	250	110	124	234	484
50–54	112	86	198	98	108	206	404
55–59	59	48	107	33	75	108	215
60–64	58	59	117	44	89	133	250
65–69	16	25	41	21	36	57	98
70+	35	54	89	27	61	88	177
Unknown	—	—	—	—	—	—	—
Total	1,338	1,079	2,417	2,798	3,224	6,022	8,439
St. John							
0–4	—	—	—	331	384	715	715
5–9	—	—	—	312	343	655	655
10–14	1	—	1	303	311	614	615
15–19	12	4	16	179	233	412	428
20–24	32	40	72	161	189	350	422
25–29	138	138	276	146	164	310	586
30–34	165	175	340	128	129	257	597
35–39	197	202	399	82	106	188	587
40–44	189	106	295	67	100	167	462
45–49	130	83	213	58	87	145	358
50–54	101	80	181	53	75	128	309
55–59	68	27	95	30	38	68	163
60–64	53	37	90	44	52	96	186
65–69	17	8	25	13	32	45	70
70+	38	32	70	30	42	72	142
Unknown	1	4	5	1	—	1	6
Total	1,142	936	2,078	1,938	2,285	4,223	6,301

Table A3.11. *Slave age structure in nine parishes, 1817 (Continued)*

	Africans			Creoles			
Age-group	Males	Fe-males	Total	Males	Fe-males	Total	Total
Port Royal							
0–4	—	—	—	436	452	888	888
5–9	—	—	—	372	399	771	771
10–14	—	—	—	358	323	681	681
15–19	33	21	54	161	172	333	387
20–24	172	117	289	127	139	266	555
25–29	440	307	747	100	123	223	970
30–34	439	406	845	74	84	158	1,003
35–39	390	260	650	41	48	89	739
40–44	266	154	420	27	35	62	482
45–49	109	83	192	22	33	55	247
50–54	94	72	166	16	23	39	205
55–59	34	27	61	7	12	19	80
60–64	51	46	97	9	11	20	117
65–69	17	24	41	1	4	5	46
70+	25	24	49	1	8	9	58
Unknown	—	—	—	—	—	—	—
Total	2,070	1,541	3,611	1,752	1,866	3,618	7,229
Portland							
0–4	—	—	—	418	489	907	907
5–9	—	—	—	433	414	847	847
10–14	—	—	—	397	376	773	773
15–19	7	3	10	292	299	591	601
20–24	56	52	108	202	225	427	535
25–29	155	154	309	193	249	442	751
30–34	289	284	573	173	173	346	919
35–39	318	248	566	145	152	297	863
40–44	262	202	464	100	110	210	674
45–49	158	97	255	68	86	154	409
50–54	115	85	200	43	60	103	303
55–59	77	70	147	32	32	64	211
60–64	55	58	113	24	30	54	167
65–69	31	34	65	5	29	34	99
70+	27	27	54	14	32	46	100
Unknown	3	2	5	—	1	1	6
Total	1,553	1,316	2,869	2,539	2,757	5,296	8,165

Table A3.11. *Slave age structure in nine parishes, 1817 (Continued)*

Age-group	Africans Males	Africans Females	Africans Total	Creoles Males	Creoles Females	Creoles Total	Total
Kingston							
0–4	—	—	—	775	809	1,584	1,584
5–9	—	—	—	828	938	1,766	1,766
10–14	6	6	12	781	855	1,636	1,648
15–19	40	46	86	484	617	1,101	1,187
20–24	237	280	517	392	487	879	1,396
25–29	589	579	1,168	335	460	795	1,963
30–34	787	771	1,558	201	391	592	2,150
35–39	571	614	1,185	130	244	374	1,559
40–44	456	480	934	84	230	314	1,248
45–49	243	292	535	55	131	186	721
50–54	174	263	437	41	91	132	569
55–59	64	108	172	17	42	59	231
60–64	57	114	171	12	47	59	230
65–69	20	26	46	6	16	22	68
70+	34	72	106	5	35	40	146
Unknown	4	2	6	5	2	7	13
Total	3,282	3,651	6,933	4,151	5,395	9,546	16,479

Sources: see p. 247

Table A3.12. *Slave age-specific sex ratios in nine parishes, 1817*

	Males per 100 females								
Age-group	St. James	St. Elizabeth	Manchester	Clarendon	Vere	St. John	Port Royal	Portland	Kingston
0–4	94.4	95.7	102.7	95.2	87.0	86.2	96.5	85.5	95.8
5–9	99.9	94.8	98.7	94.3	85.5	91.0	93.2	104.6	88.3
10–14	105.5	109.3	110.0	107.6	91.3	97.7	110.8	105.6	91.4
15–19	101.6	113.9	94.7	113.8	105.9	80.6	100.5	99.0	79.0
20–24	102.2	93.1	102.8	81.7	101.5	84.3	116.8	93.9	82.0
25–29	99.4	101.9	113.7	99.9	109.6	94.0	125.6	86.4	88.9
30–34	94.5	108.1	123.4	99.4	96.4	96.4	104.7	101.1	85.0
35–39	95.2	118.8	127.9	101.7	115.2	90.6	139.9	115.8	81.7
40–44	100.6	102.7	149.5	117.2	98.9	124.3	155.0	116.0	76.1
45–49	94.6	108.6	107.2	114.3	109.5	110.6	112.9	123.5	70.4
50–54	88.6	98.6	115.6	98.7	108.2	99.4	115.8	109.0	60.7
55–59	78.5	96.7	120.4	75.1	74.8	150.8	105.1	106.9	54.0
60–64	83.2	89.8	85.2	76.7	68.9	109.0	105.3	89.8	42.9
65–69	78.6	89.2	128.6	63.8	60.7	75.0	64.3	57.1	61.9
70+	71.7	70.9	66.7	54.1	53.9	91.9	81.3	69.5	36.4
Total[a]	96.3	101.9	111.9	97.9	96.1	95.6	112.2	100.5	82.2

[a] The sex ratios in the total are derived from the age structure data, and differ slightly from those given in Table 10, above. *Sources:* see p. 247.

Table A3.13. *Slave age-specific death rates, 1817–20 (per 1,000 per annum)*

	Africans			Creoles		
Age-group	Males	Females	Total	Males	Females	Total
St. James						
0–4	—	—	—	53.9	42.6	48.3
5–9	—	—	—	12.9	15.6	14.3
10–14	—	—	—	10.0	8.6	9.3
15–19	13.6	22.4	15.7	10.4	9.1	9.7
20–24	15.7	11.4	13.9	13.0	10.0	11.5
25–29	12.7	20.3	16.0	15.4	16.1	15.8
30–34	19.4	19.9	19.6	20.6	17.3	18.7
35–39	31.5	29.0	30.3	22.9	22.5	22.7
40–44	38.8	31.4	35.4	38.5	17.0	26.3
45–49	46.9	40.0	43.7	51.1	19.5	32.4
50–54	59.0	40.3	49.5	48.1	32.6	39.2
55–59	67.7	42.7	54.4	66.0	33.7	45.7
60–64	73.1	72.4	72.8	55.8	36.2	44.4
65–69	67.2	66.3	66.7	72.7	75.2	74.3
70+	152.1	90.4	118.1	136.3	78.3	95.5
Total	42.1	37.2	39.7	23.7	19.8	21.6
Manchester						
0–4	—	—	—	24.3	22.5	23.4
5–9	—	—	—	10.4	11.3	10.9
10–14	—	—	—	9.7	9.5	9.6
15–19	13.4	—	8.6	16.0	9.9	12.8
20–24	9.8	17.0	13.1	13.4	8.1	10.5
25–29	17.4	12.8	15.5	17.4	11.7	14.2
30–34	19.0	18.3	18.8	20.1	7.2	12.9
35–39	18.5	19.4	19.0	9.8	9.3	9.5
40–44	37.8	20.7	31.6	25.7	13.9	18.6
45–49	25.0	19.3	22.5	42.8	13.3	26.1
50–54	48.3	36.0	43.1	80.8	32.0	52.2
55–59	33.1	39.1	36.0	65.3	19.2	36.2
60–64	77.7	55.2	66.3	32.7	11.8	20.5
65–69	52.5	85.8	67.4	39.9	91.3	63.9
70+	105.4	83.8	94.4	51.3	87.0	77.6
Total	25.4	22.2	24.0	17.2	14.1	15.6
Clarendon						
0–4	—	—	—	37.1	28.5	33.5
5–9	—	—	—	13.5	15.7	15.0
10–14	—	—	—	11.1	8.6	10.1
15–19	0.0	0.0	0.0	9.2	9.8	9.7
20–24	5.5	18.8	13.0	16.0	10.1	13.0
25–29	16.3	22.1	20.1	10.2	12.8	11.8
30–34	18.2	15.4	17.9	16.8	25.9	22.1
35–39	12.7	16.7	15.3	18.6	21.0	20.5
40–44	24.5	18.7	23.4	33.1	21.5	27.7
45–49	27.6	33.7	31.8	39.6	30.2	34.8
50–54	45.6	43.2	47.3	38.7	31.5	35.3
55–59	39.5	49.9	47.3	35.3	36.1	35.9
60–64	56.0	62.1	62.6	41.7	48.7	47.3
65–69	79.7	37.0	62.2	107.1	65.7	79.2
70+	129.9	122.0	133.1	113.0	85.8	96.2
Total	28.3	29.9	29.1	21.8	21.6	21.7

Table A3.13. *Slave age-specific death rates, 1817–20* (*Continued*)

	Africans			Creoles		
Age-group	Males	Females	Total	Males	Females	Total
Vere						
0–4	—	—	—	42.0	36.5	39.1
5–9	—	—	—	16.0	16.1	16.1
10–14	—	—	—	4.7	6.9	5.8
15–19	0.0	0.0	0.0	10.5	4.5	7.6
20–24	10.8	26.1	17.7	8.5	4.8	6.6
25–29	10.4	21.1	14.3	8.9	11.5	10.3
30–34	19.3	22.3	20.7	3.4	14.1	9.3
35–39	27.0	16.2	22.5	24.8	32.8	29.0
40–44	25.4	19.7	22.8	31.0	18.4	23.9
45–49	16.3	40.5	26.7	42.4	13.4	27.1
50–54	65.5	46.5	57.2	23.8	18.5	21.0
55–59	45.2	34.7	40.5	80.8	31.1	46.3
60–64	109.2	45.2	76.9	68.2	26.2	40.1
65–69	83.3	93.3	89.4	15.9	46.3	35.1
70+	95.2	98.8	97.4	86.4	98.4	94.7
Total	31.6	31.8	31.7	20.1	18.8	19.4
St. John						
0–4	—	—	—	36.3	33.9	35.0
5–9	—	—	—	18.2	9.7	13.7
10–14	0.0	—	0.0	11.0	8.6	9.8
15–19	0.0	0.0	0.0	13.0	5.7	8.9
20–24	20.8	8.3	13.9	10.4	17.6	14.3
25–29	9.7	4.8	7.2	11.4	22.4	17.2
30–34	20.3	21.0	20.6	15.6	15.5	15.6
35–39	13.5	13.2	13.4	32.5	25.2	28.4
40–44	19.4	12.6	16.9	19.9	30.0	25.9
45–49	23.1	20.1	21.9	23.0	11.5	16.1
50–54	36.3	41.7	38.7	18.9	22.2	20.8
55–59	14.7	12.3	14.0	11.1	0.0	4.9
60–64	56.6	27.0	44.4	22.7	38.5	31.3
65–69	98.3	41.7	80.0	51.3	20.8	29.6
70+	78.9	62.5	71.4	88.9	71.4	78.7
Total	26.6	20.3	23.7	21.7	19.7	20.6
Port Royal						
0–4	—	—	—	39.0	19.9	29.3
5–9	—	—	—	7.2	9.2	8.2
10–14	—	—	—	3.7	9.3	6.4
15–19	0.0	0.0	0.0	14.5	5.8	10.0
20–24	5.8	8.5	6.9	5.2	7.2	6.3
25–29	9.1	9.8	9.4	0.0	13.6	7.5
30–34	12.1	14.8	13.4	13.5	7.9	10.5
35–39	14.5	12.8	13.8	24.4	0.0	11.2
40–44	27.6	13.0	22.2	24.7	0.0	10.8
45–49	15.3	24.1	19.1	0.0	0.0	0.0
50–54	42.6	23.1	34.1	0.0	0.0	0.0
55–59	29.4	24.7	27.3	0.0	27.8	17.5
60–64	39.2	7.2	24.1	74.1	60.6	66.7
65–69	39.2	13.9	24.4	0.0	0.0	0.0
70+	106.7	97.2	102.0	0.0	0.0	0.0
Total	22.7	18.4	20.9	18.3	12.0	15.0

Table A3.13. *Slave age-specific death rates, 1817–20 (Continued)*

Age-group	Africans Males	Africans Females	Africans Total	Creoles Males	Creoles Females	Creoles Total
Portland						
0–4	—	—	—	31.9	38.2	35.6
5–9	—	—	—	18.5	27.4	23.0
10–14	—	—	—	10.1	9.8	10.0
15–19	0.0	0.0	0.0	11.4	13.4	12.5
20–24	11.9	6.4	9.3	14.8	16.3	15.7
25–29	12.9	19.3	14.0	12.1	22.8	18.3
30–34	25.4	14.1	19.9	13.5	11.6	12.6
35–39	24.1	33.6	28.4	23.0	4.4	13.6
40–44	36.9	19.8	29.6	43.3	6.1	23.2
45–49	44.3	61.8	51.2	24.5	27.1	26.2
50–54	49.3	54.9	51.9	62.0	22.7	39.1
55–59	64.9	33.3	50.0	20.8	31.3	26.2
60–64	60.6	86.2	73.9	41.7	122.2	87.1
65–69	107.5	68.6	87.5	133.5	103.4	108.7
70+	148.1	135.8	142.4	47.6	104.2	87.7
Total	35.8	33.2	34.6	20.2	23.9	22.2
Kingston						
0–4	—	—	—	25.1	22.3	23.7
5–9	—	—	—	8.4	9.4	8.9
10–14	0.0	0.0	—	10.3	5.6	7.8
15–19	8.7	0.0	4.1	9.8	13.7	12.0
20–24	17.6	8.8	12.9	10.3	11.3	10.9
25–29	10.6	13.4	11.9	13.1	12.0	12.5
30–34	19.8	13.2	16.5	18.2	15.1	16.1
35–39	26.7	10.9	18.5	25.4	13.6	17.6
40–44	26.6	18.3	22.4	39.3	11.2	18.7
45–49	51.4	19.3	33.9	20.0	36.5	31.6
50–54	41.9	25.4	31.9	62.6	32.3	41.8
55–59	21.7	26.0	24.4	43.1	43.8	43.5
60–64	54.8	43.2	46.9	61.1	31.3	37.4
65–69	34.7	67.6	53.1	0.0	69.0	50.1
70+	71.4	43.9	52.7	0.0	42.0	36.7
Total	24.8	16.7	20.5	15.3	14.3	14.8

Sources: see p. 247.

Table A3.14. *Demographic characteristics by slave-holding size-groups in six parishes, 1817–20*

(a) St. James

Slaves per holding	Number of slaves, 1817: Africans Males	Africans Females	Africans Total	Creoles Males	Creoles Females	Creoles Total	Total Males	Total Females	Total Total
1–50	1,382	1,404	2,786	1,827	1,955	3,782	3,209	3,359	6,568
51–100	431	368	799	508	556	1,064	939	924	1,863
101–200	938	885	1,823	1,965	2,127	4,092	2,903	3,012	5,915
201–300	897	780	1,677	1,862	1,947	3,809	2,759	2,727	5,486
301–400	391	423	814	858	978	1,836	1,249	1,401	2,650
401–500	266	202	468	394	513	907	660	715	1,375
501–600	188	170	358	306	379	685	494	549	1,043
Total	4,493	4,232	8,725	7,720	8,455	16,175	12,213	12,687	24,900

Slaves per holding	% total population (1817)	% African (1817)	% Creole (1817)	% Slaves African (1817)	% deaths African (1817–20)	Males per 100 females, 1817: Africans	Creoles	Total
1–50	26.4	31.9	23.4	42.4	56.4	98.4	93.5	95.5
51–100	7.5	9.2	6.6	42.9	64.4	117.1	91.4	101.6
101–200	23.8	20.9	25.3	30.8	47.0	106.0	92.4	96.4
201–300	22.0	19.2	23.5	30.6	47.0	115.0	95.6	101.2
301–400	10.6	9.3	11.4	30.7	44.3	92.4	87.7	89.2
401–500	5.5	5.4	5.6	34.0	47.2	131.7	76.8	92.3
501–600	4.2	4.1	4.2	34.3	43.8	110.6	80.7	90.0
Total	100.0	100.0	100.0	35.0	49.8	106.2	91.3	96.3

Slaves per holding	Deaths per 1,000, 1817–20: Africans Males	Africans Females	Africans Total	Creoles Males	Creoles Females	Creoles Total	TOTAL	Births per 1,000 (1817–20)
1–50	31.4	31.1	31.2	19.3	16.4	17.8	23.5	22.5
51–100	34.0	38.9	36.3	15.7	14.4	15.0	24.2	20.6
101–200	55.4	47.1	51.4	26.5	25.2	25.8	33.7	21.1
201–300	46.1	36.3	41.5	23.3	18.1	20.7	27.0	23.0
301–400	52.0	29.2	40.1	25.3	19.8	22.3	28.1	27.7
401–500	41.4	41.3	41.3	26.2	22.1	23.9	29.8	27.9
501–600	35.5	51.0	42.8	39.2	20.2	28.7	33.6	22.1
Total	42.1	37.2	39.7	23.7	19.8	21.6	28.0	23.0

Sources: see p. 247.

Table A3.14. *Demographic characteristics by slave-holding size-groups in six parishes, 1817–20 (Continued)*

(b) St. Elizabeth

Slaves per holding	Number of slaves, 1817: Africans: Males	Africans: Females	Africans: Total	Creoles: Males	Creoles: Females	Creoles: Total	Total: Males	Total: Females	Total: Total
1–50	1,461	1,285	2,746	2,299	2,435	4,734	3,760	3,720	7,480
51–100	566	401	967	839	846	1,685	1,405	1,247	2,652
101–200	566	468	1,034	1,115	1,239	2,354	1,681	1,707	3,388
201–300	508	393	901	930	1,053	1,983	1,438	1,446	2,884
301–400	404	334	738	1,393	1,435	2,828	1,797	1,769	3,566
Total	3,505	2,881	6,386	6,576	7,008	13,584	10,081	9,889	19,970

Slaves per holding	% total population (1817)	% African (1817)	% Creole (1817)	% Slaves African (1817)	% deaths African (1817–20)	Males per 100 females, 1817: Africans	Creoles	Total
1–50	37.5	43.0	34.8	36.7	a	113.7	94.4	101.1
51–100	13.3	15.1	12.4	36.5	a	141.1	99.2	112.7
101–200	17.0	16.2	17.3	30.5	a	120.9	90.0	98.5
201–300	14.4	14.1	14.6	31.2	a	129.3	88.3	99.4
301–400	17.8	11.6	20.8	20.7	a	121.0	97.1	101.6
Total	100.0	100.0	100.0	32.0	a	121.7	93.8	101.9

[a] Data deficient.

Sources: see p. 247.

Table A3.14. *Demographic characteristics by slave-holding size-groups in six parishes, 1817–20 (Continued)*

(c) Manchester

Slaves per holding	Number of slaves, 1817: Africans: Males	Africans: Females	Africans: Total	Creoles: Males	Creoles: Females	Creoles: Total	Total: Males	Total: Females	Total: Total
1–50	1,217	812	2,029	1,035	1,069	2,104	2,252	1,881	4,133
51–100	1,099	778	1,877	850	914	1,764	1,949	1,692	3,641
101–200	951	758	1,709	963	1,021	1,984	1,914	1,779	3,693
201–300	300	247	547	275	313	588	575	560	1,135
301–400	602	499	1,101	486	517	1,003	1,088	1,016	2,104
401–500	103	84	187	108	129	237	211	213	424
Total	4,272	3,178	7,450	3,717	3,963	7,680	7,989	7,141	15,130

Slaves per holding	% total population (1817)	% African (1817)	% Creole (1817)	% Slaves African (1817)	% deaths African (1817–20)	Males per 100 females, 1817: Africans	Creoles	Total
1–50	27.3	27.2	27.4	49.1	55.7	149.9	96.8	119.7
51–100	24.1	25.2	23.0	51.6	57.7	141.3	93.0	115.2
101–200	24.4	22.9	25.8	46.3	62.1	125.5	94.3	107.6
201–300	7.5	7.3	7.7	48.2	48.7	121.5	87.9	102.7
301–400	13.9	14.8	13.1	52.3	66.4	120.6	94.0	107.1
401–500	2.8	2.5	3.1	44.1	50.0	122.6	83.7	99.1
Total	100.0	100.0	100.0	49.2	59.9	134.4	93.8	111.9

Slaves per holding	Deaths per 1,000, 1817–20: Africans: Males	Africans: Females	Africans: Total	Creoles: Males	Creoles: Females	Creoles: Total	TOTAL
1–50	26.3	26.7	26.4	16.1	15.9	16.0	21.1
51–100	22.7	14.6	19.0	16.9	13.9	15.3	17.4
101–200	30.8	23.3	27.5	17.3	11.8	14.4	20.5
201–300	22.2	24.3	23.2	29.1	17.0	22.7	22.9
301–400	21.0	24.7	22.7	12.3	12.9	12.6	17.9
401–500	25.9	19.8	23.2	21.6	15.5	18.3	20.4
Total	25.4	22.2	24.0	17.2	14.0	15.6	19.7

Sources: see p. 247.

Table A3.14. *Demographic characteristics by slave-holding size-groups in six parishes, 1817–20 (Continued)*

(d) Portland

Slaves per holding	Africans Males	Africans Females	Africans Total	Creoles Males	Creoles Females	Creoles Total	Total Males	Total Females	Total Total
	Number of slaves, 1817								
1–50	481	395	876	760	796	1,556	1,241	1,191	2,432
51–100	174	158	332	270	290	560	444	448	892
101–200	410	345	755	581	693	1,274	991	1,038	2,029
201–300	212	203	415	557	609	1,166	769	812	1,581
301–400	51	57	108	100	121	221	151	178	329
401–500	225	158	383	271	248	519	496	406	902
Total	1.553	1,316	2,869	2,539	2,757	5,296	4,092	4,073	8,165

Slaves per holding	% total population (1817)	% African (1817)	% Creole (1817)	% Slaves African (1817)	% deaths African (1817–20)	Males per 100 females, 1817: Africans	Creoles	Total
1–50	29.8	30.5	29.4	36.0	38.2	121.8	95.5	104.2
51–100	10.9	11.6	10.6	37.2	50.0	110.1	93.1	99.1
101–200	24.8	26.3	24.1	37.2	50.2	118.8	83.8	95.5
201–300	19.4	14.5	22.0	26.2	30.6	104.4	91.5	94.7
301–400	4.0	3.8	4.2	32.8	38.9	89.5	82.6	84.8
401–500	11.1	13.3	10.0	42.5	56.3	142.4	109.2	122.2
Total	100.0	100.0	100.0	35.1	45.8	118.0	92.1	100.5

Slaves per holding	Africans Males	Africans Females	Africans Total	Creoles Males	Creoles Females	Creoles Total	TOTAL
	Deaths per 1,000, 1817–20						
1–50	28.4	20.3	24.7	12.3	19.7	16.1	19.2
51–100	23.0	27.4	25.1	16.1	13.8	14.9	18.7
101–200	55.3	74.1	49.0	27.0	30.3	28.8	36.3
201–300	28.3	37.8	32.9	23.3	29.6	26.6	28.3
301–400	19.6	23.4	21.6	20.0	13.8	16.6	18.2
401–500	37.0	50.6	42.6	25.8	22.8	24.4	32.2
Total	35.8	33.2	34.6	20.2	23.9	22.2	26.6

Sources: see p. 247.

Table A3.14. *Demographic characteristics by slave-holding size-groups in six parishes, 1817–20 (Continued)*

(e) St. John

Slaves per holding	Number of slaves, 1817: Africans: Males	Africans: Females	Africans: Total	Creoles: Males	Creoles: Females	Creoles: Total	Total: Males	Total: Females	Total: Total
1–50	379	289	668	487	508	995	866	797	1,663
51–100	223	191	414	265	316	581	488	507	995
101–200	234	188	422	345	467	812	579	655	1,234
201–300	108	91	199	354	399	753	462	490	952
301–400	67	62	129	86	106	192	153	168	321
401–500	—	—	—	—	—	—	—	—	—
501–600	82	87	169	158	199	357	240	286	526
601–700	48	28	76	243	290	533	291	318	609
Total	1,141	936	2,077	1,938	2,285	4,223	3,079	3,221	6,300

Slaves per holding	% total population (1817)	% African (1817)	% Creole (1817)	% Slaves African (1817)	% deaths African (1817–20)	Males per 100 females, 1817: Africans	Creoles	Total
1–50	26.4	32.2	23.6	40.2	44.3	131.1	95.9	108.7
51–100	15.8	19.9	13.8	41.6	45.1	116.8	83.9	96.3
101–200	19.6	20.3	19.2	34.2	33.7	124.5	73.9	88.4
201–300	15.1	9.6	17.8	20.9	32.8	118.7	88.7	94.3
301–400	5.1	6.2	4.5	40.2	44.8	108.1	81.1	91.1
401–500	—	—	—	—	—	—	—	—
501–600	8.3	8.1	8.5	32.1	27.8	94.3	79.4	83.9
601–700	9.7	3.7	12.6	12.5	15.4	171.4	83.8	91.5
Total	100.0	100.0	100.0	33.0	36.2	121.9	84.8	95.6

Slaves per holding	Deaths per 1,000, 1817–20: Africans: Males	Africans: Females	Africans: Total	Creoles: Males	Creoles: Females	Creoles: Total	TOTAL
1–50	16.7	18.5	17.5	14.4	15.1	14.7	15.8
51–100	23.9	12.2	18.5	17.6	14.8	16.1	17.1
101–200	34.2	19.5	27.6	29.0	27.8	28.3	28.1
201–300	34.0	36.6	35.2	17.9	20.1	19.0	22.4
301–400	34.8	32.3	33.6	31.0	25.2	27.8	30.1
401–500	—	—	—	—	—	—	—
501–600	36.5	23.0	30.0	35.9	36.9	36.4	34.2
601–700	34.7	11.9	26.3	23.3	18.4	20.6	21.3
Total	26.6	20.3	23.8	21.7	19.7	20.6	21.6

Sources: see p. 247.

Table A3.14. *Demographic characteristics by slave-holding size-groups in six parishes, 1817–20 (Continued)*

(f) Kingston

Slaves per holding	Number of slaves, 1817: Africans: Males	Africans: Females	Africans: Total	Creoles: Males	Creoles: Females	Creoles: Total	Total: Males	Total: Females	Total: Total
1–50	2,889	3.581	6,470	4,052	5,308	9,360	6,941	8,889	15,830
51–100	393	70	463	99	87	186	492	157	649
Total	3,282	3,651	6,933	4,151	5,395	9,546	7,433	9,046	16,479

Slaves per holding	% total population (1817)	% African (1817)	% Creole (1817)	% Slaves African (1817)	% deaths African (1817–20)	Males per 100 females, 1817: Africans	Creoles	Total
1–50	96.1	93.3	98.1	40.9	48.9	80.7	76.3	78.1
51–100	3.9	6.7	1.9	71.3	77.5	561.4	113.8	313.4
Total	100.0	100.0	100.0	42.1	50.2	89.9	76.9	82.2

Slaves per holding	Deaths per 1,000, 1817–20: Africans: Males	Africans: Females	Africans: Total	Creoles: Males	Creoles: Females	Creoles: Total	TOTAL
1–50	25.0	16.7	20.4	15.5	14.1	14.7	17.1
51–100	22.9	19.0	22.3	6.7	26.8	16.1	20.5
Total	24.8	16.7	20.5	15.3	14.3	14.8	17.2

Sources: see p. 247.

Table A3.15. *Size of slave-holdings, 1832*

Slaves per holding	Westmoreland	Hanover	St. James	Trelawny	St. Elizabeth	Manchester	St. Ann	Clarendon	Vere	St. Dorothy	St. Thomas-in-the-Vale	St. John	St. Catherine
	Number of slave-holdings (Returns)												
1–5	339	495	384	300	561	162	334	218	81	69	163	124	37
6–10	107	87	113	103	141	62	120	72	19	22	43	44	12
11–20	93	62	199	88	101	61	105	40	13	14	53	30	5
21–30	34	25	25	24	51	24	60	22	3	7	12	12	1
31–40	17	11	14	11	20	26	36	17	3	5	5	5	[illegible]
41–50	12	3	15	7	20	14	25	16	2	2	10	1	[illegible]
51–100	38	22	40	37	30	54	79	33	5	7	24	15	1
101–150	19	19	18	15	15	32	37	20	4	4	14	2	1
151–200	12	18	23	20	14	8	12	12	7	3	13	4	
201–250	7	18	12	17	7	9	10	13	9	2	6	2	
251–300	8	11	6	20	5	3	5	3	4	2	1	1	
301–350	9	6	5	5	6	2	1	3	1	2	0	2	
351–400	2	1	3	1	2	1	1	2	1	0	1	1	
401–450	0	2	0	1	1	1	1	1	1	1	0	0	
451–500	1	0	1	0	1	2	1	0	0	0	0	1	
501–550	0	0	0	0	0	0	0	1	1	0	0	0	
551–600	0	0	0	1	0	0	0	0	1	0	1	0	
601–650	0	0	0	0	0	0	0	0	0	0	0	0	
651–700	0	0	0	1	0	0	0	0	0	0	0	0	
701–750	0	0	0	0	0	0	0	0	0	1	0	0	
Total	698	780	858	651	975	461	827	473	155	141	346	244	62
Mean	29	27	26	39	20	40	29	36	53	37	31	24	1

[a] The number of slaves in each group is estimated by multiplying the number of holdings b the median size (assumed to be 2, 7, 14, 24, 34, 44, 75, 125 . . . 725). The total obtained i 2,059 short of the actual total.

Source: R.R.S.

Table A3.15. *Size of slave-holdings, 1832 (Continued)*

	Number of slave-holdings (Returns)										
Slaves per holding	St. Mary	St. Andrew	Port Royal	St. David	St. George	Portland	St. Thomas-in-the-East	Kingston	Total	Estimated number of slaves[a]	Percentage of slaves
1–5	217	243	122	63	193	120	248	1,843	6,649	13,298	4.3
6–10	76	105	34	15	73	47	84	460	1,954	13,678	4.4
11–20	50	90	23	18	38	27	44	189	1,394	19,516	6.3
21–30	24	28	10	4	19	15	27	41	486	11,664	3.8
31–40	16	15	6	7	14	6	15	14	271	9,214	3.0
41–50	10	10	3	3	9	3	11	5	188	8,272	2.7
51–100	30	38	13	19	27	9	41	3	580	43,500	14.0
101–150	17	16	10	7	4	7	19	2	291	36,375	11.7
151–200	23	13	5	11	11	10	22	0	247	43,225	13.9
201–250	21	6	2	5	3	4	19	0	175	39,375	12.7
251–300	9	1	5	1	6	1	5	0	99	27,225	8.8
301–350	12	1	0	0	3	1	5	0	64	20,800	6.7
351–400	1	2	0	0	0	1	1	0	21	7,875	2.5
401–450	0	0	0	1	1	1	0	0	12	5,100	1.6
451–500	0	0	0	0	2	0	3	0	12	5,700	1.8
501–550	0	0	0	0	0	0	0	0	2	1,050	0.3
551–600	0	0	0	1	0	0	0	0	4	2,300	0.7
601–650	0	0	0	0	0	0	2	0	2	1,250	0.4
651–700	0	0	0	0	0	0	0	0	1	675	0.2
701–750	0	0	0	0	0	0	0	0	1	725	0.2
Total	506	568	233	155	403	252	546	2,557	12,453	310,817	100.0
Mean	46	25	28	49	30	29	43	5	25		

Table A3.16. *Occupational distribution of the slave population, as classified by the assistant commissioners for compensation, 1834 (percentage of parish population in each category)*

		Predial attached						Predial unattache		
Parish	TOTAL SLAVES	Head people (1)	Tradesmen (2)	Inferior tradesmen (3)	Field labourers (4)	Inferior field labourers (5)	Total	Head people (1)	Tradesmen (2)	Inferior (
Westmoreland	20,003	3.05	1.06	2.90	30.70	14.35	52.06	0.62	0.31	0.
Hanover	20,505	4.09	3.84	1.15	31.12	24.30	64.50	1.19	0.79	0.
St. James	21,761	3.61	3.80	0.87	25.94	19.87	54.09	0.97	1.24	0.
Trelawny	25,062	5.32	4.03	0.47	35.54	20.10	65.46	0.97	0.59	0.
St. Elizabeth	19,673	6.01	4.77	0.55	38.27	19.77	69.37	0.07	0.08	0.
Manchester	18,671	5.68	6.19	0.37	45.79	21.65	79.68	0.05	0.03	0.
St. Ann	25,082	5.25	4.53	0.51	46.26	17.49	74.04	0.00	0.04	0.
Clarendon	15,896	6.65	4.27	0.78	37.62	25.64	74.96	0.16	0.06	0.
Vere	8,275	6.66	5.33	0.44	42.86	21.05	76.34	0.29	0.35	0.
St. Dorothy	5,354	6.20	3.49	0.15	33.00	15.37	58.21	1.48	0.67	0.
St. Thomas-in-the-Vale	10,358	4.85	3.02	0.84	36.79	28.64	74.12	0.01	0.05	0.
St. John	6,164	4.61	2.76	0.13	33.42	14.11	55.03	2.27	1.31	0.
St. Catherine	8,488	3.32	1.63	0.72	21.81	16.72	44.20	0.32	0.11	0.
St. Mary	22,737	3.98	3.92	0.83	32.09	25.58	66.40	0.22	0.34	0.
St. Andrew	13,554	5.41	3.19	0.65	37.86	19.60	66.71	0.49	0.38	0.
Port Royal	6,128	3.48	2.59	1.00	40.62	21.08	68.77	0.08	0.00	0.
St. David	7,594	4.31	3.67	0.91	42.97	21.33	73.19	0.20	0.24	0.
St. George	11,750	2.71	2.66	1.98	37.01	27.11	71.47	0.05	0.07	0.
Portland	6,869	3.25	2.71	1.43	30.22	24.34	61.95	0.33	0.44	0.
St. Thomas-in-the-East	22,790	5.09	4.42	0.72	36.28	25.59	72.10	0.06	0.18	0.
Kingston	12,371	0.05	0.02	0.01	1.05	0.19	1.32	0.00	0.42	0.
Jamaica	311,070	4.51	3.61	0.85	34.41	20.55	63.94	0.43	0.36	0.

Source: T.71/851 (for parish totals; valuers' returns, 1 August 1834); R.M. Martin, *History* … *the Colonies of the British Empire* (London, 1834, p. 8 (for island totals).

Table A3.16. *Occupational distribution of the slave population, as classified by the assistant commissioners for compensation, 1834 (percentage of parish population in each category) (Continued)*

Predial unattached			Non predial									
Field labourers (4)	Inferior field labourers (5)	Total	Head tradesmen (1)	Inferior tradesmen (2)	Head people attached to wharves, shipping etc. (3)	Inferior people attached to wharves, shipping etc. (4)	Head domestic servants (5)	Inferior domestic servants (6)	Total	Children aged less than six years	Aged, diseased, non-effective	Runaways
11.06	3.75	16.63	0.05	0.11	0.07	0.34	1.10	8.03	9.70	12.11	8.87	0.60
7.85	3.72	13.68	0.44	0.07	0.61	0.13	2.07	1.28	4.60	11.85	5.38	
8.31	3.74	14.41	1.23	0.16	0.80	0.01	7.90	4.04	14.14	12.20	5.19	0.38
6.82	3.04	11.47	0.70	0.13	0.48	0.08	3.24	2.05	6.68	11.77	4.64	
0.75	0.40	1.31	0.00	0.00	0.10	0.00	6.82	3.48	10.40	13.97	4.96	
0.46	0.15	0.69	0.07	0.15	0.05	0.30	0.56	0.22	1.35	14.19	4.08	
0.09	0.01	0.14	0.01	0.00	0.15	0.00	5.80	2.82	8.78	14.35	2.70	
0.86	0.69	1.78	0.00	0.00	0.04	0.05	2.79	3.60	6.48	11.78	5.03	
2.02	0.81	3.47	0.19	0.07	0.07	0.07	0.46	1.43	2.29	12.94	4.95	
10.78	4.87	17.80	0.06	0.02	0.69	0.54	0.99	4.22	6.52	13.13	4.33	
0.41	0.15	0.62	0.14	0.03	0.28	0.29	3.47	3.69	7.90	11.79	4.89	0.67
17.50	6.28	27.52	0.11	0.00	0.00	0.00	0.75	0.97	1.83	11.94	3.67	
2.18	1.50	4.11	1.27	1.51	1.19	1.02	6.01	21.67	32.67	13.42	4.81	0.81
2.81	1.97	5.38	0.07	0.01	0.23	0.03	3.97	2.54	6.85	11.15	9.54	0.69
2.91	0.77	4.55	0.30	0.03	0.44	0.00	10.28	2.16	13.21	12.84	2.69	0.28
0.77	0.38	1.25	0.62	0.07	2.15	0.33	6.28	3.70	13.15	12.91	3.33	0.60
1.67	0.71	2.89	0.00	0.00	0.01	0.00	4.03	1.83	5.87	12.47	4.94	0.65
0.80	0.30	1.31	0.02	0.20	0.14	0.17	0.70	6.90	8.13	11.65	6.69	0.59
3.95	2.13	7.17	0.32	0.29	0.49	0.29	2.42	7.21	11.03	12.13	7.13	0.61
1.05	0.44	1.76	0.04	0.01	0.28	0.20	4.89	3.42	8.84	12.86	4.44	
0.35	0.00	0.77	7.08	3.38	3.11	3.51	6.66	60.98	84.72	12.18	1.02	1.29
3.75	1.64	6.29	0.57	0.25	0.46	0.29	4.14	6.13	11.84	12.54	5.04	0.35

NOTES

Note. Where *op. cit.* is used it refers back to a full citation within the same chapter.

CHAPTER 1

SLAVES, LIVESTOCK, MACHINES

1 Cynric R. Williams, *A Tour Through the Island of Jamaica* (London, 1827), p. 202.

2 Examples of lists containing the full range of characteristics are found in Old Montpelier Estate, Account Book, 1824–8 (Institute of Jamaica, Kingston) and Worthy Park, Plantation Books, 1811–37 (Jamaica Archives, Spanish Town). For examples of the distinction between creole and foreign-born cattle see Accounts Produce, Liber 51, f. 91 and Liber 62, f. 63 (Jamaica Archives, Spanish Town).

3 List of Slaves and Stock on Irwin Estate, 1820 to 1827 (Institute of Jamaica, Kingston).

4 Douglas Hall, 'Incalculability as a Feature of Sugar Production during the Eighteenth Century', *Social and Economic Studies,* 10 (1961), 348, and 'Slaves and Slavery in the British West Indies', *ibid.,* 11 (1962), 308. Cf. Eugene D. Genovese, *The Political Economy of Slavery* (New York, 1965), p. 54.

5 Dr. Collins, *Practical Rules for the Management and Medical Treatment of Negro Slaves in the Sugar Colonies* (London, 1803), p. 200; R. Bickell, *The West Indies as they are; or a Real Picture of Slavery* (London, 1825), pp. 6 and 36.

6 Hall, 'Slaves and Slavery', p. 309; Edward Brathwaite, *The Development of Creole Society in Jamaica, 1770–1820* (Oxford, 1971), p. 179; David B. Davis, *The Problem of Slavery in Western Culture* (New York, 1966), *passim.*

7 *Ibid.,* p. 459; Bickell, *op. cit.,* pp. 191–7.

8 Edward Long, *The History of Jamaica* (London, 1774), Vol. 2, pp. 356 and 377.

9 'Slaves of colour', or of mixed race; the word 'coloured' is used in the same sense. These points are discussed more fully in Chapter 9.

10 Matthew Gregory Lewis, *Journal of a West India Proprietor* (London, 1834), p. 197.

11 Thomas Roughley, *The Jamaica Planter's Guide* (London, 1823), pp. 132–4. For the facts behind this 'superstition' see G. Williamson and W. J. A. Payne, *An Introduction to Animal Husbandry in the Tropics* (London, 1965), p. 14,

and Jamaica Agricultural Society, *The Farmer's Guide* (Glasgow, 1962), p. 656.

12 Roughley, *op. cit.,* p. 333.

13 Lewis, *op. cit.,* p. 322; Benjamin McMahon, *Jamaica Plantership* (London, 1839).

14 Collins, *op. cit.,* p. 152; J. F. Barham, *Considerations on the Abolition of Negro Slavery* (London, 1823), p. 80; William Dickson, *Mitigation of Slavery* (London, 1814), p. 195; Richard S. Dunn, *Sugar and Slaves. The Rise of the Planter Class in the English West Indies, 1624–1713* (Chapel Hill, 1972), p. 320.

15 *Parliamentary Debates,* 1st Series, Vol. 2, pp. 658–9: 13 June 1804 (Wilberforce); Humboldt is discussed in Philip D. Curtin, *The Atlantic Slave Trade* (Madison, 1969), p. 29. For the United States see Jack E. Eblen, 'Growth of the Black Population in *ante bellum* America, 1820–1860', *Population Studies,* 26 (1972), 273–89.

16 Curtin, *op. cit.,* pp. 28–30.

17 *Loc. cit.;* and B. W. Higman, 'The Slave Populations of the British Caribbean: Some Nineteenth Century Variations," in Samuel R. Proctor (ed.) *Eighteenth Century Florida and the Caribbean* (Gainesville, 1975).

18 Jack E. Eblen, 'On the Natural Increase of Slave Populations: The Example of the Cuban Black Population, 1775–1900', in Stanley L. Engerman and Eugene D. Genovese (eds.) *Race and Slavery in the Western Hemisphere: Quantitative Studies* (Princeton, 1974). Cf. Franklin W. Knight, *Slave Society in Cuba during the Nineteenth Century* (Madison, 1970), p. 82; Gwendolyn Midlo Hall, *Social Control in Slave Plantation Societies. A Comparison of St. Domingue and Cuba* (Baltimore, 1971), p. 16.

19 See Eugene D. Genovese, *The World the Slaveholders Made* (New York, 1969), pp. 8–14.

20 Herman Merivale, *Lectures on Colonization and Colonies* (London, 1928: 1861 edition), pp. 303–5.

21 H. J. Nieboer, *Slavery as an Industrial System* (The Hague, 1900), p. 420. See also W. Kloosterboer, *Involuntary Labour since the Abolition of Slavery* (Leiden, 1960), pp. 206–15.

22 L. J. Ragatz, *The Fall of the Planter Class in the British Caribbean, 1763–1833* (New York, 1928), p. 239.

23 Eric Williams, *Capitalism and Slavery* (London, 1964: 1st edition, 1944), pp. 6–7; E. T. Thompson, 'Population Expansion and the Plantation System', *American Journal of Sociology,* 41 (1935), 314–26, and 'The Plantation Cycle and Problems of Typology', in Vera Rubin (ed.), *Caribbean Studies: A Symposium* (Seattle, 1960).

24 Elsa V. Goveia, *Slave Society in the British Leeward Islands at the end of the Eighteenth Century* (New Haven, 1965), p. 329. See also pp. 122 and 150.

25 Orlando Patterson, *The Sociology of Slavery* (London, 1967), p. 29. For a dissenting view see R. Keith Aufhauser, 'Profitability of Slavery in the British Caribbean', *Journal of Interdisciplinary History,* 5 (1974), 45–67.

26 But cf. Seymour Drescher, 'Le "Declin" du Système Esclavagiste Britannique et L'Abolition de la Traite', *Annales E.S.C.* (forthcoming); David Brion

Davis, *The Problem of Slavery in the Age of Revolution, 1770–1823* (Ithaca, 1975), p. 55; Roger Anstey, *The Atlantic Slave Trade and British Abolition, 1760–1810* (London, 1975), p. 51.

27 See Alexander Gerschenkron, 'Agrarian Policies and Industrialization: Russia 1861–1917', *Cambridge Economic History of Europe* (Cambridge, 1965), Vol. 6, p. 707; George L. Beckford, *Persistent Poverty* (New York, 1972), pp. 43–4.

CHAPTER 2
DISTRIBUTION OF THE SLAVE LABOUR FORCE

1 L. J. Ragatz, *The Fall of the Planter Class in the British Caribbean, 1763–1833* (New York, 1928), p. 38; Richard Sheridan, *The Development of the Plantations to 1750* and *An era of West Indian Prosperity, 1750–1775* (Barbados, 1970), pp. 44–7 and 98; Edward Brathwaite, *The Development of Creole Society in Jamaica, 1770–1820* (Oxford, 1971), p. 84; Gisela Eisner, *Jamaica, 1830–1930* (Manchester, 1961), pp. 168–9.

2 Note that 1832 is not necessarily comparable with earlier periods. Sheridan (*Development of the Plantations,* p. 44) concedes a greater diversification after 1783, but see discussion at end of Chapter 2.

3 For example, Orlando Patterson, *The Sociology of Slavery* (London, 1967), pp. 52–69.

4 R. B. Sheridan, 'The Wealth of Jamaica in the Eighteenth Century', *Economic History Review,* 18 (1965), 294; and Richard Pares, *Merchants and Planters* (Cambridge: Economic History Review Supplement No. 4, 1960), p. 70, draw attention to the series.

5 Accounts Produce (hereafter cited as A.P.), Libers 72–4 (Jamaica Archives, Spanish Town). Most of the A.P. are for the calendar year 1832. But others run from 30 Sept. 1831 to 30 Sept. 1832, and various other dates, some covering only nine months. Those which cover less than 12 months or commence earlier than 30 Sept. 1831 have been excluded. This leaves 971 A.P., but 11 of these are duplicates or cannot be related successfully to the R.R.S. and have been excluded.

6 R.R.S., Libers 115, 116, 119, 120, 124–41 (for 1832).

7 One or two returns were in fact made by resident proprietors but these seem to be anachronisms, following a series of years of returns preceding the residence of the owner.

8 Cf. L. J. Ragatz, 'Absentee Landlordism in the British Caribbean, 1750–1833', *Agricultural History,* 5 (1931), 7–24; Douglas Hall, 'Absentee-Proprietorship in the British West Indies to about 1850', *Jamaican Historical Review,* 4 (1964), 15–35.

9 A.P., Liber 73, f. 56.

10 Benjamin McMahon, *Jamaica Plantership* (London, 1839), p. 173.

11 A.P., Liber 72, fos. 213–14; Liber 73, fos. 62 and 178.

12 Even with changes in ownership, the properties can be traced readily since the A.P. almost always name the property and the owner can be traced to the R.R.S. (which rarely give property names) by using the poll tax lists in the *Jamaica Almanacks* for 1832 and 1833 and the *Claims for Compensation*

made in 1834, which give very full lists of property names.

13 See note 5 above.

14 J. Mackenzie to R. Alston, 8 May 1831, Georgia Estate, St. Thomas, Letter-books and Accounts, 1805–35, Vol. 3 (Institute of Jamaica, Kingston). Also letters of 27 Aug. 1830, 13 Mar. and 10 Apr. 1831.

15 *Ibid.,* 5 June, 10 July and 7 Oct. 1831.

16 Hamilton Brown (attorney, St. Ann) to George French, 4 Apr. and 10 May 1832, Tweedie Estate Records (Jamaica Archives, Spanish Town).

17 M. G. Kendall, 'The Geographical Distribution of Crop Productivity in England', *Journal of the Royal Statistical Society,* 102 (1939), 21–62; J. C. Weaver, 'Crop-Combination Regions in the Middle West', *Geographical Review,* 44 (1954), 175–200; J. T. Coppock, 'Crop, Livestock, and Enterprise Combinations in England and Wales', *Economic Geography,* 40 (1964), 65–81.

18 See Ward Barrett, 'Caribbean Sugar-Production Standards in the Seventeenth and Eighteenth Centuries', in John Parker (ed.), *Merchants and Scholars. Essays in the History of Exploration and Trade* (Minneapolis, 1965), pp. 164–5.

19 Cf. Douglas Hall, 'Incalculability as a Feature of Sugar Production during the Eighteenth Century', *Social and Economic Studies,* 10 (1961), 340–52.

20 Weaver, *op. cit. See also* D. Thomas, *Agriculture in Wales during the Napoleonic Wars* (Cardiff, 1963), p. 80; Leverett P. Hoag, 'The Weaver Method: An Evaluation', *Professional Geographer,* 21 (1969), 244–6.

21 Customs 12/1 (Public Record Office, London).

22 *J.H.A.V.,* 1832, p. 482, for 29 Sept. 1831 to 29 Sept. 1832. This gives an upper-limit estimate. Noel Deerr (*The History of Sugar* (London, 1949), Vol. 1, p. 199) puts the export of sugar in 1832 at 71,584 tons, or a value (using the same parameters as above) of £2,084,000.

23 Eisner, *op. cit.,* p. 299, cf. p. 302 (653 sugar factories in 1832). Cf. Douglas Hall, *Free Jamaica* (New Haven, 1959), p. 82 (646 in 1834). In 1832 679 properties were referred to as 'estates', but some of these were clearly coffee plantations (see Chapter 3).

24 Jamaica Census, 1844 (Jamaica Archives, Spanish Town).

25 *Claims for Compensation. Filed with the Assistant Commissioners for Jamaica* (n.d.). The original registers of claims and counter-claims are in the series T.71 (Public Record Office, London). For further discussion of this source see Chapter 5.

26 *J.H.A.V.,* 1847, p. 373.

27 Brathwaite, *op. cit.,* p. 146.

28 T.71/851, Abstracts of Valuers' Returns.

29 Sheridan, 'Wealth of Jamaica', p. 303.

30 R. B. Sheridan, 'The Wealth of Jamaica in the Eighteenth Century: A Rejoinder', *Economic History Review,* 21 (1968), 49.

31 Robert Paul Thomas, 'The Sugar Colonies of the Old Empire: Profit or Loss for Great Britain?' *Economic History Review,* 21 (1968), 33 and 43–4, replying to Sheridan's 1965 article, claims this similarity, and a similar labour–wealth ratio. Thomas misreads Sheridan's reference to the 1768 poll tax,

defining the non-sugar sector as consisting only of minor staples plantations.
32 See Chapter 10.

CHAPTER 3
AGRICULTURE

1 For the method of classification, see Chapter 2.
2 At the quadrat level, $r = .50$. Tables A3.1 and A3.2.
3 *P.P.*, 1832 (721), p. 11: evidence of William Taylor.
4 A. C. Barnes, *The Sugar Cane* (London, 1964), p. 107.
5 *P.P.*, 1832 (721), p. 349.
6 J. Pinkerton, *Modern Geography* (London, 1802), Vol. 2, p. 657; R. M. Martin, *History of the West Indies* (London, 1835), p. 59.
7 Edward Long, *The History of Jamaica* (London, 1774), Vol. 1, p. 456. Cf. J. B. Moreton, *Manners and Customs in the West India Islands* (London, 1790), p. 44.
8 Thomas Roughley, *The Jamaica Planter's Guide* (London, 1823), pp. 216–18, 268.
9 Long, *op. cit.*, Vol. 2, p. 226.
10 Douglas Hall, *Free Jamaica* (New Haven, 1959), p. 13.
11 Roughley, *op. cit.*, p. 215.
12 For good contemporary descriptions see *ibid.*, chapters 5–7; *P.P.*, 1832 (127), pp. 45–9: evidence of John Baillie. For modern accounts see L. J. Ragatz, *The Fall of the Planter Class in the British Caribbean, 1763–1833* (New York, 1928), pp. 56–63; Michael Craton and James Walvin, *A Jamaican Plantation* (London, 1970), chapter 5; Orlando Patterson, *The Sociology of Slavery* (London, 1967), pp. 52–69.
13 *J.H.A.V.*, 1833, p. 488.
14 *P.P.*, 1832 (127), Lords, Vol. 1, p. 67: evidence of John Baillie.
15 *Ibid.*, p. 625; Benjamin McMahon, *Jamaica Plantership* (London, 1839), p. 244.
16 *P.P.*, 1832 (127), Lords, Vol. 1, p. 67; *J.H.A.V.*, 1833, p. 488; McMahon, *op. cit.*, pp. 245–6.
17 *J.H.A.V.*, 1833, pp. 271, 488, 489, 492, 479 (*sic*). But cf. *Parliamentary Debates*, 3rd Series, Vol. 20, pp. 588–9: 14 Aug. 1833.
18 *J.H.A.V.*, 1833, pp. 488, 492.
19 Gisela Eisner, *Jamaica 1830–1930* (Manchester, 1961), pp. 298–300. Cf. *Cambridge History of the British Empire* (Cambridge, 1940), Vol. 2, p. 730.
20 The proportion of rum consumed in the island is estimated from a sample of the first 30 A.P. properties in Trelawny, arranged alphabetically. The figures are: £14,532 exported, £280 sent to Kingston and £12,376 sold in Jamaica. (Rum consumed on the estates or undisposed at the end of the year is excluded from this analysis.)
21 *P.P.*, 1832 (721), p. 80, for a contrary view.
22 Ragatz, *op. cit.*, pp. 199 and 215; *P.P.*, 1805, X (39), p. 655.
23 George W. Bridges, *The Statistical History of the Parish of Manchester* (Jamaica, 1824), pp. 3–16.

24 *Further Proceedings of the Honourable House of Assembly of Jamaica . . .*, (London, 1816), pp. 36, 99–100.
25 *P.P.*, 1832 (721), p. 349; George Richardson Porter, *The Tropical Agriculturist* (London, 1833), p. 60.
26 Samuel H. Stewart, 'A Statistical Account of the Parish of Manchester', *Jamaica Almanack*, 1840, p. 146.
27 Porter, *op. cit.*, p. 60.
28 H. T. De la Beche, *Notes on the Present Condition of the Negroes in Jamaica* (London, 1825), p. 19.
29 James Kelly, *Jamaica in 1831* (Belfast, 1838), pp. 18–19.
30 *P.P.*, 1832 (721), p. 464: evidence of William Shand.
31 W. Adlam to J. Wemyss, 7 Dec. 1819 and 1 Feb. 1820, Hermitage Estate, Letterbook, 1819–24 (Institute of Jamaica, Kingston).
32 Radnor Plantation Journal, 1822–6, pp. 239–42 (Institute of Jamaica, Kingston).
33 *Ibid.*, p. 253.
34 *Ibid.*, p. 181.
35 *Ibid.*, pp. 251–2.
36 *Ibid.*, pp. 208–10.
37 *Ibid.*, p. 241.
38 The internal organization of another large coffee plantation, Maryland, is discussed in Chapter 9.
39 Long, *op. cit.*, Vol. 2, p. 222; Stewart, *op. cit.*, p. 147.
40 Bernard Martin Senior, *Jamaica, as it was, as it is, and as it may be* (London, 1835), p. 55.
41 *Ibid.*, p. 54.
42 Porter, *op. cit.*, p. 326. See also Hamilton Brown (attorney, St. Ann) to George French, 15 Dec. 1832, Tweedie Estate Records (Jamaica Archives, Spanish Town).
43 Journal of Benjamin Scott Moncrieffe (St. Ann), planter, attorney, and horse-owner, 1828–40, Account Book, p. 39 (Jamaica Archives, Spanish Town).
44 5 Geo. IV c. 24 (Annual act).
45 See *Jamaica Almanack*, 1828, p. 140. In Manchester, for example, 12,635 head of livestock were given-in in April 1832, but only 9,872 were taxed. On coffee plantations only about 25 per cent of the livestock were taxable, whereas on pens the percentage approached 100. See Vestry Minutes, Manchester, Roll of Poll Tax, 11 April 1832, pp. 183–96 (Jamaica Archives, Spanish Town).
46 For the parish data see *Jamaica Almanack*, 1833.
47 *P.P.*, 1832 (721), p. 349; Stewart, *op. cit.*, p. 146.
48 Long, *op. cit.*, Vol. 2, p. 189.
49 Moreton, *op. cit.*, p. 58; Roughley, *cp. cit.*, p. 129.
50 Senior, *op. cit.*, p. 58; Moreton, *op. cit.*, p. 58.
51 Long, *op. cit.*, Vol. 1, p. 283; Moreton, *op. cit.*, p. 60; *J.H.A.V.*, 1833, p. 49.
52 Senior, *op. cit.*, pp. 58–9.
53 Combinations including the categories 'sundries' and 'rent' will not be discussed since the first is anomalous and the actual agricultural use of land rented is not clear. See Appendix 2 for a full list of the crop combinations.

54 For example, R. Alston to C. Scott, 29 Oct. 1832, Georgia Estate Letterbook, Vol. 3 (Institute of Jamaica, Kingston).
55 Stewart, *op. cit.*, p. 146.
56 Vestry Minutes, Manchester, 1832, p. 183.
57 R.R.S., Liber 129, f. 138.
58 A.P., Liber 73, f. 37.
59 A.P., Liber 74, f. 29; *Jamaica Almanack*, 1833, Poll tax roll: Roger Dobson.
60 R.R.S., Liber 135, f. 75.
61 Anon., *Memoir of William Wright* (Edinburgh, 1828), p. 216.
62 Matthew Gregory Lewis, *Journal of a West India Proprietor* (London, 1834), p. 66.
63 James Thomson, *A Treatise on the Diseases of Negroes* (Jamaica, 1820), p. 168.
64 Roughley, *op. cit.*, p. 155.
65 *Jamaica Almanack*, 1832, p. 151; A.P., Liber 73, f. 34 (Belvidere) and f. 172 (Greenwich).
66 A.P., Liber 73, f. 211; R.R.S., Liber 135, f. 180; *Jamaica Almanack*, 1833, Poll tax roll: John F. Nembhard; *Claims for Compensation* [1834]; *J.H.A.V.*, 1847, p. 373.
67 A.P., Liber 73, f. 78; *J.H.A.V.*, 1847, p. 373.
68 A.P., Liber 73, f. 93; *J.H.A.V.*, 1847, p. 373.
69 A.P., Liber 74, f. 37. In 1832 the owner of Windsor Castle was Archibald Dick, who was also the attorney of Dallas Castle.
70 A.P., Liber 73, fos. 108 and 139; Liber 74, f. 23.
71 *P.P.*, 1832 (721), p. 348: evidence of Robert Scott.
72 A.P., Liber 73, fos. 60, 98, 150, 162, 180, 184.
73 A.P., Liber 73, fos. 150, 166, 193.
74 Other terms used occasionally included 'farm', 'place', 'land' and 'mountain'. The eight properties named 'farms' were distributed in the same way as the pens, suggesting that they were similar to the smaller types of pen as hinted by Long and Moreton (see below). 'Place' was a rare proprietorial eponym (as in 'Fearon's Place'), while 'land' referred to outlying segments of a property (as in 'Williamsfield Land'). The term 'coffee mountain' which is common in the literature (McMahon, *op. cit.*, p. 224; R. Bickell, *The West Indies as they are* (London, 1825), p. 22; Frederic G. Cassidy, *Jamaica Talk* (London, 1961), p. 95), seems to have been a colloquial label. On the cadastral maps of the 1860–90s the label 'mountain' is common, but it refers to provision grounds or 'negro grounds' and was used in this way in the 1830s as well.
75 *Claims for Compensation* (1834); A.P. (1832); R.R.S. (1832).
76 *P.P.*, 1832 (127), Lords, Vol. 1, p. 578; Senior, *op. cit.*, p. 38.
77 Moreton, *op. cit.*, p. 58.
78 Senior, *op. cit.*, p. 38.
79 *Further Proceedings*, *op. cit.*, pp. 35, 67, 99.
80 Senior, *op. cit.*, p. 39.
81 Long, *op. cit.*, Vol. 1, pp. 283, 380.
82 Moreton, *op. cit.*, p. 58.
83 Hall, *op. cit.*, p. 10; Cassidy, *op. cit.*, p. 95.

84 Senior, *op. cit.*, p. 39. Cf. Philip D. Curtin, *Two Jamaicas* (Cambridge, 1955), p. 234, note 17.
85 *Royal Gazette* (Kingston), 6 Mar. 1819; also 23 Jan. 1819 for 'Coco-Nut-Grove Settlement', St. Ann.
86 *St. Jago de la Vega Gazette,* 29 Sept. 1832.
87 A.P., Liber 72, f. 195; Liber 73, fos. 29 and 149; Liber 74, fos. 21 and 122.

CHAPTER 4

OTHER ECONOMIC ACTIVITIES

1 Rose Hall Journal, 1817–32, Vol. 2 (Jamaica Archives, Spanish Town); Old Montpelier Estate, Account Book, List of slaves, 1 Jan. 1825 (Institute of Jamaica, Kingston); Inventories, Liber 149, f. 174 (Jamaica Archives); J. Shore and J. Stewart, *In Old St. James* (Kingston, 1911), pp. 140–51.
2 A.P., Liber 73, f. 98.
3 *Royal Gazette,* 4 Jan. 1817.
4 Cf. Gisela Eisner, *Jamaica, 1830–1930* (Manchester, 1961), pp. 167 and 173; Robert S. Starobin, *Industrial Slavery in the Old South* (New York, 1970), p. 19.
5 Inventories, Liber 140, f. 46, Liber 148, f. 36, Liber 149, ff. 99 and 174; Edward Brathwaite, *The Development of Creole Society in Jamaica, 1770–1820* (Oxford, 1971), pp. 155 and 160.
6 Inventories, Liber 142, f. 175.
7 *Ibid.*, Liber 143, f. 119.
8 *Ibid.*, Liber 141, fos. 37 and 153, Liber 142, f. 21, Liber 146, fos. 137 and 149.
9 For example, see Joseph Sturge and Thomas Harvey, *The West Indies in 1837* (London, 1838), pp. 229–30.
10 Inventories, Liber 140, f. 46.
11 *Ibid.*, Liber 148, f. 36.
12 Starobin, *op. cit.*, pp. 11 and 236, note 21. See also Richard C. Wade, *Slavery in the Cities. The South 1820–1860* (New York, 1964), pp. 33–7.
13 Based on the scattered statistics given for specific industries in Starobin, *op. cit.*, pp. 13–34.
14 Eisner, *op. cit.*, p. 30.
15 Brathwaite, *op. cit.*, p. 155.
16 A.P., Liber 73, fos. 135 and 226.
17 James Kelly, *Jamaica in 1831* (Belfast, 1838), p. 28.
18 Inventories, Liber 141, f. 27.
19 *Ibid.*, Liber 148, f. 36.
20 Brathwaite, *op. cit.*, p. 161.
21 Sidney W. Mintz and Douglas Hall, 'The Origins of the Jamaican Internal Marketing System', *Yale University Publications in Anthropology,* No. 57 (1960).
22 *St. Jago de la Vega Gazette,* 4 Feb. 1832.
23 Inventories, Liber 140, f. 81.
24 Or it may result from the system of classification used by the valuers, but the method adopted in Jamaica is uncertain. See R. E. P. Wastell, 'The History of Slave Compensation 1833 to 1845' (unpublished M.A. thesis, University of London, 1932), p. 77.

25 Brathwaite, *op. cit.*, pp. 155–6.
26 Inventories, Liber 142, f. 20.
27 Brathwaite, *op. cit.*, p. 161.
28 See Appendix 1 for the rates.
29 H. T. De la Beche, *Notes on the Present Condition of the Negroes in Jamaica* (London, 1825), p. 34.
30 Inventories, Liber 140, fos. 132 and 194, Liber 141, fos. 61, 106 and 169, Liber 147, f. 194.
31 *Ibid.*, Liber 140, f. 72.
32 *Ibid.*, Liber 140, f. 161.
33 *Ibid.*, Liber 142, f. 115.
34 But cf. *ibid.*, Liber 141, f. 155.
35 *P.P.*, 1832 (127), Lords, Vol. 1, p. 626: evidence of William Taylor. See also *ibid.*, p. 95; A.P., Liber 73, fos. 57 and 146.
36 W. Adlam to J. Wemyss, 7 Dec. 1819, Hermitage Estate Letterbook (Institute of Jamaica, Kingston).
37 De la Beche, *op. cit.*, p. 34; Benjamin McMahon, *Jamaica Plantership* (London, 1839), p. 220; Mulgrave to Stanley, 27 June 1833, Despatches, Jamaica to England, CS 102/7 (Jamaica Archives, Spanish Town).
38 *P.P.*, 1832 (127), Lords, Vol. 1, p. 549.
39 Brathwaite, *op. cit.*, pp. 155 and 160–1.
40 *P.P.*, 1832 (127), Lords, Vol. 1, p. 482: evidence of Rev. John Barry. See also Brathwaite, *op. cit.*, p. 160; Orlando Patterson, *The Sociology of Slavery* (London, 1967), pp. 161–2.
41 E. B. Forbes to Bell Forbes, 2 Sept. 1824, Letters from members of the King Family (Institute of Jamaica, Kingston).

CHAPTER 5
POPULATION DISTRIBUTION AND STRUCTURE

1 James Stephen, *Essays in Ecclesiastical Biography* (London, 1883), p. 547.
2 *Parliamentary Debates,* 1st Series, Vol. 28, p. 803: 20 July 1814.
3 See Betty Fladeland, 'Abolitionist Pressures on the Concert of Europe, 1814–1822', *Journal of Modern History,* 38 (1966), 355–73; *Parliamentary Debates,* 1st Series, Vol. 27, pp. 645–7: 2 May 1814.
4 *Ibid.,* 1st Series, Vol. 34, p. 1222: 19 June 1816, A. C. Grant (Jamaica planter).
5 James Stephen, *Reasons for Establishing a Registry of Slaves in the British Colonies* (London, 1815), p. 9, quoted in D. J. Murray, *The West Indies and the Development of Colonial Government, 1801–1834* (Oxford, 1965), p. 94.
6 C.O. 295/28, f. 250, Order in Council, 26 March 1812. See Murray, *op. cit.,* pp. 78–9.
7 R. I. and S. Wilberforce, *The Life of William Wilberforce* (London, 1838), Vol. 4, p. 176.
8 R. L. Schuyler, 'The Constitutional Claims of the British West Indies', *Political Science Quarterly,* 40 (1925), 1–36; Murray, *op. cit.,* pp. 94–7; B. W. Higman, 'The West India Interest in Parliament, 1807–1833', *Historical Studies,* 13 (1967), 10–11.

9 57 Geo. III c. 15. Minor administrative amendments were made under 1 Will. IV c. 19.

10 *A Review of the Colonial Slave Registration Acts, in a Report of a Committee of the Board of Directors of the African Institution* (London, 1820), p. 11.

11 *Royal Gazette* (Kingston), 4 January 1817.

12 *St. Jago de la Vega Gazette,* 7 July 1832. Cf. 57 Geo. III c. 15, section 4 (5d per sheet).

13 T.71/1–242 (Public Record Office, London).

14 R.R.S., Libers 1–141 (Jamaica Archives, Spanish Town).

15 *Barbados Mercury,* 20 May 1817.

16 R. E. P. Wastell, 'The History of Slave Compensation, 1833 to 1845' (unpublished M.A. thesis, University of London, 1932), pp. 117–19.

17 *J.H.A.V.,* 1832, p. 92.

18 R.R.S., Liber 137, f. 26.

19 A West Indian, *Notes in Defence of the Colonies. On the Increase and Deincrease of the Slave Population of the British West Indies* (Jamaica, 1826), p. 55. See also T.71/683, Bundle 9.

20 See Eric Williams, 'The British West Indian Slave Trade after its Abolition in 1807', *Journal of Negro History,* 27 (1942), 175–91; D. Eltis, 'The Traffic in Slaves between the British West Indian Colonies, 1807–1833', *Economic History Review,* 25 (1972), 55–64.

21 See p. 62.

22 G. W. Roberts, *The Population of Jamaica* (Cambridge, 1957), p. 4. His interpretation is supported by Gisela Eisner, *Jamaica, 1830–1930* (Manchester, 1961), p. 131, and Michael Craton, 'Jamaican Slave Mortality: Fresh Light from Worthy Park, Longville and the Tharp Estates', *Journal of Caribbean History,* 3 (1971), 12.

23 Roberts, *op. cit.,* p. 3, states that the Registration Act was 'avowedly framed to ascertain "all deductions from and additions to the former stock of slaves"'. This phrase comes not from the Jamaica Act but from Robertson's report on British Guiana: *P.P.,* 1833, Vol. 26 (700), *Slave Population. (Slave Registries),* p. 447. Cf. G. W. Roberts, 'A Life Table for a West Indian Slave Population', *Population Studies,* 5 (1952), 238–40.

24 57 Geo. III c. 15, s. 4.

25 B. W. Higman, 'Household Structure and Fertility on Jamaican Slave Plantations: A Nineteenth-Century Example', *Population Studies,* 27 (1973), 545.

26 Old Montpelier Estate, Account Book (Institute of Jamaica, Kingston).

27 William Sells, *Remarks on the Condition of the Slaves in the Island of Jamaica* (London, 1823), p. 18.

28 Robert Renny, *A History of Jamaica* (London, 1807), p. 207; John Hancock, 'Observations on Tetanus Infantum, or Lock-Jaw of Infants', *Edinburgh Medical and Surgical Journal,* 35 (1831), 343; C.O. 295/66, f. 53: evidence of Burton Williams, 18 January 1825, before the Council of Trinidad; John Morrison, *A Treatise on Tetanus* (Newry, 1816), p. 35; James Thomson, *A Treatise on the Diseases of Negroes, as they occur in the island of Jamaica* (Jamaica, 1820), p. 120; Orlando Patterson, *The Sociology of Slavery* (London, 1967), p. 101.

29 R.R.S., Liber 40, f. 216, for example.
30 See, for example, the variable practice in Worthy Park Plantation Book, 1811–17 and 1830–37, and Thetford Plantation Book, 1821–33 (Jamaica Archives, Spanish Town).
31 57 Geo. III c. 15, s. 4.
32 Edward Brathwaite, *The Development of Creole Society in Jamaica, 1770–1820* (Oxford, 1971), pp. 164–6.
33 57 Geo. III c. 15, s.1.
34 Alexander Barclay, *A Practical View of the Present State of Slavery in the West Indies* (London, 1826), p. 337.
35 R.R.S., Libers 115, 116, 119, 120, 124–41.
36 R.R.S., Liber 136, f. 77.
37 See *P.P.*, 1833, Vol. 26 (539), *Slave Registration. (Jamaica)*, p. 474; *Parliamentary Debates,* 3rd Series, Vol. 4, p. 994: 8 July 1831.
38 *P.P.*, 1832 (127), Lords, Vol. 1, p. 28; *P.P.*, 1835, Vol. 51 (235), *Slavery Abolition Proceedings,* p. 289.
39 But see the call for a census of the slave population, *J.H.A.V.*, 1831, pp. 135 and 139.
40 Great Britain: 3 & 4 Will. IV c. 73.
41 *P.P.*, 1832 (127), Lords, Vol. 1, p. 54.
42 Registers of Claims, T.71/852–914, and Compensation Valuers' Returns, T.71/685–851. The returns used were the printed *Claims for Compensation, Filed with the Assistant Commissioners for Jamaica,* published as required by Great Britain: 3 & 4 Will. IV c. 73, to enable counter-claims.
43 *Jamaica Almanack,* 1833.
44 James Robertson, *Map of the county of Cornwall, (and Middlesex and Surrey), in the island of Jamaica, constructed from actual surveys, under the authority of the Hon. House of Assembly* (London, 1804); Morris, Cunninghame and Woolridge, *A Plan . . . shewing the district and properties . . . destroyed during the late rebellion* (London, 1832); Thomas Harrison, *Cadastral Survey of Jamaica,* 1866–91 (Survey Department, Kingston). The 12,000 place names derived from these maps are much more comprehensive than the list of *Jamaica Place Names* prepared from Liddell's map of 1888 by the Institute of Jamaica.
45 G. E. Cumper, 'Population Movements in Jamaica, 1830–1950', *Social and Economic Studies,* 5 (1956), 263–7 and 277.
46 N. Gilbert and T. C. E. Wells, 'Analysis of Quadrat Data', *Journal of Ecology,* 54 (1966), 675–85; Andrei Rogers and Norbert G. Gomar, 'Statistical Inference in Quadrat Analysis', *Geographical Analysis,* 1 (1969), 370–84; H. McConnell, *Quadrat Methods in Map Analysis* (University of Iowa, 1966); P. Greig-Smith, *Quantitative Plant Ecology* (London, 1957).
47 J. T. Curtis and R. P. McIntosh, 'The Interrelations of Certain Analytic and Synthetic Phytosociological Characters', *Ecology,* 31 (1950), 453.
48 57 Geo. III c. 15, s. 1.
49 Edward Long, *The History of Jamaica* (London, 1774), Vol. 2, pp. 1, 102 and 183.
50 Statistical tests of the data, to ask whether they satisfy the assumptions of the

linear regression model, have not been carried out systematically. Measurement error has been discussed above. The quadrat data apply to a large sample (328), but those for parishes (21) and towns (26) are not all normally distributed. Systematic transformation of the data has not been attempted, though some of the demographic data for 1817–20 have been transformed to logarithms, producing superior correlations. The presence of autocorrelation should be limited, especially since time-series data are not used extensively. For the assumptions of the linear regression model, see J. Johnston, *Econometric Methods* (New York, 1963), pp. 106–8, and Jerome C. R. Li, *Statistical Inference* (Ann Arbor, 1964), Vol. 1, p. 336.

51 This total is derived from the individual returns at the Jamaica Archives: R.R.S., Libers 115, 116, 119, 120, 124–41. The London Registry Office put the total at 310,707 (T.71/680, Bundle 14, 'Summary of the Number &c. of Slaves in the Various Parishes of Jamaica', and T.71/683, Bundle 9). But this is based on only 12,236 returns (T.71/683, Bundle 19), whereas 12,453 returns were found in the Jamaica Archives series. In general, divergences between the T.71 and R.R.S. parish figures can be accounted for in terms of supplemental or late returns, hence calculations based on the R.R.S. have been preferred. Eisner, *op. cit.*, p. 130, states that 302,666 slaves were registered in 1832, but this figure seems to derive from the poll-tax givings-in (*Jamaica Almanack*, 1833).

52 Philip D. Curtin, *Two Jamaicas* (Cambridge, Mass., 1955), p. 11.

53 Robertson, *Map:* 'An Account of the Quantity and Quality of the Lands in the Respective Parishes'.

54 A. N. Strahler, 'Quantitative Slope Analysis', *Bulletin, Geological Society of America,* 67 (1956), 571–96.

55 J. Pinkerton, *Modern Geography* (London, 1802), Vol. 2, p. 657; Long, *op. cit.,* Vol. 1, p. 353.

56 Jamaica Archives, Spanish Town.

57 Frank Wesley Pitman, *The Development of the British West Indies, 1700–1763* (New Haven, 1917), p. 23. Cf. Richard C. Wade, *Slavery in the Cities. The South 1820–1860* (New York, 1964), pp. 75–9.

58 *The Watchman and Jamaica Free Press* (Kingston), 26 January and 25 May 1831. See also Wilma Williams, 'Early Kingston', *Jamaica Journal,* 5 (1971), 8; Douglas Hall, *Free Jamaica* (New Haven, 1959), p. 10.

59 See Patterson, *op. cit.,* pp. 95–6.

60 See Tables A3.6 and A3.7.

61 Great Britain: 3 & 4 Will. IV c. 73.

62 See George W. Barclay, *Techniques of Population Analysis* (New York, 1958), pp. 28–33. Cf. Sherburne F. Cook and Woodrow Borah, *Essays in Population History: Mexico and the Caribbean* (Berkeley, 1971), Vol. 1, p. 89.

63 See p. 80.

64 See Table 11. Philip D. Curtin, *The Atlantic Slave Trade* (Madison, 1969), p. 26, estimates a re-exportation of 17,800 between 1801 and 1807; this should be revised to 7,880.

65 Eltis, *op. cit.,* p. 58.

66 Kenneth M. Stampp, *The Peculiar Institution* (New York, 1956), p. 237; Robert William Fogel and Stanley L. Engerman, *Time on the Cross* (Boston, 1974), Vol. 1, p. 78.
67 *Further Proceedings of the Honourable House of Assembly of Jamaica, . . .* (London, 1816), p. 35.
68 1 Will. IV c. 25, s. 76.
69 8 Geo. II c. 6; 32 Geo. III c. 33. See also Alexander Barclay, *op. cit.,* p. 56; Brathwaite, *op. cit.,* p. 292.
70 George W. Bridges, *The Statistical History of the Parish of Manchester* (Jamaica, 1824); Lowell Joseph Ragatz, *The Fall of the Planter Class in the British Caribbean, 1763–1833* (New York, 1928), p. 17.
71 *Further Proceedings, op. cit.,* pp. 35–6, 99–100.
72 *P.P.,* 1832 (127), Lords, Vol. 1, p. 161: evidence of John Baillie.
73 Long, *op. cit.,* Vol. 2, pp. 213, 219, 222; Richard B. Sheridan, *Sugar and Slavery* (Barbados, 1974), p. 222.
74 Hall, *op. cit.,* p. 17. Sheridan, *op. cit.,* pp. 208, 210, 222, appears unaware of the confusion. Robertson in his survey of 1804 put it at 4,286 square miles.
75 47 Geo. III c. 27.
76 Bridges, *op. cit.,* p. 3.
77 *J.H.A.V.,* 1824, p. 94, and 1825, p. 305.
78 *J.H.A.V.,* 1832, p. 169.
79 Long, *op. cit.,* Vol. 1, pp. 384–404; 424–6. See also Brathwaite, *op. cit.,* pp. 86–91.
80 *J.H.A.V.,* 1831, pp. 131, 139, 247.
81 2 Will. IV c. 28.
82 X_7, X_8, X_{13}, X_{14}, X_{21}, X_{23}, X_{28}, X_{29}, X_{30}, X_{38}, X_{41}: for definitions see Table A3.1.
83 *P.P.,* 1832 (721), p. 10: evidence of William Taylor.
84 *Further Proceedings, op. cit.,* pp. 35–6.
85 R. Bickell, *The West Indies as they are* (London, 1825), p. 36.
86 Cf. D. G. Hall, 'The Social and Economic Background to Sugar in Slave Days', *Caribbean Historical Review,* Nos. 3–4 (1954), p. 163.
87 Alexander Barclay, *op. cit.,* p. 56; *P.P.,* 1832 (721), p. 350; *P.P.,* 1832 (127), Lords, Vol. 1, pp. 161–2.
88 For independent movement of the slaves see Sidney W. Mintz and Douglas Hall, 'The Origins of the Jamaican Internal Marketing System', *Yale University Publications in Anthropology,* No. 57 (1960), 1–26.
89 Alexander Barclay, *op. cit.,* p. 61.
90 H. T. De la Beche, *Notes on the Present Condition of the Negroes in Jamaica* (London, 1825), p. 34.
91 R.R.S., Liber 126, fos. 169–86, for example.
92 Stampp, *op. cit.,* p. 30; Richard Hofstadter, 'U. B. Phillips and the Plantation Legend', *Journal of Negro History,* 29 (1944), 109–24; Eugene D. Genovese, Foreword to Ulrich Bonnell Phillips, *American Negro Slavery* (Baton Rouge, 1966), pp. xii–xiii.
93 *J.H.A.V.,* 1824, p. 94; Long, *op. cit.,* Vol. 2, p. 186; Brathwaite, *op. cit.,* p. 169.

94 *J.H.A.V.*, 1817, p. 39. These statistics vary slightly from those in *P.P.*, 1833 (539).
95 Roberts, *op. cit.*, p. 71; *P.P.*, 1832 (721), p. 521.
96 See p. 107.
97 *J.H.A.V.*, 1832, pp. 92, 233.
98 *J.H.A.V.*, 1831, p. 107; Long, *op. cit.*, Vol. 2, p. 213.
99 The 1844 census recorded a sex ratio of 92.3 for the black population and 85.9 for the coloured; the decline was reversed by 1861. See Eisner, *op. cit.*, p. 155.
100 Curtin, *Atlantic Slave Trade*, p. 160. See note 64 above.
101 Brathwaite, *op. cit.*, p. 164 (who does not specify his source).
102 *P.P.*, 1832 (721), p. 521.
103 Roberts, *Population of Jamaica*, p. 70.
104 See Brathwaite, *op. cit.*, *passim*.
105 Curtin, *Atlantic Slave Trade*, p. 160.
106 J. F. Barham, *Considerations on the Abolition of Negro Slavery* (London, 1823), p. 80; Brathwaite, *op. cit.*, pp. 154 and 164.
107 James M. Phillippo, *Jamaica: Its Past and Present State* (London, 1843), p. 418. *See also* Philip D. Curtin, *The Image of Africa* (Madison, 1964), pp. 34–57, 227–53.
108 De la Beche, *op. cit.*, p. 34; Ragatz, *op. cit.*, p. 199.
109 See p. 49.
110 Ansley J. Coale, 'Estimates of Various Demographic Measures through the Quasi-Stable Age Distribution', in *Emerging Techniques in Population Research* (Milbank Memorial Fund, 1963), pp. 177–81; Ansley J. Coale and Paul Demeny, *Regional Model Life Tables and Stable Populations* (Princeton, 1966); Nathan Keyfitz, 'Changing Vital Rates and Age Distributions', *Population Studies*, 22 (1968), pp. 235–51.
111 Wastell, *op. cit.*, p. 90.
112 *P.P.*, 1803–4 (119), p. 14: circular of Duke of Portland, 23 April 1798.
113 See Higman, 'Household Structure and Fertility'.
114 Cf. Patterson, *op. cit.*, p. 106; Craton, *op. cit.*

CHAPTER 6
PATTERNS OF SURVIVAL

1 *P.P.*, 1832 (127), Lords, Vol. 2, p. 828.
2 *Further Proceedings of the Honourable House of Assembly of Jamaica* (London, 1816), p. 30.
3 Edwin Lascelles, *Instructions for the Management of a Plantation in Barbadoes* (London, 1786), p. 2.
4 Minute Book of the Society for the Improvement of West India Plantership, 1811–12, and of the Agricultural Society, 1812–16: 14 November 1812, p. 117 (University of Keele).
5 D. E. C. Eversley, *Social Theories of Fertility and the Malthusian Debate* (Oxford, 1959), pp. 54–7; K. Smith, *The Malthusian Controversy* (London, 1951), pp. 18–22, 104.

6 Edward Long, *The History of Jamaica* (London, 1774), Vol. 2, p. 386.

7 T. R. Malthus, *An Essay on the Principle of Population* (London, 1960), Vol. 1, pp. 91, 150–1; *Parliamentary Debates,* 1st Series, Vol. 8, pp. 982–3, and Vol. 9, pp. 118–32: 23 February and 16 March 1807. See also A. E. Furness, 'George Hibbert and the Defence of Slavery in the West Indies', *Jamaican Historical Review,* 5 (1965), 57–8.

8 James Thomson, *A Treatise on the Diseases of Negroes, as they Occur in the Island of Jamaica* (Jamaica, 1820), p. 8; H. T. De la Beche, *Researches in Theoretical Geology* (London, 1834), pp. 393–8.

9 Thomas Dancer, *The Medical Assistant; or Jamaica Practice of Physic* (Kingston, 1801), p. 17. Cf. C. Turner Thackrah, *The Effects of the Principal Arts, Trades, and Professions, and of Civic States and Habits of Living, on Health and Longevity* (London, 1831), p. 3.

10 Minute Book of the Society for the Improvement of West India Plantership, 14 November 1812, pp. 115–20.

11 H. T. De la Beche, *Notes on the Present Condition of the Negroes in Jamaica* (London, 1825), p. 34; *P.P.*, 1803–4, X (119), p. 13: circular of the Duke of Portland, 23 April 1798; Alfred Owen Aldridge, 'Population and Polygamy in Eighteenth-Century Thought', *Journal of the History of Medicine,* 4 (1949), 129–48.

12 De la Beche, *Present Condition,* pp. 17–18. Cf. Thomson, *op. cit.,* p. 110; *Further Proceedings, op. cit.,* p. 32; A West Indian, *Notes in Defence of the Colonies. On the Increase and Decrease of the Slave Population of the British West Indies* (Jamaica, 1826), p. 34.

13 William H. Burnley, *Opinions on Slavery and Emancipation in 1823* (London, 1833), p. x.

14 Long, *op. cit.,* Vol. 2, pp. 400–2, 435–8.

15 A West Indian, *op. cit.,* p. 18.

16 Cf. *Parliamentary Debates,* 2nd Series, Vol. 19, p. 246: 1 May 1828, the Earl of Darnley quoting M. T. Sadler.

18 See pp. 47–9.

19 These numbers are derived from the R.R.S.; they differ slightly from those found in T.71/680, Bundle 14.

20 Cf. Michael Craton, 'Jamaican Slave Mortality: Fresh Light from Worthy Park, Longville and the Tharp Estates', *Journal of Caribbean History,* 3 (1971), 5.

21 See p. 95.

22 R.R.S., Liber 115, f. 130; Liber 133, f. 40 and f. 91; Liber 135, f. 34 and f. 102.

23 See B. W. Higman, 'Household Structure and Fertility on Jamaican Slave Plantations: A Nineteenth-Century Example', *Population Studies,* 27 (1973), 527–50.

24 William Sells, *Remarks on the Condition of the Slaves in the Island of Jamaica* (London, 1823), pp. 19–21.

25 See p. 49.

26 David Mason, 'A Descriptive Account of Frambœsia or Yaws', *Edinburgh Medical and Surgical Journal,* 35 (1831), 53.

27 Dancer, *op. cit.,* p. 171.

28 James Maxwell, 'Pathological Inquiry into the Nature of Cachexia Africana,

as it is generally Connected with Dirt-Eating', *Jamaica Physical Journal,* 2 (1835), 409–35; R. Hoeppli, *Parasitic Diseases in Africa and the Western Hemisphere: Early Documentation and Transmission in the Slave Trade* (Basel, 1969), p. 117; John S. Haller, 'The Negro and the Southern Physician: A Study of Medical and Racial Attitudes', *Medical History,* 16 (1972), 238–42; John M. Hunter, 'Geophagy in Africa and the United States: A Culture-Nutrition Hypothesis', *Geographical Review,* 63 (1973), 170–95.

29 See August Hirsch, *Handbook of Geographical and Historical Pathology* (London, 1883–6), Vol. 3, p. 398; John Blackall, *Observations on the Nature and Cure of Dropsies* (London, 1813); Henry Herbert Southey, *Observations on Pulmonary Consumption* (London, 1814); Arthur Daniel Stone, *A Practical Treatise on the Diseases of the Stomach, and of Digestion* (London, 1806).

30 Hirsch, *op. cit.,* Vol. 3, p. 304.

31 Dancer, *op. cit.,* p. 93; Thomson, *op. cit.,* p. 34.

32 John Williamson, *Medical and Miscellaneous Observations, Relative to the West India Islands* (Edinburgh, 1817), Vol. 2, p. 165; Hirsch, *op. cit.,* Vol. 1, pp. 7 and 136, Vol. 3, p. 124.

33 *Ibid.,* Vol. 1, p. 401; *Jamaica Physical Journal,* Vol. 1, (1834), p. 190. Cf. William Dosite Postell, *The Health of Slaves on Southern Plantations* (Baton Rouge, 1951), p. 76.

34 J. B. Moreton, *Manners and Customs in the West India Islands* (London, 1790), p. 123; Matthew Gregory Lewis, *Journal of a West India Proprietor* (London, 1834), p. 107.

35 Anon., *Memoir of the late William Wright* (Edinburgh, 1828), p. 372; Thomson, *op. cit.,* p. 14. Cf. Philip D. Curtin, 'Epidemiology and the Slave Trade', *Political Science Quarterly,* 83 (1968), 190–216.

36 Orlando Patterson, *The Sociology of Slavery* (London, 1967), p. 111; Craton, *op. cit.,* pp. 18–20.

37 Patterson, *op. cit.,* p. 109.

38 Higman, *op. cit.,* p. 549.

39 See p. 154.

40 Joycelin Byrne, *Levels of Fertility in the Commonwealth Caribbean, 1921–1965* (University of the West Indies, 1972), pp. 58–9.

41 Long, *op. cit.,* Vol. 2, p. 435; Bryan Edwards, *The History, Civil and Commercial, of the British Colonies in the West Indies* (London, 1819), Vol. 2, p. 133; F. W. Pitman, 'Slavery on British West India Plantations in the Eighteenth Century', *Journal of Negro History,* 11 (1926), 631; Patterson, *op. cit.,* pp. 106–8; Michael Craton and James Walvin, *A Jamaican Plantation: A History of Worthy Park, 1670–1970* (London, 1970), pp. 128, 196.

42 Burnley, *op. cit.,* pp. x–xi.

43 *Further Proceedings, op. cit.,* p. 31; Dr. Collins, *Practical Rules for the Management and Medical Treatment of Negro Slaves in the Sugar Colonies* (London, 1803), p. 20.

44 Furness, *op. cit.,* pp. 57–8.

45 *A Review of the Colonial Slave Registration Acts, in a Report of a Committee of the Board of Directors of the African Institution* (London, 1820), p. 68.

46 See Tables A3.1–A3.3.

47 Table A3.12; and see p. 75.

48 *P.P.*, 1832 (721), p. 350.
49 *Further Proceedings, op. cit.*, pp. 31–2. Cf. Patterson, *op. cit.*, pp. 107–9.
50 Long, *op. cit.*, Vol. 2, pp. 353, 411–14; *P.P.*, 1832 (721), p. 467; Jack Jingle, 'The Omnibus or Jamaica Scrapbook', (Institute of Jamaica, Kingston, c. 1824), p. 230.
51 Alexander Barclay, *A Practical View of the Present State of Slavery in the West Indies* (London, 1826), p. 336.
52 See Tables 12, 15, 16 and 17.
53 See p. 116. Cf. Craton, *op. cit.*, pp. 10, 23 (but note that Craton's Table 6 fails to distinguish the age-specific fertility rates).
54 See p. 134.
55 *J.H.A.V.*, 1834, p. 317; Robert Montgomery Martin, *History of the Colonies of the British Empire* (London, 1843), p. 8; R. E. P. Wastell, 'The History of Slave Compensation, 1833 to 1845' (unpublished M.A. thesis, London University, 1932), p. 90.
56 *P.P.*, 1832 (127), Lords, Vol. 1, p. 578, Vol. 2, p. 833; *P.P.*, 1832 (721), p. 43. See also A. J. H. Bernal, *A Geographical Catechism of the Island of Jamaica* (Montego Bay, 1840), p. 9.
57 De la Beche, *Present Condition*, p. 21; R. Bickell, *The West Indies as they are* (London, 1825), p. 22; *P.P.*, 1832 (721), p. 464.
58 Samuel H. Stewart, 'A Statistical Account of the Parish of Manchester', *Jamaica Almanack*, 1840, pp. 143–4.
59 Long, *op. cit.*, Vol. 2, p. 437.
60 *P.P.*, 1832 (721), p. 43.
61 *P.P.*, 1832 (127), Lords, Vol. 1, pp. 622–5.
62 *Ibid.*, pp. 3–4, 423, 590; *P.P.*, 1832 (721), p. 19.
63 Cynric R. Williams, *A Tour Through the Island of Jamaica* (London, 1827), pp. 197–9.
64 See p. 10; and Table 1.
65 James Kelly, *Jamaica in 1831* (Belfast, 1838), pp. 28–9.
66 *P.P.*, 1832 (721), p. 470; J. Stewart, *A View of the Past and Present State of the Island of Jamaica* (Edinburgh, 1823), p. 234; De la Beche, *Present Condition*, p. 34; Benjamin McMahon, *Jamaica Plantership* (London, 1839), p. 220.
67 Bickell, *op. cit.*, p. 52.
68 Long, *op. cit.*, Vol. 2, p. 184; S. H. Stewart, *op. cit.*, p. 146.
69 *Further Proceedings, op. cit.*, p. 35.
70 *P.P.*, 1832 (127), Lords, Vol. 2, p. 828; James Bell, *A System of Geography* (Edinburgh, 1840), Vol. 6, p. 302.
71 McMahon, *op. cit.*, p. 140.
72 *Further Proceedings, op. cit.*, p. 32. Cf. W. A. Green, 'The Planter Class and British West Indian Sugar Production, before and after Emancipation', *Economic History Review*, 26 (1973), 448–63.
73 Long, *op. cit.*, Vol. 2, p. 437.
74 *Ibid.*, p. 438.
75 See Appendix 1.
76 Lowell Joseph Ragatz, *The Fall of the Planter Class in the British Caribbean, 1763–1833* (New York, 1928), pp. 79, 214.

77 *Parliamentary Debates,* 2nd Series, Vol. 15, p. 511.
78 *Anti-Slavery Monthly Reporter,* Vol. 2 (1827), pp. 10–11.
79 See Table 48, p. 216.
80 J. Stewart, *op. cit.,* p. 234; *P.P.,* 1832 (127), Lords, Vol. 1, p. 3, but cf. p. 284.
81 Cf. Edward Brathwaite, *The Development of Creole Society in Jamaica, 1770–1820* (Oxford, 1971), p. 156.
82 R.R.S., Liber 133, f. 46.
83 Richard Sheridan, *The Development of the Plantations to 1750* (Barbados, 1970), p. 43.
84 Jingle, *op. cit.,* p. 45.
85 Philip D. Curtin, *The Image of Africa* (Madison, 1964), pp. 66–86; *Edinburgh Review,* 76 (1843), 422.
86 Thomson, *op. cit.,* p. 7; John Quier, *Letters and Essays on the Small-Pox and . . . Fevers of the West Indies* (London, 1778), p. xxxii.
87 Dancer, *op. cit.,* p. 21; Colin Chisholm, *A Manual of the Climate and Diseases, of Tropical Countries* (London, 1822), p. 6.
88 James Lind, *An Essay on Diseases Incidental to Europeans in Hot Climates* (London, 1788), pp. 133–5.
89 Quier, *op. cit.,* p. xx; Bernal, *op. cit.,* p. 7; James Grainger, *An Essay on the more Common West-India Diseases* (Edinburgh, 1802), p. 91.
90 Quier, *op. cit.,* p. xix.
91 Lind, *op. cit.,* p. 212; Long, *op. cit.,* Vol. 2, p. 211; *P.P.,* 1837–8, XL (138), *Statistical Report on the Sickness, Mortality, and Invaliding Among the Troops in the West Indies,* p. 465.
92 Edwards, *op. cit.,* Vol. 1, p. 18. Cf. Long, *op. cit.,* Vol. 1, p. 288.
93 Thomson, *op. cit.,* p. 167; W. J. Titford, *Sketches Towards a Hortus Botanicus Americanus* (London, 1812). For an example of the medicinal directions given, though without any data on the complaints, recovery or characteristics of the patients, see Harmony Hall Estate (Trelawny), Hospital Book, 1823–6 (Institute of Jamaica, Kingston).
94 *J.H.A.V.,* 1833, p. 407; *ibid.,* 1832, p. 280; *Jamaica Physical Journal,* 1 (1834), 222.
95 3 Will. IV c. 17. This Act was disallowed by the Crown in 1835 (*Jamaica Physical Journal,* 2 (1835), 215). For the list of practitioners, see *ibid.,* 1 (1834) 378. *See also J.H.A.V.,* 1826, p. 144; Moreton, *op. cit.,* p. 21.
96 Thomson, *op. cit.,* p. 8; *The Barbadian,* 5 September 1826, 'A Negro Sacrifice' (Jamaica).
97 G. J. A. Ojo, *Yoruba Culture* (London, 1966), p. 177; Melville J. Herskovits, *The Myth of the Negro Past* (New York, 1941), p. 239.
98 Brathwaite, *op. cit.,* p. 214; Patterson, *op. cit.,* p. 102; H. P. Jacobs, 'The Untapped Sources of Jamaican History', *Jamaican Historical Review,* 1 (1945), 93.
99 *Parliamentary Debates,* 1st Series, Vol. 2, pp. 658–9: 13 June 1804.
100 *P.P.,* 1832 (127), Lords, Vol. 1, pp. 159, 284; J. Stewart, *op. cit.,* p. 311.
101 Cf. review of James Clark's *The Sanative Influence of Climate* in *Edinburgh Review,* 76 (1843), 425.
102 Grainger, *op. cit.,* p. 13; *P.P.,* 1832 (721), p. 350.
103 Thomson, *op. cit.,* pp. 74–5, 120; *Further Proceedings, op. cit.,* p. 31.

104 Higman, *op. cit.*, pp. 530 and 540; *P.P.*, 1832 (721), p. 350.
105 Lind, *op. cit.*, p. 212; Alexander Barclay, *A Practical View of the Present State of Slavery in the West Indies* (London, 1826), p. 344. Cf. *P.P.*, 1837–8 (138), p. 522.
106 Thomson, *op. cit.*, p. 74.
107 *P.P.*, 1832 (721), p. 461. But Chisholm (*op. cit.*, p. 17), argued that the months July–September were the most unhealthy.
108 *P.P.*, 1837–8 (138), p. 471.
109 *J.H.A.V.*, 1831, p. 161. Cf. Brathwaite, *op. cit.*, p. 287.
110 Worthy Park Plantation Books, 1811–17 and 1830–37 (Jamaica Archives, Spanish Town). See also Quier, *op. cit.*, p. xxx; Thomson, *op. cit.*, p. 14; Hamilton Brown to George French, 10 November 1832, Tweedie Estate Records (Jamaica Archives, Spanish Town).
111 R.R.S., Liber 40, f. 84.
112 Minute Book of the Society for the Improvement of West India Plantership, 14 November 1812, p. 117.
113 Curtin, 'Epidemiology and the Slave Trade'.
114 *Ibid.*, pp. 215–16; Philip D. Curtin, *The Atlantic Slave Trade* (Madison, 1969), pp. 29–30.
115 Curtin, 'Epidemiology and the Slave Trade', p. 215.
116 Curtin, *Atlantic Slave Trade*, p. 29.
117 Craton, *op. cit.*, pp. 23–7.
118 See B. W. Higman, 'The Slave Populations of the British Caribbean: Some Nineteenth Century Variations', in Samuel R. Proctor (ed.), *Eighteenth Century Florida and the Caribbean* (Gainesville, 1976); *P.P.*, 1833, Vol. 26 (539), pp. 473–7; *P.P.*, 1835, Vol. 51 (235), p. 289.
119 See Jack E. Eblen, 'On the Natural Increase of Slave Populations: The Example of the Cuban Black Population, 1775–1900', in Stanley L. Engerman and Eugene D. Genovese (eds.), *Race and Slavery in the Western Hemisphere: Quantitative Studies* (Princeton, 1974).
120 Craton, *op. cit.*, pp. 15–27.
121 *P.P.*, 1833, Vol. 26 (700), *Slave Population.* (*Slave Registries*), p. 429; C.O. 28/86, Howell to Combermere, 31 October 1817.
122 Even in Demerara: see *P.P.*, 1833, Vol. 26 (700), p. 444.
123 Jay R. Mandle, *The Plantation Economy: Population and Economic Changes in Guyana, 1838–1960* (Philadelphia, 1973), pp. 47–55.

CHAPTER 7
COLOUR, FAMILY AND FERTILITY

1 See p. 101.
2 Winthrop D. Jordan, 'American Chiaroscuro: The Status and Definition of Mulattoes in the British Colonies', *William and Mary Quarterly*, 19 (1962), 183; *idem.*, *White Over Black* (Baltimore, 1969), p. 136.
3 Magnus Mörner, *Race Mixture in the History of Latin America* (Boston, 1967); H. Hoetink, *Slavery and Race Relations in the Americas* (New York, 1973); Edward Long, *The History of Jamaica* (London, 1774), Vol. 2, p. 261.

4 Some contemporaries said that people three degrees removed in lineal descent from Negro ancestors were legally white. See Long, *op. cit.*, Vol. 2, p. 261; M. G. Lewis, *Journal of a West India Proprietor* (London, 1834), p. 106; Robert Renny, *A History of Jamaica* (London, 1807), p. 188; J. M. Phillippo, *Jamaica: Its Past and Present State* (London, 1843), p. 144. Others said that not musteephinoes but their children by whites were legally white and free. See Bryan Edwards, *The History, Civil and Commercial, of the British Colonies in the West Indies* (London, 1793), Vol. 2, p. 16; R. Bickell, *The West Indies as they are* (London, 1825), p. 111. Some musteephinoes are recorded in the R.R.S. and are specifically distinguished from mustees: for example, R.R.S., Liber 127, f. 105. See also the rather confusing discussion in Edward Brathwaite, *The Development of Creole Society in Jamaica, 1770–1820* (Oxford, 1971), p. 168.

5 J. B. Moreton, *Manners and Customs in the West India Islands* (London, 1790), p. 123.

6 Lewis, *op. cit.*, p. 79.

7 R.R.S., Liber 129, f. 186; Liber 131, f. 112.

8 Cf. G. W. Roberts, *The Population of Jamaica* (Cambridge, 1957), p. 38.

9 In the parish of St. John, Barbados, 13.8 per cent of the slaves were coloured in 1834, whereas only 12.6 per cent of births 1832–4 and 7.4 per cent of deaths were coloured: T.71/558 (Public Record Office, London).

10 J. Stewart, *A View of the Past and Present State of the Island of Jamaica* (Edinburgh, 1823), pp. 35–6. Brathwaite, *op. cit.*, p. 168, arguing from Stewart's estimate of the free coloured (35,000), uses him to derive a slave coloured population of 15,000 in 1823. But this is obtained by subtracting the free coloured from a 'possible' 50,000 coloureds, the calculation of this total not being explained.

11 Gisela Eisner, *Jamaica: 1830–1930* (Manchester, 1961), pp. 129 and 152. For a more systematic attempt to estimate the size of the free coloured population see Gerad Tikasingh, *A Method for Estimating the Free Coloured Population of Jamaica* (University of the West Indies, History Department, Seminar Paper, 1968).

12 Sheila Duncker, 'The Free Coloured and their Fight for Civil Rights in Jamaica, 1800–30' (University of London, M.A. thesis, 1960), pp. 7–10. Duncker used the Port Royal R.R.S. for 1817 and 1826, and the St. David R.R.S. for 1820 and 1829, but how the percentages for the last three years, when only increases and decreases were listed, were calculated is not stated.

13 Brathwaite, *op. cit.*, p. 168.

14 Robert W. Fogel and Stanley L. Engerman, *Time on the Cross* (Boston, 1974), Vol. 1, p. 132. Cf. Richard C. Wade, *Slavery in the Cities* (New York, 1964), p. 124.

15 Cf. Brathwaite, *op. cit.*, p. 169.

16 Jordan, *White Over Black*, p. 175; N. A. T. Hall, 'Some Aspects of the Deficiency Question in Jamaica in the Eighteenth Century', *Jamaica Journal*, 7 (1973), 37.

17 Orlando Patterson, *The Sociology of Slavery* (London, 1967), pp. 42 and 159; Elsa V. Goveia, *Slave Society in the British Leeward Islands at the End*

of the Eighteenth Century (New Haven, 1965), p. 216.

18 *P.P.*, 1832 (127), Lords, Vol. 1, p. 109; Benjamin McMahon, *Jamaica Plantership* (London, 1839), p. 164; Moreton, *op. cit.*, p. 77.

19 *Ibid.*, p. 52.

20 *Ibid.*, p. 155.

21 *Jamaica Almanack*, 1845, Part 2, pp. 84–5.

22 Eisner, *op. cit.*, p. 127; Brathwaite, *op. cit.*, p. 105; Stewart, *op. cit.*, p. 36; W. L. Burn, *Emancipation and Apprenticeship in the British West Indies* (London, 1937) p. 27; R. Montgomery Martin, *History of the West Indies* (London, 1835), p. 91; *P.P.*, 1830, Vol. 21 (582), pp. 28–33.

23 Cf. Roberts, *op. cit.*, p. 50; *Jamaica Almanack*, 1845, Part 2, pp. 84–5; Douglas Hall, *Free Jamaica* (New Haven, 1959), pp. 210–12.

24 Cf. *P.P.*, 1832 (721), p. 352.

25 See Table A3.1.

26 Census, *Jamaica Almanack*, 1845, Part 2, pp. 84–5.

27 Martin, *op. cit.*, p. 91.

28 Tables A3.3 and A3.4; and Table 48.

29 Table A3.2.

30 Cf. Wade, *op. cit.*, p. 124.

31 *J.H.A.V.*, 1824, p. 94; Long, *op. cit.*, Vol. 2, p. 186; *P.P.*, 1832 (721), p. 27; Duncker, *op. cit.*, pp. 11, 15 and 88; Brathwaite, *op. cit.*, p. 169.

32 *P.P.*, 1830 (582), p. 31; cf. p. 29.

33 James Kelly, *Jamaica in 1831* (Belfast, 1838), pp. 28–9.

34 Moreton, *op. cit.*, p. 60.

35 *Ibid.*, p. 154; McMahon, *op. cit.*, p. 134.

36 Kelly, *op. cit.*, p. 34.

37 The variables excluded from the regression equation being X_3 (slave-holding size), X_8 (sex ratio, 1817), X_{21} (percentage deaths African, 1829–32), and X_{41} (livestock per slave).

38 Excluding X_{38}, R^2 falls to .76, and X_{27} to .60.

39 Only one coloured African was noted in the R.R.S., a sambo in Kingston: Liber 140, f. 41.

40 R.R.S., Liber 130, fos. 199–203. See also A.P., Liber 73, fos. 73 and 84; and A West Indian, *Notes in Defence of the Colonies* (Jamaica, 1826), pp. 12–13.

41 See B. W. Higman, 'Household Structure and Fertility on Jamaican Slave Plantations: A Nineteenth-Century Example', *Population Studies*, 27 (1973), 527–50.

42 Emily Dodd, at Old Montpelier.

43 Long, *op. cit.*, Vol. 2, p. 335; Lewis, *op. cit.*, p. 107.

44 Brathwaite, *op. cit.*, pp. 164–6.

45 Cf. Patterson, *op. cit.*, pp. 159–66; Lewis, *op. cit.*, p. 79; Walter Jekyll (ed.), *Jamaican Song and Story* (New York, 1966), pp. 176 and 183.

46 Lewis, *op. cit.*, pp. 63 and 78.

47 Brathwaite, *op. cit.*, p. 168.

48 Cf. Patterson, *op. cit.*, pp. 159–62; Edwin Lascelles, *Instructions for the Management of a Plantation in Barbadoes, and for the Treatment of Negroes* (London, 1786), p. 20; *A Report of a Committee of the Council of*

Barbadoes, Appointed to Inquire into the Actual Condition of the Slaves in this Island (London, 1824), pp. 104, 118; Fogel and Engerman, *op. cit.* Vol. 1., p. 133; Hoetink, *op. cit.*

49 See p. 176.

50 It must be recalled that these data include only *registered* births; there may have been differential infant mortality rates for black and coloured children which would distort the pattern of fertility.

51 Fogel and Engerman, *op. cit.,*

52 See p. 144.

53 A West Indian, *op. cit.,* p. 34; *Christian Observer,* 32 (1832), 368.

54 Patterson, *op. cit.,* pp. 9 and 167.

55 Winifred M. Cousins, 'Slave Family Life in the British Colonies, 1800–1834', *Sociological Review,* 27 (1935), 35–55; Goveia, *op. cit.,* p. 235; Edith Clarke, *My Mother Who Fathered Me* (London, 1966), p. 19; Michael Craton and James Walvin, *A Jamaican Plantation* (London, 1970), p. 125; Madeline Kerr, *Personality and Conflict in Jamaica* (London, 1952), p. 93.

56 Brathwaite, *op. cit.,* p. 204.

57 The remainder of this chapter draws heavily on my papers 'Household Structure and Fertility on Jamaican Slave Plantations: A Nineteenth-Century Example', *Population Studies,* 27 (1973), 527–50, and 'The Slave Family and Household in the British West Indies, 1800–1834', *Journal of Interdisciplinary History,* 6 (1975), 261–87.

58 For a discussion of the sources for Barbados and Trinidad, see Higman, 'Slave Family and Household'.

59 See pp. 94, 113, 116, 154.

60 Old Montpelier Estate, Account Book (Institute of Jamaica, Kingston).

61 Peter Laslett (ed.), *Household and Family in Past Time* (Cambridge, 1972), p. 36.

62 *P.P.,* 1832 (127), Lords, p. 88. The full report is printed at pp. 1376–93.

63 R.R.S., Liber 27, f. 37; Liber 30, ff. 42, 49; Liber 40, fos. 83–4; Liber 48, f. 163; Liber 66, fos. 159–60; Liber 75, f. 100; Liber 85, fos. 60–1; Liber 93, f. 33; Liber 96, f. 213; Liber 100, fos. 214–15; Liber 129, fos. 28, 32; Liber 130, f. 170.

64 See E. A. Wrigley (ed.), *An Introduction to English Historical Demography* (London, 1966).

65 St. James, Copy Register, Vol. 2: Baptisms, 17 July 1816 (Island Record Office, Spanish Town).

66 Old Montpelier Account Book.

67 Joseph Sturge and Thomas Harvey, *The West Indies in 1837* (London, 1838), p. 229; *Gentleman's Magazine,* Vol. 24 (1845), Part 2, p. 419.

68 *Parliamentary Debates,* Vol. 33, p. 257: 6 April 1797. See also Goveia, *op. cit.,* p. 33.

69 Minutes of the Missions Conference, 30 November 1831 (Moravian Church Archives, Malvern, Jamaica).

70 *P.P.,* 1832 (127), Lords, p. 90; Account Book.

71 James Hakewill, *A Picturesque Tour of the Island of Jamaica* (London, 1825), plate 19.

72 Account Book; A.P., Liber 51, fos. 87, 91, 92; Liber 62, f. 63, for example.

73 *P.P.*, 1832 (127), Lords, p. 1393.
74 Hakewill, *op. cit.*, plate 19.
75 See Chapters 4 and 9.
76 *P.P.*, 1832 (127), Lords, pp. 1391, 1393.
77 *A Report of Evidence Taken at Brown's-Town and St. Ann's Bay* (Falmouth, 1837), pp. 76–8.
78 For the significance of regional/tribal origins in Trinidad, see Higman, 'Slave Family and Household'.
79 St. James, Copy Register, Vol. 2: Marriages, 25 August 1825 (Island Record Office, Spanish Town).
80 Baptisms and Marriages of Slaves, St. James, 1827–8: Marriages, 23 December 1827 (Jamaica Archives, Spanish Town).
81 R.R.S., Liber 93, f. 33; Liber 85, f. 60.
82 List of Marriages at Fairfield, Manchester, 1829–40; Carmel Church Book, 1813–37; List of the Members of the Congregation at Fairfield arranged according to the estates on which they reside, October 12th, 1824 (Moravian Church Archives, Malvern, Jamaica).
83 See Oliver W. Furley, 'Moravian Missionaries and Slaves in the West Indies', *Caribbean Studies,* 5 (1965), 3–16; J. H. Buchner, *The Moravians in Jamaica* (London, 1854).
84 This excludes all cases in which one partner was free, or in which the owner of one or both of the slaves is not stated. The period covered extends to 31 July 1834.
85 Cf. Richard Pares, *Merchants and Planters* (Economic History Review Supplement, 1960), p. 39.
86 But the nominal linkage is more difficult than in the case of the Montpelier lists, because of the Moravians' habit of attaching new christian names to the slaves.
87 For a comparison with Barbados, see Higman, 'Slave Family and Household'.
88 *Ibid.,* for a comparison with Trinidad.
89 *Jamaica Almanack,* 1817 and 1818: Poll-tax givings-in.
90 See Higman, 'Slave Family and Household'.
91 Patterson, *op. cit.,* p. 167; M. G. Smith, 'Social Structure in the British Caribbean about 1820', *Social and Economic Studies,* 1 (1953), 72.
92 Anon., 'Hope Estate, in the parish of St. Andrew, Jamaica', *Jamaica Journal,* 1 (1818), 19.
93 Cf. Patterson, *op. cit.,* p. 54; Hakewill, *op. cit.,* plate 19; B. W. Higman, 'A Report on Excavations at Montpelier and Roehampton', *Jamaica Journal,* 8 (1974), 40–5.
94 See Jack Goody, *The Developmental Cycle in Domestic Groups* (Cambridge, 1958).
95 Patterson, *op. cit.,* pp. 165–6.
96 A West Indian, *op. cit.*, p. 28. Cf. Fogel and Engerman, *op. cit.*
97 Patterson, *op. cit.*, pp. 159–70.
98 Higman, 'Slave Family and Household'; G. Debien, *Destinées d'Esclaves à la Martinique (1746–1778)* (Dakar, 1960), p. 45; Fogel and Engerman, *op. cit.,* Vol. 1, pp. 126–44.

99 See p. 48.
100 The age-specific fertility rates for 1817–25 become 89 (Types 1 and 4) and 83 (Types 3, 11 and 13). For 1825–32 these rates are 50 and 97, respectively.
101 Cf. Alfred Owen Aldridge, 'Population and Polygamy in Eighteenth-Century Thought', *Journal of the History of Medicine,* 4 (1949), 129–48; Geoffrey Hawthorn, *The Sociology of Fertility* (London, 1970), p. 32. The general results reported here are very similar to those found for late eighteenth-century Martinique by Debien, *op. cit.,* p. 58.

CHAPTER 8
MANUMISSIONS, RUNAWAYS AND CONVICTS

1 T. H. Hollingsworth, *Historical Demography* (London, 1969), pp. 105, 199–224; Michael Craton, 'Jamaican Slave Mortality: Fresh Light from Worthy Park, Longville and the Tharp Estates', *Journal of Caribbean History,* 3 (1971), 1–3.
2 The figures in Table 39 are derived from the R.R.S. A list of manumissions 1829–32 is also found in T.71/680, Bundle 14, 'Summary of the Number &c. of slaves in the various parishes of Jamaica'. These figures generally agree with those in Table 39, except that the total is 1,279, compared to 1,363.
3 T.71/683, Bundle 9.
4 See Table A3.1.
5 Edward Long, *The History of Jamaica* (London, 1774), Vol. 2, p. 322; R.R.S., Liber 140, f. 137.
6 The printed statistics are contradictory, as noted in Gisela Eisner, *Jamaica, 1830–1930* (Manchester, 1961), pp. 129–31. Cf. *P.P.,* 1832 (127), Lords, Vol. 2, p. 1394, and *P.P.,* 1833 (539), p. 474. The latter table is reprinted in Eisner.
7 Cf. Craton, *op. cit.,* p. 4.
8 R.R.S., Liber 136 (1829–32).
9 Manumissions, Liber 66, fos. 42–62, for example (Jamaica Archives, Spanish Town).
10 *P.P.,* 1832 (127), Lords, Vol. 1, pp. 24, 581. Cf. Eisner, *op. cit.,* p. 129; Orlando Patterson, *The Sociology of Slavery* (London, 1967), p. 91; Elsa V. Goveia, *Slave Society in the British Leeward Islands at the End of the Eighteenth Century* (London, 1965), p. 230.
11 Matthew Gregory Lewis, *Journal of a West India Proprietor* (London, 1834), p. 109; Edward Brathwaite, *The Development of Creole Society in Jamaica, 1770–1820* (Oxford, 1971), p. 204; Gerald W. Mullin, *Flight and Rebellion. Slave Resistance in Eighteenth-Century Virginia* (New York, 1972).
12 Brathwaite, *op. cit.,* p. 201; Patterson, *op. cit.,* p. 262; *J.H.A.V.,* 1824, pp. 189, 247.
13 T.71/851; and see Table A3.16.
14 Cf. Brathwaite, *op. cit.,* pp. 201–2.
15 The mean ages shown in Table 40 may in fact be understated, since it is difficult to be certain whether the ages given in the R.R.S. relate to the slave's age in 1832 or at the date of running away.
16 *P.P.,* 1832 (721), p. 175; *P.P.,* 1832 (127), Lords, Vol. 1, p. 610.

17 New Forest Plantation Book, 1828–97 (Institute of Jamaica, Kingston); Manchester Vestry Minutes, 11 April 1832, pp. 183–96 (Jamaica Archives, Spanish Town); R.R.S., Liber 19, f. 58; Liber 129, f. 204.
18 New Forest Plantation Book.
19 Cf. Alexander Barclay, *A Practical View of the Present State of Slavery in the West Indies* (London, 1826), p. 56.
20 Cf. U. B. Phillips, 'A Jamaica Slave Plantation', *American Historical Review,* 19 (1914), 555.
21 *J.H.A.V.,* 1831, p. 96; *P.P.,* 1831–2 (660), p. 62.
22 *P.P.,* 1832 (127), Lords, Vol. 1, p. 60.
23 Fifteen from St. Elizabeth, eleven from Trelawny, and nine from St. James (T.71/680, Bundle 14).
24 Minutes of Meetings of the Slave Court, St. Ann's Bay, 1787–1814, p. 267 (Institute of Jamaica, Kingston).
25 *J.H.A.V.,* 1825, p. 381.
26 Patterson, *op. cit.,* p. 262.
27 *P.P.,* 1831–2 (660), p. 64.
28 *J.H.A.V.,* 1825, p. 373.
29 Minutes of Meetings of the Slave Court, St. Ann's Bay, pp. 268, 378.
30 *P.P.,* 1832 (127), Lords, Vol. 1, p. 624.

CHAPTER 9
ORGANIZATION OF SLAVE LABOUR

1 See Robert W. Fogel and Stanley L. Engerman, *Time on the Cross: The Economics of American Negro Slavery* (Boston, 1974), Vol. 1, p. 209; Alfred H. Conrad and John R. Meyer, *Studies in Econometric History* (London, 1965). Cf. Elsa V. Goveia, *Slave Society in the British Leeward Islands at the End of the Eighteenth Century* (New Haven, 1965); p. 329; M. G. Smith, 'Some Aspects of Social Structure in the British Caribbean about 1820', *Social and Economic Studies,* 1 (1953), 78.
2 Stanley L. Engerman, 'Some Considerations Relating to Property Rights in Man', *Journal of Economic History,* 33 (1973), 43–65; Robert W. Fogel and Stanley L. Engerman, 'The Relative Efficiency of Slavery: A Comparison of Northern and Southern Agriculture in 1860', *Explorations in Economic History,* 8 (1971), 353–67.
3 Engerman, 'Some Considerations', p. 46.
4 D. G. Hall, 'The Social and Economic Background to Sugar in Slave Days', *Caribbean Historical Review,* Nos. 3–4 (1954), p. 168.
5 See R. Keith Aufhauser, 'Slavery and Scientific Management', *Journal of Economic History,* 33 (1973), 811–24; W. A. Green, 'The Planter Class and British West Indian Sugar Production before and after Emancipation', *Economic History Review,* 26 (1973), 448–63.
6 Edwin Lascelles, *et. al., Instructions for the Management of a Plantation in Barbadoes, and for the Treatment of Negroes* (London, 1786), p. 22.
7 Thomas Roughley, *The Jamaica Planter's Guide; or, a System for Planting and Managing a Sugar Estate, or other Plantations . . .* (London, 1823), pp. 97–119.

8 *Ibid.*, p. 61.
9 *P.P.*, 1832 (127), Lords, p. 36; *P.P.*, 1832 (721), p. 336.
10 Minute Book of the Society for the improvement of West India plantership, 1811–12 and of the Agricultural Society, 1812–16: 14 November 1812, pp. 132–3.
11 *J.H.A.V.*, 1833, p. 489.
12 See Chapters 3 and 4.
13 Fogel and Engerman, *Time on the Cross,* Vol. 1, p. 74.
14 A.P., Liber 73, f. 229; Inventories, Liber 129, f. 205 (inventory taken 7 January 1818); R.R.S., Liber 20, f. 84 (return of 28 June 1817).
15 A.P., Liber 73, f. 68; Inventories, Liber 130, f. 67 (19 March 1818); R.R.S., Liber 5, f. 6 (28 June 1817). Additional age-value profiles, not presented here, were constructed from: Inventories, Liber 130, f. 189 and R.R.S., Liber 26, f. 180; and Inventories, Liber 130, f. 35 and R.R.S., Liber 13, f. 229.
16 J. F. Barham, *Considerations on the Abolition of Negro Slavery* (London, 1823), p. 80. Cf. William Dickson, *Mitigation of Slavery* (London, 1814), pp. 195–205.
17 R.R.S., Liber 129, f. 40; A.P., Liber 62, f. 116; Liber 72, f. 180; Rose Hall Journal, 1817–32, Vol. 2 (Jamaica Archives, Spanish Town); Joseph Shore and John Stewart, *In Old St. James* (Kingston, 1911), pp. 140–51.
18 Cf. Orlando Patterson, *The Sociology of Slavery* (London, 1967), p. 61; Michael Craton and James Walvin, *A Jamaican Plantation: A History of Worthy Park, 1670–1970* (London, 1970), p. 138; Richard Pares, *A West-India Fortune* (London, 1950), p. 129.
19 Patterson, *op. cit.*, p. 61, sees 'a marked degree of interchangeability in the different occupations'. But in his sample (Green Park Estate, Trelawny, 6–10 January 1823) the only clear shifts were between the first and second gangs, since the total number of slaves was different on each day (500, 510, 518, 517, 514), perhaps a result of the hiring of jobbing gangs.
20 Rose Hall Journal, Vol. 2, 6–12 February 1832.
21 *D.N.B.; Gentleman's Magazine,* 27 (1847), 422; D. J. Murray, *The West Indies and the Development of Colonial Government, 1801–1834* (Oxford, 1965), p. 191.
22 R.R.S., Liber 131, f. 103; A.P., Liber 73, f. 61.
23 Maryland Estate Book, 1817–25: List of slaves as at 1 January 1822 (Institute of Jamaica, Kingston).
24 R.R.S., Liber 126, f. 172; A.P., Liber 73, f. 38.
25 List of Slaves and Stock on Irwin Estate, 1820 to 1827: 28 December 1821 (Institute of Jamaica, Kingston).
26 Cf. Edward Brathwaite, *The Development of Creole Society in Jamaica, 1770–1820* (Oxford, 1971), p. 155.
27 Old Montpelier Estate Account Book (Institute of Jamaica, Kingston); and see p. 161.
28 *J.H.A.V.*, 1833, p. 492.
29 *P.P.*, 1832 (721), p. 43: evidence of William Taylor. See also A West Indian, *Notes in Defence of the Colonies. On the Increase and Decrease of the Slave Population of the British West Indies* (Jamaica, 1826), p. 13.
30 *J.H.A.V.*, 1825, p. 59.

31 Hermitage Estate Letterbook, 1819–24: W. Adlam to J. Wemyss, 18 February 1822 (Institute of Jamaica, Kingston). See also Matthew Gregory Lewis, *Journal of a West India Proprietor* (London, 1834), pp. 76, 96 and 200.
32 Cf. Brathwaite, *op. cit.*, p. 154.
33 See Figures 33–36.
34 Inventories, Liber 110, f. 117; Liber 148, f. 36.
35 Inventories, Liber 149, f. 174. See also Masters Estate, *ibid.*, f. 178.
36 *J.H.A.V.*, 1833, p. 489: evidence of William Miller.
37 Georgia Estate, Letterbooks and Accounts, 1805–35, Vol. 3: C. Scott to R. Alston, 27 April 1833; J. Mackenzie to R. Alston, 7 February 1830 and 13 March 1831 (Institute of Jamaica, Kingston).
38 Hermitage Letterbook: W. Adlam to J. Wemyss, 7 December 1819.
39 *Parliamentary Debates*, 1st Series, Vol. 11, p. 506: 23 May 1808: Barham.
40 *J.H.A.V.*, 1804, p. 95.
41 Jamaica Assembly, *Journals*, 14 (1822), 72.
42 Alexander Barclay, *A Practical View of the Present State of Slavery in the West Indies* (London, 1826), p. 339. See also A West Indian, *op. cit.*, p. 19.
43 *J.H.A.V.*, 1804, p. 94; also *P.P.*, X, 1805 (39), p. 653.
44 See Table A3.11.
45 James Thomson, *A Treatise on the Diseases of Negroes* (Jamaica, 1820), p. 112. Cf. H. T. De la Beche, *Notes on the Present Condition of the Negroes in Jamaica* (London, 1825), p. 12.
46 Roughley, *op. cit.*, p. 102; Dr. Collins, *Practical Rules for the Management and Medical Treatment of Negro Slaves in the Sugar Colonies* (London, 1803), p. 116; Patterson, *op. cit.*, p. 155; Minute Book of the Society for the improvement of West India plantership, 14 November 1812, p. 119.
47 Barham, *op. cit.*, p. 79; *P.P.*, 1830–1 (120), p. 521: evidence of Hibbert. Cf. Fogel and Engerman, *Time on the Cross*, Vol. 1, p. 74, who find that in the Old South average net earnings were positive from age nine.
48 R. Bickell, *The West Indies as they are* (London, 1825), p. 36.
49 *Ibid.*, p. 32; Barclay, *op. cit.*, p. 282. Cf. Edward Long, *The History of Jamaica* (London, 1774), Vol. 2, p. 322.
50 Hermitage Letterbook: W. Adlam to J. Wemyss, 1 February 1820.
51 Collins, *op. cit.*, p. 153.
52 Barclay, *op. cit.*, p. 310.
53 Worthy Park Plantation Book, 1830–1837 (Jamaica Archives, Spanish Town); Craton and Walvin, *op. cit.*, p. 138. The 1789 list is printed in full in Brathwaite, *op. cit.*, p. 321. Craton and Walvin underestimate the size of the male field labour force since they make no allowance for the 15 men with dual occupations (those listed as 'field and distiller' or 'field and wainman', for example), finding a total of only 29.
54 Craton and Walvin, *op. cit.*, p. 172.
55 Worthy Park Plantation Book, 1830–37.
56 Goveia, *op. cit.*, pp. 231, 317; Patterson, *op. cit.*, pp. 59–64; Brathwaite, *op. cit.*, p. 174.
57 Smith, *op. cit.*, p. 65.
58 Lewis, *op. cit.*, p. 107; J. B. Moreton, *Manners and Customs in the West India Islands* (London, 1790), p. 123; Theodore Foulks, *Eighteen Months in*

Jamaica (Bristol, 1833), p. 26; Cynric R. Williams, *A Tour Through the Island of Jamaica* (London, 1827), p. 53. Cf. Frederic C. Cassidy, *Jamaica Talk* (London, 1961), p. 171; David Brion Davis, *The Problem of Slavery in Western Culture* (New York, 1966), p. 274; Goveia, *op. cit.,* p. 317.

59 *P.P.,* 1832 (127), Lords, p. 36.
60 *J.H.A.V.,* 1814, pp. 57–8.
61 *Ibid.,* p. 80.
62 *J.H.A.V.,* 1831, p. 350.
63 *J.H.A.V.,* 1821, p. 55.
64 2 Geo. IV (Private Act).
65 *J.H.A.V.,* 1832, pp. 141–2.
66 R.R.S., Liber 120, f. 134.
67 5 Geo. IV c. 21, 'An Act for removing impediments to the manumission of slaves by owners, having only a limited interest'; 1 Will. IV c. 23, 'An Act for the government of slaves', ss. 68–74, passed in 1824 and 1831 respectively.
68 Georgia Estate Letterbook, Vol. 3: C. Scott to R. Alston, 6 July 1833.
69 R.R.S., Liber 137, f. 118.
70 Lewis, *op. cit.,* p. 76.
71 Hermitage Letterbook: W. Adlam to J. Wemyss, 1 February 1820, 29 August 1820 and 30 April 1821.
72 Worthy Park Plantation Book, 1811–17, p. 250.
73 *Ibid.*
74 Craton and Walvin, *op. cit.,* p. 139.
75 Worthy Park Plantation Book, 1830–37.
76 Old Montpelier Estate Account Book. At Rose Hall, the two female slaves of colour in the field were samboes; at Maryland there was a sambo boy in the field: see p. 197.
77 Thomas Dancer, *The Medical Assistant; or Jamaica Practice of Physic* (Kingston, 1801), p. 17.
78 Goveia, *op. cit.,* p. 111, for example.
79 See p. 129.
80 F. W. Pitman, 'Slavery on British West India Plantations in the Eighteenth Century', *Journal of Negro History,* 11 (1926), 587.
81 Lowell Joseph Ragatz, *The Fall of the Planter Class in the British Caribbean, 1763–1833* (New York, 1928), p. 27. Cf. Patterson's analysis of the 'Quashee' personality type, *op. cit.,* pp. 174–81.
82 Collins, *op. cit.,* p. 196.
83 Georgia Estate Letterbook, Vol. 3: C. Scott to R. Alston, 6 July 1833; Hermitage Letterbook: W. Adlam to J. Wemyss, 17 December 1819.
84 Long, *op. cit.,* Vol. 2, pp. 404–11.
85 Shore and Stewart, *op. cit.,* pp. 140–51.
86 See p. 180.

CHAPTER 10
LEVELS OF PRODUCTIVITY

1 See discussion of these issues in Chapter 1.
2 See Lowell Joseph Ragatz, *The Fall of the Planter Class in the British Carib-*

bean, 1763–1833 (New York, 1928); Eric Williams, *Capitalism and Slavery* (London, 1964); Roger T. Anstey, 'Capitalism and Slavery: A Critique', *Economic History Review,* 21 (1968), 307–20.

3 Orlando Patterson, *The Sociology of Slavery* (London, 1967), pp. 33–51; Elsa V. Goveia, *Slave Society in the British Leeward Islands at the End of the Eighteenth Century* (New Haven, 1965), p. 329; L. J. Ragatz, 'Absentee Landlordism in the Briitsh Caribbean, 1750–1833', *Agricultural History,* 5 (1931), 7–24. But cf. Douglas Hall, 'Absentee-Proprietorship in the British West Indies to about 1850', *Jamaican Historical Review,* 4 (1964), 15–35; W. A. Green, 'The Planter Class and British West Indian Sugar Production, before and after Emancipation', *Economic History Review,* 26 (1973), 448–63; R. Keith Aufhauser, 'Profitability of Slavery in the British Caribbean', *Journal of Interdisciplinary History,* 5 (1974), 45–67.

4 Herman Merivale, *Lectures on Colonization and Colonies* (London, 1928), p. 303; Williams, *op. cit.,* p. 6; Goveia, *op. cit.,* pp. 146–51.

5 Customs 12/1 (Public Record Office, London); *J.H.A.V.,* 1834, p. 143.

6 The export data are found in Noel Deerr, *The History of Sugar* (London, 1949), Vol. 1, p. 198; Gisela Eisner, *Jamaica, 1830–1930* (Manchester, 1961), p. 240; Patterson, *op. cit.,* p. 294 (taking account of the error in dating 1810–30 in this source). The data for sugar are in tons, and for coffee in lbs.; those for the other crops have been converted using standard weights, as follows: *Rum:* puncheon equals 115 gallons, hogshead equals 57.5 gallons, cask equals 40 gallons, barrel equals 10 gallons; *Molasses:* cask equals 72 gallons; *Pimento:* cask equals 200 lbs., bag equals 115 lbs.; *Ginger:* cask equals 450 lbs.; bag equals 70 lbs. The 1832 values attributed to the standard weights are: *Sugar,* £29.12 per ton; *Rum,* £121.74 per 1,000 gallons; *Molasses,* £54.55 per 1,000 gallons; *Coffee,* £44.71 per 1,000 lbs.; Pimento, £30.00 per 1,000 lbs.; *Ginger,* £37.14 per 1,000 lbs. (See Appendix 1.) The slave population 1800–16 is based on the poll-tax givings-in inflated by 10 per cent to approximate the R.R.S. populations (p. 60).

7 See Table 3.

8 See Figure 10.

9 Ragatz, *Fall of the Planter Class,* pp. 79 and 214; Green, *op. cit.,* p. 454; Richard Pares, *A West-India Fortune* (London, 1950), p. 110.

10 Douglas Hall, *Free Jamaica* (New Haven, 1959), p. 69; Green, *op. cit.,* p. 452; Ragatz, *Fall of the Planter Class,* p. 61. See also Edward Brathwaite, *The Development of Creole Society in Jamaica, 1770–1820* (Oxford, 1971), p. 82.

11 See p. 14.

12 Eisner, *op. cit.,* pp. 289, 375. Converted to currency and 1832 prices (£15.6 sterling at 1910 prices).

13 See p. 18.

14 Natural increase is not included in the regression analysis (Table 49) because it is a function of the birth and death rates and thus cannot contribute to the explanation of the dependent variable.

15 For example, Copse Estate, Hanover (£30.32 per slave): A.P., Liber 74, f. 27; *Jamaica Almanack,* 1832, p. 151.

16 Brathwaite, *op. cit.,* pp. 86 and 146.

17 See p. 20.
18 *P.P.*, 1832 (127), Lords, Vol. 1, p. 95.
19 See p. 79.
20 *Further Proceedings of the Honourable House of Assembly of Jamaica, . . .* (London, 1816), pp. 34–5 and 67; Letters of Members of the King Family in Jamaica: Louisa M. King to Mrs. Bryan King, 15 October 1815 (Institute of Jamaica, Kingston).
21 *J.H.A.V.*, 1847, p. 373, for a list.
22 See p. 25.
23 See p. 30.
24 Ward Barrett, 'Caribbean Sugar-Production Standards in the Seventeenth and Eighteenth Centuries', in John Parker (ed.), *Merchants and Scholars* (Minneapolis, 1965), pp. 164–7.
25 Richard Pares, *Merchants and Planters* (Economic History Review Supplement, 1960), p. 25.
26 *J.H.A.V.*, 1804, p. 95.
27 *P.P.*, 1832 (127), Lords, Vol. 1, p. 133.
28 *Further Proceedings*, p. 32.
29 Around 1790, slaves on Jamaica sugar estates produced an average 1,300 lbs. of muscovado per annum (Barrett, *op. cit.*, p. 167); by 1832 they produced roughly 1,600 lbs. but it is difficult to determine how much of this increase should be attributed to the introduction of the Otaheite cane.
30 Matthew Gregory Lewis, *Journal of a West India Proprietor* (London, 1834), p. 95.
31 *Further Proceedings*, p. 35.
32 *Ibid.*, pp. 36 and 99–100.
33 See Tables 8 and 15.
34 See Table A3.2.
35 See p. 29.
36 Georgia Estate Letterbook, Vol. 3: R. Alston to C. Scott, 29 October 1832 (Institute of Jamaica, Kingston).
37 *P.P.*, 1832 (127), Lords, Vol. 1, p. 585; *P.P.*, 1835 (278), pp. 224–40.
38 A.P., Liber 51, f. 199; Liber 55, f. 141; Liber 60, f. 105; Liber 64, f. 225; Liber 69, f. 94; Liber 73, f. 43.
39 *P.P.*, 1832 (721), p. 7: evidence of William Taylor.
40 *P.P.*, 1832 (721), p. 349.
41 *Jamaica Almanacks*, 1816–33; *J.H.A.V.*, 1833, p. 48; 1 Will. IV c. 23.
42 See pp. 193–201.
43 Lewis, *op. cit.*, p. 199–200.
44 *P.P.*, 1832 (721), p. 7: evidence of William Taylor.
45 Letters of Members of the King Family: E. B. Forbes to Mrs. King, 2 September 1824; Brathwaite, *op. cit.*, p. 160; Appendix 1.

CHAPTER 11
OVERSEER DAY DONE?

1 Mary Reckord, 'The Jamaica Slave Rebellion of 1831', *Past and Present*, No. 40 (1968), 108–25; Orlando Patterson, *The Sociology of Slavery* (Lon-

don, 1967), p. 273. The statistics of the number shot and executed are inconsistent; see also T.71/680, Bundle 14.

2 Orlando Patterson, 'Slavery and Slave Revolts: A Socio-Historical Analysis of the First Maroon War, Jamaica, 1655–1740', *Social and Economic Studies,* 19 (1970), 289–325.

3 Monica Schuler, 'Akan Slave Rebellions in the British Caribbean', *Savacou,* 1 (1970), 26. Cf. Gerald W. Mullin, *Flight and Rebellion. Slave Resistance in Eighteenth-Century Virginia* (New York, 1972).

4 *J.H.A.V.,* 1832, p. 2. See also *P.P.,* 1831–2 (561), p. 183.

5 Tweedie Estate Records: Hamilton Brown to George French, 10 May 1832 (Jamaica Archives, Spanish Town). For Brown, see H. P. Jacobs, *Sixty Years of Change, 1806–1866* (Kingston, 1973), p. 60.

6 *P.P.,* 1832 (127), Lords, Vol. 1, pp. 24–5.

7 R.R.S., Liber 129, f. 6.

8 *P.P.,* 1832 (127), Lords, Vol. 1, pp. 39 and 89.

9 The following analysis is based on the data described in Chapter 7, p. 156.

10 Georgia Estate Letterbook: J. Mackenzie to R. Alston, 15 January 1832 (Institute of Jamaica, Kingston).

11 R.R.S., Liber 137, fos. 11, 123, 128, 147, 158, 173.

12 Cf. Reckford, *op. cit.*

13 T.71/680, Bundle 14, lists 175 males and 25 females shot, and 214 males but no females executed, in nine parishes.

14 See Theodore Foulks, *Eighteen Months in Jamaica; with Recollections of the Late Rebellion* (Bristol, 1833), pp. 92–4; Reckord, *op. cit.*

15 Foulks, *op. cit.,* p. 77: Order of 1 January 1832.

16 R. B. Sheridan, 'The West India Sugar Crisis and British Slave Emancipation', *Journal of Economic History,* 21 (1961), 542.

17 *J.H.A.V.,* 1832, p. 21.

18 B. W. Higman, 'The West India Interest in Parliament, 1807–1833', *Historical Studies,* 13 (1967), 1–19. See also Douglas Hall, *A Brief History of the West India Committee* (Barbados, 1971), p. 9; Roger Anstey, 'A Reinterpretation of the Abolition of the British Slave Trade, 1806–1807', *English Historical Review,* 87 (1972), pp. 324 and 331.

19 *J.H.A.V.,* 1833, p. 295.

20 Writing to Zachary Macaulay, 10 August 1832: Viscountess Knutsford, *Life and Letters of Zachary Macaulay* (London, 1900), p. 469.

21 D. J. Murray, *The West Indies and the Development of Colonial Government, 1801–1834* (Oxford, 1965), p. 203.

22 *J.H.A.V.,* 1833, pp. 295–6.

23 *Parliamentary Debates,* 1st Series, Vol. 28, p. 803: 20 July 1814.

24 James Stephen, *Essays in Ecclesiastical Biography* (London, 1883), p. 547.

APPENDIX 1
WEIGHTS, MEASURES AND VALUES, 1832

1 *P.P.,* 1832 (721), p. 307: evidence of W. A. Hankey.

2 A.P., Liber 72, f. 201; Liber 73, fos. 5, 60, 63, 84, 127; Liber 74, f. 34; Ac-

counts Current, Liber 31, fos. 56, 182 (Jamaica Archives, Spanish Town); Paisley and Windsor Lodge, Account Books, 1813–37, Vol. 3, f. 181 (Institute of Jamaica, Kingston).

3 *Ibid.*, f. 181; Accounts Current, Liber 31, fos. 56, 182.

4 Established by a Jamaica law of 1852. Douglas Hall, *Free Jamaica* (New Haven, 1959), p. 282.

5 L. J. Ragatz, *The Fall of the Planter Class in the British Caribbean, 1763–1833* (New York, 1928), p. 495.

6 *P.P.*, 1856, LV (209), pp. 3–4.

7 A.P., Liber 72, f. 201; Liber 73, fos. 60, 63, 127; Liber 74, f. 34. See also *St. Jago de la Vega Gazette*, 25 February, and 3 and 24 March 1832.

8 Accounts Current, Liber 31, f. 182; Paisley and Windsor Lodge, Account Books, Vol. 3, f. 181.

9 Douglas Hall, 'Incalculability as a Feature of Sugar Production during the Eighteenth Century', *Social and Economic Studies*, 10 (1961), 346.

10 Accounts Current, Liber 31, f. 56; Gisela Eisner, *Jamaica, 1830–1930* (London, 1961), p. 244.

11 Cf. *St. Jago de la Vega Gazette*, 18 February and 18 August 1832.

12 Eisner, *op. cit.*, p. 244.

13 A.P., Liber 73, f. 266; Liber 74, fos. 12, 29.

14 Journal of Benjamin Scott Moncrieffe (St. Ann), 1828–40, pp. 3, 9, 40, 55, 137 (Jamaica Archives, Spanish Town).

15 Bryan Edwards, *The History, Civil and Commercial, of the British Colonies in the West Indies* (London, 1794), Vol. 1, p. 303.

BIBLIOGRAPHY

1. MANUSCRIPTS

Jamaica Archives, Spanish Town

Accounts Current
Accounts Produce
Braco Estate Journal, 1795–7
Despatches, Jamaica to England
Drogging Bonds
Inventories
Journal of Benjamin Scott Moncrieffe (St. Ann), planter, attorney, and horse-owner, 1828–40; Account Book
Kingston, Parish and Poll Tax Rolls
Letters of Administration
Manchester, Parish Register, Vol. 1: Baptisms, 1816–26; Marriages, 1820–6; Burials, 1817–25
Manchester, Vestry Minutes
Manumissions
Pantrepant Estate Journal, 1834–5
Register of Baptisms, Wesley Chapel, Kingston, 1829–1902
Register of Marriages, Spanish Town, 1829–40 [Methodist]
Returns of Registrations of Slaves
Rose Hall Journal, 1817–32
St. James, Baptisms and Marriages of Slaves, 1827–8
Tweedie Estate Records
Worthy Park Estate, Plantation Books, 1811–17, 1830–7; Thetford Plantation Book, 1821–33
Writs of Dedimus to Administrators

Island Record Office, Spanish Town

St. James, Copy Register, Vol. 2: Baptisms, Marriages and Burials, 1810–25

Institute of Jamaica, Kingston

Georgia Estate, St. Thomas, Letterbooks and Accounts, 1805–35
Harmony Hall Estate, Trelawny, Hospital Book, 1823–6
Hermitage Estate, St. Elizabeth, Letterbook, 1819–24

Jingle, Jack, 'The Omnibus or Jamaica Scrap Book', [c. 1824]
Letters from Members of the King Family in Jamaica to Mrs. Bryan King in the United States, 1812–33 (Photocopy; Original in York County Historical Society, Pennsylvania)
List of Slaves and Stock on Irwin Estate, 1820 to 1827
Maryland Estate Book, 1817–25
Minutes of Meetings of the Slave Court, St. Ann's Bay, 1787–1814
New Forest Plantation Book, 1828-97
Old Montpelier Estate, Account Book, 1824–8
Paisley and Windsor Lodge, Account Books, 1813–38
Radnor Plantation Journal, 1822–6

Moravian Church Archives, Malvern, Jamaica

Carmel Church Book, 1813–37
Carmel, Diary, 1805–19
List of Marriages at Fairfield, Manchester, 1829–40
List of the Members of the Congregation at Fairfield arranged according to the Estates on which they reside, October 12th 1824
Minutes of Conference, Mesopotamia, 1798–1818
Minutes of the Missions Conference, June 1831–December 1833

University of the West Indies, Mona, Jamaica

Minute Book of the Society for the improvement of West India plantership, 1811–12 and of the Agricultural Society, 1812–16 [Barbados], (Microfilm; original at the University of Keele Library)

Public Record Office, London

T.71, Slave Registration and Compensation Records
C.O. 137, 138, 295, Despatches
Customs, 12/1

Library of Congress, Washington

Worthy Park Plantation, Jamaica, Plantation Book, 1791–1811

2. OFFICIAL PUBLICATIONS

British Parliamentary Papers

1803–4, X (119), *Papers presented to the House of Commons on the 7th May 1804, respecting the Slave-Trade*
1805, X (39) *Papers and correspondence re abolition*
1807, III (65), *Report from the committee on the commercial state of the West India colonies*
1808, XVII (178, 278, 300, 318), *Four reports from the select committee on the expediency of confining the distillation to the use of sugar and molasses only: and on relief to the growers of sugar in the West India colonies*
1830, XXI (582), *Return from slave colonies belonging to the Crown, of the population, distinguished into white, free black and coloured, and slaves;*

from 1st January 1825, and continued to the latest period
1830–1, IX (120), *Statements, calculations, and explanations submitted to the Board of Trade, relating to the commercial, financial, and political state of the British West India colonies*
1831–2, XX (381), *Report from select committee on the commercial state of the West India colonies*
1831–2, XLVII, (561), *Report of Jamaica House of Assembly, on cause of, and injury sustained in the recent rebellion*
1831–2, XLVII (660), *Slave population. (Extracts from returns relating to . . .)*
1832, XX (721), *Report from select commitee on the extinction of slavery throughout the British Dominions: with the minutes of evidence*
1832, (127), House of Lords, *Report from the select committee on the state of the West India colonies; together with the minutes of evidence*
1833, XXVI (539), *Slave registration. (Jamaica)*
1835, L (278 – II), *Papers on the abolition of slavery*
1837–8, XL (138), *Statistical report on the sickness, mortality, and invaliding among the troops in the West Indies*
1847–8, XXIII (206), *Select committee on sugar and coffee planting: Fifth report*

Jamaica

Claims for Compensation. Filed with the Assistant Commissioners for Jamaica, n.d., no place of publication
Jamaica, House of Assembly, Journals
Jamaica, House of Assembly, Votes
Laws of Jamaica

3. MAPS

Harrison, Thomas, Cadastral Survey of Jamaica, 1866–91 (Institute of Jamaica)
Kapp, Kit S., *The Printed Maps of Jamaica up to 1825* (Kingston, 1968)
Liddell, Colin, *Map of Jamaica prepared from the best authorities* (Kingston, 1888)
Morris, Cunninghame and Woolridge, *A Plan of the Parish of St. James, together with a part of the parishes of Hanover, Westmoreland and St. Elizabeth . . . shewing the District and Properties therein Destroyed during the late Rebellion* (London, 1832)
Robertson, James, *Map of the County of Cornwall (and Middlesex and Surrey), in the island of Jamaica, constructed from actual surveys, under the authority of the Hon. House of Assembly* (London, 1804)

4. PRINTED PRIMARY SOURCES

Anon., *The Contrast, as exemplified in the Lives of Mary & Hagar, two field Negroes* (St. Johns, Antigua, 1817)
Anon., *Memoir of the late William Wright, M.D., with Extracts from his Correspondence, and a Selection of his Papers on Medical and Botanical Subjects* (Edinburgh, 1828)
Anti-Slavery Reporter (London, 1827)

A West Indian, *Notes in Defence of the Colonies. On the Increase and Decrease of the Slave Population of the British West Indies* (Jamaica, 1826)

Barclay, Alexander, *A Practical View of the Present State of Slavery in the West Indies: or, an examination of Mr. Stephen's 'Slavery in the British West India Colonies': containing more particularly an account of the actual condition of the Negroes in Jamaica . . .* (London, 1826)

Barham, J. F., *Considerations on the Abolition of Negro Slavery, and the means of practically effecting it* (London, 1823)

Bell, James, *A System of Geography Popular and Scientific; or a Physical, Political, and Statistical Account of the World and its Various Divisions,* Vol. 6 (Edinburgh, 1840)

Bernal, A. J. H., *A Geographical Catechism of the island of Jamaica, and its Dependencies: with a brief outline of their History and Topography* (Montego Bay, 1840)

Bickell, Rev. R., *The West Indies as they are; or a Real Picture of Slavery: but more particularly as it exists in the island of Jamaica* (London, 1825)

Blackall, John, *Observations on the Nature and Cure of Dropsies* (London, 1813)

Bridges, Rev. George W., *The Statistical History of the Parish of Manchester; in the island of Jamaica* (Jamaica, 1824)

Burnley, William H., *Opinions on Slavery and Emancipation in 1823 . . .* (London, 1833)

Carmichael, Mrs., *Domestic Manners and Social Condition of the White, Coloured, and Negro Population of the West Indies* (London, 1833)

Chisholm, Colin, *An Essay on the Malignant Pestilential Fever introduced into the West Indian islands from Boullam, on the Coast of Guinea, as it appeared in 1793 and 1794* (London, 1795)

A Manual of the Climate and Diseases, of Tropical Countries; . . . (London, 1822)

Collins, Dr., *Practical Rules for the Management and Medical Treatment of Negro Slaves in the Sugar Colonies* (London, 1803)

Dancer, Thomas, M.D., *The Medical Assistant; or Jamaica Practice of Physic: designed chiefly for the use of Families and Plantations* (Kingston, 1801)

De la Beche, H. T., *Notes on the Present Condition of the Negroes in Jamaica* (London, 1825)

Researches in Theoretical Geology (London, 1834)

Dickson, William, *Mitigation of Slavery* (London, 1814)

Edinburgh Medical and Surgical Journal

Edwards, Bryan, *The History, Civil and Commercial, of the British Colonies in the West Indies* (London, 1794)

Foulks, Theodore, *Eighteen Months in Jamaica; with Recollections of the Late Rebellion* (Bristol, 1833)

Further Proceedings of the Honourable House of Assembly of Jamaica, relative to a bill introduced into the House of Commons, for effectually preventing the unlawful importation of slaves, and holding free persons in slavery, in the British Colonies (London, 1816)

Grainger, James, M.D., *An Essay on the More Common West-India Diseases; and the Remedies which that Country itself Produces: to which are added, some hints on the Management, &c. of Negroes* (Edinburgh, 1802, 2nd edition)

Hakewill, James, *A Picturesque Tour of the Island of Jamaica, from drawings made in the years 1820 and 1821* (London, 1825)

Hancock, John, 'Observations on Tetanus Infantum, or Lock-jaw of Infants', *Edinburgh Medical and Surgical Journal,* 35 (1831), 343–7

Jackson, Robert, M.D., *A Sketch of the History and Cure of Febrile Diseases; more particularly as they appear in the West-Indies among the soldiers of the British Army* (London, 1820, 2nd edition)

Jamaica Almanack (Kingston)

Jamaica Journal (Kingston, 1818)

The Jamaica Physical Journal, Vols. 1–3 (Kingston, 1834–6)

Johnson, James, *The Influence of Tropical Climates on European Constitutions* . . . (London, 1827, 4th edition)

Kelly, James, *Jamaica in 1831: being a Narrative of Seventeen Years' Residence in that Island* (Belfast, 1838)

Knutsford, Viscountess, *Life and Letters of Zachary Macaulay* (London, 1900)

Lascelles, Edwin, *et. al., Instructions for the Management of a Plantation in Barbados, and for the Treatment of Negroes, &c.* (London, 1786)

Lewis, Matthew Gregory, *Journal of a West India Proprietor, kept during a residence in the island of Jamaica* (London, 1834)

Lind, James, *An Essay on Diseases Incidental to Europeans in Hot Climates* (London, 1788, 4th edition)

London Medical and Physical Journal

Long, Edward, *The History of Jamaica* (London, 1774)

Martin, R. Montgomery, *The British Colonial Library. Vol. 6: History of the West Indies* (London, 1835)

Statistics of the Colonies of the British Empire (London, 1839)

History of the Colonies of the British Empire (London, 1843)

Mason, David, 'A descriptive account of Frambœsia or Yaws', *Edinburgh Medical and Surgical Journal,* 35 (1831), 52–66

Maxwell, James, 'Pathological Inquiry into the Nature of Cachexia Africana, as it is generally connected with dirt-eating', *Jamaica Physical Journal,* 2 (1835), 409–35

McMahon, Benjamin, *Jamaica Plantership* (London, 1839)

Moreton, J. B., *Manners and Customs in the West India Islands* (London, 1790)

Morrison, John, *A Treatise on Tetanus, illustrated by a number of cases* (Newry, 1816)

Nugent, Lady Maria, *A Journal of a Voyage to, and Residence in, the Island of Jamaica, from 1801–1805* (London, 1839)

Phillippo, James M., *Jamaica: Its Past and Present State* (London, 1843)

Pinkerton, John, *Modern Geography* (London, 1802)

Porter, George Richardson, *The Tropical Agriculturist* (London, 1833)

Quier, John, *et. al., Letters and Essays on the Small-Pox and Inoculation, the Measles, the Dry Belly-Ache, the Yellow, and Remitting and Intermitting Fevers of the West Indies* (London, 1778)

Renny, Robert, *A History of Jamaica* (London, 1807)

A Report of a Committee of the Council of Barbados, appointed to inquire into the actual conditions of the slaves in this island . . . (London, 1824)

A Report of Evidence taken at Brown's-Town and St. Ann's Bay, in the Parish of St. Ann's, under a commission from his excellency Sir Lionel Smith, Governor of Jamaica (Falmouth, 1837)

A Review of the Colonial Slave Registration Acts, in a Report of a Committee of the Board of Directors of the African Institution (London, 1820)

Roughley, Thomas, *The Jamaica Planter's Guide; or, a system for planting and managing a sugar estate, or other plantations in that island, and throughout the British West Indies in general* (London, 1823)

Royal Gazette (Kingston, 1817, 1819)

St. Jago de la Vega Gazette (Spanish Town, 1832)

Sells, William, *Remarks on the Condition of the Slaves in the Island of Jamaica* (London, 1823)

Senior, Bernard Martin, *Jamaica, As It Was, As It Is, and As It May be* (London, 1835)

Sloane, Hans, *A Voyage to the Islands Madera, Barbados, Nieves, S. Christophers and Jamaica* (London, 1707–25)

Southey, Henry Herbert, *Observations on Pulmonary Consumption* (London, 1814)

Stewart, J., *A View of the Past and Present State of the Island of Jamaica; with Remarks on the Moral and Physical Condition of the Slaves, and on the Abolition of Slavery in the Colonies* (Edinburgh, 1823)

Stewart, Rev. Samuel H., 'A Statistical Account of the Parish of Manchester', *Jamaica Almanack* (1840), 142–50

Stone, Arthur Daniel, *A Practical Treatise on the Diseases of the Stomach, and of Digestion; including the history and treatment of those affections of the liver and digestive organs, which occur in persons who return from the East or West Indies, . . .* (London, 1806)

Sturge, Joseph and Thomas Harvey, *The West Indies in 1837* (London, 1838, 2nd edition)

Thomson, James, M.D., *A Treatise on the Diseases of Negroes, as they Occur in the Island of Jamaica: with Observations on the Country Remedies* (Jamaica, 1820)

Titford, W. J., *Sketches towards a Hortus Botanicus Americanus* (London, 1812)

Waller, John Augustine, *A Voyage in the West Indies* (London, 1820)

Whiteley, Henry, *Three Months in Jamaica, in 1832: comprising a residence of seven weeks on a sugar plantation* (London, 1833)

Williams, Cynric R., *A Tour Through the Island of Jamaica, from the Western to the Eastern End, in the Year 1823* (London, 1827, 2nd edition)

Williamson, John, *Medical and Miscellaneous Observations, relative to the West India Islands* (Edinburgh, 1817)

Wilson, John, *Memoirs of West Indian Fever; constituting brief notices regarding the treatment, origin, and nature of the disease commonly called Yellow Fever* (London, 1827)

5. SECONDARY SOURCES

Aldridge, Alfred Owen, 'Population and Polygamy in Eighteenth-Century Thought', *Journal of the History of Medicine,* 4 (1949), 129–48

Anstey, Roger T., *The Atlantic Slave Trade and British Abolition, 1760–1810* (London, 1975)

'Capitalism and Slavery: A Critique', *Economic History Review,* 21 (1968), 307–20

'A re-interpretation of the abolition of the British slave trade, 1806–1807', *English Historical Review,* 87 (1972), 304–32

Aufhauser, R. Keith, 'Slavery and Scientific Management', *Journal of Economic History,* 33 (1973) 811–24

'Profitability of Slavery in the British Caribbean', *Journal of Interdisciplinary History,* 5 (1974), 45–67

Barrett, Ward, 'Caribbean Sugar-Production Standards in the Seventeenth and Eighteenth Centuries', in John Parker (ed.), *Merchants and Scholars: Essays in the History of Exploration and Trade* (Minneapolis, 1965)

Blake, Judith, *Family Structure in Jamaica: The Social Context of Reproduction* (New York, 1961)

Brathwaite, Edward, 'Jamaican Slave Society, A Review', *Race,* 9 (1968), 331–42

The Development of Creole Society in Jamaica, 1770–1820 (Oxford, 1971)

Buchner, J. H., *The Moravians in Jamaica: History of the Mission of the United Brethren's Church to the Negroes in the Island of Jamaica, from the year 1754 to 1854* (London, 1854)

Burn, W. L. *Emancipation and Apprenticeship in the British West Indies* (London, 1937)

Cambridge History of the British Empire, Vol. 2: *The Growth of the New Empire, 1783–1870* (Cambridge, 1940)

Clarke, Edith, *My Mother Who Fathered Me: A Study of the Family in Three Selected Communities in Jamaica* (London, 1966)

Cousins, Winifred M., 'Slave Family Life in the British Colonies, 1800–1834', *Sociological Review,* 27 (1935), 35–55

Craton, Michael, 'Jamaican slave mortality: fresh light from Worthy Park, Longville and the Tharp Estates', *Journal of Caribbean History,* 3 (1971), 1–27

Craton, Michael and James Walvin, *A Jamaican Plantation: A History of Worthy Park, 1670–1970* (London, 1970)

Cumper, G. E., 'Labour Demand and Supply in the Jamaican Sugar Industry, 1830–1950', *Social and Economic Studies,* 2 (1954), 37–86

'Population Movements in Jamaica, 1830–1950', *Social and Economic Studies,* 5 (1956), 261–80

Curtin, Philip D., *Two Jamaicas. The Role of Ideas in a Tropical Colony, 1830–1865* (Cambridge, Mass., 1955)

The Image of Africa: British Ideas and Action, 1780–1850 (Madison, 1964)

The Atlantic Slave Trade (Madison, 1969)

'Epidemiology and the Slave Trade', *Political Science Quarterly,* 83 (1968), 190–216

Davis, David Brion, *The Problem of Slavery in Western Culture* (New York, 1966)

The Problem of Slavery in the Age of Revolution, 1770–1823 (Ithaca, 1975)
Debien, G., *Destinées d'Esclaves à la Martinique (1746–1778)* (Dakar, 1960)
Deerr, Noel, *The History of Sugar* (London, 1949)
Drescher, Seymour, 'Le "Declin" du Système Esclavagiste Britannique et L'Abolition de la Traite,' *Annales E.S.C.* (forthcoming)
Duncker, Sheila, 'The Free Coloured and their Fight for Civil Rights in Jamaica, 1800–30' (M.A. thesis, University of London, 1960)
Dunn, Richard S., *Sugar and Slaves. The Rise of the Planter Class in the English West Indies, 1624–1713* (Chapel Hill, 1972)
Eblen, Jack E., 'Growth of the Black Population in *ante bellum* America, 1820–1860', *Population Studies,* 26 (1972), 273–89
'On the Natural Increase of Slave Populations: The Example of the Cuban Black Population, 1775–1900', in Stanley L. Engerman and Eugene D. Genovese (eds.), *Race and Slavery in the Western Hemisphere: Quantitative Studies* (Princeton, 1974)
Eisner, Gisela, *Jamaica, 1830–1930: A Study in Economic Growth* (Manchester, 1961)
Eltis, D., 'The Traffic in Slaves between the British West Indian Colonies, 1807–1833', *Economic History Review,* 25 (1972), 55–64
Eversley, D. E. C., *Social Theories of Fertility and the Malthusian Debate* (Oxford, 1959)
Farley, Reynolds, 'The Demographic Rates and Social Institutions of the Nineteenth-Century Negro Population. A Stable Population Analysis', *Demography,* 2 (1965), 386–98
Fladeland, Betty, 'Abolitionist Pressures on the Concert of Europe, 1814–22', *Journal of Modern History,* 38 (1966), 355–73
Fogel, Robert W. and Stanley L. Engerman, *Time on the Cross: The Economics of American Negro Slavery* (Boston, 1974)
'The Relative Efficiency of Slavery: A Comparison of Northern and Southern Agriculture in 1860', *Explorations in Economic History,* 8 (1971), 353–67
Frazier, E. Franklin, *The Negro Family in the United States* (Chicago, 1939)
Furley, Oliver W., 'Moravian Missionaries and Slaves in the West Indies', *Caribbean Studies,* 5 (1965), 3–16
Furness, A. E., 'George Hibbert and the Defence of Slavery in the West Indies', *Jamaican Historical Review,* 5 (1965), 56–70
Genovese, Eugene D., *The Political Economy of Slavery: Studies in the Economy and Society of the Slave South* (New York, 1965)
In Red and Black (New York, 1968)
Goveia, Elsa V., *Slave Society in the British Leeward Islands at the End of the Eighteenth Century* (New Haven, 1965)
Green, W. A., 'The Planter Class and British West Indian Sugar Production before and after Emancipation', *Economic History Review,* 26 (1973), 448–63
Gutman, Herbert G., 'Le Phénomène Invisible: La Composition de la Famille et du Foyer Noirs après la Guerre de Secession', *Annales E.S.C.* (1972), 1197–218
Hall, Douglas, *Free Jamaica, 1838–1865. An Economic History* (New Haven, 1959)

A Brief History of the West India Committee (Barbados, 1971)
'The Social and Economic Background to Sugar in Slave Days', *Caribbean Historical Review*, Nos. 3–4 (1954), 149–69
'Incalculability as a Feature of Sugar Production during the Eighteenth Century', *Social and Economic Studies*, 10 (1961), 340–52
'Slaves and Slavery in the British West Indies', *Social and Economic Studies*, 11 (1962), 305–18
'Absentee-Proprietorship in the British West Indies to about 1850', *Jamaican Historical Review*, 4 (1964), 15–35
Hall, Gwendolyn Midlo, *Social Control in Slave Plantation Societies. A Comparison of St. Domingue and Cuba* (Baltimore, 1971)
Hall, N. A. T., 'Some Aspects of the Deficiency Question in Jamaica in the Eighteenth Century', *Jamaica Journal*, 7 (1973), 36–41
Haller, John S., 'The Negro and the Southern Physician: A Study of Medical and Racial Attitudes', *Medical History*, 16 (1972), 238–53
Herskovits, Melville J., *The Myth of the Negro Past* (Boston, 1958).
Higman, B. W., 'The West India Interest in Parliament, 1807–1833', *Historical Studies*, 13 (1967), 1–19
'Household Structure and Fertility on Jamaican Slave Plantations: A Nineteenth-Century Example', *Population Studies*, 27 (1973), 527–50
'A Report on Excavations at Montpelier and Roehampton', *Jamaica Journal*, 8 (1974), 40–5
'The Slave Populations of the British Caribbean: Some Nineteenth Century Variations', in Samuel R. Proctor (ed.) *Eighteenth Century Florida and the Caribbean* (Gainesville, 1976)
'The Slave Family and Household in the British West Indies, 1800–1834', *Journal of Interdisciplinary History*, 6 (1965), 261–87
Hoeppli, R., *Parasitic Diseases in Africa and the Western Hemisphere: Early Documentation and Transmission by the Slave Trade* (Basel, 1969)
Hoetink, H., *Slavery and Race Relations in the Americas* (New York, 1973)
Hofstadter, Richard, 'U. B. Phillips and the Plantation Legend', *Journal of Negro History*, 29 (1944), 109–24
Hunter, John M., 'Geophagy in Africa and in the United States: A Culture-Nutrition Hypothesis', *Geographical Review*, 63 (1973), 170–95
Jacobs, H. P., *Sixty Years of Change, 1806-1866: Progress and Reaction in Kingston and the Countryside* (Kingston, 1973)
'The Untapped Sources of Jamaican History', *Jamaican Historical Review*, 1 (1945), 92–8
Jekyll, Walter (ed.), *Jamaican Song and Story. Annancy Stories, Digging Sings, Ring Tunes, and Dancing Tunes* (New York, 1966)
Jordan, Winthrop D., *White Over Black: American Attitudes toward the Negro, 1550–1812* (Chapel Hill, 1968)
'American Chiaroscuro: The Status and Definition of Mulattoes in the British Colonies', *William and Mary Quarterly*, 19 (1962), 183–200
Kerr, Madeline, *Personality and Conflict in Jamaica* (London, 1952)
Knight, Franklin W., *Slave Society in Cuba during the Nineteenth Century* (Madison, 1970)

Lammermeier, Paul J., 'The Urban Black Family of the Nineteenth Century: A Study of Black Family Structure in the Ohio Valley, 1850–1880', *Journal of Marriage and the Family,* 35 (1973), 440–56

MacDonald, John Stuart and Leatrice D. MacDonald, 'Transformation of African and Indian Family Traditions in the Southern Caribbean', *Comparative Studies in Society and History,* 15 (1973), 171–98

Marino, Anthony, 'Family, Fertility, and Sex Ratios in the British Caribbean', *Population Studies,* 24 (1970), 159–72

Mathieson, William Law, *British Slavery and its Abolition 1823–1838* (London, 1926)

Merivale, Herman, *Lectures on Colonization and Colonies* (London, 1928: 1861 edition)

Mintz, S. W. and Douglas Hall, 'The Origins of the Jamaican Internal Marketing System', *Yale University Publications in Anthropology,* No. 57 (1960)

Molen, Patricia A., 'Population and Social Patterns in Barbados in the Early Eighteenth Century', *William and Mary Quarterly,* 28 (1971), 287–300

Mullin, Gerald W., *Flight and Rebellion. Slave Resistance in Eighteenth-Century Virginia* (New York, 1972)

Murray, D. J., *The West Indies and the Development of Colonial Government, 1801–1834* (Oxford, 1965)

Otterbein, Keith F., 'Caribbean Family Organization: A Comparative Analysis', *American Anthropologist,* 67 (1965), 66–79

Pares, Richard, *Merchants and Planters, Economic History Review* Supplement, No. 4 (1960)

Parker, William N. (ed.), 'The Structure of the Cotton Economy of the Antebellum South', *Agricultural History,* 44 (1970)

Patterson, Orlando, *The Sociology of Slavery. An Analysis of the Origins, Development and Structure of Negro Slave Society in Jamaica* (London, 1967)

'Slavery and Slave Revolts: A Socio-Historical Analysis of the First Maroon War, Jamaica, 1655–1740', *Social and Economic Studies,* 19 (1970), 289–325

Phillips, Ulrich Bonnell, *American Negro Slavery* (Baton Rouge, 1966)

'A Jamaica Slave Plantation', *American Historical Review,* 19 (1914), 543–58

Pitman, Frank Wesley, 'Slavery on British West India Plantations in the Eighteenth Century', *Journal of Negro History,* 11 (1926), 584–668

'Place Names of Jamaica' (Institute of Jamaica, typescript, n.d.)

Pleck, Elizabeth H., 'The Two-Parent Household: Black Family Structure in Late Nineteenth-Century Boston', *Journal of Social History,* 6 (1972), 3–31

Postell, William Dosite, *The Health of Slaves on Southern Plantations* (Baton Rouge, 1951)

Ragatz, L. J., *Statistics for the Study of British Caribbean Economic History, 1763–1833* (London, 1927)

The Fall of the Planter Class in the British Caribbean, 1763–1833 (New York, 1928)

A Guide for the Study of British Caribbean History, 1763–1834 (Washington, 1932)

'Absentee Landlordism in the British Caribbean, 1750–1833', *Agricultural History,* 5 (1931), 7–24

Reckord, Mary, 'The Jamaica Slave Rebellion of 1831', *Past and Present,* No. 40 (1968), 108–25
Roberts, George W., *The Population of Jamaica* (Cambridge, 1957)
'A Life Table for a West Indian Slave Population', *Population Studies,* 5 (1952), 238–43
'Some Aspects of Mating and Fertility in the West Indies', *Population Studies,* 8 (1955) 199–227
Roxburgh, Adam, 'The Breeds and Breeding of Cattle in Jamaica', *Special Publications of the Institute of Jamaica, Agriculture,* No. 3 (1893), 81–90
Schuler, Monica, 'Akan Slave Rebellions in the British Caribbean', *Savacou,* 1 (1970), 8–31
Schuyler, R. L., 'The Constitutional Claims of the British West Indies', *Political Science Quarterly,* 40 (1925), 1–36
Sheridan, Richard, *The Development of the Plantations to 1750* and *An Era of West Indian Prosperity 1750–1775* (Barbados, 1970)
Sugar and Slavery. An Economic History of the British West Indies, 1623–1775 (Barbados, 1974)
'The West India Sugar Crisis and British Slave Emancipation, 1830–1833', *Journal of Economic History,* 21 (1961), 539–51
'Planter and Historian: The Career of William Beckford in Jamaica and England, 1744–1799', *Jamaican Historical Review,* 4 (1964), 36–58
'The Wealth of Jamaica in the Eighteenth Century', *Economic History Review,* 18 (1965), 292–311
'The Wealth of Jamaica in the Eighteenth Century: A Rejoinder', *Economic History Review,* 21 (1968), 46–61
'The Plantation Revolution and the Industrial Revolution', *Caribbean Studies,* 9 (1969), 5–25
'Simon Taylor, Sugar Tycoon of Jamaica, 1740–1813', *Agricultural History,* 45 (1971), 285–96
Shore, Joseph and John Stewart (eds.), *In Old St. James (Jamaica). A Book of Parish Chronicles* (Kingston, 1911)
Smith, M. G., *West Indian Family Structure* (Seattle, 1962)
'Some Aspects of Social Structure in the British Caribbean about 1820', *Social and Economic Studies,* 1 (1953), 55–79
Smith, Raymond T., 'The Nuclear Family in Afro-American Kinship', *Journal of Comparative Family Studies,* 1 (1970), 55–70
Solien, Nancie L., 'Household and Family in the Caribbean: Some Definitions and Concepts', *Social and Economic Studies,* 9 (1960), 101–6
Stampp, Kenneth M., *The Peculiar Institution. Slavery in the Ante-Bellum South* (New York, 1956)
Starobin, Robert S., *Industrial Slavery in the Old South* (New York, 1970)
Stephen, Sir James, *Essays in Ecclesiastical Biography* (London, 1883)
Thomas, Robert Paul, 'The Sugar Colonies of the Old Empire: Profit or Loss for Great Britain?' *Economic History Review,* 21 (1968), 30–45
Thoms, D. W., 'Slavery in the Leeward Islands in the Mid-Eighteenth Century: A Reappraisal', *Bulletin of the Institute of Historical Research,* 42 (1969), 76–85
Tikasingh, Gerad, 'A Method for Estimating the Free Coloured Population of

Jamaica' (University of the West Indies, History Department Seminar Paper, 1968)

Wade, Richard C., *Slavery in the Cities. The South 1820–1860* (New York, 1964)

Wastell, R. E. P., 'The History of Slave Compensation 1833 to 1845' (M.A. thesis, University of London, 1932)

Williams, Eric, *Capitalism and Slavery* (London, 1964)

'The British West Indian Slave Trade after its Abolition in 1807', *Journal of Negro History,* 27 (1942), 175–91

Zelnik, Melvin, 'Fertility of the American Negro in 1830 and 1850', *Population Studies,* 20 (1966), 77–83

6. GENERAL

Barclay, George W., *Techniques of Population Analysis* (New York, 1958)

Beckford, George L., *Persistent Poverty. Underdevelopment in Plantation Economies of the Third World* (New York, 1972)

Bender, Donald R., 'A Refinement of the Concept of Household: Families, Co-residence, and Domestic Functions', *American Anthropologist,* 69 (1967), 493–504

Best, Lloyd, 'Outlines of a Model of Pure Plantation Economy', *Social and Economic Studies,* 17 (1968), 283–326

Bogue, Donald J., *Principles of Demography* (New York, 1969)

Clark, Colin, *Population Growth and Land Use* (London, 1967)

Clarke, Edwin (ed.), *Modern Methods in the History of Medicine* (London, 1971)

Coale, Ansley J., 'The Effects of Changes in Mortality and Fertility on Age Composition', *Milbank Memorial Fund Quarterly,* 34 (1956), 79–114

'Estimates of Various Demographic Measures Through the Quasi-Stable Age Distribution', in *Emerging Techniques in Population Research* (Milbank Memorial Fund, 1963)

Coale, Ansley J. and Paul Demeny, *Regional Model Life Tables and Stable Populations* (Princeton, 1966)

Conrad, Alfred H. and John R. Meyer, *Studies in Econometric History* (London, 1965)

Cook, Sherburne F. and Woodrow Borah, *Essays in Population History: Mexico and the Caribbean* (Berkeley, 1971)

Coppock, J. T., 'Crop, Livestock, and Enterprise Combinations in England and Wales', *Economic Geography,* 40 (1964), 65–81

Curtis, J. T. and R. P. McIntosh, 'The Interrelations of Certain Analytic and Synthetic Phytosociological Characters', *Ecology,* 31 (1950), 434–55

Engerman, Stanley L., 'Some Considerations Relating to Property Rights in Man', *Journal of Economic History,* 33 (1973), 43–65

Ford, Thomas R. and Gordon F. DeJong (eds.) *Social Demography* (Englewood Cliffs, 1970)

Gilbert, N. and T. C. E. Wells, 'Analysis of Quadrat Data', *Journal of Ecology,* 54 (1966), 675–85

Goode, William J., 'Illegitimacy, Anomie, and Cultural Penetration', *American Sociological Review,* 26 (1961), 910–25

Goody, Jack, *The Developmental Cycle in Domestic Groups* (Cambridge, 1958)
Hawthorn, Geoffrey, *The Sociology of Fertility* (London, 1970)
Henry, L., 'The Verification of Data in Historical Demography', *Population Studies,* 22 (1968), 61–81
Hirsch, August, *Handbook of Geographical and Historical Pathology* (London, 1883–6)
Hoag, Leverett P., 'The Weaver Method: An Evaluation', *Professional Geographer,* 21 (1969), 244–6
Hollingsworth, T. H., *Historical Demography* (London, 1969)
Keyfitz, Nathan, 'Changing Vital Rates and Age Distributions', *Population Studies,* 22 (1968), 235–51
Laslett, Peter (ed.), *Household and Family in Past Time* (Cambridge, 1972)
May, Jacques M., *The Ecology of Human Disease* (New York, 1958)
McConnell, Harold, *Quadrat Methods in Map Analysis* (University of Iowa, Department of Geography Discussion Paper No. 3, 1966)
Rogers, Andre and Norbert G. Gomar, 'Statistical Inference in Quadrat Analysis', *Geographical Analysis,* 1 (1969), 370–84
Staples, Robert, 'Towards a Sociology of the Black Family: A Theoretical and Methodological Assessment', *Journal of Marriage and the Family,* 33 (1971), 119–38
Stewart, John Q., and William Warntz, 'Macrogeography and Social Science', *Geographical Review,* 48, (1958) 167–84
Strahler, Arthur N., 'Quantitative Slope Analysis', *Bulletin of the Geological Society of America,* 67 (1956), 571–96
Thompson, Edgar T., 'Population Expansion and the Plantation System', *American Journal of Sociology,* 41 (1935), 314–26
Weaver, John C., 'Crop-Combination Regions in the Middle West', *Geographical Review,* 44 (1954), 175–200
Wrigley, E. A., 'Family Limitation in Pre-Industrial England', *Economic History Review,* 19 (1966), 82–109
Wrigley, E. A. (ed.), *An Introduction to English Historical Demography* (London, 1966)
Wolfenden, Hugh H., *Population Statistics and their Compilation* (Chicago, 1954)

INDEX